Citizenship in Myanmar

Citizenship in Myanmar

Ways of Being in and from Burma

EDITED BY

ASHLEY SOUTH
MARIE LALL

CHIANG MAI
UNIVERSITY PRESS

ISEAS YUSOF ISHAK
INSTITUTE

First published in Singapore in 2018 by
ISEAS Publishing
30 Heng Mui Keng Terrace
Singapore 119614

For worldwide distribution except Thailand.

E-mail: publish@iseas.edu.sg
Website: <http://bookshop.iseas.edu.sg>

First published in Thailand in 2018 by
Chiang Mai University Press
239 Huay Kaew Road
Muang District, Chiang Mai
Thailand, 50200

For distribution in Thailand.

The responsibility for facts and opinions in this publication rests exclusively with the authors and their interpretations do not necessarily reflect the views of the policy of the publishers or their supporters.

ISEAS Library Cataloguing-in-Publication Data

Citizenship in Myanmar: Ways of Being in and from Burma / edited by Ashley South and Marie Lall.
   Papers originally presented at a Conference on Burma/Myanmar in Transition: Connectivity, Changes and Challenges, held in Chiang Mai University, July 2015.
   1. Citizenship—Burma.
   2. Burma—Politics and government.
   I. South, Ashley.
   II. Lall, M. C. (Marie-Carine)
Conference on Burma/Myanmar in Transition: Connectivity, Changes and Challenges (2015 : Chiang Mai, Thailand)
DS530.65 C584   2018

ISBN 978-981-4786-20-1 (soft cover)
ISBN 978-981-4786-21-8 (e-book, PDF)

Typeset by Superskill Graphics Pte Ltd
Printed in Singapore by Markono Print Media Pte Ltd

to Bellay and Viren, who put up
with our long absences

CONTENTS

FOREWORD

Most of the chapters in *Citizenship in Myanmar: Ways of Being in and from Burma* are based on papers presented at a July 2015 conference on "Burma/Myanmar in Transition: Connectivity, Changes and Challenges" held at Chiang Mai University. Additional special contributions come from six community and political leaders from Myanmar, including senior officials of Ethnic Armed Organizations.

Until recently, Myanmar studies focused primarily on democracy and human rights. With the election in 2010, the government embarked on a series of reforms to direct the country towards liberal democracy, a mixed economy, and reconciliation, although doubts persist about the motives that underpin such reforms. This has led to a new democratic system, ethnic ceasefire talks, and the victory of the National League for Democracy (NLD) in 2012. These changes have ushered in a turning point in Myanmar studies — with the focus shifting to how the liberal government will deal with both the country's past as well as the present challenges of representation and the meaning of Myanmar citizenship and national identity for the various ethnic groups in Myanmar. This book examines the practices of citizenship and the role of state and civil society in the linkages between culture, religion, speech, access to land and, most importantly, access to opportunities. The government faces major challenges in trying to unite the various ethnic and religious groups in Myanmar behind its reformist agenda.

The research included here has examined the practices of citizenship in its various aspects — including educational, cultural, religious and ethnic — to investigate whether citizenship is a political instrument for national reform or a representation of national identity. I hope this book leads to a better understanding of our neighbour, including its sociopolitical transition and the implications for regional development — and helps us to further our cooperation with Myanmar.

Associate Professor Sampan Singharajwarapan, PhD
Vice-President, Chiang Mai University

CONTRIBUTORS

Ardeth Maung Thawnhmung, Chair of the Political Science Department, University of Massachusetts at Lowell, USA.

Aung Naing Oo, a political analyst and previously leading member of the Myanmar Peace Centre.

Mikael Gravers, Associate Professor, Anthropology, Aarhus University, Denmark.

Khu Oo Reh, Vice-Chairman of the Karenni National Progressive Party.

Helene Maria Kyed, Research Fellow at the Danish Institute of International Studies, Copenhagen, Denmark.

Marie Lall, Professor of Education and South Asian Studies, Institute of Education, University College London, UK.

Jacques P. Leider, École française d'Extrême-Orient, Bangkok and Yangon.

Gerard McCarthy, Ph.D. candidate at the Australian National University, Canberra, Australia.

Nai Hongsa, Vice-Chairman of the New Mon State Party.

Nurul Islam, Chairman of the Arakan Rohingya National Organisation.

Nyi Nyi Kyaw, Postdoctoral Fellow at Centre for Asian Legal Studies at the Faculty of Law at the National University of Singapore.

P'doh Kweh Htoo Win, General Secretary of the Karen National Union.

Sai Kheunsai, the founder and editor of the Shan Herald Agency for News.

Martin Smith, an independent author and consultant.

Ashley South, independent researcher, policy analyst and consultant in Southeast Asia; Research Fellow at the Centre for Ethnic Studies and Development, Chiang Mai University.

Derek Tonkin, former British Ambassador to Thailand, Vietnam and Laos.

Matthew J. Walton, Aung San Suu Kyi Senior Research Fellow, St Antony's College, Oxford University, UK.

Yadana, Director of Braveheart Foundation, Yangon.

Source: Map of Myanmar, no. 4168 Rev. 3, June 2012, reproduced with permission of the UN Geospatial Information Sec

INTRODUCTION

Ashley South and Marie Lall

Since 2011, Myanmar has been going through a period of profound — albeit still contested — transition. Under the leadership of President U Thein Sein, the country experienced widespread if sometimes uneven reforms, including the release of most (but not all) political prisoners, a greatly improved environment for freedom of speech and association, a resurgence of the civil society sector, some economic reforms, and the start of a peace process between the government (and Myanmar Army, or Tatmadaw) and some two dozen ethnic armed organizations (EAOs) which had long been fighting for greater autonomy from the militarized and *Bama*-dominated central government.[1] This has been an unprecedented period of transition, which continued following the November 2015 elections, and April 2016 formation of a government led by Daw Aung San Suu Kyi's National League for Democracy (NLD).

Four years into the reforms, in July 2015 Chiang Mai University organized a three-day international conference on "Burma/Myanmar in Transition: Connectivity, Changes and Challenges", to discuss and assess the complex changes underway in Thailand's neighbour to the West. The conference was attended by more than 300 people, from inside Myanmar, from the border regions and Thailand, and from overseas. This book brings together chapters by academic experts, most of whom participated in a panel at the Chiang Mai conference convened by the editors. Additional contributions were elicited from colleagues working on issues of citizenship in Myanmar. The longer, analytical chapters are supplemented by six contributions provided by ethnic community and political leaders from

Myanmar, including senior officials of EAOs, who discuss what it means to be an ethnic nationality citizen of their respective states and communities, and of the larger country.[2] In the two years since the conference, authors have updated and refined their contributions, for the book to be as top-to-date as possible.

Given the genesis of this book, and the breadth and complexity of the issues, we can offer only a partial account of citizenship in Myanmar. Citizenship encompasses many different concepts, including notions of participation in meritorious social activity, as discussed in Gerard McCarthy's chapter. Other contributions survey the history of ethnic politics and citizenship in Myanmar; discuss the role of Ethnic Affairs Ministers in regional government; report on the findings of a survey into the meaning/s of citizenship in contemporary Myanmar, and in particular the roles of religion; discuss the situation of, and future status and options for, members of EAOs; describe and analyse competing narratives of identity and citizenship, in the context of Buddhist–Muslim and Rakhine–Rohingya tensions; explore notions of citizenship in provincial Myanmar; and examine scenarios and themes looking forward, in the context of various proposed frameworks for political dialogue.

The July 2015 conference was held during the run-up to elections in November that year. The polls were deemed relatively "free and fair", and the landslide victory of Daw Aung San Suu Kyi's NLD was a watershed moment. As in 1990, some two-thirds of the electorate voted for change — out with the reviled military, and in with more accountable and democratic government. In the context of the elections, debates in Myanmar have focused on the nature of citizenship: who is a "legitimate" citizen of the Union, and can vote?; how can ethnic nationality/minority communities' identities and interests best be represented, through national-level political parties or through specifically ethnic parties? What are the respective roles and relationships between ethnic elites seeking to represent non-Burman communities through civil society activism (including in the media and social work), through parliamentary politics, and through armed struggle?

The last seven years have been transformative; Myanmar is entering new and uncharted political territory. In order to better understand present directions, and possible future trajectories, one needs to study the past. Several of the chapters offered here examine how concepts and practices of citizenship developed during — and even before — the long decades of repressive military rule.

Our book explores citizenship in Myanmar in relation to three broad categories: issues of identity and conflict; debates around concepts and practices of citizenship; and inter- and intra-community issues, including Buddhist–Muslim relations. These topics help to structure the Introduction and presentation of the chapters which follow. The second part of this Introduction reviews how citizenship is discussed in political theory, and in Myanmar legal and constitutional discourse.

IDENTITY AND CONFLICT

Most of the chapter authors place particular emphasis on the situation and perspectives of ethnic nationality people in and from Myanmar (or as some still prefer, "Burma"). Questions and conflicts regarding relationships between the state and the diverse communities who live there have been at the heart of politics in this country for more than half a century. The authoritarian relationship between government and population has been, and to a significant extent remains, deeply problematic. Arguably, even more challenging have been relations between a state dominated by elements of the Burman (*Bama*) majority, and ethnic nationality communities, many members of which have not recognized the state's legitimacy, but rather experience militarized rule by central government as alien, predatory and violent.

Ethnic elites in Myanmar have generally preferred to identify their communities as "ethnic nationalities", rather than "ethnic minorities". Ethnic nationality designation is believed grant greater political status, invoking the idea of an ethnic nation, rather than a marginalized minority. Likewise, ethnic politicians have been reluctant to designate their communities as "indigenous", and therefore have not often engaged in advocacy or activism around indigenous rights issues. The chapters by ethnic political leaders demonstrate various approaches to and understandings of the notion of citizenship. A key distinction is whether and how it is possible for ethnic nationality people to be citizens of (the Union of) Myanmar, and/or of a political entity representing a ethno-national subgroup (or groups). Polities formed by and representing ethnic nationalities may be part of the union, or strive for greater independence. Historically, as Martin Smith's overview chapter describes, ethnic nationality elites in Myanmar have aspired towards political self-determination, often expressed in the context of federalism, or even in desires for outright independence. Connections between debates regarding federalism and political self-determination, and notions of citizenship, are discussed by several authors in this volume.

A key theme running through Myanmar's troubled state–society relations is the well-grounded concerns expressed by ethnic nationality (minority) communities — and not just by elites — regarding the perceived agenda among elements of the majority *Bama* community to impose a "national identity" derived from the history, culture, language, religion (Buddhism) and values of the dominant community. Historically, concerns regarding "Burmanization" (or "Myanmarfication") have been at the heart of ethnic nationality struggles for self-determination vis-à-vis a central government, which arguably since independence, and certainly since the military coup of 1962, has been dominated by Burman elites (Houtman 1999). Processes of "Burmanization" can be seen in various government policies since the 1960s, for example in the field of education (South and Lall 2016). In its strongest form, this has been a more-or-less explicit policy adopted by the militarized state, in an attempt to forge a single national unity in the country, at the expense of the identities, cultures and languages of ethnic nationality communities. This Maha *Bama* ("Greater Burma") programme is perhaps best exemplified by the wartime Burmese leader U Ba Maw's slogan of "one country, one people, one blood" (Taylor 1987). This agenda was expressed during the period of General Ne Win's "Burmese Way to Socialism" in attempts to establish a cohesive national identity for the whole country, in order to mobilize a type of "civic patriotism" intended to hold the country together in the face of what were perceived as divisive and fragmentary ethnic nationality identities (Taylor 2015). However, such a pan-Burmese national identity was historically derived from the *Bama* language and historical tradition, thus confirming and fuelling ethnic nationality concerns. Indeed, there is a widespread perception among ethnic nationality groups that Burmanization is deeply ingrained within the majority community, and reflected in attitudes of superiority and chauvinism. This is one of the greatest challenges to achieving equitable political and social progress in Myanmar, and helps to explain the widespread demands for "self-determination" articulated for many decades by the country's ethnic elites.

As noted below (in discussing the 2014 census), recent exercises in classifying ethnicity in Myanmar have tended to assume the existence of fixed categories of identity. However, before the consolidation of British colonialism in South and Southeast Asia, ethnic identities were generally diffuse, with ethnolinguistic characteristics being one among several markers of socio-political position. The political salience of ethnicity was reinforced during the colonial period (1824–1948), so that by the time of Burma's independence from the United Kingdom in 1948, ethnicity had become a defining category of political orientation. In the lead-up to independence, ethnic elites mobilized their communities in order to gain access to political and economic resources, demanding justice and fair treatment for the groups they sought to represent. During the late 1940s, there were widespread outbreaks of violence following the failure of *Bama* and minority elites to successfully negotiate a transition to independence.

State–society and armed ethnic conflicts in Myanmar have partly been structured by disagreement regarding the nature of citizenship, whether framed in ideological terms (the Communist insurgency of the 1940s through to the late 1980s) or struggles for ethnic self-determination. The complex and contested history of ethnic armed conflict in Myanmar is covered elsewhere (e.g., Smith 1999, South 2008). In this brief overview, it is sufficient to note that for many decades Myanmar has been subject to mostly quite "low-intensity" conflict between the state armed forces, and dozens of EAOs. One of the previous, military-backed government's most substantial achievements was to initiate a peace process, engaging most of the country's armed groups. Following a series of bilateral ceasefire agreements, eight EAOs joined a multilateral Nationwide Ceasefire Agreement (NCA) in October 2015. The peace process seemed to offer the best opportunity in many decades to resolve underlying issues which have long driven armed conflict in Myanmar, including the relationship between ethnic nationality citizen's and the state. However, about a dozen armed groups refused to sign the NCA, citing concerns about the agreement's lack of "inclusiveness", while often large-scale fighting continued across much of northern Myanmar, with devastating impacts on Kachin and other civilian communities. As discussed in Matthew Walton's chapter, signatories to the NCA were keen to move on to multi-stakeholder political dialogues, at the subnational and Union levels, aimed at re-negotiating state–society relations in Myanmar, and ultimately changing the constitution (which is also the aim of key actors in the electoral process, including particularly the NLD). Over the following two years, those EAOs which did not join the NCA were subject to repeated attacks by the Myanmar Army, which seemed intent on punishing non-signatory groups, and associated civilian populations (as discussed by Kyed and Gravers).

The peace process, and any resulting political dialogues, raise questions about the relationship between citizens (particularly, but not only, ethnic nationality communities) and a state which has historically been dominated by a Burman elite. Ethnic nationality elites have articulated credible agendas for greater self-determination, and autonomy within a federal union of Myanmar. (How) is it possible for individuals and communities to identify with one (or more?) distinct ethnic national identities, and/or as a citizen of a multi-ethnic union? Three of our authors address this question, offering contrasting understandings of citizenship in relation to the self-identified Rohingya community, including a contribution by a leading member of the Rohingya community in exile. One of the greatest challenges facing the new government is how to deal with inter-communal violence — a problem even more intractable than conflicts with EAOs. While ethnic insurgency can in principle be resolved through negotiations between political elites, inter-communal violence is more intractable.

CONCEPTS AND PRACTICES OF CITIZENSHIP

Demographic statistics for Myanmar remain contested, despite a census — the first in thirty-one years — held in late March and early April 2014, which calculated the population at 51.4 million people.[3] That this figure was lower than many expected is partly explained by the estimate that more than 4 million people from Myanmar were living abroad,[4] mostly as migrant workers (and/or refugees, mostly in Thailand). The census was not formally linked to questions of citizenship, and being a citizen involves more than just ethnic orientation. Nevertheless, issues of ethnic identity and citizenship are closely linked in Myanmar.

Ethnic nationality grievances include the manner in which ethnicity is officially understood and classified. While this book is not an anthropological study, it must be noted that the official 135 "national races" (*taingyintha*) recognized by the government (as discussed in the chapters by Kyed and Gravers, and Tonkin) is deeply problematic, representing arbitrary and often quite imaginary and imposed categories of identity. Nick Cheesman (2017) has demonstrated that the term and concept *taingyintha* was barely referenced in the 1947 constitution (and not at all in the Panglong Agreement of that year), and only became politically salient after the military takeover of 1962. Especially following General Ne Win's 1964 Union Day speech, "*taingyintha* obtained a hitherto unprecedented placing state lexicon" (Cheesman 2017, p. 5). Since then, citizenship in Myanmar has to a significant degree been dependent on membership of a *taingyintha*. The issue of "national races" in Myanmar therefore require some further discussion.

As Jane Ferguson (2015) has observed, censuses are classic means of (neo-)colonial control and classification, which in Myanmar:

> requires respondents to return their *lu myo*, or race/ethnicity, and the coding process makes use of a much-criticized scheme consisting of eight national races and 135 eligible subgroups. These categories have a complex political and semantic history in Myanmar, due to the ways in which ethnographic and linguistic diversity have been channelled into categorical frameworks by both colonial and post-colonial regimes. These categories have also acquired different kinds of meaning and resonance as a result of ongoing political-resistance movements. (Ferguson 2015)

There is some confusion regarding the genesis of the "135 national races", which Cheesman (2017, p. 9) describes as "emerging haphazardly and episodically … internally inconsistent". These are not listed in the 1982 Citizenship Law (see below), which established ethnicity (*taingyintha* status) as key to citizenship but states only that "nationals such as the Kachin, Kayah, Karen, Chin, Burman, Mon, Rakhine or Shan and ethnic groups as have settled in any of the territories included within the state as their permanent home from a period anterior to 1185 B.E., 1823 A.D. are Burma citizens … [and that] The Council of State may decide whether any ethnic group is national or not." The subsequent 1983 census listed more than 135 categories,[5] but some of these were redundant or returned as empty, which may explain the origin of the 135 *lu myo*.[6]

The enumeration of these categories serves to create the forms of ethnicity, through making historically arbitrary markers of race concrete and relevant to accessing symbolic and political resources. These categories are derived ultimately from British colonial era classifications (Taylor 1982; Ferguson 2015). The Crisis Group[7] likewise criticized the census methodology, according to which respondents were only able to self-identify as one category (or as "other") — regardless of the complexity of many people's mixed ancestry. Furthermore, the census lists were full of technical inconsistencies, with confusion between dialect and language names, and clan subgroups, and ethnic categories (Ferguson 2015).

Other groups were not listed at all, especially those of South Asian origin (e.g., the Gurkhas and Panthay Muslims, and of course the Rohingya). Furthermore, people living in areas not under government control were not counted (the numbers being estimated), and nor were migrant workers from Myanmar living overseas,[8] nor refugees living in Thailand, Bangladesh, China or Malaysia. Results of the census were controversial for example among the Kachin community, many of whom rejected the strange and arbitrary categories used to enumerate them.[9] Due to sensitivities around the ethnic breakdown of Myanmar's demographics, detailed figures on ethnicity had not been made available at the time of publication. This delay *may* indicate that numbers of self-identifying ethnic nationality citizens are lower than those claimed by some ethnic activists — either due to problems with the census methodology (undercounting of ethnic citizens), and/or to overly optimistic estimates on the part of some ethnic advocates.

The census revealed that 89 per cent of the enumerated population is Buddhist; 6.3 per cent self-identified as Christian (with substantial populations in Chin, Kachin and Karenni States), 0.8 per cent animist (mainly in Karenni and Shan States), and 2.3 per cent were Muslims[10] — but this number rises to about 4.3 per cent, including those not enumerated (including the Rohingya). The latter figure is only 0.4 per cent above the 1973 and 1983 Census figures of 3.9 per cent, regarded by some critics as spurious.[11]

INTER- AND INTRA-COMMUNITY ISSUES

As the (albeit incomplete and problematic) census data indicates, Myanmar is highly diverse ethnically, and this complexity extends to intra-group dynamics. For example, there are a dozen Karen ethnolinguistic subgroups consisting of Buddhists, Christians, animists and Muslims, living in urban, peri-urban, and rural areas. In several cases, particular subgroups within "minority communities" have historically assumed leading roles and sought to reimagine and reproduce a heterogeneous ethnic group in the stylized image of particular cultural and linguistic practices. Furthermore, in many parts of Myanmar, ethnic groups such as Karen and Shan coexist with smaller minority communities like the Mon, PaO, and Lahu. This raises questions about how self-determination for the dominant ethnic group potentially affects the identities and interests of such "minorities within minorities". A further trend in shifting demographics within the states and regions is the internal migration of non-indigenous groups, diluting the traditional character of ethnic states.[12]

It has generally been estimated that non-Burman communities make up at least 30 per cent of the population.[13] However, this begs the question of how ethnicity is defined, and by whom. Identification with a particular (or mixed) ethnic category (e.g. "Karen", "Kachin", or "Karen-Kachin") may be relatively unproblematic on a day-to-day basis, in terms of social orientation. Nevertheless, there a risk of reinforcing unhelpful essentializations of ethnic identity in Myanmar. Ethnicity is a fluid category, subject to reimaginations over time, and/or in different contexts. The classic anthropological study to this effect is Edmund Leach's work on the relationship between Kachin and Shan communities in Upland Burma in the 1950s, and the manner in which the two groups shade into each other, depending on local socio-economic factors.[14]

While the fixing of ethnic identity may be convenient for administrative and political elites, this often does not reflect lived realities (see Sadan 2013). This is particularly so for children of "mixed-race" relationships. Myanmar ID cards ("Citizenship Scrutiny Cards") continue to record citizens' ethnic identity, and official ethnicity remains a key element in leveraging access to political and economic resources, including through elections for ethnic nationality representatives in State and Regional parliaments, and Special Administrative areas. Such deep-rooted conventions help to orientate Burmese politics around sometimes exclusionary categories. It is partly for this reason that previous governments (in particular, the Ne Win regime in its various guises[15]) have sought to promote alternative axes of political identification — e.g., "civic patriotism" in relation to a (supposedly ethnically neutral) state, and/or different ideological orientations (e.g., varieties of more-or-less democratic socialism). However, as discussed, such projects have often been undermined and discredited by the unacknowledged capturing of official/civic narratives of history and tropes of culture by elements of the Burmese historical tradition, and the implicit or explicit identification of *Bama* discourse and identity with that of the state. Further problems arise when elements of one community — particularly if this is the majority group — seek to police which identity categories are acceptable and legitimate, and which not. In contemporary Myanmar, this problem is particularly acute in the case of Muslim communities in Northern Rakhine State who self-identify as *Rohingya* — an ethnic category (*lu myo*) rejected by many Burmese (not just *Bama*/Burman) Buddhists. It is important to note in this context that the Buddhist Rakhine community has long suffered discrimination and marginalization on the part of a state dominated by the Burman majority. Rakhine nationalist understandably feel uneasy when attention is focused on the situation of Muslim communities in southwest Myanmar, when the local Buddhist population has also suffered greatly.

Also interesting is the situation of groups such as the *Dawei* — who speak a distinct dialect of Burmese, and some members of which claim status as a distinct *lu myo*, not just a subgroup of the *Bama*. Indicating the complexity of the issues, there are communities around the southern Tanintharyi town of Myeik (long a commercial rival of Dawei, to the north), who claim a further subcategory of *Myeik* (or *Beik*) identity.[16] In accord with principles of self-determination (and the ability of individuals and groups to call themselves what they want), it will be necessary for a healthy future Myanmar to create space, and make available resources, to explore and disseminate such local perceptions and histories. Potentially more problematic is how such different identity groups can and should be represented politically.[17]

The Muslim community is also diverse. Myanmar's Muslims include the extremely vulnerable *Rohingya* community — a politically charged categorization, which generates heated debate in political and civil society (including within the Rakhine Muslim communities themselves) as well as in academic circles.[18] Other Muslims groups include the Kaman, who have long been regarded as citizens of the country, but face particular problems "sandwiched" between the much larger Rakhine and *Rohingya* populations.

While a few scholars have looked at issues of majority-minority relations and identity politics in Myanmar (e.g., Houtman 1999), relatively little attention has focused on the issue of citizenship in Myanmar (exceptions being Lall et al. 2014). Most scholarly activity in this field has focused on the vexed "Rohingya issue" (addressed in this book particularly in the chapters by Leider and Tonkin, and the contribution from a Rohingya scholar-activist, Nurul Islam). The contributions presented here seek to deepen debates regarding citizenship and its meaning in modern Myanmar, to include a wider range of issues and approaches. These include Nyi Nyi Kyaw's chapter on the Kaman.[19]

CITIZENSHIP IN POLITICAL THEORY — A VERY BRIEF OVERVIEW

There are many definitions of citizenship — but at its most basic, citizenship focuses on the relationship between the individual and the state (Turner 2006). Any understanding of the concept usually encompasses three different aspects:

> Citizenship as status, which denotes formal state membership and the rules of access to it; citizenship as rights, which is about the formal capacities and immunities connected with such a status; and in addition citizenship as identity, which refers to the behavioural aspects of individuals acting and conceiving of themselves as members of a collectivity, classically the nation *or* the normative conceptions of such behaviour imputed by the state. (Joppke 2007, p. 38)

This definition also reflects Kivisto and Faist's (2007) notion of citizenship as establishing the boundaries of the political community, defining who is in and who is out based on access to political life, as well as a sense of belonging through national identity. Citizenship therefore denotes membership to a polity — in this case a particular state, membership of which involves a reciprocal set of rights and duties. The formal expansion of citizenship rights has evolved from the civil to the political, and further to the social sphere (Kivisto and Faist 2007). The ideal of self-governance as a key component of citizenship was based on the equality and equal liberty of all citizens, which derives historically from Hobbes and Rousseau. One of the debates (Heater 2004; Mitra 2012) which has emerged in the largely Western literature is the link between citizenship and democracy — whereby it is questioned if true citizenship can exist outside of a democratic system, in the absence of political and civil rights to participate in the affairs of state, an approach to citizenship based on social contract theory. However, even in the absence of political participation there is a relationship between the state and the individual — even if rights are not fully guaranteed under a liberal-democratic social contract. For example, in post-colonial countries, which are not always democratic, the challenge of establishing a commonly agreed concept of citizenship has largely hinged on issues of defining national identity, as opposed to rights, duties and political participation. Thus the salience of ethnicity in discussions of citizenship in Myanmar. Benhabib's (2005, p. 675) definition of citizenship in the modern state as "the collective identity of citizens along the lines of shared language, religion, ethnicity, common history and memories; the privileges of political membership in the sense of access to the rights of public autonomy; and the entitlement to social rights and privileges" is useful in post-colonial contexts, as it emphasizes the role identity plays as part of citizenship and acknowledges that these in themselves are diverse. In fact, many Asian post-colonial countries made the establishment of a common national identity across ethnic, religious and linguistic boundaries a political priority, often using education as a political tool[20] to foster an (often) artificial unity (Lall and Vickers 2009). Arguably, General Ne Win's attempts at constructing a pan-Burmese civic patriotism can be understood in this way. However, rights such as political participation and freedom of expression, and accompanying responsibilities such as the duty to pay tax, are still important, as is a general sense of legitimacy for the government. Subrata Mitra expands on the relationship between citizenship and identity, arguing that only when both the legal and moral right to belong are combined can a sense of legitimate citizenship develop. His point that the modern state has to work with traditional society is crucial in cases where there are diverse linguistic, ethnic and religious overlapping identities (as in Myanmar), which existed well before the modern state was imposed:

> Just as the legal right to citizenship is accorded by the state, identity and following from it, the moral right to belong, is what people give to their claims to citizenship. When both converge in the same group, the result is a sense of legitimate citizenship where the individual feels both legally entitled and morally engaged. If not, the consequences are either legal citizenship devoid of a sense of identification with the soil, or a primordial identification with the land but no legal sanction of this. (...) Orderly, legitimate citizenship is possible only if the concept is co-authored by the modern state and traditional society. (Mitra 2008, p. 4)

The relationship between national identity and citizenship differs from country to country. Further complexity is added by the notion of subnational citizenship: identity with a community (which itself may claim to be a nation) which does not map onto the state, at least according to internationally recognized borders. As noted in discussing the definitions above, identity is a key element of citizenship. Yet mature notions of citizenship go beyond issues of (ethnic) identity, as various groups within one state might have differing, overlapping identities — ethnic, linguistic or religious — yet should still be able to relate to an overarching concept of citizenship. Kymlicka and Norman (2000) have discussed the concepts of citizenship in diverse societies, finding that — depending on the system — minorities sometimes are awarded special rights and sometimes have to play by the rules of the majority. These issues are very much in play as Myanmar emerges from half a century of military rule, and should form the basis of a national political conversation regarding the relationship between state, society and citizens.

It is therefore useful to look at what a social contract means in light of reforms in Myanmar. Early social contract theorists, such as Hobbes, Locke and Rousseau, were concerned with ideas of social cooperation and, to a greater extent, of political obligation that rested with the state on the one hand and the individual on the other. Social contract theories tried to establish why citizens would and should accept authoritative governments and obey the law. Today however, social contract theories take the existence of the modern state as a given. According to Rawlsian philosophy, in order for the social contract to work, citizens have to take part (or be able to take part) in public life. Consequently society is obligated to help with the construction of institutions, and cannot leave this responsibility to the state alone. The contract rests on reciprocity and both sides have to take part for it to work. This reciprocity is also at the basis of the legitimacy of the modern state. The state has to justify its existence through its normative role, i.e., what it should do with regard to meeting the needs of individual citizens. There is therefore an element of state responsibility, where the state regulates public policy-making in order to meet the social, economic and political needs of its citizens. In light of this, we look briefly at the 2008 Myanmar Constitution that sets out an implicit social contract governing relations between citizens and the state.

CITIZENSHIP IN MYANMAR LEGAL AND CONSTITUTIONAL DISCOURSE

Despite its many problems, and widespread unpopularity particularly among ethnic communities, the text of the 2008 Constitution is a key document in discussing citizenship in Myanmar.[21] Citizenship in the 2008 Constitution is described in Chapter VIII: "Citizen, Fundamental Rights and Duties of the Citizens" (Articles 345–90). The Union offers citizenship to all those who are born of parents who both hold Myanmar citizenship, or those who on the day the Constitution came into effect already held Myanmar citizenship.[22] It goes on to list rights such as equal treatment before the law, equal opportunities in public employment, occupation, trade, etc., and the non-discrimination against women including mothers. The Constitution also promises non-discrimination on the basis of race, religion or sex in appointing or assigning civil service personnel — with the caveat that in those cases where the job is suitable for men only, only a man should be appointed. Other rights, such as freedom of expression and the rights to settle anywhere in the Union, are also granted *if* not contrary to the laws enacted for Union security. The rights offered by the constitution in Chapter VIII can be suspended in times of invasion, insurrection and emergency.

The list of citizens' duties is much shorter, and includes the duty to abide by the Constitution, safeguard the territorial integrity of the Union, undergo military training, enhance unity and peace amongst the national races, help bring about a modern and developed nation, and pay taxes. With regard to political participation, Article 369 (Chapter VIIIA) guarantees the right to elect and be elected to the Parliaments. More details can be found in Chapter IX ("Election") and Chapter X ("Political Parties"). According to Article 406, political parties are allowed in accord with the law to organize freely and compete in the election. "Organisations and associations" can be founded (Article 354c) and people have the right to get elected (Article 369). This is particularly important given the decades where Myanmar did not allow for political participation — a crucial part of citizenship, and political parties such as the NLD were repressed.

Thus the 2008 Constitution does enshrine rights and duties, and the right to political participation figures quite prominently in the text — even though the environment for such participation remains restricted by other laws — and extra-legal practices — governing integrity of the Union and national security. Emerging from a historical context where neither rights nor duties were enshrined and respected, and political participation in the form of opposition generally engendered lengthy prison sentences, these provisions are relatively progressive. Nevertheless, many political stakeholders in Myanmar continue to demand fundamental changes to, or even the abolition of, the 2008 Constitution. Concerns focus in particular on how the Constitution entrenches the role of the Myanmar Army (for example, granting the Tatmadaw 25 per cent of seats in all legislatures, including State/Regional assemblies), and the manner in which the charter centralizes power under the Union government, in contrast to many ethnic stakeholders' demands for a more federal state (notwithstanding the 2008 Constitution's provision for Ethnic Affairs Ministers, as discussed by Ardeth Maung Thawnhmung and Yadana).

In order to understand how issues of citizenship play out in contemporary Myanmar, it is necessary to refer to the legal frameworks which have governed citizenship in Myanmar in the past, and forms the basis of laws today. Although this collection of essays is not primarily a legal-constitutional study, we offer an introduction to the two citizenship acts that have governed who is part of the Myanmar polity.

BURMA — KEY CONSTITUTIONAL AND LEGAL DOCUMENTS

The Union Citizenship (Election) Act, 1948

The 1948 Citizenship Acts was based on sections 10, 11 and 12 of the 1947 Constitution of the Union of Burma, defining a citizen as:

1. Any person whose parents belong or belonged to any of the indigenous races of Burma; or
2. Any person, born in any of the territories included within the Union, at least one of whose grandparents belong or belonged to any of the indigenous races of Burma; or
3. Any person born in any of the territories which included within the Union, of parents both of whom are or if they had been alive at the commencement of this Constitution would have been, citizen of Burma; or
4. Any person born in any of the territories which at the time of birth was included within the British colonial dominions and who has resided in any of the territories included within Burma for a period of not less than eight years in the ten years preceding the date of commencement of this Constitution or immediately preceding 1 January 1942 and who intends to reside permanently there in and who signifies his election of citizenship of the Union in the manner and within the time prescribed by law, shall be a citizen of Burma.

(Adapted and reproduced from Tun Tun Aung 2007, pp. 270–71).

During the 1970s, the 1948 Citizenship Act was reviewed for six and a half years, and in 1982 a new Citizenship Law was enacted. In a speech at the

President's house on 8 October 1982 General Ne Win explained that the new law was written to protect Burma from foreign subjugation.[23] He distinguished between "true nationals", guests and those born of mixed unions, and explained the difference between citizens, guests who have registered for citizenship (i.e., associate citizens) and guests who have not registered for citizenship within the legal time frame (i.e., naturalized citizens). Ne Win emphasized that since the grandchildren of associate and naturalized citizens would become full citizens in the future, there would only be full citizens within two generations:

> There are three types of citizens at present as said earlier. There will be only one type in our country at some time in the future; that is there will be only citizens.... When the grandchild is given citizenship, he will, just like any other citizen, become a full citizen. (Ne Win 1982)

Ne Win's vision has yet to be realized. The law and its current application is explained below.

The 1982 Citizenship Law

The 1982 Citizenship Law, which is still in effect, contains special provisions for ethnic groups who came into the country after the beginning of the first Anglo-Burmese War. Under the 1982 Citizenship Law there are two types of citizenship: Native Citizenship and Legal Citizenship. *Native Citizens* are nationals such as Kachin, Kayah, Kayin, Chin, Bamar, Mon, Rakhine, Shan and other ethnic groups who have been settled in the territory of Myanmar since 1823, as well as their descendants. No one can revoke their citizenship without a strong reason.

Legal Citizens are not nationals, but qualify to become citizens of Myanmar according to the legal framework. The third generation of residents who arrived before 1948 will be issued a "Certificate of Citizenship" automatically even though they are not "nationals". Within the *legal citizenship* category there are of two sub-types:

1. Associate Citizens: People who became Myanmar citizens according to the 1948 citizenship law.
2. Naturalized Citizens: People who had been residing in Myanmar before independence (4 January 1948) and their descendants, who have strong supporting evidence and documents that they were eligible for citizenship under the 1948 citizenship law.

According to the 1982 Citizenship Act, only a person whose parents had naturalized citizenship, or a certificate of citizenship, or a certificate of guest citizenship can be a citizen.

It can be seen from the above that the status of Myanmar citizenship was well "protected" (or guarded), making it almost impossible for foreigners to gain equality with those who can claim decent by blood. In the absence of a social contract of any kind (at least before the advent of the 2008 Constitution), and given the lack of access to rights in general, the "right to live in one country", i.e., Myanmar, seems to have been a fundamental part of citizens' identity. This is reflected in Lall's chapter on youth and citizenship. It is interesting to note that the battle of who qualifies under the 1982 Citizenship act is not over, as reflected in the chapters on the Rohingya and Rakhine State by Leider and Tonkin, as well as the contribution by Nurul Islam.

The chapters of this book address various aspects of citizenship, allowing readers to understand this concept better in the Myanmar context of social and political transition. The contributions from ethnic political leaders and academic authors are summarized below.

CHAPTER OVERVIEWS

The book consists of nine chapters, plus six contributions from political leaders in and from Myanmar. Interspersed throughout the book, these shorter contributions vary in style and tone (and length). While sometimes less nuanced academically than the chapters written by scholars, these pieces are valuable in revealing and illustrating how political leaders from six of Myanmar's ethnic communities (and citizens groups) understand issues of citizenship. This book constitutes the first time that such local (albeit elite) voices have been presented in juxtaposition with academic analyses of issues around citizenship and ethnicity in Myanmar.

Nai Hongsa, Vice-Chairman of the New Mon State Party, sketches the history of armed conflict in Myanmar and identifies underlying causes. He concludes by arguing for a strong federal union as the way forward. Nai Hongsa highlights some of the reasons why achieving a sense of citizenship in Myanmar are so fraught, including the existence of sometimes conflicting allegiances to both ethnic group and the larger union. Nevertheless, he is optimistic about the possibility for unity and progress. *Sai Kheunsai, the founder and editor of the Shan Herald Agency for News*, contributes a lively and witty personal piece, offering insights into the meaning of ethnic citizenship in Burma/Myanmar. He describes the challenges and complexities of identifying both with a "minority" ethnic group (which nevertheless is a majority in its own State), and with the larger national community. *Khu Oo Reh, Vice-Chairman of the Karenni National Progressive Party*, provides a historical overview and account of ethnic nationality citizens' strong feelings of identity and community. He too is optimistic about the prospects for a federal union. *U Aung Naing Oo, a political analyst and previously leading member of the Myanmar Peace Centre*, is an ethnic Burman who has spent much time among ethnic nationality communities. He describes his struggle as a democracy activist in coming to terms with a new Myanmar of which he can be proud. *P'doh Kweh Htoo Win, General Secretary of the Karen National Union*, was interviewed by Ashley South on 11 August 2016. He spoke about the challenges faced by Karen and other ethnic nationality people, in achieving equality and citizenship. P'doh Kweh Htoo advocates for an approach to federalism which allows for territorial self-determination, and also the rights of ethnic nationality people (for example, in relation to language use), wherever they live in the country. He also spoke about the challenges of building trust between Karen and other ethnic nationality communities, and *Bama* majority, and government. *Nurul Islam, Chairman of the Arakan Rohingya National Organization* discusses the situation of the Muslim Rohingya community, and their claims to citizenship. Given the recent issues in Rakhine State, a Rohingya voice on this issue is particularly important.

The longer, scholarly chapters are grouped around the three broad themes introduced above: issues of identity and conflict in relation to citizenship; debates specifically around concepts and practices of citizenship; and inter- and intra-community issues, including Buddhist–Muslim relations. Chapter 1 (Ethnic Politics and Citizenship in History) by *Martin Smith*, an independent author and consultant, sets the scene, analysing how ethnic conflict and different perceptions of national identity, politics and citizenship have remained integral challenges in state-building and national life in Myanmar since independence in 1948. One of the most ethnically diverse countries in Asia, a hopeful future was predicted for the new nation. However, armed conflict swiftly broke out in the post-colonial state, and conditions of internal warfare have been sustained through every era of national politics, as a diversity of different state and non-state actors have struggled to achieve a constitutional system that reflects the aspirations, identities and citizenship rights of all peoples. This overview chapter describes how, since 2011, a new democratic system of government has been introduced in Myanmar — albeit one in which the military still wield great influence. Smith analyses ceasefires agreed between the government and ethnic armed groups since 2012. This and the victory of the NLD in the 2015 general election have added to the hopes for change. However, as the search for solutions continues, new challenges are emerging and old problems have in some cases worsened. These include renewed fighting in the Kachin and Shan States; Buddhist–Muslim violence that has spread from the Rakhine State; disenfranchisement from voting rights or citizenship for over million people of perceived Indian or Chinese ancestry; and the displacement of a further 350,000 civilians from their homes. He argues that it remains vital that crises and historic failings in ethnic politics are addressed if Myanmar is to achieve peace, democracy and nationality rights for all peoples.

Chapter 2 (Representation and Citizenship in the Future Integration of Ethnic Armed Actors in Myanmar/Burma), by *Helene Kyed*, Research Fellow at the Institute of International Studies, Copenhagen, and *Mikael Gravers*, Associate Professor, Anthropology, Aarhus University, continues the discussion of ethnic politics, armed conflict and citizenship. This chapter discusses the future integration of EAOs in a post-conflict in Myanmar, and the importance of *de facto* citizenship to ethnic populations in this process, and the problems this presents given continued large-scale fighting across much of the country, between the Myanmar army and NCA non-signatory groups. This chapter discusses different possible paths for integration, at least for those groups and associated communities which have ceasefires with the government, including in the context of security sector reform, as political parties, in relation to local governance, regarding economic integration and as civil society organizations. Integration needs to consider citizenship issues at the local level, including questions of who represents ethnic people, as individuals and groups.

Chapter 3 (National Political Dialogue and Practices of Citizenship in Myanmar), by *Matthew J. Walton*, Aung San Suu Kyi Senior Research Fellow, St Antony's College, Oxford University, moves the discussion from issues of ethnicity and conflict, towards broader topics of citizenship and state–society relations in a changing Myanmar. Walton argues that developing a broader understanding of a diverse range of citizenship skills and practices is particularly important in the context of Myanmar's rapid political change. Practices of citizenship would include various perspectives on what citizenship entails (the different rights and responsibilities), the roles of state and civil society groups in fostering citizenship, and expectations of citizen participation (including the role of the state in facilitating participation). Particularly important are the many "skills" of citizenship that go beyond basic rights and responsibilities, that are applicable to citizens and government officials in different ways. This chapter considers practices of citizenship primarily in relation to the national political dialogue process, the forum that (in some form or another) will shape

Myanmar's political future. It explores two aspects of citizenship that draw attention to critical limitations of the current political dialogue framework. The first concern is related to political communication: what are the accepted methods of "speaking" and modes of engagement in the dialogue? How do these accepted methods privilege particular groups and individuals and how can other participants be sure that their voices can be meaningfully "heard"? The second issue is that of transformative citizenship and participation: how is the dialogue process organized so that it can generate new notions of belonging in Myanmar and new relationships among citizens and between citizens and leaders? Can it be constructed in a way that would lead more directly and effectively to the development of capable, empathetic, savvy, and inter-connected citizens? For Walton, the national political dialogue process represents an opportunity to not only restructure the country politically, but also to set examples and reinforce precedents of practices of citizenship. For this to happen, the process must be broadly inclusive, meaningfully participatory, and sensitive to the diverse experiences, needs, and perspectives of Myanmar's population.

The next two chapters look at specific issues in relation to citizenship in Myanmar, from the perspective of government authority, and the country's youth. Chapter 4 (Citizenship and Minority Rights: The Role of "National Race Affairs" Ministers in Myanmar's 2008 Constitution) by *Ardeth Maung Thawnhmung*, Chair of the Political Science Department, University of Massachusetts at Lowell, and *U Yadana*, Director of Braveheart Foundation, examines the significance and implications of the post created by the 2008 Constitution for National Race Affairs Ministers, in the post-military government of Myanmar. The authors focus on the processes that have led to greater recognition and enhancement of National Race Affairs Ministers, and the implications of this role for the protection and expansion of minority rights, and the promotion of citizenship rights. However, these position remains precarious, and the performance of individuals depends of their social, economic and ideological backgrounds.

Chapter 5 (Myanmar's Youth and the Question of Citizenship), by *Marie Lall*, Professor of Education and South Asian Studies, Institute of Education, University College London, is framed by an understanding that citizenship in Myanmar under military rule has always been defined from above. In light of the post-2010 reforms, this chapter examines views from below — specifically how young people across Myanmar define citizenship, in the context of education. One of the most prominent cross-cutting themes emerging from the primary research reported here is that of patriotism and nationalism, often linked to culture, religion and sometimes to language.

This includes a growing sense of Buddhism as part of the national identity that serves to discriminate/divide rather than unite. A very large number of respondents within the Buddhist ethnic groups — i.e., not only Bamar respondents — equated citizenship with religion, or seemed to think that in order to be Myanmar one has to also be Buddhist. Equal rights for all was another key theme. There were however, regional and ethnic differences on whether the fairness was based on sharing resources (Bamars) or a federated concept of ethnic rights and national rights (other ethnic nationalities). Many of these rights focused on freedom of culture, religion, speech, access to land, and most importantly access to opportunities.

Chapter 6 ("The Value of Life": Citizenship, Entitlement and Moral Legibility in Provincial Myanmar), by *Gerard McCarthy*, a Ph.D. candidate at the Australian National University, further explores relationships between religion, social position and notions of citizenship, through an examination of the spiritually imbued ideas of "nation" and "citizenship" that emerge through the work of Buddhist welfare groups in provincial Myanmar. Based in Taungoo, Bago Region, McCarthy's ethnographic study follows these groups and their ideas about "compassionate mindedness" and "moral obligations" that are evoked in their work with medical patients, flood victims, the elderly and the deceased. Whilst these groups promote what may appear to be normatively praiseworthy values of "self-reliance" and "care for others", McCarthy notes the ease with which such moral claim-making around generosity and care are deployed to the exclusion of Muslims who are labelled as "stingy" and violent — especially with the rise of social media in recent years. Even as the Myanmar state expands into spheres of welfare in the coming years, McCarthy argues that the thin notions of entitlement from the state and thick sense of obligations to fellow citizens that are embedded within the work of these groups are likely to form the basis of important cleavages around citizenship and political community in Myanmar.

The final three chapters explore different aspects of the often fraught, and sometimes violent, relationships between Muslim communities in Myanmar, and other groups, and the government. They should be read in conjunction with the contribution by the Rohingya scholar-activist, Nurul Islam. Chapter 7 (Conflict and Mass Violence in Arakan (Rakhine State): The 1942 Events and Political Identity Formation) by *Jacques P. Leider*, École française d'Extrême-Orient, Bangkok and Yangon, presents original research and analysis regarding mass atrocities which took place in Arakan/Rakhine State during the months of April and May 1942, when the British administration broke down and the Japanese regime was not yet established. Both the Buddhist and the Muslim communities were responsible for killing and persecuting members of the other community. The 1942 acts of ethnic cleansing were never thoroughly investigated or addressed. Each community kept its own memory of the tragic events that fed later discordant nationalist narratives. The chapter compiles available information on the 1942 violence, its historical context and the diverging and often partial retellings and interpretations. The mutual acts of aggression led to killings and forced displacement, and increased inter-ethnic hostility. This episode is highly relevant still, because it helped to determine the civic awareness and political orientations of Buddhists and Muslims during the early post-war period.

Chapter 8 (Exploring the Issue of Citizenship in Rakhine State), by *Derek Tonkin*, former British Ambassador to Thailand, Vietnam and Laos, examines the issue of citizenship for the Rohingya in Rakhine State. Tonkin notes that in 1948 Muslims were as entitled as anyone else to be granted citizenship automatically, provided they belonged to any of the national races (last tabulated at the 1931 Census), or to apply for citizenship on the basis of the length of their residence. However, the provision of a "National Registration Certificate", even to those who were automatically entitled, was lethargic in Arakan, and few of those who had made application for citizenship ever received an official response. Nonetheless, the Burmese authorities made no difficulties about agreeing to the repatriation in 1979 and the early 1990s of Muslims who had fled for safety into Bangladesh. When the 1982 Citizenship Act came into force, there was still no substantive change in the status of Muslims in Arakan, for those who were already citizens were guaranteed under both the 1974 Constitution and the Act that their status would be unchanged. Unfortunately, the decision seems to have been taken only in Rakhine State that holders of National Registration Certificates would not be automatically issued with new IDs, as happened elsewhere, but that holders would need to be examined for entitlement because of the prevalence of forged and improperly acquired documents. Around 1990, the authorities started to issue temporary "White Cards" (which in 2015 was abruptly cancelled) but took no action to examine entitlement. Only about 20 per cent of some 450,000 "White Card" holders in Arakan had (at the time of writing) taken up new green-coloured cards describing the holder as persons "whose citizenship will be scrutinized". Tonkin describes how the NLD government established a special commission to resolve the problems affecting Rakhine State, arguing that external pressures are unlikely to be productive, unless they support the government's objectives of peace, stability and economic development.

Chapter 9 (Myanmar's Other Muslims: The Case of the Kaman) by *Nyi Nyi Kyaw*, Postdoctoral Fellow at the Centre for Asian Legal Studies at the

Faculty of Law at the National University of Singapore, examines the rise of anti-Muslim sentiments and violent and sectarian conflicts since 2012. He demonstrates how the issue of the Rohingya understandably became the dominant topic in discourse and advocacy regarding Myanmar Muslims, especially outside the country. However, he draws attention to the plight of the Kaman Muslims, who are officially recognized as an ethnic community in Myanmar, but often find themselves marginalized and discriminated against. This final chapter discusses how Kaman identity has been constructed, problematized and reconstructed, largely due to the impact of sectarian violent conflicts in Rakhine State in 2012, and analyses how the small Kaman community has sought to survive due to their status sandwiched between Rakhine Buddhists and Rohingya Muslims.

Notes

1. On the reform process in Myanmar, see Lall (2016).
2. The editors thank all who contributed to the book, including the copyeditor, Michael Woods, and of course the conference organizer and inspiration, Adjarn Chayan Vaddhanaphuti.
3. The census was financed by international donors to the tune of US$75 million, and implemented with the help of the UN Population Fund.
4. According to the UN Population Fund, "UN Estimates 4.25 Million Myanmar-born People Now Live Abroad" <http://www.irrawaddy.com/news/burma/un-estimates-4-25-million-people-from-burma-now-live-abroad.html> (accessed 29 January 2017).
5. Perhaps derived from the 135 or 136 groups identified in the 1931 Census (Cheeseman 2017, p. 8).
6. Also, in the late 1980s, Gen Ne Win tasked the Burma Historical Commission with elucidating a list of ethnic identities in the country, based on the 1973 census (Mary Callaghan, personal communication).
7. Crisis Group, "Counting the Costs: Myanmar's Problematic Census", Crisis Group Asia Briefing 144, 15 May 2014.
8. Failure to enumerate migrant workers may explain the relatively low number of men in the census data.
9. Laur Kiik (2016), p. 213.
10. "The Union Report: Religion — Census Report Volume 2-C" <www.dop.gov.mm> (accessed 11 November 2016).
11. According to Derek Tonkin (personal communication, 10 December 2016), "the Islamic population in Rakhine State (enumerated and unenumerated at the 2014 Census) is approximately 1,120,000 (includes Kaman and non-Rohingya:

estimated 1.09 million unenumerated plus 28,631 enumerated), while outside Rakhine State it is 1,118,864 (1,147,495 total enumerated nationally, but less the 28,631 enumerated in Rakhine State). This suggests that the number of self-identified Rohingya are not more than 50 per cent of all Muslims in the country, and possibly slightly less. But this takes no account of those who might choose to identify as Rohingya outside Rakhine State if it were safe and possible for them to do so."

12. For example, in western Kachin State in 2009 the military-connected Yuzana Company was reported in local media to be planning the resettlement of up to 200,000 *Bama* people to work on plantations in the Hukawng Valley: Laur Kiik (2016), p. 227.

13. The CIA's World Factbook estimates: Burman 68 per cent, Shan 9 per cent, Karen 7 per cent, Rakhine 4 per cent, Chinese 3 per cent, Indian 2 per cent, Mon 2 per cent, other 5 per cent <https://www.cia.gov/library/publications/the-world-factbook/geos/bm.html> (accessed 25 April 2016).

14. Leach (1954).

15. Taylor (2015).

16. According to sources in the Dawei National Party, there are about 1 million Dawei citizens in Tanintharyi Region, which would include most of those currently regarded as Burmans (Field Notes 28 August 2016).

17. C.f. the Nung community of northern Kachin State, regarded by many Kachin nationalists (and Rawang leaders) as part of the Rawang Kachin subgroup, but some members of which want to claim a distinct Nung *lu myo* status.

18. According to Jacques Leider (2015), "the quasi-monopoly that the term 'Rohingya' enjoys in the media today, did not yet exist in the early 1950s".

19. For an overview of Muslim communities in Myanmar, and intra-communal relations in the context of citizenship and the constitution, see Nyi Nyi Kyaw (2015).

20. The use of education as a political tool is not confined to Asia. In Western industrialized societies, education has been used historically (and arguably still is today) to create an "imagined" (or even "artificial") unity. Generally, however, education's role as a political tool is most visible in postcolonial countries where in a short span of time diverse ethnic, linguistic and religious communities had to be joined together under the banner of a new nation state.

21. The 2008 Constitution came into being after a highly controversial referendum. The new constitution put in place the mechanism through which the structural change, including the 2010 elections, could take place.

22. See below for details on the 1948 Union Citizenship (Election) Act and 1982 Union Citizenship Act.

23. <http://www.netipr.org/policy/downloads/19821008_Gen-Ne-Win-speech-on-Citizenship-Law.pdf>.

References

Benhabib, Seyla. "Borders, Boundaries, and Citizenship". *Political Science and Politics* 38, no. 4 (2005): 673–77.

Cheesman, Nick. "How in Myanmar 'National Races' Came to Surpass Citizenship and Exclude Rohingya". *Journal of Contemporary Asia* 47, issue 3 (2017): 461–83 [DOI: 10.1080/00472336.2017.1297476].

Ferguson, Jane M. "Who's Counting? Ethnicity, Belonging, and the National Census in Burma/Myanmar". *Bijdragen tot de Taal-, Land- en Volkenkunde* 171 (2015): 1–28.

Heater, D.B. *A Brief History of Citizenship*. New York: New York University Press, 2004.

Houtman, Gustaaf. *Mental Culture in Burmese Crisis Politics: Aung San Suu Kyi and the National League For Democracy*. Monograph 33. Tokyo: Institute for the Study of Languages and Cultures of Asia and Africa Tokyo University of Foreign Studies, 1999.

International Crisis Group. *Counting the Costs: Myanmar's Problematic Census, Asia Report*. Brussels: International Crisis Group, 2015.

Joppke, Christian. "Beyond national models: Civic integration policies for immigrants in Western Europe". *West European Politics* 30, no. 1 (2007): 1–22.

Kivisto, Peter and Thomas Faist. *Citizenship: Discourse, Theory, and Transnational Prospects*. New Jersey: John Wiley, 2007.

Kymlicka, Will and Wayne Norman, eds. *Citizenship in Diverse Societies*. Oxford: Oxford University Press, 2000.

Lall, Marie. *Understanding Reform in Myanmar: People and Society in the Wake of Military Rule*. London: Hurst Publishers, 2016.

——— and Edward Vickers, eds. *Education as a Political Tool in Asia*. London: Routledge, 2009.

———, Thei Su San, Nwe Nwe San, Yeh Tut Naing, Thein Thein Myat, Lwin Thet Thet Khaing, Swann Lynn Htet and Yin Nyein Aye. *Citizenship in Myanmar: Contemporary debates and challenges in light of the reform process*. Yangon: Myanmar Egress, 2014 <http://marielall.com/wp/wp-content/uploads/Myanmar-Egress-Citizenship-FINAL-as-sent-out.pdf> (accessed 28 May 2016).

Laur Kiik. "Conspiracy, God's Plan and National Emergency: Kachin Popular Analyses of the Ceasefire Era and its Resource Grabs". In *War and Peace in the Borderlands of Myanmar: The Kachin Ceasefire, 1994–2011*, edited by Mandy Sadan, pp. 205–35. Copenhagen: NIAS Press, 2016.

Leach, Edmund. *Political Systems of Highland Burma: A study of Kachin social structure*. London: G Bell & Son, 1954.

Leider, Jacques. "Competing Identities and the Hybridized History of the Rohingyas". In *Metamorphosis: Studies in Social and Political Change in Myanmar*, edited by Renaud Egreteau and Francois Robinne, pp. 151–78; Singapore NUS Press 2015.

Mitra, Subatra. "Level playing fields: The Post-colonial State, Democracy, Courts and Citizenship in India". *German Law Journal* 9, no. 3 (2008): 343–66.

Ne Win. "Translation of the speech by General Ne Win". *The Working People's Daily*, 9 October 1982 <http://www.burmalibrary.org/docs6/Ne_Win's_speech_Oct-1982-Citizenship_Law.pdf>.

Nyi Nyi Kyaw (2015).

Sadan, M. *Being and Becoming Kachin: Histories Beyond the State in the Borderworlds of Burma*. Oxford: British Academy and Oxford University Press, 2013.

Smith, Martin. *Burma: insurgency and the politics of ethnicity*. New York: Zed Books, 1999.

South, Ashley. *Ethnic Politics in Burma: States of Conflict*. Oxon: Routledge, 2008.

———— and Marie Lall. *Conflict and Schooling: ethnic education and mother tongue-based teaching in Myanmar*. Yangon: The Asia Foundation, 2016.

Taylor, R. "Perceptions of Ethnicity in the Politics of Burma". *Southeast Asian Journal of Social Science* 10, no. 1 (1982): 7–22.

————. *The State in Burma*. London: Hurst Publishing, 1987.

————. *General Ne Win: A political biography*. Singapore: Institute of Southeast Asian Studies, 2015.

Tun Tun Aung. "An Introduction to Citizenship Card under Myanmar Citizenship Law". 現代社會文化研究 [Modern Socio-cultural Research] 38 (2007): 265–90 <http://dspace.lib.niigata-u.ac.jp/dspace/bitstream/10191/6399/1/01_0053.pdf> (accessed 29 May 2016).

Turner, B.S. "Citizenship and the Crisis of Multiculturalism". *Citizenship Studies* 10, no. 5 (2006): 607–18.

1

ETHNIC POLITICS AND CITIZENSHIP IN HISTORY

Martin Smith

Different perceptions over identity, politics and citizenship have continued throughout Myanmar/Burma's modern history.[1] Such differences were partially structured during the colonial era of government, and they have diversified into new forms since independence in 1948 as a host of different state and non-state actors have struggled to achieve a national political system that reflects the aspirations and identities of all peoples. Failure in the accomplishment of such a fundamental task has underpinned the legacy of ethnic conflict and state failure that continues to face the country. Into the twenty-first century, the national landscape has remained divided. While the national armed forces, known as the Tatmadaw, have come to dominate government and unitary political systems in the centre of the country, a variety of ethnic-based opposition groups have kept alive very different visions of identity, citizenship and statehood in the surrounding borderlands.

Since 2011, a new multi-ethnic, multi-party political system is being introduced through such elements as ethnic peace talks, parliamentary politics and constitutional reform. The advent to government of the National League for Democracy (NLD) in March 2016 provides further momentum to the processes of change. As dialogue takes place, this is bringing on to the national stage differences of opinion and deep crises in ethnic politics that have long needed to be addressed if national peace and stability are to be achieved.

Political transition, however, is neither prescriptive nor a one-way street. As steps towards democracy continue, the difficulties in achieving solutions have been compounded as long-standing crises reveal new complexities or, in some cases, even worsen. Setbacks in ethnic politics during the past six years include a resurgence of armed conflict in the Kachin State and Kachin, Kokang, Shan and Ta-ang (Palaung) regions of the Northern Shan State; Buddhist–Muslim violence that has spread from the Rakhine State to other parts of the country; disenfranchisement from voting rights or citizenship for over million people of perceived Indian or Chinese ancestry; accelerating land-grabbing and competition for the control of natural resources; and the displacement of a further 350,000 civilians from their homes in the Kachin, Rakhine and Shan States.

Clearly, political transition from Tatmadaw-based government is still at a beginning, not at an end. It is vital, therefore, that in the coming years the root causes of the political conflicts and disagreements that have long divided the country are recognized and addressed. As Myanmar's isolation recedes, informed debate about many long-neglected challenges is increasing, and this is helping to support reconciliation during a critical time of national change. But until inclusive peace and reforms reach to all peoples, state failure and national instability are only likely to continue.

BACKGROUND: INTERNAL CONFLICT AND NATIONAL DISUNITY

State instability in Myanmar has been underpinned since independence from Great Britain in 1948 by a challenge the political scientist Josef Silverstein described over three decades ago as "the dilemma of national unity" (Silverstein 1980). In trying to explain this impasse, nationalist politicians have sought to blame the country's problems on a debilitating inheritance from colonial rule when the "3 Ms" (merchants, missionaries and military) had significant, and frequently divisive, socio-political impact. According to the late prime minister U Ba Swe: "In order to separate them culturally from the Burmese (sic), they converted the Karens to their religion and also created a separate literature and privileges for them" (quoted in Von Der Mehden 1963, p. 191).

As, however, the era of Western colonialism fades, such arguments do not explain why many of the most fundamental challenges in building peace and democracy are yet to be addressed in Myanmar. Now in the fourth era of government since 1948, conflict and humanitarian suffering have continued for over six decades, undermining national stability and blighting communities across the country during all political eras: i.e., parliamentary democracy (1948–62); Tatmadaw-backed socialism (1962–88); Tatmadaw dictatorship (1988–2011); and quasi-civilian democracy (2011–present). Even finding a common language to describe the ethnic identities and political goals of Myanmar's peoples has proven difficult. "Ethnic politics is the obverse of the politics of national unity" was the introduction to one study in the military socialist era by the historian and political analyst Robert Taylor (Taylor 1982, p. 7). More recently, Taylor has argued that the contemporary "politics of ethnicity in Myanmar" in the post-2011 era is a case of "refighting old battles, compounding misconceptions" (Taylor 2015).

For social scientists, too, there is sad irony in the intensity of ethnic conflicts in Myanmar. Half a century ago, it was among the Kachin people that the anthropologist Edmund Leach demonstrated in his pioneering *Political Systems of Highland Burma* that "ethnic" identities should not be considered primordial or innate; rather, he argued, they are constantly evolving or being formed in any state or society (Leach 1954). More recently, Mandy Sadan has furthered understanding of the developing character of ethnic identities within the country, describing the experience of "being and becoming Kachin" (Sadan 2013).

Equally pertinent, it is important to recognize that there are conceptual differences between terms for ethnicity in the English and Burmese languages. In particular, "nationality" or "national race" has been used since independence to refer to a "people" or "ethnic" grouping considered to have a distinctive history, language or identity, including the Bamar (Burman) majority, that is considered indigenous to the country. But as the Transnational Institute (TNI 2014) has explained, the Burmese language concepts of "*lu myo*" ("kinds of people" or "race") who are regarded as "*taingyinthar*" ("sons/offspring of the geographical division") are complex, controversial in political and citizenship terms, and do not translate easily into English.

The collective result of these different perceptions is that across the decades some very conflicting views have been expressed about the peoples of Myanmar and the foundations upon which the modern state is being built. For instance, Senior General Than Shwe, chairman of the military State Peace and Development Council (SPDC), stated in a 2002 address to the University for Development of National Races: "Thanks to the unity and farsightedness of our forefathers, our country has existed as a united and firm Union and not as separate small nations for over 2,000 years" (SPDC 2002). In contrast, many ethnic minority parties claim independent traditions for non-Bamar peoples, who make up an estimated third of the country's 53 million population. "There is undoubtedly no community of language, culture or interests between the Shans and the Burmese (sic) save religion, nor is there any sentiment of unity which is the index of a common national mind", claimed the Shan State Independence Army (SSIA) soon after its 1959 founding (SSIA 1959). More recently, the twelve-party United Nationalities Federal Council (UNFC) reiterated the long-standing demand by many nationality organizations for a genuine "federal union" of all peoples after the ethnic conflict and discrimination since independence:

> In the general analysis of the political situation of our country, which is composed of various ethnic nationalities, we find that civil war has been raging in the country for nearly 70 years, due to the forcible practice of chauvinism and fake union system by successive governments in power. (UNFC 2014).

Given this long history of conflict, it is important to stress that there is no integral reason to suggest that the exceptional political violence in Myanmar since independence was in any way pre-ordained. Indeed post-colonial "Burma" was expected to have one of the brightest futures of any emerging state in Asia. As neighbouring China and India demonstrate, ethnic diversity is not, in itself, the cause of war nor an impediment to nation-building or challenges over citizenship. Rather, experiences in different parts of the modern world show that there are usually other reasons why civil war may become so intense in post-colonial countries such as Myanmar.

In the post-Cold War era, especially, internal wars have become the most prevalent form of armed conflict. In such cases, a World Bank study led by Paul Collier found that three conditions are likely to be central to the risk of sustained conflict in lands in post-colonial transition: a multi-ethnic society or "ethnocratic state" where one nationality group forms an absolute majority; destabilizing "root causes" that cause the initial resort to violence, such as weak institutions, poverty, and the battle for control of resources; and, finally, military organizations that become the "perpetuating forces" in the field (Collier et al. 2003, pp. 53, 57).

By all these definitions, Myanmar has been a land entrapped in such cycles of conflict since independence in wars that have endured and diversified through every era of government. Other than Kuomintang (KMT) military activities in the 1950s[2] and two decades of Beijing support to the Communist Party of Burma (CPB) from the late 1960s,[3] international influence or cross-border interference have been slight. Such internal wars, however, do not mean that Myanmar has always been on the brink of collapse. Indeed, rather than war being a situation of breakdown, there can be surprising stability in the status quo between opposing parties caught in a "conflict trap"; many modern states have emerged through protracted times of civil war.

In this sense, Mark Duffield's conflict analysis (Duffield 2001) of "emerging political complexes" rather than "complex political emergencies" is especially apt in Myanmar's case, suggesting "social transformation" more than "social regression" during the experiences of internal warfare. In support of such a "social transformation" view, a distinctive feature of Myanmar's conflict impasse is the self-sustaining way in which an often remarkable diversity of armed movements professing political and ethnic goals have been able to continue their struggles, underpinning an unusually durable paradigm of conflict "as a way of life" in both government and opposition circles (Smith 1999, 2007; South 2008). But, as David Keen has noted (Keen 2001), such conditions of endless war come with a heavy national price. Key stakeholders may see no imperative to change their behaviour; "prolonging a war may be a higher priority than winning it"; and, especially resonant in Myanmar's case, "conflict generates ethnicity" (Keen 2001, pp. 2, 8).

Finally, in view of the terrible sufferings since independence, there remains the enigma of how the social vibrancy and ethnic diversity of present-day Myanmar have survived through the long years of conflict. As censorship is reduced and international doors open, the dynamism of community life is evident in every part of the country. In consequence, it can be argued that the political failures since independence are those of national governance and the institutions of state, not those of local communities or peoples. Indeed it is very often the "societies" — for example, Bamar, Kachin, Mon, Buddhist, Christian or Muslim — that appear stronger at the grassroots levels. As Tom Kramer has noted (Kramer 2011), the reality is that civil society never truly went away during the long years of conflict under military rule. In this respect, post-colonial Myanmar represents a striking example of the political phenomenon, described by Joel Migdal and others, known as "weak state, strong societies", where central government has been unable to impose its will, except by the use of force (Migdal 1988).

In summary, as the country now embarks on another era of political change, the dilemmas of building national unity, reform and citizenship rights that include all peoples still remain. Conflict continues, and many communities still feel excluded from national political life. As the co-founder of the Metta Development Foundation, Lahpai Seng Raw, recently summarized: "Peace requires the people. It is a social state and cannot be developed by military men" (Seng Raw 2015).

THE LEGACY OF COLONIAL GOVERNMENT

A multi-ethnic land located on a strategic crossroads in Asia, Myanmar is inextricably linked to its neighbours through a long history of transmigration and cultural interchange. This heritage remains evident in the twenty-first century in many social and ethnographic fields, from the prevalence of Buddhism to the diversity of Tibeto-Burmese languages.

To construct a unifying narrative, military officials have projected their claims for the starting points in Myanmar state history back to the ruling monarchs Anawrahta, Bayinnaung and Alaungpaya, who lived seven centuries apart between the eleventh and eighteenth centuries. For contemporary purposes, however, most of the dynamics and fault lines in the structures of national politics are more appropriately dated to the era of British colonial rule in the nineteenth and twentieth centuries when Thant Myint-U argues "the making of modern Burma" took place (Myint-U 2001). As the historian Michael Aung-Thwin has written, the British "pacification of Burma" imposed a system of "order without meaning" (Aung-Thwin 1985, p. 258), an ad hoc situation that, it can be argued, still continues today.

Two characteristics, in particular, during the British annexation and governance of the territories that constitute present-day Myanmar have had lasting, and often detrimental, implications for ethnic politics and citizenship in the post-colonial union.

First, British Burma was administered as a province of the Indian Empire until 1937, a demarcation that imposed inhibitions on the development of the modern state and encouraged immigration to accelerate from India and, on smaller scale, China. By 1931, the Census of India records that the Indian population had passed one million out of an estimated country population of 14,650,000 (Bennison 1933, pp. 176–77). According to Robert Taylor (Taylor 2015, p. 1), such rapid migration led to fears, especially in Arakan (the present-day Rakhine State) and the ethnic Bamar heartlands, of being colonized "twice", first by the British and then by "South Asia", fuelling political consciousness and the rise in Burmese nationalism. As Taylor wrote: "Race, or ethnicity, compounded by religion, was a powerful theme in the Burmese nationalist movement in the 1920s, 1930s and 1940s" (ibid.).

The result of such socio-political stirring was a rising tide in communal tension that led to anti-Indian (and to a lesser extent anti-Chinese) violence in 1930 and 1938, and also in the Saya San rebellion during 1931 in which hundreds of people lost their lives. Eventually, an estimated half a million Indians fled the country during the Second World War, pursued by nationalists of the Burma Independence Army (BIA). Although it would be simplistic to ascribe present-day violence to particular events under colonial rule, a worrying precedent had been set for the identity and citizenship rights of those perceived to be of Chinese or Indian "*kala*" (a pejorative term for foreigner) ancestry — a negative view that still exists in many parts of the country today.

The second unhelpful legacy from colonial rule has been equally destabilizing in ethnic politics: the development of a diarchic system of government that divided Myanmar's peoples. Among the Bamar majority, the administrative structures under the royal court were abolished by the colonial authorities and replaced by the village tract system from British India. However, while a system of parliamentary home rule was introduced in what became known as "Burma Proper" or "Ministerial Burma", the borderland territories that are largely home to non-Bamar peoples were, in the main, left under their traditional rulers in a "Frontier Areas Administration" that came under the British Governor. As a result, British Burma was set on two different tracks of national governance in which different perceptions of identity and politics continued to evolve.

In explanation of the colonial system, it can be argued that the British administration reflected the realities of *de facto* autonomy that then existed among such peoples as the Chin, Kachin, Karen, Karenni, Shan, Ta-ang and Wa. The perception, however, in nationalist circles that British rule significantly advantaged non-Bamar peoples is not born out by the evidence. Indeed the late Duwa Zau Rip, a signatory to the 1947 Panglong Agreement that helped bring the new "Union of Burma" into being, several times told this author that it was the belief that the Kachin people had not progressed as equals under British rule, which encouraged his delegation to listen to the late independence leader Aung San and sign this historic treaty of equal union among the country's peoples.

In reality, British Burma was permeated with administrative inconsistencies that highlighted ethnic differences but did not provide solutions. In particular, while non-Bamar peoples (notably Chins, Kachins and Karens) were preferred into ethnic-based units in the colonial Burma Army, little was done to address nationality aspirations on the ground. Karen populations, for instance, were divided between five districts of British Burma; requests from Kachin and Shan leaders for independence were ignored; the Chin/Zo peoples were separated between India and Burma; and, in a territorial exception that still has political resonance, the Karenni states were never fully incorporated into British Burma (Smith 1999, pp. 44–59).

With time and inter-community dialogue, it is possible that many of these political differences could have been resolved.[4] The potential, however, for peaceful transition was undermined by the devastating consequences of the Second World War. For while Aung San's BIA initially joined on the side of Imperial Japan, the Kachins, Karens and other non-Bamar peoples generally stayed loyal to the Allied Forces. Significant loss of life occurred. There was Bamar–Karen violence in the south of the country, Buddhist–Muslim conflict in Arakan, and a major exodus of ethnic Indians, providing troubling warnings of the instabilities about to come. Equally destabilizing, it was during the upheavals of the 1940s that many of the "root causes" and "perpetuating forces" evolved that have underpinned the divisions in national politics ever since. This was reflected in the rise of a generation of national leaders who remained hardliners until the end of their days, including General Ne Win (Tatmadaw, Burma Socialist Programme Party [BSPP]), Thakin Ba Thein Tin (CPB), and General Bo Mya (Karen National Union [KNU]).

In the hurried British departure, the achievement of a political system that found agreement among all peoples proved an impossible task. With the CPB and KNU boycotting the 1947 general election, this challenge was made even more difficult due to the assassination (by the gang of a political rival) of Aung San whose "unity in diversity" slogan had become the independence rallying call. Eventually, a new constitution was drawn up, with power to be divided in a bicameral legislature between the former Ministerial Burma and ethnic nationality territories in the Frontier Areas. This, however, proved to be as unsatisfactory as the "order without meaning" structures of British rule.

Among many inconsistencies: the Shan and Karenni States were allowed the right of secession (Articles 201–206) after a ten-year period; the new Kachin State did not receive this right in exchange for the inclusion of more territory; the Chins only received a "special division"; the designation of Karen rights and territory was left to be decided after independence; such nationalities as the Mon, Rakhine, Pao, Ta-ang and Wa were left without distinctive recognition; and, as Josef Silverstein pointed out, "federalism" was not actually mentioned in the new constitution, despite appearing to be its main intention (Silverstein 1980, pp. 185–205).

Even the famed Panglong Agreement of February 1947 had its flaws. Today it is mostly remembered for its symbolism as an accord of national unity. However, only Chin, Kachin and Shan leaders were represented at the five-day meeting, and sentiment has always been widespread among non-Bamar peoples that the promises of autonomy and equality agreed at Panglong have never been delivered upon.[5]

For this reason, the calls by Aung San Suu Kyi for "Panglong spirit" and the "second struggle for independence" have been among her most popular declarations since she emerged on the national stage during the 1988 pro-democracy protests (Aung San Suu Kyi 2011, p. 5; NLD 2015, p. 5). Such unity calls have allowed all peoples a role in the country's national struggles in history: firstly, against colonial rule and, subsequently, military rule. For citizens long deprived of a political voice, it is a struggle for democracy and ethnic rights that is still continuing today. One of the first acts of Aung San Suu Kyi's NLD government has been to initiate a new process, known as the "Twenty-first Century Panglong", as the party's primary platform in seeking to bring ethnic peace and reform to the country. Memory of better times in the past continue to have powerful resonance in national politics today.

PARLIAMENTARY DEMOCRACY AND THE FIRST CYCLE OF CONFLICT: 1948–62

There are many hopes during Myanmar's present national transition that the long-standing cycles of conflict in ethnic politics will soon be ended. However it is important to remember that, far from peace and reform initiatives being a new idea, there have been several moments of optimism before. As today, new processes have been started at the beginning of each new era of government, notably in 1948–50, 1962–64, 1988–90 and 2011–13. However, on each occasion, failure ultimately led to new cycles of conflict that, over the years, have made the achievement of solutions more difficult.

Conflict and militarization in national politics first took root during the upheavals around independence and transition to a new system of parliamentary democracy, headed by the Anti-Fascist People's Freedom League (AFPFL) government of Prime Minister U Nu. As instability spread across the country, the CPB began armed insurrection in March 1948; mutinies split the fledgling Tatmadaw; and, within a year, a host of ethnic-based parties had taken up arms, including Karen, Karenni, Mon, Pao and Rakhine forces. Unsuccessful peace talks took place with the KNU during 1949, and other peace initiatives followed. These included U Nu's "Arms for Democracy" call in 1958 and peace talks again with the KNU by General Ne Win's "Military Caretaker" administration in 1960, shortly before power was returned to Prime Minister U Nu.

On the surface, the political situation may have appeared chaotic. But, from the upheavals of these years, new "political complexes" evolved that have dominated national politics ever since. Over half a century later, many of the leading ethnic armed organizations in contemporary politics date their foundations back to nationality movements that evolved during the parliamentary era. Long-standing parties include the KNU (1947), Karenni

National Progressive Party (KNPP: 1957), New Mon State Party (NMSP: 1958) and Kachin Independence Organisation (KIO: 1961).

Undoubtedly, however, the most important force to emerge during the AFPFL era was the Tatmadaw, which developed under General Ne Win as the most powerful institution in the country before seizing control of government in 1962. Ultimately, General Ne Win's "Burmese Way to Socialism" was to end in failure. But, as Mary Callahan has highlighted, it was Ne Win's fears of ethnic schisms and national disunity that were a primary factor in the Tatmadaw's rise to power during the parliamentary era of the 1950s (Callahan 2003).

Ne Win's ascendancy set in motion two key consequences that have since had deep impact on national politics and perceptions of ethnicity and citizenship. Previously, these had been loosely defined under the 1947 Constitution.[6] The first important consequence was the increasing "Burmanization" of the Tatmadaw and marginalization of non-Bamar peoples from official positions in government. Although Chin, Kachin and Karen units in the Tatmadaw had remained loyal to the Union following the outbreak of the CPB insurrection, General Ne Win ousted the Karen General Smith Dun as commander-in-chief just before the outbreak of the KNU uprising in January 1949, prompting many of the Karen troops, as well as one Kachin battalion, to join the armed struggle against the central government.

These events remain highly controversial in national politics today. But whoever was to blame, such incidents underpinned Ne Win's distrust of non-Bamar peoples and inheritance from the colonial era of a "two-wing" army formed along nationality lines: one of Bamars and one of non-Bamars (Callahan 2003, pp. 95–96). Ethnic-based battalions were ended during the 1950s, and it has since become difficult to find any non-Bamar, or non-Buddhist, above the rank of major in the Tatmadaw leadership. "One blood, one voice, one command" became the Tatmadaw's guiding ideology, deepening a sense of estrangement from the armed forces and government among many minority communities.

The second consequence of Ne Win's dominance was the Tatmadaw's drift into national politics. In the early years of conflict, such motivation was prompted by perceived threats to territorial integrity and the new country's borders, including a Mujahid insurgency along the Arakan frontier and the invasion of several thousand KMT troops into the Shan State after the communist victory in China. By the mid-1950s, both emergencies had largely been contained, but they fuelled General Ne Win's belief that, while politicians dithered and opposition groups wrought national instability, only the Tatmadaw was defending the new nation.

In the late 1950s, this perception caused Ne Win to develop a new concern: a fear of the break-up of the Union itself. The risks, he believed, were underscored through factionalism among political parties and the right of secession for the Shan and Karenni States that had been written into the 1947 Constitution. This unusual clause, which could be enacted after a ten-year period, prompted Ne Win to pressure the Shan and Karenni *sawbwas* (princes) to sign away their traditional rights during his "Military Caretaker" administration during 1958–60 when he briefly assumed office (Smith 1999, pp. 179–94).

Far from being a temporary measure, however, Ne Win's premiership proved a trial run. Following the return of Prime Minister U Nu to elected government in 1960, new armed struggles accelerated in the Kachin and Shan States, while a "federal seminar" movement gained momentum among politicians in the towns. Finally on 2 March 1962, as pressures for ethnic reform increased around the country, Ne Win seized power in a military coup. "Federalism is impossible: it will destroy the Union", *The Times* of 3 March quoted Ne Win as saying.

Thus ended the fourteen-year experiment with parliamentary democracy. From this moment, "federalism" became a taboo word in government circles during half a century of Tatmadaw rule. A new era of state nationalism now began in which the delineations of ethnic identity and citizenship were much more tightly circumscribed.

THE SECOND CYCLE OF CONFLICT AND THE ARAKAN CRISIS: 1962–88

Despite the repressive character of Ne Win's government, there initially appeared potential for political dialogue after he first seized power when CPB, KNU, KNPP, KIO, NMSP and other armed opposition delegations came to Yangon for a national "peace parley" during 1963–64 (Smith 1999, pp. 206–13). Any hopes were short-lived, however. Following the peace failure, Ne Win rapidly moved ahead with seeking to impose his "Burmese Way to Socialism", an unusual mix of Marxist, Buddhist and nationalist principles. The consequences were far-reaching and, within a few years, multi-ethnic Myanmar had become one of the most isolated and monolithic states in the world.

There were two main elements to the structures of government under BSPP rule: political and military, both of which have impact on the configurations in national politics until the present day. In political terms, a degree of symmetry was delineated on the political map under the 1974 Constitution, with seven ethnic "States" for the largest minorities (Chin, Kachin, Karen, Kayah [Karenni], Mon, Rakhine and Shan) and seven "divisions" (today "regions"), where the Bamar majority mostly live. In reality, however, the new political system was a one-party state controlled by serving or former military officers. The Tatmadaw ran administration down to the township level in parallel to the BSPP; the media, education and much of the economy was nationalized; the teaching of minority languages largely stopped beyond fourth grade in schools; and missionaries and most foreign business people were excluded from the country.

Meanwhile, on the military front, the Tatmadaw began all-out counter-insurgency campaigns, including the notorious "Four Cuts" that was first introduced in the mid-1960s. Similar to the "strategic hamlet" operations of U.S. forces in Vietnam, the aim was to clear all parts of the country from armed opposition groups in chessboard fashion, one by one (Smith 1999, pp. 258–62). By the mid-1970s, the "Four Cuts" campaign had largely driven out insurgent units from Bamar-majority areas in the centre of the country. But in other areas armed resistance often continued, and many borderlands became strongholds of opposition forces with very different aspirations to Ne Win's BSPP.

Here, in the anti-government *maquis*, nationality forces largely divided between those aligned with the CPB on the China frontier and those in the National Democratic Front (NDF, formed 1976), headquartered in KNU territory on the Thai border.[7] With control of much of the economy, many of the "liberated zones" administered by such forces as the CPB, KNU, KNPP, NMSP, KIO and Shan State Army (SSA, founded 1964) became quasi mini-states, maintaining their own governments, laws and educational systems which promoted their own views of ethnic identity and statehood. Inhabitants, for example, of KNU-controlled areas on the Thailand border were regarded as "citizens" of the "free state" of Kawthoolei.

It is important to stress, then, that armed opposition territories were by no means bastions of liberty or unity during the BSPP era. The challenges of conflict resolution in Myanmar have never been simply Bamar majority versus ethnic minority affairs. Black-market trading was often the main source of income; illicit narcotic production fuelled its own wars; many organizations were dominated by military rather than political leaders; and conflicts also broke out between opposition groups themselves. The BSPP era also saw armed movements develop among smaller nationality groups, including Kokang, Kayan (Padaung), Lahu, Naga, Pao, Ta-ang and Wa. Eventually, however, a majority of nationality forces settled upon the agreement of a "federal union" at the NDF's Third Plenary Central Presidium in October

1984 (Smith 1999, pp. 385–89), and this has remained the basic political demand for most ethnic-based movements until the present day.

Few records exist of the scale of community dislocation during the BSPP era. Events in Myanmar were rarely reported in the outside world and, even today, there are inhabitants in the borderlands who have never been registered as citizens of the post-colonial state. Rather, when international reporting of population movement did occur, it tended to focus on peoples of perceived Chinese, Indian or Muslim ancestry who became caught up in nationalist pressures after Ne Win seized power. With the imposition of the "Burmese Way to Socialism", an estimated 300,000 Indians and 100,000 Chinese left the country during 1963–67, many of whom had played important middleman roles in the national economy. Then in 1967 anti-Chinese violence broke out in Yangon at the height of the Cultural Revolution in China, prompting Beijing to begin two decades of armed support to the CPB which was able to build new strongholds along the Yunnan province border.

Against this backdrop, different examples can be picked out of ethnic challenges during the BSPP era that have resonance today. With fighting a daily occurrence, many borderlands remained conflict zones where villagers frequently had to move, with refugee numbers — especially Karen, Karenni and Mon — increasing in neighbouring Thailand. In terms of community displacement and citizenship, however, it was undoubtedly in the Rakhine State, the former Arakan, that the most problematical emergency was developing for ethnic rights and conflict resolution today.

The background to the Arakan crisis is complex. It is not in doubt that there have long been different Muslim communities in the territory. But the socio-ethnic landscape became rather more complicated under colonial rule when immigration from India increased. Arakan also has a tradition of independence and, until today, nationality movements — both electoral and armed — remain active among the Buddhist Rakhine population. Buddhist–Muslim violence first broke out during the Second World War, and conflict then escalated at independence when a Mujahid movement sought either secession or the separation of Muslim-majority territories into East Pakistan. By the early 1960s, however, peace agreements had largely been put in place by the U Nu government with the Mujahid groups, and the crisis only took on its contemporary forms following Ne Win's coup when a new movement, the Rohingya Patriotic Front (RPF), began armed struggle asserting an ethnic "Rohingya" identity for the Muslim cause in the Arakan borderlands.

Until today, the etymology of "Rohingya" remains controversial, as Jacques Leider has analysed (Leider 2014; see also the chapters by Leider and Tonkin and the contribution by Islam in this volume). All peoples should have the right to self-identity as they choose, and the Rohingya term was gaining political currency during the parliamentary era after 1948. Not all Muslim leaders, however, agreed with the promotion of a Rohingya identity, preferring to be called "Arakanese Muslims".[8] The Rohingya term was also rejected by many among the Rakhine population who feared that it could be used as a pretext for secessionist claims or to encourage illegal immigration from East Pakistan — from 1971 Bangladesh. RPF leaders nevertheless believed that, in the country's highly ethnicized politics, local Muslims need a distinctive nationality identity, as much as religious, if they are to gain legal traction on the country's political map.[9]

The acceptance of an ethnic Rohingya identity was one of many developments in ethnic politics that General Ne Win was determined to forestall during his time in government. Under the 1974 Constitution, Arakan gained state recognition under the Buddhist "Rakhine" name, and this was followed four years later by the government's heavy-handed Nagamin census operation when over 200,000 Muslim refugees fled across the Naaf river border into Bangladesh. There was also a counter-insurgency motive as the Tatmadaw sought to secure the northern Rakhine State from a number of communist, Rakhine and Muslim organizations embedded in the tri-border region with Bangladesh and India (Smith 1999, pp. 241, 308–309). In subsequent years, however, the BSPP government intensified its pressures on Muslim communities with the 1982 Citizenship Law, still in existence today, that restricts full citizenship to only eight major groups in the country — "Kachin, Kayah, Karen, Chin, Burman, Mon, Rakhine and Shan" — along with other nationality peoples who can prove ancestry before the first British annexation in 1823 (TNI 2014). There was no mention of "Rohingya".

The outcome of these events in the contemporary Rakhine State has left the country with one of its most intractable dilemmas. Systematic repression, sparked off in the BSPP era, may have gained the Rohingya movement a new support and international profile that it had previously been lacking. But this has been little consolation for Muslim inhabitants on the ground. Until today, there has been no official acceptance of nationality status or citizenship rights for those who self-identify as "Rohingya", and successive governments in Myanmar have continued to reject them as "Bengalis". This means, as Jacques Leider has highlighted, they have become a people without legal recognition in a country where "issues like ethnicity, history and cultural identity are key ingredients of legitimacy" (Leider 2014, p. 24).

By the late 1980s, however, the crisis in Arakan was just one of many challenges facing the BSPP government as the "Burmese Way to Socialism" declined towards a precipitate close. The national economy was in free-fall; armed conflict continued in the borderlands; and in 1987 Myanmar was accepted into Least Development Country status by the United Nations as one of the world's ten poorest nations. The following year General Ne Win resigned, and the BSPP quickly collapsed in the face of pro-democracy protests across the country. After a quarter century of Ne Win's experiment with autarchic socialism, Myanmar was a land in ethnic conflict and still very far from national peace.

MILITARY RULE AND THE THIRD CYCLE OF CONFLICT: 1988–2011

The third era of conflict in national politics occurred during the government of the military State Law and Order Restoration Council (SLORC; subsequently SPDC). As confusion reigned around the country, it appeared for a brief moment that the structures of national government might undergo seismic change. Thousands of students and democracy activists fled into borderlands controlled by ethnic forces after the SLORC assumed power; in 1989 Myanmar's oldest insurgent group, the CPB, collapsed due to ethnic mutinies; and in May 1990 the SLORC oversaw Myanmar's first general election in three decades which was convincingly won by the NLD. Once again, however, any optimism proved short-lived. The NLD's election victory was downplayed by the ruling generals, and the SLORC-SPDC era was to last almost as long as its BSPP predecessor in leaving another imprint of Tatmadaw rule on the country.

Despite the reform impasse, some important reconfigurations did take place in national politics during the SLORC-SPDC era. With the Tatmadaw still in government control, the three-cornered struggle between the BSPP, CPB and NDF was, in many respects, superseded by a new triangulation between the SLORC-SPDC, NLD and different ethnic nationality forces. Reflecting this equation, the demand for "tri-partite dialogue" was widely promoted, including by the United Nations and other international voices. But, as in previous political eras, no inclusive or "tri-partite" process for national reconciliation ever developed. Instead, military rule intensified while new conflicts and divisions emerged in the national landscape.

Faced with countrywide opposition, Senior General Than Shwe and the Tatmadaw leaders took time to entrench as they developed a plan for national transition to a new system of what they termed "disciplined democracy".

This first saw light with the 1993 start of a government-controlled National Convention to draw up a new constitution and the creation of the mass Union Solidarity and Development Association (USDA), which in 2010 became the present-day Union Solidarity and Development Party (USDP). Progress, however, was intermittent, and the convention did not finish its work until 2008. Transitional plans, in fact, only gathered momentum with the 2003 announcement by the prime minister and military intelligence chief General Khin Nyunt, shortly before his arrest, of a seven-stage "roadmap" to democracy. Over a decade later, Myanmar is still in the seventh and final stage of the SPDC's roadmap vision.

In the meantime, there were some important changes in ethnic politics during the SLORC-SPDC era. As the Tatmadaw struggled to maintain national dominance, life was never static on the ground. Seven particular issues stand out, with resonance still felt until today.

The first was the changing pattern of deadlock in the political field. The military government's suppression of the nascent democracy movement was relentless, putting back the NLD's accession to national office by a quarter of a century. Throughout the SLORC-SPDC era, the NLD leader Aung San Suu Kyi and other democracy supporters remained under frequent arrest or imprisonment, but this did not quell pro-democracy activism around the country. As in previous political eras, resistance took on two forms: aboveground and underground. While the NLD and 88 Generation Students attempted to continue political campaigning in the towns, over thirty MPs-elect joined the exodus by democracy activists into the ethnic borderlands. Here, in a new alignment in opposition politics, another cycle of anti-government fronts was agreed in NDF-controlled territories. Of these, the main alliance became the National Council Union of Burma (NCUB), formed in 1992 in KNU-controlled territory, and included the National Coalition Government Union of Burma of exile-MPs, headed by Aung San Suu Kyi's cousin Dr Sein Win.

This scale of countrywide opposition led to a second key feature of SLORC-SPDC government: the changing landscape in ethnic conflict. In 1989, in what initially appeared a "divide and rule" bid to win time, the SLORC leaders announced a nationwide ceasefire initiative for the first time since General Ne Win's failed "peace parley" back in 1963–64. Restricted to ethnic-based organizations, the ceasefire offer was initially aimed at new nationality forces, spearheaded by the Kokang-based Myanmar National Democratic Alliance Army (MNDAA) and United Wa State Army (UWSA), that were formed in the aftermath of the CPB mutinies. But, from a slow beginning, the peace initiative proved to be one of the most successful elements under SLORC-SPDC government, eventually spreading to sixteen of the main ethnic forces, including the KIO, SSA (North), NMSP and other NDF groups.

This unexpected breakthrough led to the first tentative end to fighting in many borderland areas in several decades, allowing outside visitors to arrive. From the late 1990s, the first non-governmental organizations (NGOs) were allowed to form and, through faith-based groups and such new NGOs as the Metta Development Foundation and Shalom (Nyein) Foundation, the spread of peace — in northeast Myanmar especially — helped underpin the public revival of civil society groups that had operated beneath the radar during the BSPP years. Indeed, Senior General Than Shwe stated that the ethnic ceasefires were the most distinguishing feature of the SLORC-SPDC era. "National unity has been fostered", he claimed in the state-controlled *New Light of Myanmar* on 27 February 1998.

It is important to stress, then, that the conflict picture was by no means even or settled across the country. Despite the ceasefires along the China border, fighting still continued with the KNU, KNPP and non-ceasefire members of the NDF and NCUB alliances, especially in southeast Myanmar, and this was reflected in the continuing exodus of refugees and migrants from the country. Meanwhile, as the political impasse continued in urban areas, periodic efforts at pro-democracy protest were swiftly suppressed, and this was graphically highlighted by the security crackdown on the 2007 "Saffron Revolution" led by Buddhist monks in Yangon. In essence, the national landscape could be described as one of ceasefires without peace.

The conflict impasse also had impact on a third new aspect in ethnic politics: the right of nationality parties to form. After a ban of nearly three decades, ethnic-based parties were now permitted back on the official political map, but, as with the NLD, the outcome was ambiguous. The Shan Nationalities League for Democracy (SNLD), for example, won the second largest number of seats in the 1990 election but, like its NLD ally, also suffered years of repression by the security services. This, however, did not end joint initiatives with the NLD, including the 1998 formation of the Committee Representing the People's Parliament. Subsequently, in 2002 the SNLD and eight other ethnic-based parties formed a United Nationalities Alliance (UNA), whose members boycotted the 2010 general election along with the NLD. In their absence, a number of other nationality parties came forward to contest the 2010 polls, some of which did well at the ballot box. But the UNA has since remained the main campaigning voice for pro-federal reform, and it was generally the SNLD and other UNA supporters that were the most successful among ethnic-based parties during the 2015 polls; in contrast, those that had stood in the 2010 election were identified too closely with the SPDC past and fared poorly (TNI 2015*b*).

The fourth and fifth key areas of change during the SLORC-SPDC era — the economy and international geopolitics — quickly became interconnected and were prime elements in the military government's restructuring. Whereas previous governments had never gained real control over the national economy, SLORC-SPDC officers were determined to bring such important natural resources as timber, gold and jade under central administration. The government's Border Areas Development Programme, started in 1989, never led to significant investment, but the ethnic ceasefires quickly provided the platform for business opportunism to take off, especially in the China borderlands where different sides were complicit in the expansion in trades underway.[10]

Simultaneous with this new promotion of "market-oriented" reform, the SLORC generals ended Ne Win's isolationist policies and opened the door to political and economic relations with Asian neighbours. In part, these decisions were in response to sanctions by governments in the West, where the regime continued to be regarded as an international pariah. Informal trades had long existed in many borderland areas but, with government access, the new revenue streams soon became a game-changer for the embattled regime. Initially, the SLORC focus was on China and Thailand, but in 1997 Myanmar became a full member of the Association of Southeast Asian Nations (ASEAN) and, in the following years, business and political ties became closer with governments in Asia where a policy of "constructive engagement" was preferred to Western boycotts.

Seen from the perspective of communities on the ground, however, the headlong rush by powerful business interests into their territories was not a sign of progress. Rather, many new projects quickly became a cause of new grievance. Not only were many borderlands still conflict zones, but there was rarely consultation or benefit for the local peoples. Concerns were then exacerbated by a number of mega-deals agreed with Asian neighbours during the last years of the SPDC government. These included the China-backed Myitsone dam in the Kachin State and the oil and gas pipelines from the Rakhine State through the Shan State to Yunnan province. Once again, nationality parties feared that their peoples were going to be left behind, politically and economically, during a time of national change.

Community worries were also raised by a sixth issue in ethnic politics during the SLORC-SPDC era: the Tatmadaw's behaviour on the security front. No official policy was ever announced but, parallel to the spread of ceasefires, militia programmes were accelerated as part of a long-term "regional clearance" strategy to remove opposition forces from the ethnic borderlands — not by politics but by building up local militias (Pyi Thu Sit) on the government side. Such auxiliary or paramilitary forces have existed since independence, but during the SLORC-SPDC era the creation of pro-government militias steadily increased, a number of whose leaders were involved in business and won seats for the USDP in the 2010 general election. As Kim Joliffe has analysed, the result is a divided landscape in the borderlands where "ethnic armed conflict and territorial administration" overlap (Jolliffe 2015).

Matters then came to a head in April 2009 when, without discussion, the SPDC ordered all ceasefire groups to transform into Border Guard Forces (BGFs) under Tatmadaw control. The stronger forces refused, including the KIO, SSA (North), UWSA, NMSP and MNDAA, but their rejection was followed by a Tatmadaw offensive against the MNDAA to impose a BGF in the Kokang region. Many of these events received little media or political attention at the time.[11] But over 200 people were killed, and 37,000 refugees, most of whom were ethnic Chinese, fled into Yunnan province, leaving a legacy of distrust over Tatmadaw motives in northeast Myanmar that has proven difficult to dispel. Many parts of the Kachin and northern Shan States that were at relative peace during the SLORC-SPDC era are conflict zones today.

As fighting and human rights abuses continued, the final legacy from the SLORC-SPDC era was the significant increase in the number of internally displaced persons (IDPs) and refugees, most of whom were non-Bamar peoples. It is difficult to be precise about numbers. In addition to an estimated 400,000 IDPs in the southeast borderlands, there were eventually around 150,000 refugees in official camps (mostly Karen, Karenni, Mon and Shan) and upwards of 2 million migrants (both legal and illegal) in Thailand by the first decade of the twenty-first century.[12] A constant stream of civilians also left from the Kachin State into China and the Chin State into India, many of whom subsequently made their way onto Thailand, Malaysia and further countries abroad.

International concerns also deepened in 1992 when, in a repetition of the 1978 exodus, 260,000 Muslim or Rohingya refugees fled into Bangladesh from the Rakhine State during another Tatmadaw security clampdown.[13] Unlike 1978, many have never been able to return home. However, with the government subject to Western boycotts, international leverage was small in Myanmar during the SLORC-SPDC era. Indeed in 2005 the Global Fund to Fight AIDS, Tuberculosis and Malaria took the extraordinary decision to leave from Myanmar, and greater awareness of the precarious humanitarian situation in the country only reached the international stage in the most terrible circumstances in May 2008 when 140,000 people died during Cyclone Nargis that swept across the Ayeyarwady Delta. Government services were inadequate and simply unable to cope.

The national landscape therefore hardly looked promising as the SLORC-SPDC era of government began to wind down. A general election was held in November 2010, following a constitutional referendum in the aftermath of Cyclone Nargis. But the outcome was disputed, and no agreements had been reached by the government with opposition groups on political or military transition. Repression of the NLD continued until election day; the new constitution underpinned the Tatmadaw's "leading role in national politics"; critical issues in citizenship and ethnic rights had yet to be addressed; and, in the aftermath of the BGF debacle, the ethnic ceasefires looked under increasing strain. In short, after over two decades in government, the stepping down of Senior General Than Shwe and the SPDC did not appear likely to herald in a new era of peace and democracy.

NATIONAL TRANSITION AND THE FOURTH CYCLE OF CONFLICT: 2011–16

Against many expectations, political reforms initiated after the quasi-civilian government of President Thein Sein assumed office in March 2011 led to the most important experience of countrywide transition since the earliest days after independence in 1948. Tatmadaw dominance still continued through reserved seats in the legislatures and control of three ministries (defence, border and home affairs); the life of the first parliament (2011–16) was overshadowed by the ruling USDP-Tatmadaw nexus; and the strength of business groups connected to Tatmadaw interests and families was further enhanced. Certainly, it was never likely that Myanmar would be transformed from an international pariah to democratic arcadia overnight.

Nevertheless, from a tentative beginning, hopes for reconciliation and reform slowly strengthened as the years passed by. Among critical changes: political prisoners were mostly released; restrictions on the media and freedom of expression were gradually lifted; Aung San Suu Kyi and the NLD entered parliament through 2012 by-elections; bridges were built with Western governments that began to drop economic sanctions; and President Thein Sein announced the goal of a new "nationwide ceasefire agreement" (NCA) with ethnic armed groups. As he promised in London in July 2013: "Very possibly, over the coming weeks, we will have a nationwide ceasefire and the guns will go silent everywhere in Myanmar for the first time in over sixty years" (Thein Sein 2013). Subsequently, Thein Sein embraced the goal of a "federal" system of government, and hopes for more rapid reform towards democracy were heightened by the NLD victory in the 2015 general election. With the NLD's accession to government in March 2016, political transition to democracy appeared complete after decades of military rule.

Many uncertainties, however, remained about the country's future. The difficulty was that, despite the NLD's victory and promise of nationwide peace, there had been no clear moments of inclusive reform for all peoples under the Thein Sein government. Rather, after decades of military rule, opposition fears lingered that Tatmadaw interests were still seeking to delay deeper reforms by steering political dialogue on to two different tracks; one through parliament and the other through its control of ethnic ceasefire talks. Indeed commander-in-chief Senior General Min Aung Hlaing said in a rare international interview before the 2015 polls that the Tatmadaw's role in government would continue for some time: "It could be five years or ten years — I couldn't say" (Fisher 2015).

As perceived evidence of Tatmadaw stone-walling, parliamentary efforts were blocked by military officials to amend two key clauses in the 2008 Constitution before President Thein Sein stood down: article 59(f), a citizenship rule that bars candidates with foreign relatives from becoming president (i.e., Aung San Suu Kyi whose two sons have UK passports), and article 436, which effectively allows the Tatmadaw control over charter reform because it is reserved 25 per cent of all seats in the legislatures.

Meanwhile Thein Sein's nationwide ceasefire initiative had also made slow progress. While ceasefires spread in the southeast of the country to include the KNU, KNPP and SSA (South), the seventeen-year ceasefire of the KIO broke down in June 2011 and conflict increased throughout Thein Sein's presidency in adjoining Kokang, Shan and Ta'ang areas. Eventually, a partial "NCA" signing ceremony was hurried through in October 2015 before President Thein Sein stood down, but only eight armed opposition organizations took part. With conflict continuing in several border regions, many nationality leaders distrusted Tatmadaw intentions and preferred to wait until after the general election when, it was hoped, a more sympathetic government would take office. At the same time, arguments continued over who should be represented in any "nationwide" peace accord. While the Tatmadaw recognized sixteen groups, the main ethnic alliance of the United Nationalities Federal Council proposed up to twenty-one organizations. In particular, the Tatmadaw rejected the inclusion of three forces, the Arakan Army (AA), Ta'ang National Liberation Army (TNLA) and Kokang-MNDAA, the last of which had refused the Tatmadaw's order to transform into a BGF in 2009. In essence, rather than the achievement of peace under the Thein Sein government, a new cycle of conflict appeared to be unfolding.

As the political manoeuvrings continued, these uncertainties created a major dilemma for opposition parties: were the 2008 Constitution and NCA intended as procedural straightjackets to maintain Tatmadaw dominance or could they develop into innovative processes for inclusive dialogue and national reform in the following years? These questions initially appeared to be thrown into confusion by the results of the 2015 general election which the NLD won by a landslide, gaining 79 per cent of the electoral seats. Not only had the USDP been routed, but the NLD also did well in many nationality areas at the expense of ethnic-based parties. As the Transnational Institute highlighted, the only conclusion that could be drawn from such a countrywide result was that citizens from very different backgrounds, whatever their political or nationality perspectives, had voted for the NLD because they considered the party's victory as the surest way to end USDP-Tatmadaw rule (Transnational Institute 2015*b*). The NLD's "time for change" slogan was a powerful call.

The NLD, however, was entering very uncharted waters. It was the first government since 1960 that could claim to have been elected by the people. It also marks the first time since independence that the major parties among the Bamar majority — in this case the NLD and Tatmadaw — are working together in government. Other than faith-based groups, there is no other national institution of socio-political significance standing in the organizational wings. But whether the NLD can steer a way between Tatmadaw interests and the different expectations of the people is yet to be seen. Huge challenges lie ahead as the NLD attempts to usher in a new era of democratic freedoms. In the meantime, four areas can be highlighted from the Thein Sein era that are likely to influence the path of ethnic politics in the coming years: political, economic, societal, and humanitarian.

First, under the new constitutional system, the ethnic landscape has become at its most diverse in national representation since independence in 1948. Since the SLORC-SPDC stepped down, over 100 ethnic-based parties have been active, whether electoral, in ceasefires or not, and initiatives by NGO and community-based groups have multiplied across the country (Smith 2015, pp. 138–52). Such diversity is, to some extent, reflected in the new political map under the 2008 constitution, increasing the representation of ethnic identity in the three forms of legislature (lower and upper houses of parliament, state/region assemblies). The seven ethnic states and seven regions (formerly divisions) are retained from the 1974 constitution, but six new "self-administered" areas have been designated for the Danu, Kokang, Pao, Ta-ang and Wa populations in the Shan State and Naga in the Sagaing region. In addition, twenty-nine electoral seats are reserved for "national race" populations in states and regions where they form smaller minorities.[14] This means that twenty different nationalities are now officially represented in one form or another in ethnic politics (not, though, the Rohingya identity).

The prospect of parliamentary change, however, was not matched by conflict change during the Thein Sein era. From 2012, government ceasefires were agreed with such forces as the KNU, KNPP and SSA (South) in southeast Myanmar as well as with Chin and Naga groups on the India border, but the situation markedly deteriorated in several areas in the northeast and northwest of the country where ceasefires had been initiated under the SLORC-SPDC. Here fighting initially began with the breakdown of the KIO ceasefire in June 2011 in a dispute that began over a China-backed dam on the Taping river, but conflict subsequently spread across Kachin, Shan, Ta-ang and Kokang regions of the northern Shan State, prompting some of the fiercest battles witnessed in decades. The result was increasing community displacement and distrust, becoming a prime factor in the decision by most UNFC members not to sign the government's NCA until it includes all regions and parties. Fears of Tatmadaw "divide-and-rule" continued to run deep and, as President Thein Sein stood down in March 2016, inclusive political dialogue had yet to begin.

Optimism, nevertheless, grew following the 2015 general election that the issues of ethnic peace and reform might be resolved during the lifetime of an NLD-led parliament. Nationality parties did not do as well in the 2015 polls as they had done in 2010. This was partly due to the number of ethnic-based parties; fifty-five stood, often splitting the nationality vote, of which just ten won seats in the legislatures (Transnational Institute 2015*b*, p. 7). However, given the decisive scale of the NLD's victory, nationality leaders recognized that the new government was a popular choice that they would have to work with in seeking progressive change. Equally important, with both the NLD and President Thein Sein advocating "federal" reform, consensus appeared to be growing over a mutual language for the country's future political path. It was recognized that much work was still needed to agree on what kind of federalism might succeed in Myanmar. But in general, the underlying disagreement in national politics has always been more basic: i.e., between "unitary" and "union" systems of governance. The question thus remained as to whether Tatmadaw leaders would allow political reforms that devolve real autonomy to the ethnic states and regions. Since 1962, military officers have always rejected any decentralization or diminution of their powers. Of all Myanmar's challenges, this may well become the most defining in national politics during the next decade.

This led to a second area of concern in ethnic politics: the direction of the economy under the country's new political system. President Thein Sein initially won praise for suspending the US$3.6 billion Myitsone dam in the Kachin State for the duration of the first parliament (2011–16), but otherwise, as Global Witness (GW) and other environmental organizations pointed out, land-grabbing and natural resource exploitation further accelerated during his era of government (GW 2015*a*, 2015*b*; TNI 2013). Different sides to the conflicts continued to be involved in such trades as logging, gold and jade. However the scale of profiteering by companies linked to Tatmadaw interests notably increased, and there was further growth in the number of business investors from such countries as China, Japan and Thailand who were very aware of the economic potential of Myanmar's borderlands. This saw the take-off of such mega projects as the oil and gas pipelines from the Rakhine State coast to China, the Kaladan Multi-modal Transit Transport Project with India, and the Dawei Development project with Thailand.

Consultation, however, with local populations was minimal, and unrest over the manner of economic change was undoubtedly a contributory factor to the slow pace of peace talks and resumption of conflict in the Kachin and northern Shan States.[15] Unease was also reflected in protest among electoral parties and civil society organizations that became increasingly active during the Thein Sein era. For this reason, sentiment grew that the agreement of equitable economic rights for all peoples has become an important barometer for adjudging democratic reform under Myanmar's new political system.

In many respects, the manifestations of public unrest over economic developments were connected to a third key area of change during the Thein Sein government: the growth in community activism. After decades of military rule, popular responses were to be expected at the community level, with many citizens keen to express their rights and views. But, as national transition continued, the socio-political situation hardly stabilized. In the past four years, the security services have made frequent arrests during civilian protests over economic projects and land seizures that are perceived to adversely affect local communities. At the same time, while consensus has grown about the need for ethnic reform, several nationalities have increased their political demands, with such groups as the Pao, Ta-ang and Wa wanting larger territories and the creation of state-level administrations under the union government.

Among the Bamar majority population, too, a notable feature of the Thein Sein era was the emergence of a new nationalist movement, the "Ma Ba Tha" or Organization for the Protection of Race and Religion, that is led by Buddhist monks. A particular target of the Ma Ba Tha movement are the country's minority Muslims, and the Ma Ba Tha's campaign found apparent support from both the Thein Sein government, which passed four "Race and Religion Protection Laws", and the NLD which failed to appoint a Muslim as a candidate during the 2015 general election.[16]

Against this backdrop, the 2014 Population and Housing Census failed to improve inter-community relations or clarify the challenges in understanding ethnicity and citizenship in the country. Indeed many nationality leaders feared that it could become as unhelpful in understanding identity issues as the last major census, conducted by the colonial government, back in 1931 (Transnational Institute 2014). Not only did the census go ahead with the flawed "135 national races" designation of the SLORC-SPDC government, but release of the results was held back because of difficulties in data assessment and fears over negative reaction. Among a number of failings, the census questions confused the number of ethnic groups among such peoples as the Chin, Kachin and Karen by including dialect and identity classifications that are not always recognizable or locally used. This, in turn, led to worries that miscounting could lead to political under-representation for non-Bamar peoples if the census is used as a basis for territorial delineations and future reforms.

Nowhere were such community-level tensions more obvious than in the Rakhine State. As the International Crisis Group (ICG) analysed, serious Buddhist–Muslim violence first broke out in the territory during 2012 before spreading to other parts of the country, causing significant loss of life and community displacement (International Crisis Group 2013, 2014). Communal tensions then flared up again over the 2014 census, which raised sensitive questions over the identities of ethnic Indians, Chinese and other inhabitants whose ancestry is not considered to be indigenous under the 1982 Citizenship Law. Bowing to pressures (and sometimes violence) by Buddhist nationalists, the census went ahead without allowing local Muslims to self-identify as "Rohingya" — only as "Bengali". This marginalization was then followed by further anti-Muslim protests and the government's decision to revoke temporary or "white" identity cards, most of which were held by Muslims, meaning that they were not allowed to vote in the 2015 general election.[17]

For the Muslim population of the Rakhine State, especially those who identify as Rohingya, the consequences of the deterioration in inter-communal relations during the Thein Sein era have proven a disaster, a regressive situation that has since gone from bad to worse. Many Buddhist Rakhines also believe themselves a disadvantaged minority within the Myanmar State, and the Arakan

National Party did notably well in the 2015 polls. However the plight of the Muslim community in the Rakhine State cannot be minimized. During the Thein Sein government, over 250 people (mostly Muslims) lost their lives in conflict, another 140,000 civilians (also mostly Muslims) were displaced from their homes, and up to one million disenfranchised from voting and full citizenship rights (International Crisis Group 2013, 2014, 2015).

It was not, however, only in the Rakhine State where such xenophobic or "anti-foreigner" sentiment showed itself during Thein Sein's presidency. Following the resumption of conflict with the MNDAA in the Chinese-speaking Kokang region in early 2015, government officials also appeared to play an anti-Chinese card by claiming the right of "national defence" and winning the Tatmadaw rare popular support among the ethnic Bamar majority (Transnational Institute 2015a). Hundreds of casualties were reported, around 80,000 people displaced, and a military response was threatened from Beijing when five citizens were killed in an airstrike that landed across the China border. Eventually, the Thein Sein government apologized for the loss of life in Yunnan but, a few weeks later, the state media aired the same anti-Chinese sentiment when criticizing the ceasefire UWSA that controls territories to the south. On 18 May 2015, the Global New Light of Myanmar claimed that administrative positions in the UWSA "are being taken by ethnic Chinese and local culture is being swallowed and overwhelmed by the Chinese one". Clearly, the rights of the many citizens of Chinese identity in contemporary Myanmar also need to be protected and resolved.[18]

Finally, as continued fighting and community displacement highlighted, the fourth major area of concern from the Thein Sein era is social and humanitarian. After decades of conflict, the country has some of the poorest health and welfare indicators in Asia. Myanmar was ranked 148th of 188 countries in the UNDP's 2015 Human Development Report; it is the world's second largest producer of illicit opium; treatable and preventable illnesses such as malaria, TB and HIV are rife; unbridled business practices have been furthering poverty and displacement; and there are estimates of over 800,000 internally displaced persons as well as over 3 million refugees and migrants abroad. According to UNOCHA figures for March 2016, around 1 million people needed humanitarian aid across the country; 140,000 IDPs were in the Rakhine State and over 100,000 in the Kachin State, displacement numbers that have since continued to increase.[19] But of unregistered peoples or those who have moved deeper into the borderlands, there were no reliable figures at all.

Thus, as the NLD prepared to assume office, the national stage was delicately set. As any visitor to the country could witness, considerable changes had taken place under Thein Sein's presidency during the previous five years; modernity and urban life increasingly reflected the pace of Asian neighbours; and decades of international isolation were at an end. In ethnic politics, however, many of the most fundamental problems that had divided the country since independence still remained. After nearly three decades in political opposition, it had now fallen to an NLD government to take national peace and reform forward if democratic transition is to succeed.

AN END TO CONFLICT? THE NLD ERA AND BEYOND

It is still early to make conclusions about the NLD era of government. Both domestic and international expectations were high as party officials took on government positions in March 2016. However, after a year in office, it was clear that the new administration was encountering many of the same challenges that had beset its predecessors in earlier political eras. Speculation was rife, with NLD officials often reticent about explaining government policies and decisions. Since party members had little governmental experience, the public was initially willing to make allowances for the NLD's hesitation. But as the months passed by, concerns began to be expressed about two political trends that had not been widely anticipated in advance: first, rather than seeking radical change, the NLD government seemed more intent on building upon the political landscape left by the Thein Sein administration; and second, as the NLD tried to balance government between the different interests in the country, the party's primary concern appeared to be maintain favour with the Tatmadaw and its influential commander-in-chief Senior General Min Aung Hlaing. As the 2008 Constitution had intended, the Tatmadaw remained a powerful influence in national administration and decision-making. In effect, there was not so much an NLD government in Myanmar as a hybrid NLD-Tatmadaw government.

Initially, the NLD seemed to be trying to side-step some of the restrictions imposed by the 2008 Constitution. A symbolic move was the creation of a new post of State Counsellor for Aung San Suu Kyi who had been blocked from becoming president. A new Advisory Commission on Rakhine State was also formed, headed by former UN Secretary-General Kofi Annan, and the new government appeared to put the achievement of ethnic peace high on its political agenda. Doubts about the NLD's ethnic policies had been raised before the polls,[20] and some of the initial decisions of the party (such as governmental appointments) appeared to be echoing the token, rather than meaningful, actions of Bamar-majority governments in the past. Nevertheless, nationality leaders did not regard this as an insuperable problem, provided that the party uses its mandate to support an inclusive path towards national peace and reform.[21]

Hopes of imminent change then reached a peak with the NLD's holding of a Union Peace Conference, known as the 21st Century Panglong or Panglong-21, at the end of August 2016. Although the AA, MNDAA and TNLA were still excluded, most ethnic armed organizations and political parties were represented among the over 800 participants, who included leaders of the NLD, Tatmadaw, KNU, KIO, NMSP and SNLD. For a brief moment, it appeared that for the first time since independence representatives of the key actors in the country's political conflicts could be brought together, and delegates left in good spirits to plan further meetings that would keep the NLD's Panglong-21 initiative alive.

From this point, expectations rapidly declined, and some of the fiercest fighting in many years erupted in several parts of the country. All sides accused one another in a blame-game that still continues. Nationality parties were convinced that the escalation started when the NLD apparently gave the green light to the Tatmadaw to enforce the NCA as the only way to achieve peace in the country. Whether the Tatmadaw was already in preparation for such moves is uncertain, but the intensity of the Tatmadaw's operations in the Kachin and northern Shan States, with fighter aircraft and attack helicopters, still caused widespread surprise. The KIO, AA, MNDAA and TNLA in a new "Northern Alliance" hit back with military strikes of their own that continued into 2017. As another 50,000 civilians were displaced from their homes, the impact of the fighting was to seriously undermine confidence in the new government and the NLD's ability to steer national policies along a peaceful path. The Chinese government, too, was alarmed by the new escalation in conflict that had serious impact on Chinese nationals and interests in the Yunnan border area (Sun 2017).

Meanwhile, following attacks on the police by a militant Islamist group in the Rakhine State, a new military front also opened along the Bangladesh frontier where the Tatmadaw launched an intensive security operation targeting the local Muslim population (ICG 2016). More than 1,500 homes were reportedly destroyed, another 70,000 refugees fled across the border and over 80 people died, prompting an international outcry over Myanmar's treatment of the Rohingya cause. UN agencies, Western governments and Asian neighbours all raised voices in concern, with the Tatmadaw, NLD government and Buddhist nationalists all being accused of complicity in the ill-treatment of minority Muslims and what was alleged to be a systematic campaign to force those claiming to be of Rohingya identity from the country.[22] In March

2017, the UN Human Rights Council adopted a resolution to investigate the situation in the border territory.[23]

Finally, it appeared that Myanmar's Rohingya crisis would become the focus of serious international study and attention. But, for many citizens, the shock assassination in January 2017 of U Ko Ni, a prominent Muslim and the NLD's leading constitutional lawyer, had already undermined any hopes of imminent reform. Few doubted that nationalist hardliners were sending a clear warning to anyone considering further change.[24] On Union Day, 27 March 2017, Senior General Min Aung Hlaing publicly warned against international intervention and reiterated the Tatmadaw's determination to continue in its task of "ensuring the stability, unity and development of the country".[25]

Such events marked a sobering end to the NLD's first year in office. For the moment, they do not appear to have deflected the country's transitional path towards peace and democracy, but they remind that an unaddressed legacy of grave challenges still need to be addressed in many spheres of national life. A second Panglong-21 was held in May but progress was slow. As at independence in 1948, ethnic politics and citizenship are national issues of paramount concern, and fundamental human rights continue to be denied to many people. After so many decades of conflict, it is therefore essential that the current opportunities for national change are not wasted. The need is for all sides to work constructively together rather than pursuing self-interest, as has happened so often in the past. Myanmar's troubled history warns that failure will only result in another cycle of instability, conflict and national under-achievement.

Notes

1. Agreement over common terms for "nationality" or "ethnic" rights and identity can be problematical. Controversy has also followed the use of "Burma" or "Myanmar", which can be considered alternative forms in the Burmese language. Historically, "Burmese" has been used in English as a term for such issues as language, culture and citizenship, while "Burman" — more recently "Bamar" — for the majority nationality group. For a discussion, see e.g., Transnational Institute (2014).
2. See, e.g., Gibson and Chen (2011).
3. See, e.g., Smith (1999).
4. The initial British idea was for a two-speed evolution to independence, with the Frontier Areas remaining under British administration until amalgamation with Ministerial Burma could be agreed.
5. Clause Five declared: "Full autonomy in internal administration for the Frontier Areas is accepted in principle."

6. The 1947 Constitution, articles 10–11, defined citizens as persons whose parents belong to an "indigenous race", have a grandparent from an "indigenous race", are children of citizens, or lived in British Burma prior to 1942.

7. Nationality parties also gained a propaganda victory in the late 1960s when the deposed prime minister U Nu fled with several colleagues to the Thailand border to ally with the KNU and his former ethnic opponents in the short-lived "National United Liberation Front" (Smith 1999, pp. 273–93).

8. There is also another minority people in the Rakhine State, the Kaman, who are mostly Muslim.

9. This background is based upon interviews with RPF, Muslim, Rakhine, communist and other leaders in Arakan from the mid-1980s. For a contemporary account by this author of the frontier-world in the BSPP days, see: Martin Smith, "Sold down the river: Burma's Muslim borderland", *Inside Asia* 9 (July–August 1986).

10. For an analysis of the logging trade in which government, business, Chinese and ethnic armed groups were involved, see, e.g., Global Witness, "A Disharmonious Trade: China and the continued destruction of Burma's northern frontier forests", 2009 <https://www.globalwitness.org/en/archive/disharmonious-trade-china-and-continued-destruction-burmas-northern-frontier-forests/> (accessed 25 May 2016).

11. For a history of the Kokang conflict, see, e.g., Transnational Institute (2015a).

12. For refugees and displacement in Thai border areas, see reports of the Thailand Burma Border Consortium which began recording numbers from the mid-1980s. See, e.g., Border Consortium (2014).

13. For a report at that time, see, e.g., Amnesty International (1992).

14. The complete list: Bamar (5), Karen (5), Chin (3), Shan (3), Pa-O (2), Rakhine (2), Lisu (2), Akha, Intha, Kachin, Kayan, Lahu, Mon, Rawang (1).

15. On a lesser scale, armed struggle also resumed in the Rakhine State where the Arakan Army (established 2009) was seeking to gain a foothold.

16. See, e.g., Hanna Hindstrom, "NLD Blocked Muslim Candidates to Appease Ma Ba Tha: Party Member", *The Irrawaddy*, 31 August 2015.

17. For a snapshot of protests, see, e.g., Yen Snaing, "Week of protests planned against suffrage for white card holders", *The Irrawaddy*, 5 February 2015; AFP/Reuters, "Myanmar nullifies temporary ID cards after nationalist protest", 11 February 2015; Andrew Marshall, "In Rohingya camp, tensions mount over Myanmar plan to revoke ID cards", Reuters, 17 February 2015.

18. For an analysis of the Chinese population and Yunnan connections, see, Y. Li (2015).

19. <http://www.unocha.org/myanmar>.

20. See, e.g., Lall et al. (2015).

21. See, e.g., Seng Raw (2016).

22. See, e.g., "Foreign Officials 'Deeply Troubled' by Findings of UN Report",

Reuters, 6 February 2017; "More than 1,000 feared killed in Myanmar army crackdown on Rohingya — U.N. officials", Reuters, 6 February 2017.

23. Feliz Solomon, "The U.N. Has Agreed to Investigate Myanmar's Alleged Abuse of Rohingya", *Time*, 24 March 2017.

24. The exact circumstances of U Ko Ni's assassination are yet to be revealed, but those arrested point to military connections and "extreme nationalism": see, e.g., Aung Zaw, "Who Was Behind U Ko Ni's Assassination?", *The Irrawaddy*, 27 February 2017.

25. Htet Naing Zaw, "Army Chief: Tatmadaw Will Prevent Political Intervention on Rohingyas' Behalf: The 72 Armed Forces Day in Naypyidaw", *The Irrawaddy*, 27 March 2017.

References

Amnesty International. *Human Rights Violations against Muslims in the Rakhine (Arakan) State.* London: Amnesty International, 1992.

Aung San Suu Kyi. *BBC Reith Lecture.* BBC, 5 July 2011.

Aung-Thwin, M. "British 'pacification' of Burma: Order without meaning". *Journal of South East Asian Studies* 16, no. 2 (1985): 245–61.

Bennison, J.J. *Census of India, 1931.* Rangoon: Government Printing and Stationery, 1933.

Border Consortium, The. *Protection and Security Concerns in South East Burma/ Myanmar.* Wanida Press: Bangkok & Yangon, 2014 <http://www.theborder consortium.org/media/54376/report-2014-idp-en.pdf> (accessed 20 May 2016).

Buchanan, J., T. Kramer and K. Woods. *Developing Disparity: Regional Investment in Burma's Borderlands.* Amsterdam: TNI-BCN, 2013.

Callahan, M. *Making Enemies: War and State Building in Burma.* Ithaca: Cornell University Press, 2003.

Collier, P., V.L. Elliott, Havard Hegre, Anke Hoeffler, Marta Reynal-Querol, Nicholas Sambanis. *Breaking the Conflict Trap: Civil War and Development Policy.* Oxford and Washington: Oxford University Press and World Bank, 2003.

Duffield, M. *Global Governance and the New Wars: The Merging of Development and Security.* London: Zed Books, 2001.

Fisher, Jonah. "Myanmar's strongman gives rare BBC interview". BBC, 20 July 2015.

Gibson, R. and W. Chen. *The Secret Army: Chiang Kai-Shek and the Drug Warlords of the Golden Triangle.* Singapore: John Wiley & Sons, 2011.

Global Witness. *Guns, Cronies and Crops: How Military, Political and Business Cronies Have Conspired to Grab Land in Myanmar.* London: Global Witness, 2015*a*.

———. *Jade: Myanmar's "Big State Secret".* London: Global Witness, 2015*b*.

International Crisis Group. "The Dark Side of Transition: Violence Against Muslims in Myanmar". *Asia Report* 251. International Crisis Group, 2013.

————. "Myanmar: The Politics of Rakhine State". *Asia Report* 261. International Crisis Group, 2014.

————. "Myanmar's Electoral Landscape". *Asia Report* 266. International Crisis Group, 2015.

————. "Myanmar: A New Muslim Insurgency in Rakhine State". *Asia Report* 283. International Crisis Group, 2016.

Jolliffe, K. *Ethnic Armed Conflict and Territorial Administration in Myanmar*. Yangon: The Asia Foundation, 2015.

Keen, D. "War and peace: what's the difference?". In *Managing Armed Conflicts in the 21st Century*, edited by A. Adebajo and C.L. Sriram. London: Frank Cass Publishers, 2001.

Kramer, T. *Civil Society Gaining Ground: Opportunities for Change and Development in Burma*. Amsterdam: Transnational Institute, 2011.

Lall, M., Nwe Nwe San, Theint Theint Myat and Yin Nyein Aye. *Myanmar's ethnic parties and the 2015 elections*. Yangon: EU and IMG <http://www.networkmyanmar.org/images/stories/PDF19/Lall-MEP.pdf> (accessed 25 May 2016).

Leach, E. *Political Systems of Highland Burma: A Study of Kachin Social Structure*. London: G. Bell & Son Ltd, 1954.

Leider, J. "Rohingya. The name. The movement. The quest for identity". 28 January 2014 <http://www.networkmyanmar.org/images/stories/PDF17/Leider-2014.pdf> (accessed 20 May 2016).

Li, Y. "Yunnanese Chinese in Myanmar: Past and Present". *Trends in Southeast Asia* no. 12/2015. Singapore: ISEAS – Yusof Ishak Institute, 2015.

Migdal, J. *Strong Societies and Weak States: State-Society Relations and State Capabilities in the Third World*. Princeton: Princeton University Press, 1988.

Myint-U, T. *The Making of Modern Burma*. Cambridge: Cambridge University Press, 2001.

National League for Democracy. "Election Manifesto". Authorised Translation <http://www.burmalibrary.org/docs21/NLD_2015_Election_Manifesto-en.pdf> (accessed 26 May 2016).

Sadan, M. *Being and Becoming Kachin: Histories Beyond the State in the Borderworlds of Burma*. Oxford: The British Academy and Oxford University Press, 2013.

Seng Raw, Laphai. "Strengthening civil society in peace building: evolving perspectives from South East Myanmar". Paper presented at Aid & International Development Forum, 13 February 2015.

————. *The Need for Peace and Inclusion*. Amsterdam: Transnational Institute, 2016.

Shan State Independence Army. "Communique of the Revolutionary Council". 1959.

Silverstein, J. *Burmese Politics: the Dilemma of National Unity*. New Brunswick: Rutgers University Press, 1980.

Smith, M. *Burma: Insurgency and the Politics of Ethnicity*. 2nd ed. London: Zed Books, 1999.

————. *State of Strife: The Dynamics of Ethnic Conflicts in Burma.* Policy Studies no. 36. Singapore: Institute of Southeast Asian Studies, 2007.

————. "Ethnic Politics in a Time of Change". In *Myanmar: The Dynamics of an Evolving Polity*, edited by D. Steinberg. Boulder: Lynne Rienner Publishers, 2015.

South, A. *Ethnic Politics in Burma: States of Conflict.* Abingdon: Routledge, 2008.

State Peace and Development Council. "Information Sheet". Yangon: Myanmar. C-2103 (I), 30 January 2002.

Sun, Y. *China and Myanmar's Peace Process.* United States Institute of Peace. March 2017.

Taylor, R. "Perceptions of Ethnicity in the Politics of Burma". *Southeast Asian Journal of Social Science* 10, no. 1 (1982): 7–22.

————. "Refighting Old Battles, Compounding Misconceptions: The Politics of Ethnicity in Myanmar Today". *ISEAS Perspective* 2015/12. Singapore: ISEAS – Yusof Ishak Institute, 2015.

Thein Sein. "Myanmar's Complex Transformation: Prospects and Challenges". Paper presented at Chatham House, London, 15 July 2013.

Transnational Institute. "Developing Disparity: Regional Investment in Burma's Borderlands". Amsterdam: Transnational Institute, 2013.

————. "Ethnicity without Meaning, Data without Context: The 2014 Census, Identity and Citizenship in Burma/Myanmar". *TNI-BCN Burma Policy Briefing* 13. Amsterdam: Transnational Institute, 2014.

————. "Military Confrontation or Political Dialogue: Consequences of the Kokang Crisis for Peace and Democracy in Myanmar". *TNI Myanmar Policy Briefing* 15. Amsterdam: Transnational Institute, 2015*a*.

————. "The 2015 General Election in Myanmar: What Now for Ethnic Politics?". *TNI Myanmar Policy Briefing* 17. Amsterdam: Transnational Institute, 2015*b*.

United Nationalities Federal Council. "Statement of UNFC Council: First Meeting of UNFC First Congress". 22 October 2014 <http://www.burmaenac.org/wp-content/uploads/2016/01/statement_20141022.pdf> (accessed 26 May 2016).

Von Der Mehden, F.R. *Religion and Nationalism in Southeast Asia: Burma, Indonesia, the Philippines.* Madison: University of Wisconsin Press, 1963.

2

REPRESENTATION AND CITIZENSHIP IN THE FUTURE INTEGRATION OF ETHNIC ARMED ACTORS IN MYANMAR/BURMA

Helene Maria Kyed and Mikael Gravers

INTRODUCTION

In this chapter, we discuss the future integration options for ethnic armed actors in the Myanmar/Burma peace process, and link this to questions of citizenship and representation. The focus is not only on the future political positions of the ethnic armed organizations (EAOs) and their leaders, but also on the possible civilian roles for the many middle and lower ranks. The future positions of the latter have received scant attention in the nationwide ceasefire negotiations and in national media coverage of the peace process. Based on interviews in 2014, focused particularly on armed actor integration, as well as on qualitative research in 2016 on the provision of justice by the two main EAOs in Mon and Karen States, we explore a number of possible roles that EAO actors could assume.[1] We focus particularly on their roles as security and justice actors, as civil servants, political party members, businessmen and members of civil society organizations.[2] Many of these roles can draw on already existing experiences of the EAOs as *de facto* local government actors in the areas they control. In addition, the options we outline are inspired by the international literature on "Demobilization, Disarmament and Reintegration" (DDR) (Munive and Jakobsen 2012; Muggah 2005; McMullin 2013*b*).

Debating the future integration options — denoting a shift from "combatant" to "civilian" identity — for ethnic armed actors, we argue, are significant to create trust in the peace process as well as to ensure longer term sustainable peace. Without concrete livelihood options and forms of recognition, there is a real risk that armed actors will be unsupportive of the peace process (Muggah 2005). Simultaneously, integration of EAO personnel and ethnic minorities more generally, into state structures can be important for fostering notions of national citizenship in a way that is inclusive of ethnic minorities' cultural, social, economic and political rights. This implies carefully linking ex-combatant reintegration with wider local governance and security sector reform as well as addressing how ethnic political representation by EAOs can promote *de facto* citizenship. Thus, we argue for the need to link EAO reintegration to questions of citizenship and representation.

In line with the critical literature on citizenship, we approach citizenship not only as a set of formal rights and status — i.e. as *de jure* legal citizenship — but also as a set of practices (Isin and Wood 1999; Isin and Turner 2002). This means paying attention to the actual fulfilment of rights for the diverse members of the nation-state, and to the forms of identification, conduct and attitude that are prescribed *de facto* as the ideal nation-state citizen. Using this approach scholars have illustrated how certain groups of people — ethnic groups, minorities, indigenous people, etc. — are systematically excluded from access to resources and recognition, despite their legal citizenship status. This *de facto* group-differentiated citizenship has, according to the critical scholars, happened under the pretence of the modern universal, individualist concept of citizenship, which places particularistic forms of identification and cultural modes of being as inferior to national belonging or to one central national identity. A way to undo *de facto* forms of group discrimination, it is argued, is to accommodate multiple forms of identification and collective claims to rights within the concept of citizenship (Kymlicka 1995; Ong 1999; Isin and Turner 2002; Kabeer 2005). This debate resonates with core concerns in Myanmar. Although in this context it has not been a universal individualist concept of citizenship that has *de facto* marginalized minority ethnic groups, the Bamar majority military government (1962–88) promoted an ideology of a unitary state based on one supra-Myanmar corporate national identity. Although this national identity comprised the eight major "national races", it *de facto* worked to foreground Bamar identity as the basis of national belonging. The process of *ethnicism* (Gravers 1999) has inhibited a common national identification. According to Taylor (2005) ethnicity was reified during colonial rule, whereas the army secured the state and created a nation. However, it was not colonialism alone, but also the military's often brutal practices of "Burmanization" which created a long lasting mutual distrust and violent ethnic boundary-making inhibiting nation-building (Gravers 1999).

The EAOs have for decades fought for ethnic groups' self-determination. Their armed struggle has been legitimized as the protection of ethnic minorities against military incursions, and as a fight for the *de facto* assurance of ethnic minority rights, including culture and customs, against what many ethnic organizations have seen as government strategies of "Burmanization" (Lewis 1924; Walton 2013). "Burmanization" denotes efforts to assimilate ethnic groups under one national identity, defined on the basis of the culture of the majority Bamar/Burman group (Walton 2013, p. 11; Taylor 2005). Non-Burman culture was equated with national disloyalty and disunity. This logic informed military campaigns against EAO resistance (ibid., p. 13). Simultaneously, ethnic nationalities, especially in EAO areas, have been the most disenfranchised in terms of political rights, and have had much less, if any, access to central government provided social rights (Callahan 2007; Walton 2013, 2015; Holliday 2014). This underscores *de facto* group-differentiated citizenship. Conversely, EAOs, and civil society organizations (CSOs) linked to the EAOs, have to varying degrees provided social services, including security and justice provision, in the areas they control (McCartan and Jolliffe 2016; Joliffe 2015). Formal recognition and integration of these services as part of the peace process can potentially promote the *de facto* citizenship rights of ethnic nationalities, and can also contribute to assuring future positions for combatants. How this can be achieved will be strongly influenced by the kind of political system that the parties can agree on in the peace process.

In the current nationwide ceasefire process, the EAOs are seeking a federal system, which will imply a high degree of self-determination and decentralization. The previous military-backed government, which led the ceasefire process from 2011, agreed to discuss federalism, and also the new NLD (National League for Democracy) government has promised a federal democracy with equal rights and autonomy (BNI 2015). Federalism is being discussed in the political dialogue that began in January 2016 as part of a nationwide ceasefire agreement. However, it is still unclear how much self-determination federalism will imply, and although the national army has now accepted the concept of federalism, it seems to cling on to a discourse that highlights national integration and unity to the detriment of the decentralization of power.[3] Another challenge is the question of who will represent the ethnic nationalities groups in a political settlement and in

future integration efforts. Today the EAOs' emphasis on continuing to bear
arms likely reflects current mistrust in the peace process, but it also indicates
the historically embedded link between armed defence and ethnic identity
politics. This raises the question of how the EAOs are able to transform
themselves from armed defenders to civilian representatives of ethnic group
rights. Increasingly they do not hold a monopoly on ethnic representation,
and their legitimacy may be further challenged with the growing number of
ethnic political parties and CSOs who equally claim to defend ethnic rights.
These political questions have mainly been addressed towards EAO leaders.
What is seldom asked is what will happen to the lower and middle-ranked
ethnic armed actors. In this chapter we combine the wider question of
representation with integration of lower ranking actors, and how each may
contribute to *de facto* citizenship for ethnic groups.

Before discussing integration options, we provide a short background to
the conflict and the peace process, linking each to questions of citizenship
and representation.

FROM ARMED CONFLICT TO CONTESTED PEACE: THE VEXED QUESTION OF ETHNICITY

Ethno-nationalist conflict has marred Myanmar since Independence from
British colonial rule. Approximately twenty EAOs claim to represent
the different ethnic groups and sub-groups. During their armed struggle
ethnic-based identity politics has focused on the cultural and political self-
determination and protection of the ethnic minorities, combined with conflicts
over the control of trade and resources. Most EAOs have political wings and
have administered their own micro-states, including departments of education,
health, justice, forestry, agriculture, and local defence.

As discussed in detail by Martin Smith (this volume), the course of
the seven decades of conflict is complex, but overall it was sparked by the
unfulfilled promise of federalism after Independence, which was further
underscored by the colonial reification and politicization of ethnicity (see also
Walton 2013; Taylor 1982). Although the 1948 Citizenship Law supported
equal citizenship to all national races, the first post-independence Burmese
leaders' claim to represent the interests of all residents in the country did
not convince the ethnic organizations. This distrust, which was supported
by military incursions into ethnic areas, laid the roots of the long civil war.
When the military under General Ne Win took power in 1962, antagonisms
intensified. Ne Win demanded unconditional surrender of the EAOs and
his idea of order, which was a corporate state of one single nationality,

rejected the demands for federalism (Callahan 2003). During this period different discourses and strategies of "Burmanization", further undermined ethnic citizenship rights (Walton 2012; Gravers 1999; Taylor 2005). *De facto* membership of the nation became conditional on assimilation of Burman-ness, whereas non-Burman ethnicity was conflated with disloyalty to the nation. Citizenship was *de facto* restricted to those adopting Burmese ways and culture, and who were loyal to the regime. Although citizens of Burmese ethnic identity also lacked *de facto* political and social rights, Walton (2012, p. 13) argues that non-Burmese groups have been subject to greater suspicion, violence and limited access to rights, as they "do not naturally possess a true Burmese heritage". This logic infused educational policies and also military strategies, which also strengthened the EAOs' emphasis on cultural identity as "an act of survival in a context of sustained violence and reinforced cultural assimilation" (ibid., p. 14).

The 1982 Citizenship Law, which was passed in this era, and which is still in power today, has supported Burmanization in practice. It provides *full citizenship:* "Nationals such as Kachin, Kayah, Chin, Karen, Burman, Mon, Rakine, or Shan and *other ethnic groups* as have settled within the state as their present home before 1823 are Burmese citizens." Other ethnic groups were not specified in the law. However, in 1990 the military government announced the existence of (but did not specifically list) 135 Myanmar "indigenous peoples" (*taingyintha*), in the state-controlled *Working Peoples Daily* newspaper. Despite its cloudy origin and status it seems to function as a semi-legal and political instrument of inclusion/exclusion in relation to the 1982 law. Two other categories of citizenship are the *associate citizenship* for persons who acquired citizenship through the 1948 Union Citizenship Law; and *naturalized citizenship*, which refers to persons born in Burma and who can prove they lived in Burma before 4 January 1948 and applied for citizenship after 1982. For all three categories, it can be difficult for a person to find evidence of ancestry more than half a century back, which also relates to the fact that numerous ethnic minorities do not have the required forms of national documents and registration to assert citizenship (Transnational Institute 2014).

People not listed as one of the 135 *taingyintha*, such as Bengalis, Pakistanis, Chinese, and Indians are therefore not considered to be "national races".[4] Thus, Tamil Hindus and Muslims from the former British India have had increasing difficulties in obtaining a form of citizenship or even a green Identity Card for National Verification. During ongoing research among Karen Muslims in the Karen State we found they were registered as "Bengalis" in their household registers — despite the fact that they speak fluent Pwo, are well integrated and have been there for more than 100 years. Some of their parents had folded cards (associate citizenship) or even pink cards, but cannot renew or obtain any form of citizenship.

Thus, even *de jure* citizenship is uncertain for many persons. Another controversial issue concerns those persons with mixed ethnicity or race, because the law stipulates that a person can only register under one ethnic category: in the past, if one parent is Bamar this will likely be registered by the authorities, thus favouring the number of people belonging to the majority group. This has also sparked discontent among the ethnic organizations, as it reduces the number of registered minority persons.[5]

The idea behind the 1982 law was a unitary Myanmar nation subsuming all ethnic groups under one national identity, which according to Taylor (1982, pp. 19–20) reflected an attempt by the military regime to downplay the hitherto prevalence of ethnic and religious differences in politics, which has colonial roots. However, because the policies that attempted to de-ethnicize politics, were implemented by a Bamar majority army government, they were seen by the ethnic organizations as strategies of Burmanization. Also at the centre of these policies were attempts to extend central state control to the border areas, and thus make national integration superior to ethnic pluralism (Taylor 1982, p. 20). This was supported by major offensives during Ne Win's rule, which considerably weakened many EAOs.

When the State Law and Order Restoration Council (SLORC) took over power from Ne Win, after pro-democracy protest in 1988, ceasefires were made with at least sixteen EAOs (1989–97) (Jolliffe 2015, pp. 18–19), but these did little to change the conditions of citizenship for the ethnic minorities (Kramer 2010; Zaw Oo and Win Min 2007; Callahan 2007; and Smith 2006). The ceasefires focused on economic and military matters, granting trade concessions and some territorial control, and allowed the groups to still carry arms, but the EAOs' political demands for federalism were not met. For this reason some EAOs, like the Karen National Union (KNU) did not agree. While the ceasefires did bring some development projects that improved the lives of villagers, they also ended up strengthening the illicit businesses and territorial control of the Army (Oh 2013, p. 11; see also Martin Smith's chapter in this volume). Also they split up some of the EAOs, further weakening their position. In 2009 the 1990s ceasefire groups became subject to the Border Guard Force (BGF) initiative, which followed the new 2008 Constitution's demand for a single army (Keenan 2013). The deal involved salaries, social benefits, and continued armament, but it also came with no political settlement and improvement of ethnic citizenship. Consequently, many EAO leaders refused the deal, resulting in renewed cycles of fighting.

After the 2010 elections when the military proxy Union Solidarity and Development Party (USDP) came into power, the new President U Thein Sein declared a surprising political and economic reform agenda, which also included a strong commitment to make peace with the EAOs. In 2012 bilateral ceasefires were signed with a majority of the EAOs, followed by negotiations towards a nationwide agreement, which also included promises to discuss the political demands of the EAOs. In terms of citizenship, the reform process since 2011 has supported greater freedoms and equal rights of citizens, but the status of ethnic minorities remains ambiguous. The 2008 Constitution assures freedom of religion and support for ethnic minority languages and customs, but simultaneously allots a special position to Buddhism as the religion of the majority (article 361).[6] Also the language of the Bamar majority is defined as the official language (article 450) (ibid., pp. 410–11). These aspects point to how the *de facto* promotion of cultural rights is still perceived as inferior to majority privileges. Importantly, the political and cultural rights of ethnic minorities are not linked, leaving out a deeper acceptance of the political self-determination demands of ethnic groups. In contrast, the Constitution defines the main national causes as "non-disintegration of the union", "non-disintegration of national solidarity" and "perpetuation of sovereignty" (ibid., p. 407), which could be used against federalism. According to Holliday (2014, p. 411), this reflects a continued emphasis on unity above all else, which makes it difficult for ethnic leaders to claim particular political rights in the sphere of governance. As Kymlicka (1995) argues, to ensure "horizontal multicultural citizenship" there must be political accommodation of ethnic diversity, beyond cultural rights. These matters are significant to consider in the peace negotiations.

NATIONWIDE CEASEFIRE NEGOTIATIONS

Nationwide ceasefire negotiations began in 2013 with sixteen EAOs, and in August 2015 all parties agreed on a Nationwide Ceasefire Agreement (NCA) text. However, on 15 October 2015 only eight of the EAOs signed, including the KNU and other Karen groups. The rest of the groups refused. Their official reason was not that they disagreed with the NCA text, but that the USDP government did not recognize all existing groups (on more complex reasons behind the decision not to sign, see Martin Smith's chapter, this volume).[7]

The NCA text promises a union based on the principles of federalism and democracy, which can be seen as a major gain for the EAOs. However, what kind of federalism this will entail is not spelled out in the NCA, but depends on the result of the inclusive political dialogue that began in January

2016 and that is still ongoing as of March 2017. Also federalism will need constitutional changes. Many key questions remain open in the NCA: how much power can the EAOs claim, and what would be the geographical markers of ethnic as well as multi-ethnic areas? What kind of local governance arrangements and sub-national power-sharing could a federal system imply for the EAOs and the ethnic populations in general? Also the NCA leaves open for future negotiations, the roles and positions of EAO members in the security sector, as security sector reform and DDR are still to be discussed. In terms of economic power-sharing such as the equal distribution of resources and land rights, the NCA also does not provide any concrete guarantees, although it promises that any new larger development projects will only be rolled out after consultation with EAOs and ethnic communities. In short, although the NCA reflects that the parties have come a long way in agreeing on basic principles, many areas remain uncertain when it comes to the future position of EAO members and the rights of ethnic citizens. This breeds insecurity and mistrust about the future, especially among lower ranks and mid-level commanders,[8] as well as among some members of the ethnic populations.[9] These matters may also constitute another reason for why some groups have not signed.

The unclear position of the powerful army with respect to federalism is another area of uncertainty. Army generals still seem to pledge that the EAOs come under one army.[10] Also the failed efforts in parliament to change the Constitution towards more decentralization in 2015, points to the army's reluctance to accept federalism.[11] Changing the Constitution requires the support of the military representatives in parliament, still constituting 25 per cent of the seats. Intensified fighting in Shan and Kachin States since 2015 has further given rise to insecurity about the army's commitment to peace.

A final area of insecurity is the political changes since the NLD came into power in April 2016. The NLD has given high priority to the peace process and has explicitly stated its support for federalism, but it is unclear how much central power it will decentralize to the ethnic states, and what position it will grant the EAOs. The peace conference convened under the NLD government in late August 2016 was more inclusive of EAOs, including those that had not signed the NCA, but the conference did not lead to any concrete results and political agreements. As of March 2017, no new EAOs have signed the NCA, which means that they are excluded from the political dialogue, although bilateral talks are ongoing. Another matter, which we will discuss below, is that there are a growing number of non-armed representatives of the various ethnic groups, including ethnic political parties and CSOs. Although the ethnic political parties did not obtain many seats in the 2015 elections, they still constitute significant alternative forces, which could challenge the role of the EAOs as legitimate stakeholders in the political negotiations with the government (South 2014). Also, a number of ethnic CSOs have raised complaints about the lack of popular inclusion in the peace process.[12] There is a sense that the EAOs are becoming more marginalized in the political process and the reforms that are taking place alongside the peace process. Political marginalization could run the risk of renewed cycles of armed conflict, especially if EAOs are unable to get concrete benefits through the political dialogue, not only politically, but also in terms of SSR and economic survival for their members. A related concern is the question of the EAOs' capacity to govern in a federal system, and thence what governance roles they could play. Next, we discuss these matters of political integration, along with other options.

INTEGRATION OPTIONS AND CITIZENSHIP

In the DDR literature (re)integration is the process through which fighters change their identity from "combatant" to "civilian", and change their behaviour by ending the use of violent means and increasing activities that are sanctioned by the mainstream community (Torjesen 2013). We make a call for a combination of different *integration* options, which considers the heterogeneity of interests and rank levels: livelihood options are indeed important for sustainable peace, but needs to be combined with power-sharing arrangements that also consider political positions for the EAOs as well as the wider distribution of economic resources and power in ethnic areas. In what follows, we explore also the future options for EAO actors as service providers, based on already existing practices. We focus on five options: (1) integration in the sense of a recognition of EAO actors as security and justice providers; (2) political party integration; (3) civil service and local government positions; (4) job creation and the formalization of large-scale businesses, and; (5) CSOs. We consider the possibilities and dilemmas of these options, and link them to questions of citizenship and representation.

Security and Justice Sector Integration

In Myanmar, it is likely that some form of military integration will occur, but we suggest that this is combined with wider Security Sector Reform (SSR), including the police and the judiciary. SSR in other contexts has involved the integration of EAO members into national and regional (state-level) police branches, as well as into village defence and dispute resolution forums

(Knight 2009). Less discussed in the DDR literature is the integration of EAO actors into the judiciary, based on already existing arrangements and practices (Sivakumaran 2009). Even when national police and courts are not present, there is seldom a total security and justice provision vacuum in conflict or ceasefire areas: armed and non-armed local security forces and dispute resolution actors, with varying levels of legitimacy and effectiveness exist. This is also the case in Mon and Karen States.

The KNU and the New Mon State Party (NMSP) have their own justice systems, which are institutionalized from central to township level. They have their own laws, covering civil and criminal cases, prisons as well as a quite extensive transfer system from the village levels inside the areas they control (McCartan and Jolliffe 2016; Kyed forthcoming; Harrisson and Kyed 2017). They do not have professionally trained judges and do not use lawyers, but elected justice committee members are expected to use arbitration and apply the written law. The KNU has independent judges, whereas the NMSP justice committees comprise members from the administrative and military wings. These systems have existed since the 1970s, with varying levels of presence and human resources due to the contours of the armed conflict (Harrisson and Kyed 2017). Since 1991, the KNU has also had the Karen National Police Force (KNPF), including a criminal investigation department, which is supposed to investigate crimes, make arrests and provide public security (McCartan and Jolliffe 2016).

According to research conducted in 2016, the EAO justice systems constitute the preferred option or back-up when disputes and crimes cannot be resolved by village leaders. Village leaders and/or village justice committees transfer cases to the EAO courts at township level when cases are too difficult to handle at the village level, when perpetrators repeat offences or when decisions made at village level are not abided by. The EAO justice systems are seen to be central to maintaining order, punishing larger crimes, and ensuring that disputes do not escalate at the village level. Interviewed village leaders, stated that the EAO systems support their capacity to enforce decisions in criminal and civil matters within the village, because they can warn perpetrators and disputing parties that the case will be transferred to the EAOs if they do not abide by local decisions. By contrast, it is almost unthinkable to use the official state justice system, which is mistrusted, difficult to access, associated with corruption and feared. Villagers value that the EAO systems use the local ethnic languages and recognize local customary norms and the preference for mediation and negotiated settlements. The EAOs grant a large jurisdiction to village leaders and local justice committees, and also allow these to make their own by-laws or village rules, such as prohibitions on alcohol abuse and sale. The EAOs back these village rules in the sense that if village leaders are unable to enforce punishments of perpetrators, they can forward these to the EAO systems. In fact, when compared with Myanmar government administered areas, we found that the NMSP and the KNU have a much more institutionalized link between higher courts and the village dispute resolution fora. They have a system of appeal and transfer, including the sharing of case records, which does not currently exist in the Myanmar system (Kyed forthcoming).

Importantly, we found that the stability created with the ceasefires since 2012, have enabled the KNU and the NMSP to strengthen and reform their justice systems, rather than leading to an increase in Karen and Mon villagers using the Myanmar system. This strengthening includes efforts to establish stronger links between the EAO courts and the villages located in former combat zones on the frontline with Myanmar controlled areas (Harrisson and Kyed 2017). The KNU has provided training for judges in human rights and the rule of law, as well as empowered the Karen Women's Organization (KWO) to deal with gender-based violence cases and marriage disputes at the village level. They have helped to establish village justice committees in places where KNU-aligned village chairmen previously had to operate secretly, due to fear of Tatmadaw attacks, often at the expense of not being able to deal with crimes and resolve social disputes. In one Northern Karen State village, officially situated within Myanmar administered boundaries, for instance, the KNU was able to openly operate since 2013, including to disseminate its laws and encourage village leaders to form justice committees, codify their village laws, and forward serious crimes to the KNU. The KWO leader in this village said: "Before this time we had rules, but no one followed them. But after this time the KNU gave us authority to write the rules and now we can enforce them".[13] Since 2012, the KNPF has also been strengthened with training and new recruits, and officers are now supposed to be present in all KNU townships and districts.[14] Both the KNU and the NMSP have also revised their laws to fit with current requirements, especially with regards to drugs. Due to the increase in drug abuse since the 2012 ceasefires, the NMSP and the KNU are now strongly engaged in prosecuting drug traffickers, and especially the NMSP is focused on drug rehabilitation. In 2015, the KNU also passed a land policy, which has a specific chapter on land dispute resolution at village levels and above.

Currently, there is no official recognition of these justice systems by the Myanmar government, and their future role has still not been discussed in the post-ceasefire political dialogues. In fact, there is a growing tendency for the state-level governments to criticize these systems, asserting that they are illegal, likely because they are seen as challenging the official state system.[15] This is especially seen as critical when the EAO systems arrest and prosecute offenders who have committed crimes outside of their immediate areas of control, or when they decide criminal offences involving persons from another ethnic group than their own. Conversely, the EAOs' strengthening of their systems, including into villages that lie on the blurred territorial borderline with Myanmar-administered areas, can be seen as a strategic aspect of ceasefire state-making, which could strengthen their position in a future federal system.

Lack of recognition and insecurities around jurisdictional boundaries are the core challenges facing the EAO justice systems, which at times compromises the quality of the justice provided. For instance in Northern Karen State the KNU is often forced to operate mobile courts, to set up temporary prison cells at outposts, and it is not always possible to summon the judges and the police to decide cases, so instead soldiers or other administrative staff make judgements. Whereas mobile courts means that the system is flexible and able to adjust to the circumstances on the ground, it can also mean that legal procedures are not always followed. The NMSP equally suffers from human resource constraints, and justice committee members have varying knowledge of the law. Some members do not even have the written laws, and in both EAOs there was an expressed desire for more legal awareness and capacity building (Harrisson and Kyed 2017).

Recognition of the EAO justice systems could contribute significantly to making the systems more stable and transparent, as this would also allow for more open operations as well as skills training. When debating future SSR for Myanmar as part of the peace process it would be relevant to discuss the integration of already existing EAO policing and justice actors into new reformed institutions, especially given that they enjoy considerably more legitimacy than the current Myanmar institutions. Such integration can support the fulfilment of ethnic groups' *de facto* right to justice and security, because such mechanisms work closer to people, speak the local language and also recognize local justice preferences and customs. Whereas customary law is recognized in Myanmar, this only regards family law matters, not criminal offences, and it does not include the recognition of ethnic-based or customary courts as part of the judiciary (Kham 2014, p. 3; Crouch 2016, p. 92). The justice systems of the KNU and the NMSP reflect in some respects a state legal system, with written laws and judges, but they also draw on customary rules and mediation. For justice and security sector reform to become an integration option for armed actors that serves the *de facto* and *de jure* citizenship of ethnic nationalities, there is a need for a widely inclusive debate on dispute resolution and protection preferences that also involves ordinary ethnic citizens, village leaders and CSOs, along with the EAOs. Here it is important to draw on empirical knowledge, as described above, of already existing practices. As other similar contexts show, it is unsustainable in a peace and reform process to exclude existing systems and those practices that are considered to work on the ground (Albecht et al. 2011). Rather it is more viable to find ways of reforming and aligning non-state mechanisms with the wider judicial system.

POLITICAL PARTY INTEGRATION

EAOs could transform into political parties, which would make them "protectors" or representatives of ethnic communities through competitive political (rather than mainly armed) means. Political integration could also involve combatants joining existing political parties. This transformation typically targets higher-ranks. However, it can also give lower and middle-ranks a conduit for political expression so as to realize personal, social and economic goals through non-violent means (Mitton 2008, p. 202).

Most of our Karen and Mon interviewees supported political integration of EAOs, but there were also some concerns about their skills to run party apparatus and about their militarized political culture. One Buddhist monk, a supporter of the Ploung-Sgaw Democratic Party (PSDP), which was founded by Karen youth activists, stated: "The leaders [of EAOs] are not ready to be politicians in a democracy. They are not educated and civilized, but speak in a too rough manner like military way. They do not understand that democracy is to be representative of the people."[16] Another concern is the extent to which the EAOs are willing to transform into political parties without a political deal towards federalism that also secures them political power outside of competitive politics. According to Kempel, Aung Tun and Aung Tun (2014, p. 24), they are currently reluctant, because they already see themselves as legitimate representatives of ethnic communities.

A core challenge here is the growing heterogeneity of, and indeed rivalry between, ethnic political parties that also claim to represent ethnic groups. For instance three parties in Mon State and four in Karen State all ran for the November 2015 elections. The EAOs do not have a monopoly as defenders of ethnic rights and culture, and therefore transforming into political parties is not a guarantee that the EAOs will come out of the peace process with secure political positions (Lall et al. 2015).

The NLD landslide victory in the 2015 elections reduced the representation of most ethnic parties in the parliament, as many ethnic nationalities chose to vote for NLD, which also had ethnic candidates. This regarded not least the Mon parties, among which only one party obtained a seat at national level and two at state level. Also only one Karen political party got a seat in the state level parliament, and therefore there are no Karen party representatives at national level. Significantly, interviews suggest that the KNU advised their constituencies to vote for NLD because they consider the Karen political parties to be close to the army. Other observations suggest that ethnic nationalities voted for NLD because they believe a change of the political system requires a strong national party in government, rather than a range of smaller parties. The failure of the majority of ethnic parties to merge and create alliances (Kempel, Aung Tun and Aung Tun 2014, p. 22), likely also had a bearing on voter behaviour. Time will show whether this trend will favour or not the EAOs political representation vis-à-vis the ethnic political parties. The relative clout of the EAOs and potential rivalries over who are the true and most legitimate representatives of ethnic groups will likely become clearer as the post-NCA political dialogue, which also involves ethnic political parties, progresses. At the same time the peace transition could compel the EAOs into closer collaboration, incorporating or merging with existing parties (ibid., p. 24).

Ethnic political alliances and divisions raise important questions about the prospects for group-based ethnic citizenship and the fulfilment of ethnic minorities' social and political rights. Who can claim to represent the ethnic nationalities in the multi-party democracy? And how would this work within a federal system? These questions also need to consider the multi-ethnicity of the ethnic nationalities states: although for instance Mon and Karen States may be populated by a majority of Mon and Karen ethnicities respectively, there are also numerous other ethnic groups, not least in the larger towns.[17] Whereas many representatives potentially multiply efforts to promote the rights of minorities, divisions can also undermine the political clout of ethnic representatives in the national arena and at state level, as is now already evident with the 2015 election results.

To avoid splitting the ethnic vote in the future, some of the existing party representatives that we spoke with suggested that alliances could be built between EAO parties and existing ones. For instance, one Karen People's Party (KPP) representative asserted: "the KNU leaders can become party officials in the KPP or they could make their own party and then we can make an alliance. This would mean a strong constituency, because KNU has support in the villages and KPP is strong in towns."[18] However there were also contrasting views, such as by the Mon Democratic Party (MDP — now renamed Mon National Party (MNP)), whose chairman did not support

NMSP becoming a political party. However, he welcomed its members to join MNP (Lall et al. 2015).

Another option for political integration is to motivate individual EAO combatants and commanders to join existing parties, many of whom share their political goals. Already there are some examples of "self-integration", like the chairman of the MNP (in 2014), who is an ex-commander of the NMSP. Also the Karen State Democracy and Development Party was formed by people close to the DKBA leadership. The MDP chairman told us that his party does not represent the NMSP, but considers it an ally and he maintains personal relations. In general, however, it is unclear to what extent current ethnic parties support the EAOs and to what extent individual EAO members support them and are willing to lay down arms by joining them (Kempel, Aung Tun and Aung Tun 2014, p. 24).

A related concern is the political legitimacy of the EAOs in ethnic constituencies. According to South (2012) many ethnic communities in Karen conflict-affected areas display strong support for the KNU, yet there is concern that this is not the case in other Karen constituencies. Some EAO leaders fear losing popular support and control over client populations during the peace process, especially as civilians resettle in government-controlled areas. Simultaneously, some citizens living in EAO-controlled areas were deprived of their political right to vote in the 2015 elections, as there was no government administration there. This underscores a sense of marginalization caused by EAO control, thus potentially delegitimizing the EAOs politically. Transformation into political parties as part of a disarmament process will arguably only be attractive to the EAOs if they believe they are able to mobilize enough votes. In other contexts, such insecurity of popular legitimacy has led to a combination of political integration in the form of electoral competition with power-sharing arrangements and the granting of higher positions to ex-combatant leaders within the existing government and state apparatus (Torjesen 2013; Mitton 2008). The question is whether the other ethnic political parties and indeed the NLD government would agree to giving special political positions to EAOs. This question arguably harks back on the extent to which the EAOs are seen as privileged representatives of ethnic minorities as groups, rather than as individual citizens, who can choose their representatives through electoral politics.

Political integration also needs to consider the gains for lower ranks (Torjesen 2013, p. 6). If lower ranks do not feel that they benefit from and are represented through the political integration of higher ranks then there is a risk of violent remobilization (Christensen and Utas 2008). According to Spear (2007) one of the problems in other contexts is that many ex-combatants do not regard being in political opposition as providing for them economically, at least not sufficiently. This calls for a consideration of other integration options.

SOCIAL SERVICE PROVISION AND LOCAL GOVERNMENT POSITIONS

Integration of ex-combatants into local government service provision and administration is not only a matter of job-creation, but is also important for reconciliation (Jolliffe 2014, 2015). Overall, this implies aligning *de facto* governance arrangements in EAO-controlled areas with post-conflict sub-national governance reform. This is similar to the points made about the justice sector, as discussed above. In addition to justice provision, the EAOs, along with a range of EAO-linked community-based organizations (CBOs), have to varying degrees had administrations as well as social service delivery in the areas of health, education, agriculture, land tenure and so forth. Instead of viewing these as oppositional to state-building, they should be seen as an asset in consolidating and improving service delivery to citizens during the implementation of the NCA and beyond. Examples of collaboration at the local level already exist, such as between the NMSP education sector and the Mon State Parliament in mixed NMSP and government-controlled areas around the introduction of Mon language in schools (Lall and South 2013). Jolliffe (2015) also highlights informal collaboration and accommodation between EAO and government administrations in some areas, which could support future alignments in sub-national governance. This can be contrasted with situations where the rolling out of government schools, clinics, and administrations staffed by Burmans, in ethnic areas has created antagonisms and fears that the government is taking over control before a political settlement is reached. At worst it is seen as Burmanization: it signals that ethnic representatives are excluded from government, which creates mistrust in the peace process and in governance reform in general. As Derksen (2014, p. 2) argues, it is important not only to focus on high-level political settlements: "translating national power-sharing into local arrangements that give the main local actors access to power and resources will be crucial" to sustainable peace.

Integration of ex-combatants in sub-national governance, and recognition of EAO services, need to consider the great variety of local governance set-ups across the ethnic states, which have changed over the course of the conflict. Along with a separation of government and EAO-controlled areas, there are several areas with mixed local government. Here both EAOs and government village headmen operate, sometimes along with village leaders accountable to other armed fractions.[19] It is important that these matters are discussed in the political dialogue, focusing also on the question of what will happen with existing personnel within *de facto* governance arrangements and the power positions they hold. Although South (2012) questions the governance capacities and technical expertise of EAO personnel, many public government officials face similar challenges. This calls for extensive nationwide civil service training. As experiences from elsewhere show, it is important to carefully balance the integration of ex-combatants, as a means to mitigate local power conflicts, with the inclusion of ethnic civilians, so that integration does not become exclusionary and seen as the granting of special privileges to armed actors (Ansori 2012).

These matters are important to citizenship in two ways. First, reliance on already existing capacities can enhance the *de facto* fulfilment of service delivery, like the right to education and health. Second, inclusion of ethnic minorities in the civil service and administration can enhance trust in and familiarity with the governance system, for instance by enabling local dialects to be spoken and reducing the fear that public officials discriminate against minorities due to them being of another ethnic group.

ECONOMIC INTEGRATION AND RIGHTS

Economic integration means moving combatants away from livelihood support mechanisms associated with military networks, towards employment in public and private sectors, in addition to various income-generating activities. Typically, this option is targeted at lower-ranks. It covers many different mechanisms like vocational and agricultural training, job placement, education, income generation through microcredits, and public works schemes (McMullin 2013*a*). Apart from providing an income that moves them away from combat or criminality, a job can give ex-combatants a sense of pride in supporting their families and thus aid their psychological and social reintegration (Specht 2003). In previous years DDR programmes have moved away from an exclusive focus on ex-combatants to involve whole communities in joint community development and reconstruction work, where civilians and ex-combatants participate and get on-the-job training (e.g., for building schools, clinics, roads and wells) (Munive and Jakobsen 2012, p. 362). These joint schemes can lessen distrust and increase tolerance between combatants and different conflict-affected groups, which are important for reconciliation (Specht 2003, p. 96).

Economic integration needs to consider that EAOs already have numerous economic activities in the territories they control, ranging from cross border trade, mineral extraction, agriculture, to illegal businesses like drugs and gambling. Simultaneously, the Army has also made incursions into the EAO territories or the borders around them, including illicit businesses, sometimes with the aid of people's militias. Moreover, new businesses and large foreign investments are being rolled out. Economic reintegration, and its relationship to promoting the rights of ethnic citizens, should not be divorced from considerations of such "ceasefire economies" (Woods 2011), which are deeply embedded in networks of power and contestations over control of territories and resources. Key combatants have often enjoyed the benefits of the ceasefire economy, and this position can be hard to break. Some of our interviewees stated that the armed conflict has created a kind of "lost generation" of people who have known little but war and military conduct, and who see few opportunities to join the licit economy. This calls for what Specht (2003) terms a "political economy of peace", which involves closing off illicit routes to economic gain in order to integrate ex-combatants into a licit economy. This requires a deep understanding of wartime economies and of the extent to which combatants' activities have or have not benefitted ethnic communities. For instance the Karen Peace Force general that we spoke with had used the 1995 ceasefire deal to commence agricultural and infrastructural projects that also benefitted the population in his area. Building on such experiences by formalizing, and indeed regulating, ex-combatants' existing economic activities could be an important entrance point to integration that also supports communities. However, there is cause for concern that such activities are balanced more towards personal enrichment and/or to secure the survival of armed groups. The balance between *de facto* supporting ethnic economic rights and personal interests is unclear and inevitably varies from EAO to EAO and from brigade to brigade. One interviewee argued for the importance of strengthening Karen business corporations to assist the Karen in creating businesses, so as to avoid monopolization by foreigners. However, his concern was that the KNU has already established such a corporation, which he feared was not broadly inclusive of all Karen businesses.

Economic integration and employment creation are therefore matters that go beyond ex-combatants. According to our interviews there is a real worry in Mon and Karen States that the new businesses that have emerged over the past years, which are predominantly owned by the Bamar majority or by foreigners, do not hire local Karen and Mon. Although this may be because many Mon and Karen rather seek higher paid jobs in Thailand, as part of a strong pattern of labour migration, while new companies hire Burmese migrants, who migrate due to low job opportunities in their own regions, especially Bago, this tendency still plays into prevailing notions of ethnic minority discrimination. Not only may this tendency make it difficult for ex-combatants and returning internally displaced persons (IDPs) to get jobs, it also challenges ideas about the consolidation of economic opportunities for ethnic groups inside their own states. These matters are crucial to citizenship in the sense of the right to and control over development, resources and land in ethnic nationalities areas. In this area it is still unclear to what extent the EAOs and their economic activities *de facto* support the economic rights of ethnic communities.

CIVIL SOCIETY ORGANIZATIONS

CSOs enjoy an expanding space for operation in Myanmar, and as international donor flows are increasing inside the country there will be a growing demand for local NGOs as partners in development. Also in EAO areas in southeast Myanmar there has been a long history of CSOs, including religious organizations, which have provided humanitarian aid. In one respect the new ethnic CSOs, like with the political parties, could be seen as challenging the EAOs' local legitimacy, because many of them claim to represent those civilians who did not participate in the armed struggle. Conversely, many of the CSOs in the conflict areas have operated under the protection of the EAOs and therefore have deep alliances. The possibility of CSOs becoming spaces for ex-combatant integration into civilian life is not something one reads about in the DDR literature, but in Myanmar this could be relevant. This became clear in Mon State when we met the Ramanya Peace Foundation (RPF), established after the 2012 NMSP ceasefire. Two of its founders were former NMSP members, and essentially they had "self-integrated" by setting up RPF. It now receives international funding to support projects in the areas of water and sanitation, women's empowerment, rule of law, and leadership training in NMSP areas. Similar examples exist, with ethnic CSOs not only being service providers, but also engaging with culture and language.

CSOs are important to the citizenship of ethnic nationalities, both in terms of promoting cultural and political rights and in the sense of service delivery to remote and conflict-affected areas, not least in a transitional phase before more stable and reformed local government institutions can operate. For combatants CSOs can serve as a conduit for self-transformation into civilian service providers, and they can be an asset, because they often have strong contacts and alliances in the areas that have been controlled by EAOs. However, as in the other areas of integration competition for resources and over the representation of ethnic communities cannot be ruled out.

TOWARDS A CONCLUSION

In this chapter we have argued that there is a need in Myanmar to discuss the future reintegration options for members of EAOs, and link this not only to conventional DDR processes, but also to questions of citizenship and representation of ethnic nationalities. As experiences from elsewhere show, it is important that members of armed groups can envision viable integration options after the end of a conflict so as to establish trust in the peace process and achieve sustainable peace (Derksen 2014; Spear 2007). Along with a national political settlement about federalism, there is a need for concrete integration options, which focus both on livelihood as well as on sub-national governance power-sharing. This is important not least in a context like Myanmar where the EAOs and EAO-linked organizations have for decades run their own micro-states within the state, including the delivery of various social services as well as justice and security provision. The existing experiences and skills of EAO members, such as justice committee members, administrators, teachers and so forth, should be approached as assets for rather than as obstacles to peace, reconciliation and development. Especially the integration of EAO personnel into reformed state structures, and as part of local governance arrangements is also important for citizenship.

When we speak about citizenship this is not only in the sense of legal status, albeit important, but also in terms of *de facto* access to rights (economic, political, cultural and social) and as *de facto* forms of belonging and identification. Given the history of "Burmanization" in Myanmar, which has meant that the majority Bamar have tended to occupy official state positions, and ethnic minorities have felt discriminated against in terms of access to basic rights, the integration of EAOs into the state apparatus and recognition of their existing roles, can potentially help create trust in the state. It also holds the potential for enabling improved services to ethnic minorities, especially if integration is combined with skills training and capacity building. Currently, the trust in EAO justice systems, for instance, as opposed to mistrust in the Myanmar justice system, underscores that ethnic nationalities prefer accessing services that are sensitive towards their needs and preferences for justice, including the use of ethnic languages. Integration into state institutions can also foster reconciliation if and when service providers from both sides of the conflict divide work together for instance around specific service delivery. This is already seen in the education sector in Mon State. Tensions, however, remain for instance in the field of justice where the Myanmar state-level governments are increasingly treating EAO service provision as illegal and as a challenge to the official state system. This hampers the EAO's capacity to provide quality justice, because they must operate partly secretly and sometimes in a mobile fashion.

When speaking about integration into local governance and service delivery there is a need to consider the shorter and longer term perspective. It is clear that the political dialogue about federalism will take several years, and this raises the question of the interim phase inside ceasefire areas like those of the KNU and the NMSP. We suggest that there could be strong benefits, also in the longer term, from recognizing EAO systems in the interim phase. This means allowing locally legitimate service delivery, including justice provision, to operate openly and with formalized support from not only the EAOs, but also the Myanmar state and international actors supporting development and peace. This could mean that, for instance the EAO justice committees could function more transparently and predictably if they did not have to be insecure about jurisdictions or operate partly secretly. There is opening in the NCA for "Interim Arrangements" around development and service delivery. The NCA recognizes that EAOs "have been responsible for development and security in their respective areas" and stipulates that signatory EAOs and the Myanmar state coordinate "matters regarding peace and stability and the maintenance of the rule of law" and the "eradication of illicit drugs" (NCA quoted in McCartan and Jolliffe 2016, pp. 22–23). However, the NCA does not provide a plan for how such arrangements could be implemented. This needs to be decided among the stakeholders in the political dialogue. In addition, the NCA emphasizes coordination between EAOs and the Myanmar state rather than vesting total authority in the EAOs to perform governance functions. This leaves some ambiguity given the reality of parallel systems, and it could also underscore existing fears among EAO actors that their state-like structures could be challenged through Myanmar state expansion, even if this is through collaboration (Harrisson and Kyed 2017).

When speaking about integration and citizenship it is important to be aware of the economic and political power interests at play. It is not always entirely clear where the balance lies between supporting ethnic communities and serving EAOs' own power interests. It is therefore important that the integration of EAO personnel does not translate into the exclusion of other members of ethnic nationalities. The rights and preferences of local villagers must be included and respected.

In the chapter, we also raised questions about representation, as important in considerations especially of the political integration of EAO actors. An important question for the future is the extent to which the EAOs in Myanmar can continue to claim the same legitimacy in light of the wider political transition and the increase in other non-armed ethnic representatives, who make similar claims, like political parties and CSOs. For EAOs to support sustainable peace this may require that the EAOs — or individual members — transform themselves into political parties or join existing ones, and/or that they achieve special positions in state and sub-national governance arrangements.

Finally, and more generally, it is important to begin to discuss what form of ethnic citizenship would be relevant in a federal set-up, which is still not clear among the EAOs and the government. This could include several models, but overall there is a need to discuss the pros and cons of either a group- or individual-based form of citizenship. One solution could be a kind of *de jure* multicultural group-based citizenship, which accommodates group differences as horizontally incorporated under national citizenship. Such a solution can support the recognition of particular, and partly autonomous, ethnic political and juridical institutions, but also raises important questions about how each of the groups will be represented and by whom. Also geographic delineation of ethnic identity could face important challenges, given that the current states are internally multi-ethnic. Another solution is to continue with the current individual-based citizenship, along with the recognition of ethnic culture and customs, but then important insurances of the decentralization of power and resources as well as of the *de facto* access to rights by ethnic nationalities are crucial. As argued by scholars on citizenship it is significant in multi-cultural and multi-ethnic settings that cultural recognition is accompanied by political rights and power-sharing, so as not to undermine minorities (Kymlicka 1995; Isin and Turner 2002).

Notes

1. We also draw on insights from other studies of Mon and Karen armed organizations (Gravers 2015; Joliffe 2014, 2015; Kempel and Nyein 2014; McConnachie 2014; Oh 2013; Smith 2006; South 2003).

2. The research in 2014 was short-term and concentrated on a selected number of interviews with actors that we encountered in Hpa-An (Karen State) and Moulmein (Mon State), who were members of armed groups, local leaders and persons involved in the peace process, including religious leaders, to get their opinions about the future roles and positions of the ethnic armed actors. These were distributed as follows. In Karen State: 2 Karen Buddhist monks, 2 Karen political party representatives, 1 ward administrator in Democratic Karen Buddhist Army (DKBA) area, 1 Karen National Union (KNU) Liaison officer and ex-combatant, 1 KNU splinter group leader, 1 leader of Karen development CSO and 3 group interviews (Karen ANSA ex-combatants in

village for disabled, 2 Karen youth and environmental networks). In Mon State: 2 Mon political party leaders, 2 New Mon State Party (NMSP) liaison officers, 1 Mon women's group organization, 1 Mon/NMSP development CSO and 2 religious leaders. In Yangon we interviewed representatives from the Myanmar Peace Center, the Myanmar Peace Support Initiative as well as had several informal conversations with academics and journalists. The selection of interviewees was based on access possibilities. The research in 2016 was part of a four-year-long research project on "Everyday Justice and Security in the Myanmar Transition" (EverJust), which focuses on the provision of justice in Myanmar government and EAO-controlled areas. Ethnographic fieldwork was carried out in one NMSP-controlled area, and in two areas controlled by the KNU, which included in-depth interviews with EAO justice providers, administrators and soldiers, as well as numerous interviews with ordinary villagers and village leaders. The fieldwork also covered participant observation of court and justice committee hearings.

3. This was evident on 25 June 2015 where the Military MPs voted against the direct election of the head ministers of states and regions (see <http://www.dvb.no/news/parliament-deals-fatal-blow-to-suu-kyis-presidential-bid-burma-myanmar/53105>).

4. See Chapter 8 this volume for details. The list is flawed. Some are missing, others not existing. Cheesman (2015), pp. 210–14 describes how the law was used as a "law and order" instrument.

5. This information is based on interviews conducted by Mikael Gravers in 2014 and 2015.

6. The passing of four "Race and Religion Protection Laws" in May and August 2015, which focus on monogamy, religious conversion, interfaith marriage, and population control, have also been seen to protect Buddhism by restricting and preventing Buddhist women from marrying men of other faiths (see White 2015).

7. On this official reason, see Larry Jagan, "Ceasefire Masks Flawed Peace Process", DVB, 14 October 2015 <http://www.dvb.no/news/ceasefire-masks-flawed-peace-process-burma-myanmar/58165> (accessed 20 May 2016).

8. See, for instance, a statement to the Karen News (26 August 2015) by a General in the Karen National Defence Organization (KNDO): "Karen General Urges Ethnic Leaders Not To Sign Nationwide Ceasefire Until Gov't Agrees To Political Roadmap" <http://karennews.org/2015/08/karen-general-urges-ethnic-leaders-not-to-sign-nationwide-ceasefire-until-govt-agrees-to-political-roadmap.html/> (accessed 20 May 2016).

9. On the doubts about the NCA among for instance Shan youth, see <http://english.panglong.org/how-do-we-know-this-time-it-will-benefit-us-shan-state-youth-share-perspectives-on-ceasefire-signing-2/>. Similarly, forty Karen CSOs have expressed doubts about the NCA (see Saw Yang Naing, "Burma's Peace Process: The Factional Pieces Pushing Pen to Paper", *The Irrawaddy*, 8 October

2015 <http://www.irrawaddy.com/news-analysis/burmas-peace-process-the-factional-figures-pushing-pen-to-paper.html>.

10. This was confirmed at the political dialogue meeting in January 2016 when the army chief reiterated the demand that all the armed actors in the country should come under one singular army, inviting the EAOs to join the Tatmadaw as the only army in the country (Nyein Nyein, "Notable absences as Political Dialogue begins in capital", *The Irrawaddy*, 16 January 2016 <http://www.irrawaddy.com/burma/notable-absences-as-political-dialogue-begins-in-capital.html>; DVB, "Army Chief invites rebels to join Burma Army", 12 January 2016 <http://www.dvb.no/news/defence-chief-invites-rebels-to-join-burma-army/60260>; Lun Min Mang, "Peace Conference Widens Divisions and Troubles NLD", *Myanmar Times*, 20 January 2016 <http://www.mmtimes.com/index.php/national-news/nay-pyi-taw/18563-peace-conference-widens-divisions-and-troubles-nld.html>).

11. On 25 June the Military MPs rejected the 436 Amendment Bill, which would have changed the Constitution so that constitutional changes would require 70 rather than 75 per cent of the parliamentary votes. Since the military now holds 25 per cent of the seats in parliament, any constitutional changes depends on military votes. On the same day the military MPs also voted against changes of section 262 of the Constitution, which included a proposal for the election of state and region ministers by the state parliaments, rather than them being appointed by the president. The failure to approve this amendment sent a clear signal of military opposition to the decentralization of power and sharing of authority (see Ei Ei Toe Lwin, "MPs hold little hope for next constitutional amendment proposals", *Myanmar Times*, 30 June 2015 <http://www.mmtimes.com/index.php/national-news/15268-mps-hold-little-hope-for-next-constitutional-amendment-proposals.html>.

12. See Ye Mon and Lun Min Mang, "CSOs call for Political Dialogue Halt", *Myanmar Times*, 6 January 2016 <http://www.mmtimes.com/index.php/national-news/18345-csos-call-for-political-dialogue-halt.html>.

13. Interview, KWO village leader, 27 September, 2016.

14. The ceasefire gave a space for reforming the KPF, which also comprise some retired Karen National Liberation Army (KNLA) soldiers (EverJust interview, KNU Justice Department, March 2016). Today the KNPF has an estimated force of 600 officers, and in 2016, 200 new officers graduated from training (McCartan and Jolliffe 2016, p. 21).

15. Currently the NMSP is accused by the Mon State Government for extortion, narcotic arrests, military recruitment training and justice-related projects outside of their territory (Min Paing 2016).

16. Interview, Buddhist Monk, Hpa-An, 12 January 2014.

17. The exact ethnic composition is unknown as such figures have still not be made public from the 2014 census, as this is regarded by the outgoing USDP government as a politically sensitive issue that could compromise stability. The census may reveal a higher number of ethnic minorities which could increase

their political claims vis-à-vis the majority (see Pyae Thet Phyo, "Census Data could 'shatter' transition stability, says official", *Myanmar Times*, 24 February 2016 <http://www.mmtimes.com/index.php/national-news/nay-pyi-taw/19137-census-data-could-shatter-transition-stability-says-official.html>.

18. Interview, 15 January 2014.
19. Interview, EAO member, January 2014.

References

Albecht, P., H.M. Kyed, D. Isser and E. Harper, eds. *Perspectives on involving non-state and customary actors in Justice and Security Reform*. Rome and Copenhagen: International Development Law Organisation and Danish Institute for International Studies, 2011.

Ansori, M.H. "From Insurgency to Bureaucracy: Free Aceh Movement, Aceh Party and the New Face of Conflict". *Stability of Security and Development* 1, no. 1 (2012): 31–44.

BNI. "NLD promises federal union with equal rights and autonomy". *Mizzima: News from Myanmar*, 15 October 2015 <http://mizzima.com/news-election-2015-election-news/nld-promises-federal-union-equal-rights-and-autonomy> (accessed 20 May 2016).

Callahan, M.P. "Political Authority in Burma's Ethnic Minority States: Devolution, Occupation, and Coexistence". *Policy Studies* 31. Washington, D.C.: East-West Center, 2007.

Cheesman, N. *Opposing the Rule of Law: How Myanmar's courts make law and order*. Cambridge: Cambridge University Press, 2015.

Christensen, M.M. and M. Utas. "Mercenaries of Democracy: the 'Politricks' of Remobilized Combatants in the 2007 General Elections, Sierra Leone". *African Affairs* 107, no. 429 (2008): 515–39.

Crouch, M. "Personal Law and Colonial Legacy". In *Islam and the State in Myanmar*, edited by M. Crouch. Oxford: Oxford University Press, 2016.

Derksen, D. "Reintegrating Armed Groups in Afghanistan". *Peacebrief* 168, Washington, D.C.: United States Institute for Peace (USIP), March 2014.

Gravers, M. *Nationalism as Political Paranoia in Burma: An Essay on the Historical Practice of Power*. London: Curzon, 1999.

———. "Disorder as Order: The Ethno-Nationalist Struggle of the Karen in Burma/Myanmar — a discussion of the dynamics of an ethnicized civil war and its historical roots". *Journal of Burma Studies* 19, no. 1 (2015): 1–27.

——— and F. Ytzen, eds. *Burma/Myanmar: Where Now?* Copenhagen: NIAS Press, 2014.

Harrisson, A. and H.M. Kyed. "Ceasefire Statemakings: Justice provision in Karen and Mon armed group controlled areas". Unpublished paper presented at the Myanmar Update Conference, 17–18 February 2017, Australian National University.

Hill, R. and L. Bowman. "Police Reform Programs: Links to Post-Conflict Reconstruction and Social Stability in Violent and Fragile States — Building responsiveness and the connection to local civilian needs — public security as good governance". 2016 <http://www.thecornwallisgroup.org/pdf/CXI_2006_08_Hill.pdf> (accessed 20 May 2016).

Holliday, I. "Addressing Myanmar's Citizenship Crisis". *Journal of Contemporary Asia* 44, no. 3 (2014): 404–21.

Isin, E.F. and B.S. Turner. *Handbook on Citizenship Studies*. London: Sage Publications, 2002.

Isin, E.F. and P.K. Wood. *Citizenship and Identity*. London: Sage, 1999.

Jolliffe, K. *Ethnic Conflict and Social Services in Myanmar's Contested Regions*. Yangon: The Asia Foundation, 2014.

———. *Ethnic Armed Conflict and Territorial Administration in Myanmar*. Yangon: The Asia Foundation, 2015.

Kabeer, N. *Inclusive Citizenship: Meanings and expressions*. London: Zed Books, 2005.

Keenan, P. "The Border Guard Force. The need to reassess the policy". *Briefing Paper* 15, Chiang Mai: Burma Centre for Ethnic Studies, July 2013.

Kempel, S. and A.T. Nyein. *Local Governance Dynamics in South East Myanmar*. Swiss Agency for Development Report, 2014 <https://mdricesd.files.wordpress.com/2015/08/paper-local-governance-dynamics-aug-2014.pdf> (accessed 20 May 2016).

Kempel, S., C.M. Aung Tun and Aung Tun. *Myanmar Political Parties at a time of transition. Political Party Dynamics at the national and local level*. Yangon: Pyioe Pin Programme, 2014.

Kham, Y.N. "An Introduction to the Law and Judicial System of Myanmar". *Myanmar Law Working Paper Serious*, No. 001. Singapore: National University of Singapore, March 2014.

Knight, M. *Security Sector Reform: Post-Conflict Integration*. Birmingham: GFN-SSR, University of Birmingham, 2009.

Kramer, T. "Ethnic Conflict in Burma: The Challenge of Unity in a Divided Country". In *Burma or Myanmar? The Struggle for National Identity*, edited by I.L. Dittmer. Hackensack, NJ: World Scientific, 2010.

Kyed, H.M. "Community-based Dispute Resolution. Exploring Everyday Justice in Southeast Myanmar". DIIS and IRC, forthcoming.

Kymlicka, W. *Multicultural Citizenship: a Liberal Theory of Minority Rights*. Oxford: Clarendon Press, 1995.

Lall, M. and A. South. "Comparing models of non-state ethnic education in Myanmar: the Mon and Karen national education regimes". *Journal of Contemporary Asia* 44, no. 2 (2013): 298–321.

Lall, M., New New San, Theint Theint and Yin Nyein Aye. *Myanmar's ethnic parties and the 2015 elections*. Yangon: EU and IMG, 2015.

Lewis, J. "The Burmanization of the Karen people : a study in racial adaptability". PhD dissertation, University of Chicago, 1924.

McCartan, Brian and Kim Jolliffe. *Ethnic Armed Actors and Justice Provision in Myanmar*. Yangon: The Asia Foundation, October 2016.

McConnachie, K. *Governing Refugees. Justice, Order and Legal Pluralism*. Oxon and New York: Routledge, 2014.

McMullin, J. *Ex-Combatants and the Post-Conflict State: Challenges of Reintegration*. New York: Palgrave Macmillan, 2013*a*.

———. "Integration or separation? Stigmatisation of ex-combatants after war". *Review of International Studies* 39, no. 2 (2013*b*): 385–414.

Min Paing, "NMSP received 28 complaint letters from Mon State Gov't". Mon News Agency, October 2016 <http://monnews.org/2016/10/03/nmsp-received-28-complaint-letters-from-mon-state-govt/> (accessed 14 November 2016).

Mitton, K. "Engaging disengagement. The political reintegration of Sierra Leone's Revolutionary United Front". *Conflict, Security and Development* 8, no. 2 (2008): 193–222.

Muggah, R. "No Magic Bullet: A Critical Perspective on Disarmament, Demobilization and Reintegration (DDR) and Weapons Reduction in Post-conflict Contexts". *The Round Table* 94, no. 379 (2005): 239–52.

Munive, J. and S.F. Jakobsen. "Revisiting DDR in Liberia: Exploring the power, agency and interests of local and international actors in the 'making' and 'unmaking' of combatants". *Conflicts, Security and Development* 12, no. 4 (2012): 359–85.

Oh, S. *Competing Forms of Sovereignty in the Karen State of Myanmar*. ISEAS working paper, no. 1/2013. Singapore: Institute of Southeast Asian Studies, 2013.

Ong, I. *Flexible Citizenship. The Cultural Logics of Transnationality*. Durham and London: Duke University Press, 1999.

Sivakumaran, Sandesh. "Courts of Armed Opposition Groups". *Journal of International Criminal Justice* 7 (2009): 489–513.

Smith, M. *Burma. Insurgency and the Politics of Ethnicity*. London: Zed Books, 1999.

———. "Ethnic Participation and Reconciliation in Myanmar: Challenges in the Transitional Landscape". In *Myanmar's Long Road to National Reconciliation*, edited by T. Wilson. Singapore: Institute of Southeast Asian Studies, 2006.

South, A. *Mon Nationalism and Civil War in Burma: The Golden Sheldrake*. London: Routledge, 2003.

———. *Burma's Longest War: Anatomy of the Karen Conflict*. Amsterdam: Transnational Institute, Burma Center Netherlands, 2011.

———. *Prospects for Peace in Myanmar: Opportunities and Threats*. Oslo: PRIO, 2012.

Spear, J. "From political economies of war to political economies of peace: The contribution of DDR after wars of predation". *Contemporary Security Policy* 27, no. 1 (2007): 168–89.

Specht, I. "Jobs for Rebels and Soldiers". In *Jobs After War: A Critical Challenge in the Peace and Reconstruction Puzzle*, edited by E. Date-Bah. Geneva: ILO, 2003.

Taylor, R. "Perceptions of Ethnicity in the Politics of Burma". *Southeast Asian Journal of Social Science* 10, no. 1 (1982): 7–22.

———. "Do States make Nations? The Politics of identity in Myanmar revisited". *South East Asia Research* 13, no. 3 (2005): 261–86.

TBC (The Border Consortium). *Protection and Security Concerns in South East Burma/Myanmar*. Bangkok: Wanida Press, 2014.

Thawnhmung, A.M. *The "Other" Karen in Myanmar. Ethnic Minorities without Arms*. Lanham: Lexington Books, 2012.

———. "Beyond Armed Resistance: The Non-insurgent Members of Ethno-national Groups in Burma". *Policy Studies* 62. Washington, D.C.: East-West Center, 2011.

Torjesen, S. "Towards a theory of ex-combatant reintegration". *Journal of Security & Development* 2, no. 3 (2013): 1–13.

Transnational Institute. "Ethnicity without Meaning, Data without Context. The 2014 Census, identity and citizenship in Burma/Myanmar". *Burma Policy Briefing* 13. Washington, D.C.: The Transnational Institute, February 2014.

Walton, M.J. "The 'Wages of Burman-ness': Ethnicity and Burman Privilege in Contemporary Myanmar". *Journal of Contemporary Asia* 43, no. 1 (2013): 1–27.

———. "The Disciplining Discourse of Unity in Burmese Politics". *Journal of Burma Studies* 19, no. 1 (2015): 1–26.

White, C. *Protection for Whom? Violations of International Law in Myanmar's New "Race and Religion Protection Laws"*. Washington: Georgetown Institute for Women, Peace and Security, 2015.

Woods, K. "Ceasefire capitalism: Military–private partnerships, resource concessions and military-state building in Burma–China borderlands". *Journal of Peasant Studies* 38, no. 4 (2011): 747–70.

Zaw, O. and W. Min. "Assessing Burma's Ceasefire Accords". *Policy Studies* 39, Washington, D.C.: East-West Centre, 2007.

THE WAY FORWARD FOR PEACE, STABILITY AND PROGRESS IN BURMA/MYANMAR

Nai Hongsa
Vice Chairman, New Mon State Party

OVERVIEW OF MYANMAR

Burma, or Myanmar, is a fortunate country in many ways. It has a warm and wet tropical climate, with adequate rainfall that encourages many kinds of plants to flourish. The land is blessed with fertile low-land plains, plateaus and high ground with gentle slopes, where many varieties of vegetables can be grown. In terms of natural resources, it has timber and bamboo forests; many waterfalls and rivers in the hills that have potential for generating hydro-electric power; underground there are mineral deposits, including gold, silver, copper, iron, and lead; there are gemstones such as rubies, sapphire and jade; and deposits of fossil fuels of coal, petroleum and natural gas.

It is also well positioned to benefit from international trade and commerce, having a long coastline with sites suitable for deep-sea ports, and archipelagos where all kinds of marine life thrives. With a land area of 260,000 square miles supporting a little more than 51 million inhabitants, the country does not suffer from a high population density. With all of these benefits, one would expect Burma to be an affluent nation, and at one time it did in fact have the highest living standard of Southeast Asian countries. However, from being the "rice bowl of Asia", Burma is now listed as one of the world's

Least Developed Countries (LDC). The following traces the main threads of Burma/Myanmar's recent history that have led to this situation.

The Union of Burma/Myanmar is inhabited by numerous ethnic groups, many with the characteristics of an independent nationality, such as having a substantial population living together in a defined area, with their own distinct language, literature, culture, custom and historical development. Prior to the British colonial era — and even during that era — some of these groups had their own kingdoms contemporaneously with the largest of the ethnic groups, the Burmans. In such a complex country, it is perhaps not surprising that there has been discord and armed conflict for nearly seventy years between the ethnic Burman (who have controlled the government) and the other ethnic nationalities. Almost all the ethnic nationalities have been in armed resistance at some time against successive central (Burman) governments. Some of the major ethnic groups being, alphabetically: Aka, Chin, Kachin, Karen, Karenni (Kayah), Kuki, Kokang, Lahu, Mon, Naga, Palaung (Ta'ang), Pa-oh, Rakhine (Arakanese), Shan, and Wa. There are even some ethnic Burman groups which have waged armed struggle against the government.

But the conflict in Myanmar has not always been associated with diverse ethnicities — during the latter half of the twentieth century there were a number of groups based in political ideologies, such as the Red Flag Communist Party-Burma (CPB), White Flag Burma Communist Party (BCP), and the Parliamentary Democracy Party/Burma Patriotic Army. However, despite these groups receiving external support, they did not persist as have those groups based on the struggle for ethnic/national freedom and rights. The organizations based on ethnic/national freedom have never received any notable external assistance, they have persisted primarily as a result of the contributions of time and resources from their own people. Their lengthy existence is a testament to the fact that the issue of identity/nationality runs deeper than overt political issues of class and democratic struggle.

CAUSES OF THE ARMED STRUGGLE IN MYANMAR

1. The most obvious question for those not acquainted with Myanmar's recent history is: "Why have the prominent non-Burman nationalities been engaged in armed resistance against the central government for so long?". The basic answer is because the successive governments in power, espousing chauvinism/ultra-nationalism, have employed force to attempt to deny the rights of the other ethnic nationalities in order to

absorb them into, or subjugate them by, the dominant ethnic Burman group. Some of the evidence supporting this assertion is as follows: The provision for using spoken and written Burman language as the only official language in the Union means other languages serve no practical purpose. At least until recently, only the Burmese language has been taught in state schools all over the Union, from primary to university levels. Government schools teach only the Burmese language to children in villages in the remote border areas, children who have never previously heard or seen the Burmese language. Historically, other ethnic languages have not even been officially allowed in the primary schools in the non-Burman ethnic areas. Under the military government that seized power in 1988, when military officers learned that some of the nationalities were teaching their own national languages in schools in their own areas, at their own expense, they often ordered the teaching to stop. (This also happened much later, during the years of 2005 and 2006 in Mon and Shan regions.) It is our view that they were doing this systematically, knowing that language is a central aspect of culture, so destroying the language effectively destroys the culture — and the sense of identity that goes with the culture. Over time, ethnic groups could thus become "Burmanized".

2. During its time in power, the military government that seized power in 1988 set up a National Theatre House and Padonma Theatre House in Rangoon/Yangon, and a National Theatre for Upper Burma in Mandalay. These theatres maintained and promoted Burman culture by holding yearly competitions for traditional singing, dancing and composing, and awarding prizes to competitors. This government also set up the so-called "Cultural University". However, there was absolutely no promotion of cultures of the ethnic nationalities other than Burman.

3. In the maintenance and promotion of historical evidence relating to nationality, the government promoted research into the history of the Burman nationality only, and destroyed the histories of the other nationalities. School history books record only the history of the Burman nationality — there is absolutely no mention of the histories of the other ethnic nationalities.

4. As a part of the concealing of history, there is also discrimination in the maintenance of historical buildings. In order to highlight Burman history, the military government has spent considerable sums of money to meticulously maintain the old city of Pagan. They rebuilt the feudal palaces which had disappeared for hundreds of years in Mandalay, Shwebo and Bago. Yet on the other hand, the military government in 1991 destroyed

the best of the palaces of the Shan chiefs, the Kyaingtong Palace, which was still in good condition and had been a highlight of Shan history. In 2006, the military government closed down Thibaw Shan chief's palace to prevent people from visiting. In 2007, Nyaung Shwe Shan chief's palace was renovated — but turned into a Buddhist museum. Rebuilding the palace of the Burman king, Bayint Naung, in Bago, who ruled only for thirty years, was a conspiracy by the government to conceal Mon kingdoms and dynasties that had existed for nearly a thousand years. This promotion of the Burman language, literature, culture and heritage at the expense of other ethnic nationalities is designed to eliminate these latter groups.

All over the world ethnic nationalities attempt to ensure the survival of their culture into the future, and people sacrifice their lives to do so. It is instructive for the Burman people to remember how they themselves worried and struggled when Burman language and literature waned under the rule of the British, and have empathy for the other nationalities in Myanmar. It is this lack of empathy on the part of the Burmans in power that has caused some ethnic nationalities to commence armed resistance not long after independence. Instead of erroneously blaming the British for the instigation of Myanmar's internal conflict, it would be helpful if the Burman people re-examined and re-evaluated the attitudes and actions of those Burman leaders in power following independence.

The history of the entire territory of the current Union of Burma/Myanmar shows that it was at one time made up of the contemporary kingdoms of Mon, Burman, Arakanese and Shan peoples, and the self-administered lands of the Kachin, Karen, Karenni, Chin, Wa, etc. During the era of absolute monarchy, it was normal practice for the strong nations to attack and annex the lands of the weaker national groups for vassalage. However, when the British colonialists annexed the country into their empire, all the ethnic nationalities became slaves of the British. After living as fellow slaves for over a hundred years, the ethnic nationalities realized that any one nationality could not succeed in breaking out from serfdom, so they joined together to drive out the colonialists. In the joining of forces, all the ethnic nationalities became brothers, and the Burman leaders promised to equally share power and opportunities when victory was achieved.

When it became impossible for the British to go on controlling the entire country due to a combination of factors, they decided to give independence to the plains, or Burma Proper, and retain the hill areas.

However, the hill peoples of Chin, Kachin and Shan negotiated with the Burman leader Bogyoke Aung San and concluded the Panglong Agreement in 1947 to achieve independence at the same time, and establish a Union of States (Federal Union) based on national equality and self-determination of all the nationalities.

However, when independence was finally achieved, the Burman took over the entirety of Burma Proper, and states and "special divisions" were created for the hill peoples, under the control of Burmans. The peoples of the plains, the Karen, Pa-oh, Mon and Arakanese (Rakhine), who had struggled together for independence, were not given the opportunities and levels of independence they expected. When they made demands for some levels of autonomy, force was used to suppress them.

Since the Burman leaders had failed to keep their promise, armed resistance from the non-Burman nationalities began. Though only the Karen, Karenni, Mon and Arakanese initially took up arms, later on all of the prominent nationalities joined in the resistance. It is evident that the ensuing civil war was the result of the chauvinism/ultra-nationalism of the Burman leaders in power, and not because of the narrow nationalism and extremism of the non-Burman nationalities or as a result of actions by the British. In the analysis of the ensuing civil war, we find the following key points of development.

When the civil war, which had broken out following independence was ten years old, in 1958, the "Clean" Anti-Fascist People's Freedom League (AFPFL) government led by U Nu invited all the armed resistance organizations to work together for peace and progress of the country, within a democratic framework and with respect for the aspirations of the people, and wiping out past happenings from the slate. In that move, the slogan "Exchange of Arms for Democracy" was used. In response to this initiative, three organizations which had taken up arms due to a lack of democracy, surrendered — the Pa-oh, Mon and Arakanese — and participated in the "Exchange of Arms for Democracy". These organizations set up political organizations to participate in the 1960 general elections. In these elections, sadly, they encountered widespread vote stealing, cheating, intimidation and threats, and only a few of their candidates were elected. However, the non-Burman nationality members of parliament and leaders were able to work together and drafted a Federal Constitution which was submitted to replace the fake Union Constitution. With growing demands for a democracy, the Tatmadaw (armed forces) leader General Ne Win seized power on 2 March 1962, on the pretext that the country was on the brink of falling into chaos, and ruled the country as a military dictatorship for many years. During his time, the rights of the ethnic nationalities were largely annulled or greatly reduced.

In 1963, General Ne Win's military government invited all the armed groups fighting against the government for peace talks. However, as the government's position was "Exchange of Arms for Peace", almost all the organizations did not accept it. The Karen Revolutionary Council (KRC) led by Saw Hunter Thahmwe and Colonel Lin Htyn was one of the few to join with the junta, but after two months Colonel Lin Htyn was murdered and his troops became disorganized. The leader of the Red Flag Communist Party (RFCP), Thakin Soe, tried to take advantage of this apparently good opportunity, but was arrested and jailed, leading to the demise of the RFCP. Over time, General Ne Win's military government greatly increased the strength of the Tatmadaw in an effort to wipe out the resistance forces. Using the "Four Cuts Strategy" of encirclement and annihilation, the government forces launched military operations in many areas, using large amounts of the state budget for the offensives. This military expenditure drained funds that would otherwise have gone to education, health, transport and infrastructure, and is one of the main reasons behind Burma's current impoverishment and lagging development.

Under the Four Cuts Strategy, government troops destroyed thousands of villages and forced the villagers to live in concentration camps so as to to cut off links between the local people and the resistance forces. This period is well known for the extent of the atrocities and widespread human rights violations that occurred. The military forced the villagers to porter for the troops, used them as "human mine sweepers", stole household possessions, slaughtered farm animals, destroyed crops and summarily executed persons suspected of having any connection with resistance forces. When the people could no longer bear these outrages, the so-called Four-8 Mass Movement broke out and General Ne Win was forced to resign from his position as leader of the government.

During the subsequent time of the so-called Second Coup d'état, in the era of the State Law and Order Restoration Council (SLORC) and the State Peace and Development Council (SPDC) the military government led by Senior General Saw Maung, Vice Senior General Than Shwe and General Khin Nyunt, made extensive ceasefire agreements with the ethnic nationality resistance organizations. When the ethnic nationality organizations called for political dialogue, the military replied that as they were a government that had seized state power, they could not decide on political matters, but instead promised that there would be political dialogue after a government elected by the people had emerged. It further had said that after the Constitution had been written, elections would be held and, during the ceasefire period before the political dialogue could held, the resistance organizations should do development work in their own areas.

However, during the ceasefire period in 2005, the military government forcibly disarmed the Palaung State Liberation Organization (PSLO) and the Shan State National Army (SSNA). In 2008, it again disarmed the so-called Red Pa-oh, or Shan State Nationalities Liberation Organization (SSNLO), by force. After fraudulently adopting the Constitution in 2008 and when preparations for holding elections were made, it stopped talking about holding political dialogue. On the other hand, it started to tell the ceasefire organizations to let the older members form political parties for contesting the elections, and to make the younger ones transform either into the Border Guard Force or people's militia. It threatened to regard any organization refusing to do its bidding as an enemy and to annihilate it. Under these circumstances, organizations without a sufficiently strong revolutionary ethos fell under the control of the military government.

In the above discussion of efforts by successive Burman governments supposedly towards peace and stability, we find that they actually evaded resolving problems peacefully through negotiation with the armed resistance forces, and consistently tried to disarm, demobilize or subdue them by stratagem or force. The ethnic organizations that could not accept the SLORC and SPDC military governments' treacherous attempts to turn all the ceasefire organizations into their underlings, formed, with the ethnic resistance organizations which had carried on armed resistance, first the Committee for Emergence of Federal Union (CEFU) and then in 2011 the United Nationalities Federal Council (UNFC), and resumed armed resistance. The alliance unified previously dispersed forces and became a strong organization. Realizing that the problem could not be resolved by military means, U Thein Sein's government made overtures for peaceful resolution of the political problem after a ceasefire. The government eventually held negotiations with the UNFC for one year and with the Nationwide Ceasefire Coordination Team (NCCT) for one year and five months. However, as a satisfactory result was not gained, the government continued to hold negotiation with the Senior Delegation of the ethnic resistance forces. All these activities were not negotiations relating to political matters, but only protracted negotiations for a nationwide ceasefire in order to be able to hold political dialogue peacefully. We can say that the negotiation has become protracted like this because the Burman government is still not able to relinquish chauvinism/ultra-nationalism.

In the final analysis, the conflict in Myanmar arose because of the rejection of the aspirations of the non-Burman nationalities in Myanmar. The chauvinism/ultra-nationalism of the Burman leaders in power over the past fifty years has exacerbated the ethnic situation. The Tatmadaw's control of government and continuing suppression or elimination of human rights has alienated pro-democracy groups. A side effect of the Tatmadaw's desire to dominate and subjugate has been the diverting of funds and youthful energy from the wider economic sphere into militaristic goals. Not only has the state's income been reduced as a result of lost productivity due to conflict, but a large proportion of that shrinking budget is being used for the military rather than productive social sectors like education, healthcare, transport and infrastructure.

In order to resolve Myanmar's problems, a genuine Federal Union must be established that fosters the continuing existence of the culture and identity of ethnic groups such as the Mon. To do this will require addressing those root causes of armed conflict, particularly ethnic aspirations and human rights. The Tatmadaw will need to transform into the armed forces of this Federal Union, relinquish their involvement in civil administration and state legislature, submit to civilian control under a democratic government, and reduce the economic burden resulting from its unnecessary size (Myanmar has the largest army in Southeast Asia). If this begins to occur, we will see the Union of Burma/Myanmar progress rapidly in an environment of peace and stability.

3

NATIONAL POLITICAL DIALOGUE AND PRACTICES OF CITIZENSHIP IN MYANMAR

Matthew J. Walton

Citizenship is undoubtedly one of the more contentious issues in Myanmar today. Much of the discussion focuses on the boundaries of national inclusion, of deciding which groups are officially considered citizens, either according to the 1982 Citizenship Law or according to various other metrics. Most prominent in these discussions is the status of the Rohingya, but the subject is also relevant for other groups on the margins that might either be in danger of being excluded in the future or might be considered for inclusion in the future (such as some Chinese populations). While this is an important aspect of Myanmar's contemporary politics, this chapter focuses instead on an aspect of citizenship that is often ignored: its practice.

The practice of citizenship would include various perspectives on what citizenship entails (the different rights and responsibilities), the roles of state and civil society groups in fostering citizenship, and expectations of citizen participation. This latter category refers not only to ways in which citizens would expect to be able to participate in the political process, but also expectations of the state in facilitating that participation. A discussion of the practice of citizenship should also include attention to the many "skills" of citizenship that go beyond basic rights and responsibilities. While these are potentially applicable to all citizens, this chapter seeks to highlight the ways in which differently positioned individuals might be expected to develop and display different citizenship skills, especially government officials.

Developing a broader understanding of a diverse range of citizenship skills and practices is particularly important in the context of Myanmar's rapid political change. Since at least the 2008 constitutional referendum, the country's citizens have been expected to participate in politics in a variety of ways that were not only not available to them previously, they were actively denied by military-led governments. The result is a situation in which the meaning and content of citizenship is either limited among citizens or expressed in ways that do not necessarily accord with centralized notions of citizenship and participation in Myanmar or with international norms.

An instructive example can be found in a series of studies on citizenship conducted by the research and education organization Myanmar Egress. The researchers note that for field work in 2012 and 2013, they found it necessary to focus on educated middle and lower class respondents. They had found, during similar field work among villagers in the Delta region in 2010, that respondents did not have much of an opinion on citizenship or that to them, citizenship was "simply holding an ID card" (Lall et al. 2014, p. 7). Practices of citizenship (beyond merely submission to the state's authority) were obviously not cultivated by previous governments and the state today has a role to play in acculturating citizens to certain collective processes. But there is also a danger of imposing a centrally generated conception of citizen participation that might expand inclusion in certain ways only to further cement other barriers to meaningful participation by not recognizing existing understandings or practices of citizenship that do not align with the state's expectations or with notions of citizenship common in other countries. In contrast, this chapter advocates for close attention to the design of institutionalized pathways to citizen participation that are themselves shaped by the diverse range of understandings and practices of citizenship in Myanmar.

This chapter considers the practice of citizenship primarily in relation to the national political dialogue process (now officially called the 21st Century Panglong Conference), arguably the forum that (in some form or another) will shape Myanmar's political future. While the national political dialogue is not the only place to analyse or address practices of citizenship and citizen political participation, its centrality in Myanmar's politics during the country's transition makes it an excellent case study. Additionally, many of the critical aspects of citizenship practice raised in this chapter are completely ignored in the current political dialogue framework, making it a useful starting point for a critical analysis.

There has been impressive progress over the past few years in the development of a national political dialogue framework that is broadly inclusive, consensus-based, and oriented towards expanded participation, focused predominantly on structure, timelines, inclusion of different groups, and decision-making processes. While these are all important elements, there has been virtually no attention to two issues that could limit the effectiveness of the dialogue's attention to inclusion. The first concern is related to political communication: what are the accepted methods of "speaking" and modes of engagement in the dialogue? How do these accepted methods privilege particular groups and individuals and how can other participants be sure that their voices can be meaningfully "heard"?

The second issue is that of transformative citizenship and participation: how is the dialogue process organized so that it can generate new notions of belonging in Myanmar and new relationships among citizens and between citizens and leaders? Is there a related danger that the "transformation" that the dialogue as currently constructed will foster is merely a continuation of already existing hegemonic projects? In seeking to ensure that the national political dialogue process that emerges in Myanmar can effectively address the country's most deeply entrenched divisions and antagonisms, it should not ignore the methods and arrangements that lead more directly and effectively to the development of capable, empathetic, savvy, and inter-connected citizens.

The chapter begins with a brief overview of the national political dialogue process in Myanmar, including its guiding framework that was developed at the end of 2015. It then deals with the topics of political communication and transformative citizenship in turn, as subjects that are virtually unaddressed by the existing framework and plans for future 21st Century Panglong Conferences. In exploring these two subjects, the chapter draws on insights from the discipline of political theory, especially debates on deliberative democracy.

MYANMAR'S NATIONAL POLITICAL DIALOGUE PROCESS

Myanmar's national political dialogue (NPD) has grown out of the ongoing ceasefire process that was initiated by President Thein Sein after he took office in 2011. While many different ethnic armed groups have signed bilateral ceasefires with the Burmese government over the past two and a half decades, the missing component to these ceasefires has always been a lasting political settlement. Most ethnic armed groups seem to be in agreement that the primary purpose of their resistance has been to achieve a fundamental reorganization of the Myanmar state along the lines of a "true" federal union, with recognition of ethnic cultural rights and certain constitutionally authorized levels of autonomy at the state and region level. Many had been promised this political settlement in past ceasefires but the previous military government had never moved forward with the process. Thus, clear timelines related to the convening of the NPD were incorporated into the Nationwide Ceasefire Agreement (NCA).

The NCA was signed on 15 October 2015 and even though it was signed by only a portion of the ethnic armed groups that had been involved in negotiations, this triggered the deadlines that it contained for beginning the NPD. By 15 December 2015, the political dialogue framework was completed (as mandated at sixty days after the signing of the NCA) and the first Union Peace Conference was held in Naypyitaw on 12–15 January (again, mandated to occur within ninety days of signing and to be held every four months after that for a period of three to five years).

The fact that many important ethnic armed groups were not signatories to the NCA has meant that those who drafted the framework for the NPD have had to find ways of including non-ceasefire participants. Although they have stated this intention, it has not yet been realized. The framework was drafted by a nine-member committee, with equal representation from the government, political parties, and ethnic NCA signatories and although stipulations in both the NCA and the resulting framework call for increased participation of women, the drafting committee was all male (The Republic of the Union of Myanmar President Office 2015). (The implications of this point will be considered more below.) The framework laid out the formation of the Union Peace Dialogue Joint Committee (which would manage the process and be composed of equal representatives from the government, parliament, military, ethnic NCA signatories, and representatives of political parties) and of various working groups according to the NPD agenda. Currently, that agenda is separated into six categories: political, social, economic, security, land/natural resources, and other. The framework also gives general guidance on convening the triannual Union Peace Conferences.[1]

The framework includes a number of basic principles, including the establishment of a union based on liberty, equality, and fraternity; to give equal rights to all citizens; to settle differences of opinion within the NPD in a spirit of sincerity and honesty; and to have a minimum level of 30 per cent female participation at all levels of the NPD. It stipulates that the triannual Union Peace Conferences will include 700 delegates, with 75 from the government, 75 from the parliament, 150 from the military, 150 from the ethnic armed groups, 150 from registered political parties, and an additional

50 each from "ethnic representatives" and "others who should participate". These last 100 are to be selected in equal proportion by the government, ethnic armed groups, and registered political parties.

While ultimately the drafting of Myanmar's NPD framework occurred behind closed doors with a small group of people on a tight deadline, it had been informed by a much longer process of public consultation over several years. The Nationwide Ceasefire Coordination Team (NCCT, a negotiating team formed by the ethnic armed groups in October 2013) put forward its proposal for a process that would both mirror and update the 1947 Panglong Conference, one of the country's founding political moments.[2] The Peace and Politics Implementation Committee of the Parliament, composed of 56 political parties, put forward its own framework in November 2014, in an attempt to create a stronger role for Parliament in the peace process (Shwe Yi Win Htet 2014). Several other groups, including the National League for Democracy (NLD), developed political dialogue frameworks that were made public in full or in part between 2012 and 2015. While there is no way of knowing exactly how these previous framework proposals influenced the eventual framework, it does include some key elements of them.

Yet, for all of its laudable attention to federalism and a more inclusive process, certain critical aspects of citizen participation, notably, institutionalized impediments to meaningful participation, are unaddressed in either the framework or the broader process up to this point. As Daw Aung San Suu Kyi sought to assume leadership of the dialogue process from the previous government, she announced in April 2016 that she would convene a "21st Century Panglong Conference", to mirror her father's foundational 1947 Panglong Conference. However, far from expanding participation, the initial guidelines issued by the government indicated *more limited* participation, with only political parties that had won seats being allowed to participate, a restriction that was met with criticism from ethnic organizations (Lun Min Mang 2016*a*). Facing complaints from many groups, the government eventually adopted an approach to the conference that made it more of a collective discussion, rather than a decision-making forum. While this meant that nothing substantive emerged from the meeting (a point of frustration for some), it also meant that the general sentiment from most observers was that it had been a limited success (mostly by not being a larger debacle) (Ei Ei Toe Lwin 2016*b*).

Since that first meeting, however, the government seems to have adopted a stricter policy and, possibly frustrated with not seeing as much progress as it had expected, has tightened criteria for inclusion (Sam Aung Moon 2017). While in the lead-up to the second conference, state- and local-level dialogues proliferated as opportunities to air grievances and discuss policy reforms (Shan Herald Agency News 2017), the process for channelling these perspectives to the national level — and most importantly, to government decision-making at the highest levels — remains unclear. This suggests that the new government's process is likely to be characterized by some of the same limitations as the previous government, and that they do not have an appreciation of how to make the country's political dialogue meaningfully participatory or transformative. The following sections consider some of the ramifications of these missing components.

POLITICAL COMMUNICATION

The national political dialogue framework mandates for broad inclusion of representatives of key stakeholders in Myanmar's political process. It is perhaps understandable that, despite inclusive rhetoric, this has so far been an elite-led process. But even among elites, there is reason to attend to questions of the appropriate methods or modes of communication and expression in the public, political sphere, and whether the privileging or presumption of certain modes of communication reinforces inequality or further extends already institutionalized exclusion. And if privileged elites can be excluded from public discourse, it is even easier for those with limited political influence or standing to be shut out of the process. This section draws on theories of deliberative democracy to better understand the impediments to developing more inclusive processes of democratic communication. It seeks to address not just methods of public "speaking" and participation but also the circumstances under which various voices can be "heard", both publicly and by key decision-makers.[3]

Political theorist Iris Marion Young (2000) has argued for a model of "communicative" democracy, where different cultural forms of expression are valued as public discourse, opening up space for modes of speech other than argumentation, including greeting, narrative, and storytelling. This approach would take seriously the fact that most modern political systems privilege modes of communication that are either more natural for or are socialized to dominant groups, thereby reinforcing the political exclusion of already marginalized groups. Remedies would require institutional changes to political systems and processes that would allow other forms of communication (and thus, other "voices") to be more effectively heard and acknowledged by political decision-makers.

Presenting a different argument, political theorist Seyla Benhabib (1996) develops a model of deliberative democracy that rejects alternative modes of communication as applicable to or appropriate for the public sphere. She argues that public reasons need to be given in accordance with the rule of law, which has a rhetorical structure of its own and requires a particular type of argumentation. This would mean that the forms of communication that Young wishes to highlight and include may be valid in certain contexts but that effective democratic political discourse must adhere to common standards that come from the nature of law and the ways in which it is justified. To incorporate diverse perspectives, Benhabib instead builds on the notion of the "counter-public". In this model, a political society would carve out spaces where non-dominant groups can still challenge the tendency towards a unitary, hegemonic public sphere, but retain a standard of expression and deliberation appropriate to public speech and policy-making.

Considering Young's and Benhabib's theories in the context of Myanmar does not imply that non-dominant groups in the country are incapable of public deliberation through argumentation; this is obviously not true. However, Benhabib's development of the counter-public model seems at best to be what the designers of the NPD framework imagine as a way for civil society groups and local communities to be able to engage with the NPD process; even this is unclear, as the exact channels for civil society input have yet to be clarified by those who are leading the process. Furthermore, there are several reasons why Young's model might be more appropriate for Myanmar.

First, various dimensions of social hierarchy in the country mean that argumentation is either frowned upon or seen as the purview of elites, men, one's seniors, or the highly educated.[4] The norms that make argumentation unacceptable or improper when done by certain groups (for example, young people, women, or those without formal education) obviously hinder the free exchange of ideas and specifically the expression of non-dominant points of view. Even when members of these groups are accepted into public forums and speak in accordance with these norms of argumentation and dispute, they are often not recognized as participants.[5] Female participants in the first Union Peace Conference (which, although aspiring to a 30 per cent female participant level only achieved 7 per cent) complained of regularly encountering dismissive attitudes. One woman's comments through multiple sessions were not included in the official record until she physically took the computers of the facilitators and typed in her statements herself. Another had to take a male facilitator to task for "diluting points put across by female speakers" (Thin Lei Win 2016). Even when women ostensibly had a place at the table, their perspectives were not adequately recognized or recorded, a concern that has continued to plague planning meetings related to the dialogue and other political processes (Hogan 2017).

Equally importantly for the Myanmar case, we can easily identify distinctions in the modes of public expression and representation between different ethnic groups and likely between other identity groups as well. One example is the way in which elders from non-Burman communities tend to express their grievances. Rather than list their concerns in relation to specific laws or procedures, they might instead contextualize a contemporary situation of injustice within a historical trajectory of personal and collective experiences, or highlight an expectation of recognition over a more tangible policy concern (Nyan Hlaing Lynn 2016). This type of communication can have deep resonance for their lived experiences of oppression and injustice and can also function as a way of preserving or strengthening communal identity. It is also an example of a historically situated narrative that Young would like to see acknowledged as a recognized speech act with political relevance, but which is more often than not merely dismissed as older generations unwilling to move on from the past. Dismissal of this type of speech act is common in statements by Burman government officials and advisors and the author has heard similar sentiments from foreign observers, including some of those advising on the peace process.

Seyla Benhabib rightly points out that modern democratic states must accept the fact that true mass deliberation (where all can participate regularly and equally) simply is not possible. She seeks to address this constraint by advocating for a "plurality of modes of association" (1996, p. 73). This is, in essence, a call for a vibrant and diverse civil society sphere, but one in which people would be members of multiple interlocking and overlapping networks and associations, making sure that discussions on important public policy issues would take place within, between, and across identity and interest groups. This would create the "public conversation" that deliberative democracy aspires to, by allowing people to gain access to the government and other decision-makers in a variety of different ways.

Again, it appears to be something similar to Benhabib's model that is the implicit point of reference in most of the draft political dialogue frameworks that were put forward and in the current NPD framework. That is, there is no question as to whether or not civil society groups have a place in the dialogue: they do. However, the formalized avenues for engagement are not clearly defined yet for civil society and other community groups and many have worried that the result will be a replication of the ways in which civil society groups have only been allowed to be involved in superficial ways in other discussions and negotiations connected to the peace process (Radio Free Asia 2016). Even more pertinent for the topic at hand is the worrying question as to whether the dialogue (and other political processes and venues in Myanmar's political arena) is structured in such a way that allows the diverse modes of communication of the country's different groups to be properly "heard".[6]

Cultivating practices of citizenship that can be effective in furthering national reconciliation in Myanmar will require taking into consideration these alternate modes of expression. But creating space for them in the institutions and processes created as part of the national political dialogue is only one step. And in fact, it will be a relatively pointless step if it is not complemented by active training in the complementary citizenship skills that would allow others to really be able to listen to and appreciate both what is being expressed in these narratives and the modes of expression. That is, in addition to training citizens in various modes of participation, political leaders and decision-makers also need to be trained in the skills that would enable them to engage respectfully and productively with a diverse group of citizen constituents.

Too often discussions of the duties and practices of citizenship assume that these apply only (or primarily) to the mass of citizens, not necessarily to political officials. In fact, not only should political leaders be bound by the same expectations as their fellow citizens, it is useful to think about the ways in which elected officials and other government officials practise a distinct type of citizenship, one that should have higher standards of inclusion, patience, and empathy. There is no lack of negative examples among Myanmar's recent political leadership. One of the most egregious was former Minister for Livestock, Fisheries, and Rural Development U Ohn Myint's bullying of villagers in January 2014, when he threatened to slap and imprison people who were questioning him (Ei Ei Toe Lwin 2014). But in fact, the kind of listening training that Iris Young's arguments point to would go much deeper, along the lines of training officials to be able to appreciate and learn from the different communicative styles of Myanmar's diverse population. Discussions about the transformative aspects of democratic practice or citizenship usually refer to those who are participating in politics from grassroots levels and becoming more empowered or engaged. But in the case of Myanmar, an even more important transformative process must occur among government and military officials. And it is both revealing and productive to think about these practices as practices of citizenship, appropriate to different roles in the country.

TRANSFORMATIVE CITIZENSHIP

One of the holy grails of democratic studies is the idea of transformative citizenship. Many have theorized about how democracy could be transformative or how engaged citizenship could transform relationships between citizens and government. But it is difficult to really track this concept, for obvious reasons. It is important to acknowledge, however, that most (if not all) practices of citizenship are transformative to some degree in that they have effects on individual practitioners and on communities. That is, they affect the ways in which political leaders understand their roles and responsibilities as well as the ways in which non-elite citizens understand their own efficacy and position as autonomous individuals who are also members of multiple collective identity groups (including the national community).

A national political dialogue process that consists of regularly held 21st Century Panglong Conferences of 700 elite representatives mostly drawn from a few centrally important institutions actually reflects multiple views on citizenship, none of them transformative in empowering or ennobling ways. It further privileges direct political participation and decision-making for a select few, while imposing a set of passive citizenship practices on the vast majority of the population. A meaningful voice in political decision-making (particularly about their own affairs) is the central complaint of almost every interest group in Myanmar, from ethnic armed groups to women's organizations to opposition parties to student unions. Yet almost every step of the process leading to the current NPD framework (from initial negotiations between a small government team and ethnic armed group leaders through to the drafting of the final framework by a nine member, all male group behind closed doors) has reinforced the notion that for most, citizenship is primarily a non-participatory notion, merely the act of being represented. And this type of citizenship cannot be transformative in the sense of turning people into more active, knowledgeable, inter-connected, and empathetic members of a political community.

What types of citizen engagement might be potentially transformative? A study by Ank Michels in 2011 looked at the presumed benefits of citizen participation in democratic governance. Michels finds that the positive effects of expanded participation are noticeable primarily to those actually taking part, which should not be surprising. The study specified these benefits as coming in the form of "knowledge, skills, and [democratic] virtues" (2011, p. 290). This insight helps to distinguish between the effects of different types of "democratic innovations", for example referendums and deliberative forums. While referendums seem to result in more direct policy influence, deliberative forums would contribute more to individual citizen development, not to mention the embeddedness that seems to be so critical in the citizen–political community relationship.

The designers and advocates of Myanmar's peace process and NPD process have frequently congratulated themselves for fostering an "open dialogue culture" (Slow 2016). While this may be the case relative to the closed-off nature of previous military regimes, the NPD framework creates minimal opportunities for deliberative forums that would invite mass participation. As a result, any potentially transformative benefits would be restricted — at best — to the small group of elites participating in the Union Peace Conferences. While the NPD's designers have also continued to insist that civil society will play an important role in the political dialogue, this role (not to mention the opportunities for participation by citizens who do not have political or civil society affiliations) has not been specified beyond being occasional and consultative rather than participatory and transformative. The expansion of local forums and consultations has been at least a partial response to this concern, but as mentioned above, without clear indications of how the discussions and insights from these gatherings will be channelled into political decision-making, they are not fulfilling the goal of making the national political dialogue a meaningfully inclusive process.

The simple lesson here is that, for citizenship to be transformative in an empowering way, it must be participatory. And this notion is supported by the activities of countless civil society organizations (CSOs) and NGOs that have been working in Myanmar and on its borders for decades on projects that have sought to include people in the political process, whether through creating refugee camp councils with explicit guidelines for marginalized group representation, organizing farmers to articulate and present their grievances to MPs in Naypyitaw, or demanding that ethnic political authorities hold regular public meetings in which people's concerns can be aired and leaders held to account.

The transformative possibilities of political participation can also be found in one of Myanmar's earliest examples of contemporary political philosophy. U Hpo Hlaing, an advisor to Myanmar's last two kings, Mindon and Thibaw, wrote the *Rajadhammasangaha* in 1878 as a manual of advice for King Thibaw. In it, he advocated for a political assembly as a way of guarding against the likelihood of a single individual with absolute power being guided by certain negative biases or hindrances. In Burmese these are called *agati* and include desire, anger, fear, and ignorance. U Hpo Hlaing wrote:

> if a number of people get together for any sort of action, there can be no question of following the *agati* way. In such assemblies what one man does not know another will; when one man has feelings of hate, another will not; when one is angry, another will be calm. When people have agreed

in a meeting and preserve their solidarity, there will be no need for fear. For these reasons, we must affirm that if a number of people conduct their business in an assembly there is no way in which the four wrong ways can be followed. (Bagshawe 2004, p. 174)

While U Hpo Hlaing's primary interest in the *Rajadhammasangaha* was to convince the monarch of the value of an assembly to guide his decision-making, elsewhere I have sought to build on his logic to consider the converse of the process, in which engaging in collective discussion with a focus on building mutual understanding and, ideally, consensus, could positively affect participants' own moral development:

> Collective decision-making, undertaken under ideal institutional structures, can open individuals to alternate or opposing perspectives, eroding their own self-interest and functioning as a moral practice in itself. When in the assembly, an individual's bias is revealed and he or she can see not only the perspective of another but also the benefit for the entire community of a particular decision, democratic participation can become a morally transformative activity itself." (Walton 2014, p. 42)

National political dialogue forums could thus become a place for transformative citizenship, but only if they are broadly participatory. This would require not just regular 21st Century Panglong Conferences attended by political elites, but the further development of open and inclusive political forums at multiple levels, all designed with sensitivity to the communication impediments described in the previous section.

Iris Young's warnings about the pitfalls of certain understandings of democracy sometimes seem as if they were written with Myanmar in mind. One type of public rhetoric that concerns her is appeals to the "common good", which can simply be a way of masking the continuation of the status quo and of the inequality and differential privilege it perpetuates (Young 1997). For the phrase common good, simply substitute "national politics" (as opposed to party politics), "unity",[7] or any other phrase that Burmese political elites use that subtly or not-so-subtly suggests that they are selflessly striving for the benefit of all while others are working selfishly for their own benefit.

Furthermore, in cases where a common good exists (or is *presumed* to exist), there is no need for "transformations from self-regarding to enlarged thought" (Young 2000, p. 42). That is, those making appeals to the common good or to unity believe that these sentiments already exist or could be brought into existence without any fundamental changes in their own perspectives and attitudes. An example can be seen in a criticism of President Thein Sein and Daw Aung San Suu Kyi made by a Burmese political commentator who noted that both dignitaries had simply given speeches to the January 2016 Union Peace Conference and then left, rather than staying to listen or participate further (Lun Min Mang 2016*b*). A Myanmar colleague noted to me that the same was again true for the most prominent speakers at the August 2016 21st Century Panglong Conference, with the notable exception of President U Htin Kyaw, who attended and listened throughout, seemingly modelling the type of behavior that must be expected from all political decision-makers at these alleged "dialogues". There can be no personal transformation where, as has been the case among military leadership for decades, prominent individuals believe that their job is merely to lecture, instruct, and admonish, rather than listen and learn through participating in a mutually transformative discussion.

By contrast, the type of open public communication Young advocates for would see every political encounter as a potential opportunity for both personal and collective growth, as moments to practise engaged, empathetic, and transformative citizenship. This type of citizenship practice would not privilege what is held in common, it would preserve plurality and respect difference as a source of creativity and growth. It is important to recognize that in this process the goal is not to transcend difference. Rather, the intention is to create a scenario in which one learns from another person who is expressing her experience, confronts that different perspective as a way of further revealing the partiality of one's own perspective, and has to articulate one's own expressions of self- or group-interest into appeals that can be heard and acted on in the public sphere.

The "common good" is a particularly pernicious appeal in Young's view, and especially in contexts of significant social or economic inequality, where it can mask exclusion, as appeals to the common good are really appeals to support the dominant position. Appeals to the common good, national interest, or unity can narrow the field of political debate and the political agenda by silencing disagreement. Myanmar's evolving NPD process should be monitored with attention to the ways in which an emphasis on the common good, unity, or the other watchwords of discipline and order *exclude* voices from the public sphere or from public consideration. There can be no transformative aspect of citizenship when processes of political participation do not allow for the sharing and consideration of dissenting views.

Another argument for transformative democratic politics comes from Benjamin Barber (2003), whose "strong democracy" emphasizes not only the personal transformations that might occur, but the transformation of conflict itself, a point that would seem to be particularly pertinent to Myanmar's situation. For Barber, conflict is inevitable, so rather than seeking to eliminate it, repress it, or simply tolerate it, democratic institutions ought to seek to make it a *productive* aspect of modern political life. This would happen through public political engagement, through encountering the "Other" in the political arena, not as an adversary but as a fellow citizen. Conflict would produce the conditions under which one could practise the expansion of the self that seems to be so critical to accounts of transformative citizenship, which, as explained above, paradoxically happens by recognizing the specificity and limited reach of our own particular experiences and views.

Myanmar's decades-long conflict continues to be the motivator for its current peace process and NPD. But very few aspects of the peace process or the NPD have been conducted as public political engagement of the type that Barber suggests could transform not only perspectives on conflict, but views on community and belonging. Negotiations have taken place between elites largely behind closed doors, with the public results being either periodic joint statements or agreements or gaudy signing ceremonies in which fundamental disagreements are unacknowledged or papered over. Note that this does not mean that a goal of Myanmar's NPD should not be to end the armed conflict that has brought decades of suffering to its population, merely that instances of conflict and disagreement should not be condemned or avoided. Statements such as Daw Aung San Suu Kyi's admonishment to new MPs reported in Frontier Myanmar on 25 February 2016 that Parliament is not "a boxing ring to host fights between people of different opinions" could potentially discourage the kind of public, reasoned disagreement that would seem absolutely necessary for the development of a political culture in Myanmar that will welcome voices of dissent but seek to channel it in productive ways.

CONCLUSION

Myanmar's national political dialogue process is not only the vehicle for fundamental political restructuring in the country; it also sets examples and reinforces precedents of practices of citizenship. A broadly participatory process, designed with attention to the ways in which different modes of political expression can actually be heard and appreciated by decision-makers would seem to be necessary in order to make the dialogue potentially transformative for all participants. As it was formulated throughout 2016 and remains in 2017, it is an elite-dominated proceeding that instead reinforces at best a model of passive political engagement for most citizens. This chapter has suggested that, given the nature of the grievances of those who have felt excluded from Myanmar's political process for decades, it would be wise to reconfigure the national political dialogue so that it can be a vehicle for the development of new models of broad political participation. Only in this way will it be able to act as a catalyst for the creation of an inclusive national identity rather than the imposition of an enforced unity and harmony. In doing so, Myanmar's leaders will need to recognize and cultivate a diverse set of practices of citizenship, not only in the national political dialogue process but in every one of the country's evolving political institutions.

It is true that there is virtually no country in the world that designs political institutions so that alternate modes of communication can be effectively "heard" or that seeks to make processes of citizenship both inclusive and transformative at every level. This chapter advocates for radical alterations in both understandings of and practices of citizenship that will not be easy to implement in Myanmar. However, the country is at a transitional and transformative point in its political history and the national political dialogue process has been designed to fundamentally change its political structure, potentially contributing to the success or failure of its broader democratic reform. Given the nature of the political grievances of those who have been excluded from Myanmar's politics for decades, it makes sense to design key political institutions in a way that would expand participation and increase the chances for marginalized voices to be effectively "heard". Now is the time to be aspirational, to describe the kind of government people want, the kind of public sphere that people want, the kind of citizens people want to become, and the type of political community that might, over time, develop into a community of mutual trust and benefit, rather than simply a community of fate.

Notes

1. An unofficial English translation of the document, entitled "The Framework for Political Dialogue" can be found at <http://www.eprpinformation.org/files/recent-events/the-framework-for-political-dialogue-unofficial-translation--22dec2015--eng.pdf> (accessed 25 February 2016). A useful infographic showing the various components of the NPD and the proportional representation of different groups can be found at <http://peaceanddialogueplatform.org/files/slider/pdf-QArvIl-Burma_Myanmar_Agreed_FPD_%28January_2016%29.pdf> (accessed 25 February 2016).
2. Pictorial representations of their proposed roadmap and structure can be found at <http://peaceanddialogueplatform.libguides.com/content.php?pid=475880&sid=3896998> (accessed 23 February 2016).
3. I have looked to the deliberative democracy literature to ground this analysis

because it has developed in large part as a school of thought that attends to the ways in which a diversity of public perspectives can be incorporated into political discussions and the design of political institutions and processes. This seems to me to be particularly relevant for the Myanmar case, where a primary complaint (not only from minority ethnic groups, but from a variety of marginalized groups) has been the lack of meaningful inclusion of people's views and concerns in political decision-making. There are similar reasons why I have chosen to draw on only a few thinkers within this field, most notably Iris Marion Young. To my mind, Young's insights regarding political communication are pertinent to the criticisms currently levelled against the National Political Dialogue and, as such, are particularly useful for thinking about practices of participatory citizenship in relation to this central process. My intention is not to argue that Young's ideas are the *most* relevant for Myanmar's context, indeed, it might be useful to see further comparative studies. But here I have made a choice here to be relatively focused on a few thinkers and ideas, for purposes of simplicity and clarity.

4. While this phenomenon has not been the subject of much academic study, anecdotal analysis has increased in recent years, alongside personal narrative such as Htet Moe Nwe Win (2016).

5. A troubling example that demonstrates the power of these norms even at the highest levels is that of NLD MPs being chastised by senior party leadership not to ask difficult questions in Parliament that might make the government look bad (Ei Ei Toe Lwin 2016*a*).

6. A relevant example can be found in the United States, where Native Americans have worked for centuries to be given the space to express their political grievances to representatives of the U.S. government in ways that they deem culturally appropriate. But the significance of their communication is often lost on political figures who have never been taught how to effectively listen to a political actor who is not communicating with a clear thesis and logical points of argument, ideally backed up by a brief and focused, bullet-pointed position paper.

7. I have argued elsewhere that there is a discourse of "unity" in Burmese politics that is used in a disciplining way to silence dissent or alternate perspectives; it is effectively deployed by actors across the political spectrum, from the military to the ethnic armed groups to the NLD (Walton 2015).

References

Bagshawe, L.E. "Rajadhammasangaha". Online Burma/Myanmar Library. 2004 <www.ibiblio.org/obl/docs/THE_RAJADHAMMASANGAHA.pdf> (accessed 20 February 2016).

Barber, Benjamin. *Strong democracy: Participatory politics for a new age.* 2nd ed. Berkeley, CA: University of California Press, 2003.

Benhabib, Seyla. *Democracy and Difference: contesting the boundaries of the political.* Princeton, N.J.: Princeton University Press, 1996.

Ei Ei Toe Lwin. "'Don't ask tough questions' — Checks on power out the window as NLD exerts its majority". *Myanmar Times*, 7 October 2016*a* <http://www.mmtimes.com/index.php/national-news/nay-pyi-taw/22959-don-t-ask-tough-questions-checks-on-power-out-the-window-as-nld-exerts-its-majority.html> (accessed 30 January 2017).

————. "Not without wrinkles, peace conference lauded for taking landmark 'first steps'." *Myanmar Times*, 5 September 2016*b* <http://www.mmtimes.com/index.php/national-news/22313-not-without-wrinkles-peace-conference-lauded-for-taking-landmark-first-steps.html> (accessed 30 January 2017).

————. "Minister to be investigated over comments to villagers". *Myanmar Times*, 5 February 2014 <http://www.mmtimes.com/index.php/national-news/9459-govt-investigating-minister-over-comments-to-magwe-villagers.html> (accessed 23 November 2015).

Hogan, Libby. "Advocates push for more women's voices in peace process". *Democratic Voice of Burma*, 3 January 2017 <http://www.dvb.no/news/advocates-push-womens-voices-peace-process/73410> (accessed 30 January 2017).

Htet Moe Nwe Lwin. "Dreams for our daughters and sons". *Tea Circle*, 10 August 2016 <https://teacircleoxford.com/2016/08/10/dreams-for-our-daughters-and-sons/> (accessed 30 January 2017).

Lall, Marie, Thei Su San, Nwe Nwe San, Yeh Tut Naing, Thein Thein Myat, Lwin Thet Thet Khaing, Swann Lynn Htet and Yin Nyein Aye. *Citizenship in Myanmar: Contemporary debates and challenges in light of the reform process*. Yangon and Bangkok: Myanmar Egress and FNS, 2014.

Lun Min Mang. "Panglong framework debated in Yangon". *Myanmar Times*, 13 June 2016*a* <http://www.mmtimes.com/index.php/national-news/yangon/20805-panglong-framework-debated-in-yangon.html> (accessed 15 June 2016).

————. "Peace conference widens divisions and troubles NLD". *Myanmar Times*, 20 January 2016*b* <http://www.mmtimes.com/index.php/national-news/nay-pyi-taw/18563-peace-conference-widens-divisions-and-troubles-nld.html> (accessed 25 February 2016).

Michels, Ank. "Innovations in democratic governance: How does citizen participation contribute to a better democracy?". *International Review of Administrative Sciences* 77, no. 2 (2011): 275–93.

Nyan Hlaing Lynn. "Min Zin: 'It is essential that the democratic transition not be derailed'". *Frontier Myanmar*, 23 September 2016 <http://frontiermyanmar.net/en/min-zin-it-is-essential-that-the-democratic-transition-not-be-derailed> (accessed 30 January 2017).

Radio Free Asia. "Myanmar NGOs seek postponement of peace talks". *Radio Free Asia*, 7 January 2016 <http://www.rfa.org/english/news/myanmar/myanmar-ngos-01072016142835.html> (accessed 25 February 2016).

Sam Aung Moon. "Second Panglong meet looks set to be a lonely affair". *Myanmar Times*, 11 January 2017 <http://www.mmtimes.com/index.php/national-news/24490-second-panglong-meet-looks-set-to-be-a-lonely-affair.html> (accessed 30 January 2017).

Shan Herald Agency News. "Shans prepare for next '21ˢᵗ century Panglong conference'". *Shan Herald Agency News*, 13 January 2017 <http://english. panglong.org/2017/01/13/shans-prepare-for-next-21st-century-panglong-conference/> (accessed 30 January 2017).

Slow, Oliver. "Aung Naing Oo: The patient peace advocate". *Frontier Myanmar*, 29 February 2016 <http://frontiermyanmar.net/en/aung-naing-oo-the-patient-peace-advocate> (accessed 22 July 2017).

Walton, Matthew J. "Buddhism in Contemporary Myanmar". In *Myanmar: Dynamics and Continuities*, edited by David I. Steinberg. Boulder: Lynne Reinner, 2014.

———. "The Disciplining Discourse of Unity in Burmese Politics". *Journal of Burma Studies* 19, no. 1 (2015): 1–26.

Young, Iris Marion. *Intersecting voices: Dilemmas of gender, political philosophy, and policy*. Princeton, N.J.: Princeton University Press, 1997.

———. *Inclusion and Democracy*. Oxford: Oxford University Press, 2000.

4

CITIZENSHIP AND MINORITY RIGHTS
The Role of "National Race Affairs" Ministers in Myanmar's 2008 Constitution

Ardeth Maung Thawnhmung and Yadana[1]

INTRODUCTION

In Myanmar, "national races" settled in the territory of Myanmar since 1823 and their descendants are automatically eligible for the first type of citizenship (see introduction by Lall and South). There are currently 136 such groups that are officially recognized as "native" or national races (one group was added at the end of U Thein Sein government). However, not many of them share the vision and values of a Burman/Buddhist "national identity" forged upon them by the state dominated by Burman elites. Successive military governments have dealt with minority nationalities' grievances and aspiration for self-determination and federalism by crushing forces that refused to acknowledge the legitimacy of militarized and centralized state. Creating a shared identity among these nationalities has been a major challenge for post-independence Myanmar government which saw federalism as synonymous with separatism and a path leading to the disintegration of the union. Armed groups and leaders of ethnic communities on the other hand saw federalism as the best solution to be a part and citizens of the Union of Myanmar.

The 2008 Constitution attempted to deal with these grievances by offering some limited provisions for national minorities. First, the existing seven regions and seven states (which are named after seven dominant minority groups) are given limited legislative and administrative powers. Second, autonomous zones/regions are given ethnic nationalities that constitute a majority in two adjacent townships. Six such groups, Wa, Pao, Palaung, Danu, Kokang in Shan State and Naga from Sagaing are qualified for this. Thirdly, the minority that constitutes 0.1 per cent of the populations of the country's total population and reside in any given region/state are to be represented by their respective "national race affair" ministers. There were twenty-nine such positions. Studies have examined the role and performances of regional governments and the self-autonomous zones (SAZs) under U Thein Sein government.[2] However, there have not been any studies that examine the role and implications of ethnic affairs ministers in Myanmar. To what extent these ethnic affairs ministers (referred to as "national race affairs" ministers) are able to represent their members' interests? How much power and authority do they have? Were they able to forge a common identity of multi-ethnic states while promoting their cultures and identity and addressing grievances of their respective constituents?

Our aim here is to provide a critical analysis of the position of the national race affairs ministers by looking their evolving role and responsibilities under U Thein Sein government between 2011 and 2015. We also assess the implications of the post for minority rights, citizenship rights, and the prospects for national reconciliation among the country's minority ethnic nationalities especially under the National League for Democracy (NLD) government which won a landslide victory in the 2015 elections. We first demonstrate the ability of ethnic affairs ministers — known formally as National Race Affairs Ministers (NRAMs) — to formally enhance their own positions and open up a space in Myanmar's political landscape. We also highlighted a number of concerns, including their ambiguous roles. They are based on ethnicity that is not only arbitrarily drawn, but also are based on outdated data. The paper is based on the second author's extensive engagement with NRAMs over the past four years; the first author's personal interactions, interviews, and conversations with three NRAMs; and a survey of eight NRAMs undertaken by the second author.

MINORITY RIGHTS AND CITIZENSHIP

The promotion and protection of the rights of persons belonging to minorities has been integral responsibility and significant priority of the

High Commissioner and OHCHR (UN Human Rights Office for High Commissioner 2012, p. 11) Some governments in culturally diverse countries, such as Canada, India, South Africa and members of European Union, officially recognize ethnic and linguistic "minority" or "group" rights as well as individual rights in order to accommodate diversity and help prevent or ameliorate communal tension and conflicts.[3] There has, however, been a debate over whether the provision of minority rights helps protect ethnic culture and identity and prevent inter-communal conflicts. For instance, the "liberal integrationist" approach stresses that individual rights should form the basis of constitutional principles in ethnically diverse countries, since individual rights guarantee freedom of religion, speech, and association, regardless of group membership or ethnic or religious affiliation.[4] According to this line of argument, minority communities do not require special assistance as long as their members are guaranteed individual rights to freely practise their culture and religion. In addition, this "ethnically blind" approach would eliminate ethnicity as a basis for political mobilization, encourage political parties to appeal to broader constituencies across different nationalities, create new allegiances across different ethnic groups, and promote inter-ethnic cooperation. U Nu, the first prime minister of independent Burma, emphasized the key role of individual rights in cementing bonds among all the nation's cultural communities (Silverstein 1980, p. 151).

Other commentators, such as Young 1990, Taylor 1992, and Kymlicka 1995, stress the importance of "minority" or "group" rights for providing leverage for culturally disadvantaged minorities. They argue that the very existence of minority groups — not to mention their culture and language — is at risk without protection and special assistance by government. According to this line of reasoning, the provision of minority rights is the key to assuaging distrust of a dominant group by minority communities and strengthening the latter's identification with the nation-state. Advocates for minority rights argue that governments should make special efforts to help preserve minority religious and cultural groups by funding bilingual education in schools as well as ethnic associations and festivals, exempting them from laws that disadvantage them because of their religious practices, and recognizing minority religious holidays. Other special considerations that might be extended to historically disadvantaged minority groups include self-governing status for territories where they are dominant, resource sharing, special representation rights and reserved seats in executive or legislative forums, and implementing policies that give them preferential treatment with respect to education, employment, government scholarships and bank loans. Examples of these measures are the "affirmative action" policies in the United States that give preferential treatment to African-Americans, and Malaysia's New Economic Policy that gives preferential treatment to the country's majority Malay population (see, e.g., Lee 2005). Historically, however, official policies towards minority groups have varied depending on the political context of individual countries and on whether minority groups are considered to be "native" or "immigrant" populations. In principle, there are differences between "national minorities", or previously self-governing, territorially concentrated cultural groups that have been incorporated into a larger state, and "polyethnic minorities" who are immigrants (Kymlicka 1995). Those two types of minorities also tend to differ with respect to the claims they make on the state. According to Kymlicka (1995), while national minorities tend to focus on securing self-governing rights in order to manage their own affairs within a given territory, polyethnic minorities focus on rights that promote integration into the larger society. These goals can overlap, however, as both groups can make claims for self-government as well as greater integration within federal institutions.

In some countries, such as Canada and the United States official policies that favour the rights of minority groups to self-government and special representation have enlarged the space for political participation and have strengthened individuals' ties with the nation-state. At the same time, however, the last decade has witnessed the backlash against in this accommodationist trend, especially noticeable in Europe, where the model has come under intense pressure in countries that had (officially or semi-officially) recognized and granted specific entitlements to minority cultures (Torbisco-Casals 2016, p. 377). In other places, such as military government in Myanmar and Suharto Indonesia, outright repression or half-hearted reforms have further exacerbated tensions between governments and minority groups and have only heightened their desire for secession (Smith 1999; Bertrand 2009). Against this background, we seek to examine how minority rights are stipulated in the 2008 Myanmar Constitution and to assess how they have been implemented. We also analyse their implications for minority rights, citizenship rights, and the prospects for national reconciliation among the country's minority ethnic groups.

THE 2008 MYANMAR CONSTITUTION: CITIZENSHIP AND MINORITY RIGHTS

The emphasis of the Myanmar military regime on creating a path towards "disciplined democracy" is reflected in the rather constrained and ambiguous language of the provisions made for individual and minority rights in the 2008 Constitution. Article 348, for instance, stipulates that "the Union shall not discriminate [against] any citizen of the Republic of the Union of Myanmar, based on race, birth, religion, official position, status, culture, sex and wealth." Article 349 stipulates that citizens shall enjoy equal opportunity in the areas of public employment, occupation, trade, business, technical know-how and vocation, and in the arenas of art, science and technology. However, citizens can only express and freely publish their convictions and opinions, assemble peacefully, form associations and organizations, and develop their respective languages, literature, culture, religion, and customs, *as long as they do not undermine "the laws, enacted for Union security, community peace and tranquility or public order and morality."*[5]

Eligibility for different types of citizenship, however, is determined by the 1982 citizenship law, which prescribes that members of cultural groups who are officially designated as *taing yin thar* have immediate rights to full citizenship. The law defines *taing yin thar* (translated from Burmese as "sons/offspring of the geographical division") as a cultural group present in what is now known as Myanmar before the first British annexation of Burma began in 1823 (Transnational Institute 2014, p. 5). The 1982 law outlines two additional but less privileged categories of citizens: "associate" citizens (who qualified for citizenship under the previous 1948 citizenship law) and "naturalized" citizens (who have been in Myanmar for three generations). Those with associate citizenship, for instance, had the right to earn a living but could not occupy any government office.[6] Likewise, naturalized citizens are prohibited from holding any important political office and from serving in the armed forces.[7]

The 2008 Constitution contains provisions that can be interpreted as group rights *for taing yin thar* members who constitute a certain threshold percentage of the total populations in the country and territorially concentrated in a given region/state. These include the devolution of limited legislative powers to seven states and seven regions, the establishment of six SAZs, and twenty-nine newly created posts for ethnic affairs ministers. The constitution retains Myanmar's seven divisions (renamed as regions) and seven ethnic states as basic administrative and territorial units. The seven ethnic states are named after the seven largest minority groups — Shan, Kayin, Kayah, Chin, Mon, Rakhine, and Kachin — that constitute a majority in their respective territories, while the seven regions represent areas of mixed ethnicity but with a dominant Bamar population. None of these regions and states is ethnically homogeneous. In addition, they are uneven in size, ranging from Shan State, with 155,801 square kilometres to the smallest entity, Karenni State, with 11,733 square kilometres. Shan State itself includes many smaller minority groups including Wa, Pao, Kokeng, Palaung, and Danu. On the other hand, it is estimated that only a third of the Karen people live in Karen State; the remainder are spread over various parts of Lower Burma.[8] In like manner, there are a sizeable population of Kachin in Shan State, or Chin in Rakhine State, or Mon in Kayin State.

In order to represent minority groups living outside their respective ethnic states or regions where they constitute a majority, the Constitution created elected posts for NRAMs who are tasked with the responsibility to represent their constituents, who may constitute as little as 0.1 per cent of the country's total population and are residents of a given region (estimated to be 51,500 people).[9] Unlike other representatives who are elected from their respective townships, NRAMs are to be elected by their constituencies across the whole state or region. In addition, six additional groups that constitute a majority in at least two adjacent towns in any given state or region were given the status of autonomous region (Danu, Pao, Kokang, Pao in Shan State and Naga in Sagaing Region) and autonomous division (Wa in Shan State).[10]

There has not been any study that examines the role and implications of the NRAMs. Below, we offer a critical analysis of NRAMs under U Thein Sein government, and assess their role in the promotion of minority rights and citizen rights. We argue that while the NRAM under U Thein Sein government were able to gain formal recognition for their position, and collectively pushed for issues that are related to minority ethnic groups to the forefront of the national policy agenda, the position is fraught with challenges not only because their ambiguous and limited roles, but also because the nature of the position which is based on arbitrary and contested categories.

THE NATIONAL RACE AFFAIRS MINISTERS (NRAMs)

NRAMs are created for any *taing yin thar* (including Bamar majority) who constitutes about 0.1 per cent of the country's total population and reside in any given region (estimated to be 51,500 people).[11] Given their dispersed settlement across the country, the Karen people, the second largest minority group in Myanmar, has the largest number of designated ethnic affairs ministers (five in total from Yangon, Ayeyarwaddy, Bago, Tenintharyi, and Mon State). Bamar, who constitute the largest ethnic nationality or 68 per cent of the population, are also represented by five elected officials, due to the prevalence of members of the majority community in ethnic nationality designated States. Shan State — by some way, the largest in the Union — has the largest number of ethnic affairs ministers (a total of seven representing Bamar, Inn, Lisu, Lahu, Aka, Kachin, and Kayan communities), followed by Kachin State with four. Rakhine and Kayah States host one NRAM each, and Chin State has none.

Thus, according to the provisions of the Constitution and the 1993 population census, twenty-nine representatives were elected in 2010 as NRAMs. Twenty were members of the military-backed ruling party, the Union Solidarity and Development Party (USDP), and the rest belonged to political parties representing their respective ethnic groups. Most were retired (an average age of 65 years old) and were former government officials or civil servants. More precisely, seven were former civil servants, five were high-ranking military and police officials, six were retired schoolteachers, one was a retired university rector, three were lawyers, and seven were business owners. Only one, Daw Khin Pyone Yee (a Shan minister from Kachin State), was a woman.

See Appendix Table 1 for a list of NRAMs for states and regions in Myanmar. Appendix Table 2 shows NRAMs and their ethnic representation. Appendix Table 3 shows personal profiles of NRAMs.

Expansion of the Rights and Privileges of NRAMs

Analysing the first five years of the quasi-civilian period of government, it is clear that not only were NRAMs able to secure privileges and rights commensurate with their constitutional position, but they were also able to expand their roles and activities. Although the 2008 Constitution recognizes them as regional and state level *cabinet ministers*, after regional cabinets were formed, they tended to be treated as *elected members of state or regional legislatures*. Consequently, they were given lower salaries and privileges than those usually accorded to state and regional cabinet ministers. Most were never invited to attend cabinet meetings. In addition, because NRAMs lacked their own designated budget, they depended on the interest and generosity of the chief ministers of their states in carrying out some of their activities.

As a result of these anomalies, in 2011 NRAMs approached Myanmar's Constitutional Tribunal to decide on their status as regional and state ministers. At a hearing held on 14 December 2011 the tribunal ruled in favour of the NRAMs, but the judgement was not acknowledged by the Union government. NRAMs thus submitted another petition the following year. On 28 March 2012 the Constitutional Tribunal rejected the Union Government's decision, but was again ignored by the government. The ministers' first collective attempt to discuss shared grievances and fight for their rights took place at an NRAM consultation workshop in September 2012, where the eighteen attendees issued a joint petition to the Union Government. In their recommendations, they urged the government to respect the decision by the Constitutional

Tribunal, to recognize their right to participate in the peace-making process, and to give regional governments clear instructions regarding the formation of ethnic affairs ministries.[12]

Two days after the workshop, the president invited the NRAMs to an official meeting in Naypyidaw. He also offered them a "direct channel" to consult with him on ethnic affairs. The president's change of heart may have had to do with the need to court support from the ministers, who together enjoyed a large constituency base, especially in a period when tensions were developing between government and parliament over the status of parliamentary commissions (Robinson 2012).

Eventually, the NRAMs were able to secure the status, salaries, and privileges accorded to other regional and state cabinet ministers.[13] They also successfully challenged section 48 of the Region or State Government Law that stipulates that "chairmen of self-autonomous regions and ethnic affairs ministers should only attend invited cabinet meetings" by arguing that the law contradicts the constitution where NRAMs are named as "ministers" without any discriminatory qualifications applied.[14]

The second area where the NRAMs formed a collective lobby is the teaching of minority ethnic languages in government schools. With the help of civil societal groups and international non-governmental organizations (INGOs), the teaching of ethnic languages at government schools was approved by the president in 2013, albeit only out of normal school hours.[15]

The third area in which they achieved collective success relates to the passing of a law in April 2015 that recognizes the rights of ethnic nationalities or *taing yin thar*. This law, The Protection of National Races, mandates the formation of a National Race Affairs ministerial position with its own separate budget at Union level, and guarantees the right of *taing yin thar* to be informed and have their consent obtained for major development programmes and extractive activities in their respective areas.[16] Shortly after taking power in 2016, the NLD administration implemented the Protection of National Races law (passed by the national parliament in 2015 under the previous administration), by creating the Ministry of Ethnic Affairs and appointed Naing Thet Lwin of the Mon National Party — an NLD ally — as minister of ethnic affairs. It should be acknowledged, however, that the 2015 Law for the Protection of the Rights of Ethnic Nationalities has yet to be supplemented by the appropriate by-laws and detailed regulations that would fit it for implementation.[17] On a positive note, however, the NLD has shown its commitment towards national reconciliation by forming the Ministry of National Race Affairs while simultaneously reducing the number of ministries from thirty-six to twenty-one to cut cost and redundancy.[18]

In addition to these three areas, the NRAMs also collectively submitted their recommendations to the committee responsible for drafting the National Land Use Policy, urging that customary land practices be incorporated in the policy. Many upland ethnic communities have communal landholding practices which are not recognized under the new Farm Land Law of 2012, making them vulnerable to displacement by large-scale private business ventures. Land grabbing by private companies and government agencies proceeded at an unprecedented pace in the 1990s in the country's minority ethnic areas. Kachin and Northern Shan States in particular have experienced high levels of land grabbing by Chinese companies seeking land to grow rubber, cassava, and other cash crops.[19] According to official statistics, in 2013 a total of 377 domestic companies were allocated 2.3 million acres of "vacant, fallow, and virgin" land, and a further 822 companies or individuals were allocated 0.8 million acres of forest lands (Andersen 2015). On top of this, the Ministry of Agriculture and Irrigation (MOAI) plans to convert 10 million acres of "wastelands" to commercial agricultural production between 2000 and 2030.

Some collective endeavours failed to materialize, however. In 2013, the NRAMs made a request to the Union Government to let them participate formally in ceasefire negotiations between the government and ethnic armed groups. However, their proposal was turned down by Union Minister U Aung Min, who promised them a role in the peace-building process in the post-ceasefire period.

The (Ambiguous) Roles and Responsibilities of NRAMs

Despite their success in gaining a formal recognition for their position and for collective advocacy on a few issue areas, the main responsibilities of ethnic affairs ministers remain vague in both the 2008 Constitution and the Region or State Government Law. Section 10(B) of the Law merely authorizes the president to "assign duties" to *taing yin thar* representatives to deal with "matters related to *Taing Yin Thar*". Section 12 sets out the chain of command, stipulating that regional and state ministers shall be responsible to their respective chief minister, and through them to the president.[20] Consequently, there are many diverse interpretations of the roles and expectations appropriate to the NRAMs.

Four areas can be identified in which most NRAMs have been active. These are:

1. Preserving the culture, literature and identity of particular ethnic groups;

2. Promoting welfare and development issues in the constituencies they represent;
3. Advocating for their constituents and directing them to the appropriate channels to address their grievances; and
4. Mediating between armed groups and the government.

Six of out the eight ministers who filled out our survey questionnaires agreed that these duties are generally associated with NRAMs.[21] All eight respondents said that they were able to perform "some" of these duties. One minister noted that he had mediated in talks between the government and armed groups; offered financial assistance to schools; and helped persuade the relevant authorities to lower their admission standards regarding health and education training and accept high school graduates with low grades. Another minister mentioned his efforts to promote his group's literary and cultural practices and to resolve land disputes. Yet another commented that he was able to help constituents through the process of forming and registering for new organizations, building roads and providing access to drinking water, and repairing schools. One respondent, who was appointed regional minister for workers affairs in his area, proudly recalled mediating between owners and workers at a number of garment factories with a view to reaching a common agreement on daily wages — although this clearly came under his workers affairs rather than his role as ethnic affairs minister.

Although they were officially barred from mediating in ceasefire negotiations, a few ethnic affairs ministers in Karen areas served as intermediaries between armed groups and state/regional or Union level government, and have helped bring Karen communities across different geographical areas to the table. One example of this process is the formation of the Karen Unity and Peace Committee (KUPC), initiated by prominent Karen community leaders including several ethnic affairs ministers, with the aim of forming a form which captures and recognizes some of the Karen communities' great diversity when contributing to the political dialogue process. KUPC is composed of all the Karen political parties, the major Karen armed groups, civil societal groups, and bodies representing Karen from across different areas. Its main goal is to draft a comprehensive paper that would advance political dialogue. The final report incorporated reports from five regions (Ayeyarwaddy, Yangon, Bago, Tenintharyi, and Mon) plus the Karen State, the area controlled by the KNU, and Upper Burma.

All eight of the NRAMs surveyed cited budgetary constraints; a lack of autonomy; a shortage of staff; the failure of department heads, personnel, and office clerks to perform their roles conscientiously; and a lack of coordination among departments as obstacles to carrying out their duties successfully.

For instance, NRAMs who were able to implement the teaching of minority languages in government schools faced a variety of financial and institutional challenges. Towards the end of U Thein Sein period, quite a few respondents working on the teaching of minority ethnic languages in government school mentioned to us that the government has cut down the budget on the second year of policy implementation. One regional MP from Mon State stated that the government reduced its financial support for language teachers from 30,000 kyat per month to 10,000 kyat per month.[22] Many communities lack the human and financial resources to develop curricula and textbooks that would suit their local context. In some communities, it is proved an insurmountable challenge to teach literacy skills to children whose parents no longer speak the language. The offering of language classes outside of regular school hours is also an unrealistic proposition for parents and students who are already hard-pressed for time through taking "extra tuition" and helping with household tasks.[23]

One minister also listed the lack of security in his constituency as a restraining factor. Overall, however, respondents were optimistic about the role of NRAMs and stressed that they would be able to accomplish their duties more effectively if they were given greater autonomy (*loke pine kwint*), a realistic budget, if they were treated with more respect by government departments and agencies — and if the country was operating more fully under the rule of law.

Some respondents hold that while NRAMs are not responsible for raising funds to build schools or hospitals for their constituents (areas that fall under the jurisdictions of the Ministries of Education and Health), they should be advocating for their communities by serving as a bridge between their constituencies and the appropriate ministers.[24] For instance, while they are not expected to investigate disputes arising from the confiscation of lands worked and owned by their constituents, NRAMs should be putting those affected in touch with land investigation committees. They should promote the wellbeing of their people by liaising with the relevant ministries and INGOs and local NGOs to implement employment projects, build infrastructure, schools and clinics, and to help preserve the culture and identity of their communities by hosting New Year festivities and the respective National Days of their ethnic nationalities.[25]

Explaining Variations in the Performance, Capacity, and Influence of Ethnic Affair Ministers

Because NRAM is a newly created position with many responsibilities that are ambiguous or unclear, it is still too early to assess their impact and influence.

In addition, the lack of clearly defined roles and responsibilities for NRAMs has resulted in their being engaged in varied and diverse activities. The analysis of the performance of NRAMs presented here is tentative and based on our own observations and interactions with ministers, and the self-evaluations provided by eight of them who served under U Thein Sein government.

The variations we found in their influence, performance and capacity can be tentatively explained by a number of factors:

1. their prior work experience and institutional backgrounds;
2. individual ideological and personal attitudes (level of commitment and attitude to the job);
3. their relationship with their chief minister;
4. their party affiliation; and
5. the nature and composition of the constituencies they represent.

Five of the eight ministers who filled out the survey agreed that the performance of NRAMs is mediated by these five factors. It should be noted however that while these factors are important, the needs of their constituents would remain unfilled if ministers lacked the willingness to serve and represent their communities.

Let us discuss these five factors in order. First, in Myanmar, the higher one's position in the military or the civil service, the more likely one is to exercise influence. Six out of the twenty-nine ministers had had prior careers as senior military and police officers or civil servants. Jubilee San Hla, a Karen affairs minister from Bago, for instance, held the post of regional commissioner (General Administration) for Bago before being appointed an NRAM, and is the president of the Veterans of the General Administration Association. Serving general administrative officials at regional and township level were his juniors when he was active in the service. Compared to his NRAM colleagues who were retired educators or police officials (police fall under the control of the General Administration in the chain of command), Jubilee San Hla garnered respect and deference from both administrative officials and cabinet ministers in Bago Region. Other ministers who enjoyed a comparable level of influence are U Khin Kyuu (Bamar minister, Kayin State), who served as chairman of the Kayin State Peace and Development Council; U Thet Win (Bamar minister, Mon State), a retired army colonel with a long career of service in the diplomatic corps; U Naing Win (Bamar minister, Shan State), another retired colonel; and U Saw Tun Aung Myint (Kayin minister, Yangon Region), a former senior naval officer. In contrast to these figures, Duwa Zuk Dung and U Peter Thaung Sein, both of whom had no prior experience in higher administration, but had participated in the development of the 2008 Constitution (as representatives of ethnic groups and a legal expert group, respectively), faced difficulties in working with departmental officials who refused to recognize their authority. Again, having prior positions in high-level civil and military posts is a necessary but not a sufficient factor in meeting constituents' needs — more important is a sense of public service and a high level of commitment to serving the community.

Second, high energy levels, an outgoing personality, and personal courage and integrity were positive attributes for ministers who were seeking to advance their claims on behalf of constituents. A further desideratum is a strong background in legal and constitutional matters. Some personal attributes may cut both ways — being outspoken and publicly critical of official policies may be valued by one's constituents, but may be viewed less positively by the regional chief minister or the Union Government. U Zaw Aye Maung, who was well known for his open criticism of both regional and central government, was given repeated warnings by both the chief minister and Speaker of the Yangon Regional Parliament. However, despite — or perhaps, because of — this, he was one of the only two ethnic affairs ministers who were re-elected in 2015.[26]

Third, the nature of a minister's relationship with their regional or state chief minister is also relevant in terms of procuring support for one's constituency. Some NRAMs, including Jubilee San Hla from Bago, Saw Tun Aung Myint (Yangon), U Thet Win (Mon), U Sein Oo (Kayah) and U Khin Kyuu (Kayin), developed good relationships with their chief ministers. Jubilee San Hla enjoyed a particularly good relationship with his chief minister, who assisted him with arrangements for the celebration of the Karen New Year, training teachers for Karen language instruction, and the publication of a Karen language textbook.

Fourth, although some ministers argue that non-USDP members can accomplish more than lawmakers from the ruling party, who faced greater institutional restrictions and are subject to hierarchical administrative structures in addressing the needs of their constituents, other observers argue that USDP ministers can deliver more because the USDP is better financed than other parties and has the heft to deliver infrastructure projects and other services to their constituencies. There is a marked lack of information in this area, and more research is needed to assess these alleged variations in capacity and resources between USDP and non-USDP ministers.

Last but not least, the character and demographic makeup of the various constituencies represented by NRAMs is also an important factor in explaining variations in their performance. For instance, Jubilee San

Hla was the only Karen affairs minister who has succeeded in reactivating a regionwide Karen Culture and Language Committee to implement the teaching of the Karen language in government schools; he was able to achieve this because the Bago Region which he represented has a predominantly Sgaw Karen population of 370,000. By contrast, Ayeyarwaddy, which has the largest Karen population outside Karen State has a mix of Pwo and Sgaw Karen peoples, making it more difficult for the local Karen affair minister to introduce a uniform Karen language textbook and script.[27] Most of the ministers who have successfully taken advantage of the new law offering the teaching of ethnic languages in government schools have done so with the help of long-established organizations such as cultural and literary societies, Buddhist monasteries, and Christian churches. Their educational activities are thus very localized, depending on the history of the involvement of these civil societal and other groups.

In addition to constraining factors such as these, some ministers failed to fully utilize their positions to represent their constituencies because they have been given other portfolios, thus diluting their efforts as NRAMs. U Tun Aung Myint of the Kayin People's Party was given the post of assistant Yangon mayor. Similarly, Zaw Aye Maung took up an additional position as minister for information for Yangon. These additional positions have meant that a number of ministers have been unable to attend effectively to their main responsibilities as NRAMs.

HOW SUSTAINABLE IS ETHNICITY BASED SOLUTION TO THE MINORITY GRIEVANCES?

Eligibility for NRAMs have been based on outdated and unreliable population figures compiled under the military government, and the contested categories of 135 officially designated *taing yin thar*. There are currently 136 officially recognized *taing yin thar* groups who are automatically eligible for full citizenship, but the government's position has been challenged by language experts, scholars, and leaders of ethnic minority groups because of the arbitrary way in which these ethnic boundaries have been drawn. For instance out of these 136 groups are macro-ethnic categories such as Kachin, Kayin, Chin and Naga which are collective names for various subgroups which are listed as separate ethnic groups. Some ethnic minority leaders also challenge the official categories which either exclude or undermine the status of their groups (Transnational Institute 2014).

The government, in collaboration with the United Nations Population Fund (UNPF), conducted a nationwide population census in 2014, but has yet to release the data on ethnic and religious groups. These figures are important because they will determine the sizes of ethnic nationalities as well as the groups that will be eligible for NRAM positions and SAZs.[28]

The fact that the NRAMs' position is based on their membership of a particular ethnic group means that their survival — and that of the communities they represent — remains precarious, depending on the findings of the 2014 census on the ethnic make-up of the country. That was the reason that many ministerial candidates lobbied hard during the census period to encourage voters to list their own group as their primary ethnic identity so that they could continue to enjoy representation. Depending on the results, some positions might be dissolved and new ones created. For instance, unofficial results from the 2014 census reveal that the Bamar population is lower than 0.1 per cent in Kayah, which would lead to the elimination of the ministerial position in the state. On the other hand, Taung-yoe from Shan State has claimed that their population exceeds the minimum percentage required to have one NRAM.

Inevitably, attempts have been made to benefit a minister's own ethnic group at the expense of others. Daw Dwe Bu, a Kachin and member of the Pyithu Hluttaw, has argued before the Constitutional Tribunal that Rawang and Lisu should no longer have rights to representation since Lisu is merely one of the twelve subgroups of Kachin, an ethnic nationality which is composed of six major groups.[29] She argued that appointing Rawang and Lisu ministers in Kachin and Shan States would not only reduce the number of people who self-identify as Kachin, but would be unfair to other subgroups such as Jing Hpaw, Lao Vao, La Chyik and Zai Wa, who have never had ministerial representation. However, the Constitutional Tribunal rejected her petition, responding that such concerns should be raised during the election period by submitting a formal complaint to the Election Commission, and that the tribunal did not have a remit to deal with matters under the jurisdiction of the commission. The constantly changing political and ethnic landscape in Myanmar, and the arbitrary nature of how ethnicity is defined, has shed light on the concern expressed by the liberal integrationist approach to minority and group rights discussed above. The post, in this particular incidence, seems to create more problems for inter-ethnic cooperation than offering solutions.

IMPLICATIONS FOR CITIZENSHIP AND MINORITY GROUPS

Given the newly created nature of the position, the short tenure of democracy (or quasi-democracy) in the country, and small sample size of respondents (which is confined to ministers under U Thein Sein government), and the inconclusive nature of our findings, it is difficult to offer a systematic assessment of how the office of NRAM has enhanced the concept of multi-ethnic citizenship and improved the status of ethnic minorities in Myanmar. Further research is needed in order to develop a more systematic assessment of the factors that would explain the variations in the performance of individual NRAMs and the relationship between the position and the promotion of citizenship rights. In addition, it is important to remember that any assessment of NRAMs would not in itself offer a comprehensive picture of the current situation of minority rights in Myanmar. This would need to include an evaluation of the performance of regional assemblies and civil societal groups.

These things aside, a number of conclusions can be drawn regarding the role of NRAMs in the promotion of citizenship and minority rights in Myanmar. There can be no doubt that, as a group, NRAMs under U Thein Sein government succeeded in closing the gap that became evident between their constitutional status and their actual standing when they first assumed office. Since their posts were created, they expanded their roles and their activities to become increasingly regularized and institutionalized. Some ministers promoted and empowered citizens' participation in politics by helping them address their grievances and directing them into the appropriate channels. They contributed to laws that attempt to protect citizenship rights, especially in minority areas. They were instrumental in promoting public awareness of ethnic minority issues including the teaching of minority languages in government schools, in pushing for the establishment of an NRAM ministry at Union level, and in advocating for non-violent resolution for ongoing regional conflicts.

NRAMs can certainly use their position to help promote the cause of minority ethnic groups, and help strengthen the process of national reconciliation and peace-building among ethnic nationalities. These activities can help promote citizenships rights of minority ethnic groups by allowing citizens to freely preserve their language and culture, to actively participate in politics (through voting or engage for peace movements and ceasefire negotiations), and to promote minority rights (by requiring extractive industries to obtain free prior informed consent from local populations, and by exercising autonomy over language and education policy).

Second, while NRAMs have successfully fought to secure their status and position in line with the constitution, the extent to which these newly elected ministers can utilize their powers to represent the interests of the people remains to be seen. It remains to be seen whether and to what extent newly elected ethnic affairs ministers can continue to build on the achievements of their predecessors and gain greater recognition for and protection of Myanmar's minority ethnic groups.

The background of elected NRAMs in 2015 indicates a more diverse group. Many of the new NRAMs have worked in professions outside government, politics, and military, and some have maintained a low profile in public life until the elections results were known in November 2015. A majority of them (thirteen or 45 per cent) come from private business sectors, while nine or 31 per cent of them worked in government. Seven of them (or 24 per cent) are farmers. While only one woman was elected in 2010, four women were elected for the NRAM in 2015. The role and significance of NRAMs will nonetheless be determined by the policy of the NLD given the centralized nature of the NLD party operation, and the overwhelming number of seats won by the NLD at the expense of USDP and minority ethnic political parties. For instance, the NLD has not only replaced the USDP as the party with the largest number of NRAMs in 2015, but also took away a few NRAM seats that were previously occupied by minority ethnic political parties (e.g., two seats occupied by Kayin People's Party in Bago and Yangon, and one seat occupied by Mon National Party in Kayin State). The number of NRAMs representing minority ethnic parties has been reduced from seven parties in 2010 (Rakhine, Chin, Mon, In thar, Kayin, Kayn, Shan) to five parties (mostly from Shan State, including Shan, Lisu, Ahkha, Lahu, TaiLai). The NLD's appointment and nomination of members minority ethnic groups (Chin, Shan, Kayin, Kachin) as presidential candidate or as Speakers or Deputy Speakers of the national parliament and its acknowledgement and formation of the Ministry of National Race Affairs have initially dispelled some concerns expressed by many minority ethnic leaders about ranking of ethnic issues in NLD's agenda, but the NLD has remained elusive on how much power and authority should be given to NRAMs, regional governments, and SAZs. Specifically, it is not yet clear how much the NLD government is willing to allow the NRAMs to exercise their authority and autonomy, and on which issues. Some observers and minority ethnic leaders are concerned that the nominations of a Karen as the Speaker, Kachin and Rakhine as Deputy Speakers of the national parliament, and a Chin as the Vice-President (2) may give the NLD a legitimate reason not to involve other ethnic leaders in the National Reconciliation and Peace Process anymore.

There is also a legitimate concern that some NRAMs will inevitably end up becoming "ineffective", focused on expanding their personal rights and privileges rather than protecting the rights of ethnic minorities. The lack of clearly defined roles and responsibilities for NRAMs also makes it easier for their respective governments to assign them responsibilities that do not have anything to do with their respective communities or for their constituents to have high and unrealistic expectations of them. Their positions also remain precarious and could potentially fuel inter-ethnic tension as they are based on arbitrarily drawn categories that are subject to contest.

In conclusion, while the newly created title of NRAM has the potential to enhance multicultural citizenship and a shared sense of common identity among Burma's ethnic nationalities by protecting and promoting the culture — and even survival — of ethnic minority groups, their position remains precarious given the lack of clearly defined roles and responsibilities and arbitrarily drawn categories upon which their position is based.

APPENDIX

TABLE 1
States and Regions in Myanmar

State/Region	Area in sq. km	Number of NRAMs
Shan	155,801.3	7
Kachin	89,041.8	4
Kayin	30,383.0	3
Mon	12,296.6	3
Sagaing	93704.8	2
Ayeyarwaddy	35,031.8	2
Yangon	10,276.7	2
Kayah	11,731.5	1
Rakhine	36,778.0	1
Magwe	44,820.6	1
Mandalay	37,945.7	1
Bago	39,402.3	1
Tanintharyi	44,344.9	1
Chin	36,018.8	0
Total		*29*

TABLE 2
NRAM Representation and Ethnic Group

Ethnic group	Number of NRAMs
Bamar	5
Kayin	5
Chin	3
Shan	3
Rakhine	2
Lisu	2
Pa-oh	2
Kachin	1
Rawan	1
Lahu	1
Kayan	1
Mon	1
Inn thar	1
Aka	1
Total	*29*

TABLE 3
Profiles of National Race Affairs Ministers

Name	Ethnicity represented	State/Region	Party	Date of Birth
Khin Maung Swe (2011–15)	Bamar	Kachin	USDP	30 March 1940
Khin Maung Myint (2015–)			NLD	5 February 1967
Gum Rein Dee (2011–15)	Rawan	Kachin	USDP	28 July 1950
U Yan Nam Pone (2015–)			NLD	12 March 1946
Khin Pyone Yee (2011–15)	Shan	Kachin	SNDP	18 July 1942
U Sai Sein Lin (2015–)			NLD	10 October 1958
Ah Si (2011–15) (2015–)	Lisu	Kachin	USDP	16 July 1957
Ah ti Yaw Han (2015–)			NLD	6 January 1977
Sein Oo (2011–15) (2015–)	Bamar	Kayah	USDP	21 September 1950
U Hla Myo Swe (2015–)			USDP	20 December 1967
Khin Kyuu (2011–15) (2015–)	Bamar	Kayin	USDP	8 March 1952
U Tayza Tut Hlaing Htwe (2015–)			NLD	7 September 1980
Khun Than Myint (2011–15)	Pao	Kayin	USDP	
U Khun Myoe Tint (2015–)			NLD	9 December 1965

Name	Ethnicity represented	State/Region	Party	Date of Birth
Naing Chit Oo (2011–15)	Mon	Kayin	Mon People's Party	6 December 1948
U Min Tin Win (2015–)			NLD	18 June 1945
Thet Win (2011–15)	Bamar	Mon	USDP	27 March 1949
U Shwe Myint (2015–)			NLD	24 February 1965
Khun Pe Mya (2011–15)	Pao	Mon	USDP	15 July 1948
Daw San Wint Khaing (2015–)			NLD	5 August 1947
Saw Aung Kyaw Thein (2011–15)	Kayin	Mon	USDP	7 March 1949
U Aung Myint Khaing (2015–)			NLD	5 February 1979
Salai Hla Tun (2011–15)	Chin	Magwe	NUP	
U Hla Tun (2015–)			NLD	25 July 1951
Sai Maung Hla (2011–15) (2015–)	Shan	Mandalay	USDP	1937
U Sai Kyaw Zaw (2015–)			SNLD	26 December 1950
Duwa Zuk Dung (2011–15)	Kachin	Shan	USDP	19 July 1942
Duwa Zuk Dung (2015–)			Independent	19 July 1942 (74)
Win Myint (2011–15)	Inn-thar	Shan	Inn-thar Party	15 January 1950
Dr Tun Hlaing (2015–)			NLD	1 September 1949

continued on next page

Name	Ethnicity represented	State/Region	Party	Date of Birth
Naing Win (2011–15)	Bamar	Shan	USDP	5 February 1944
Dr Aung Than Maung (2015–)			USDP	6 January 1952
Lawrence (2011–15)	Kayan	Shan	Kayan People's Party	
U Khun Aye Maung (2015–)			NLD	15 January 1979
Yaw Wi (2011–2015)	Lisu	Shan	USDP	27 August 1955
Gu Sar (2015–)			Lisu National Development Party	11 August 1966
Peter Thaung Sein (2011–15)	Ahkha	Shan	USDP	23 August 1958
U Ah Bay Hla (2015–)			Ahkah National Development Party	8 August 1955 (61)
Samuel Shan (2011–15)	Lahu	Shan	USDP	16 October 1958
Yaw Tha (2015)			Lahu National Development Party	5 July 1968
Ko Ko Naing (2011–15)	Chin	Rakhine	USDP	15 July 1968
U Bone Bwe (2015–)			NLD	4 January 1974
Jubilee San Hla (2011–015)	Kayin	Bago	Kayin People's Party	19 February 1937
Daw Naw Bwe Say (2015–)			NLD	
Saw Harvey (2011–15) (2015–)	Kayin	Tanintharyi	USDP	23 March 1946
Saw Luke (2015–)			NLD	30 March 1950

Name	Ethnicity represented	State/Region	Party	Date of Birth
U Saw Htun Aung Myint (2011–15)	Kayin	Yangon	Kayin People's Party	19 February 1942
Daw Pan Thinzar Myoe (2015–)			NLD	5 July 1979
U Zaw Aye Maung (2011–15) (2015–)	Rakhine	Yangon	RNDP	2 September 1959
Noh Than Kup (2011–15)	Chin	Sagaing	CPP	30 August 1955
U Lal Taung Thang (2015–)			NLD	22 June 1952
San Shwe (2011–15)	Shan	Sagaing	USDP	
Daw Mwe Mwe Khin (2015–)			Talaing National Development Party	22 December 1962
Mann Than Shwe (2011–2015)	Kayin	Ayeyarwaddy	USDP	11 December 1937
Daw Moe Mya Mya Thu (2015–)			NLD	11 August 1949
Ba Kyuu (2011–15)	Rakhine	Ayeyarwaddy	USDP	15 March 1951
U Tin Saw (2015–)			NLD	27 May 1950

Notes

1. Funding for this project is supported by the United States Institute for Peace.
2. See, for instance, Hamish Nixon, Cindy Joelene, Thet Aung Lynn, Kyi Pyar Chit Saw and Matthew Arnold. *State and Region Government in Myanmar* (Yangon: The Asia Foundation and Myanmar Development Research Institute – Centre for Economic and Social Development, 2013); and Thet Aung Lynn and Mari Oye *Natural Resources and Subnational Governments in Myanmar: Key considerations for wealth sharing* (Yangon: The Asia Foundation, International Growth Centre, and Myanmar Development Research Institute – Centre for Economic and Social Development, 2014).
3. Minority rights applied to members of racial, ethnic, religious, linguistic or gender and sexual minorities. Different countries however have different policies on what constitutes "minority rights". See, for instance, Will Kymlicka (2015). The EU recognized minority rights has found article 2 of the Treaty on European Union, but it has been criticized for failing to adhere to its commitment to protecting minority rights. See Barten (2016).
4. See, for instance, Trudeau (1992, 2011).
5. Constitution of the Republic of the Union of Myanmar 2008, Ministry of Information.
6. Yegar (2002) notes that associate citizenship is granted to the offspring of mixed marriages between ethnic Burmans and members of immigrant communities, and to the spouses of ethnic Burmans. It also applies to anyone who had lived in Burma for five consecutive years, or for eight out of ten years preceding 1942 or before independence in 1948. To obtain associate citizenship, the application must be pending on the date the 1948 Act came into force.
7 Yegar (2002) notes that a third category, "naturalized citizenship", is generally reserved for members of immigrant communities who can furnish "conclusive evidence" of entry and residence before Burma's independence on 4 January 1948, who are fluent in one of the national languages, and whose children were born in Burma.
8. Karen are spread throughout the Yangon, Ayeyarwaddy, Tanintharyi, and Bago Regions, as well as Mon State, see, for example, Thawnghmung (2012).
9. Section 161(b) of the Constitution mentions that "Representatives of the Region Huttaw, each is elected from each national race determined by the authorities concerned as having a population which constitutes 0.1 per cent and above of the population of the Union, of the remaining national races other than those who have already obtained the respective Region or a Self-administered Area in the Region". Constitution of the Republic of the Union of Myanmar, Ministry of Information, English version, 58. The figure of 51,500 is derived from 0.1 per cent of the 51.5 million population of Myanmar in the 2014 Population and Housing Census (TNI 2015, p. 7).
10. These new entities are given legislative rights as long as they are do not conflict

with Union and state laws. In principle, they enjoy comparable powers of jurisdiction and limited autonomy. In practice, these groups enjoy a wide variety of power and authority, ranging from the fiercely independent Wa (who control the second largest armed forces in Myanmar, and operate like a state in two of its regions) to the KoKaung (which has recently been fighting the Bamar military) to the Pao, who have done relatively well in preserving their own identity and culture, to the compliant Danu.

11. See note 9.
12. This summary is based on the second author's extensive role in coordinating, organizing, and facilitating activities conducted by the NRAMs.
13. The Law of Emoluments, Allowances and Insignia of Office for Representatives of the Region or State (Notification No. 3/2011 of the State Peace and Development Council) sets out the rights of ministers of a region or state.
14. Information based on the second author's extensive engagement with NRAMs, July 2015.
15. For more information about the teaching of ethnic minority languages in areas populated by minority groups, see, e.g., South and Lall (2016).
16. Pyidaungsu Hluttaw Law No. 8/2015, 24 February 2015, "Law protecting the rights of 'Taing Yin Thar'."
17. Interview with No Than Kap, "We Desperately Need an Ethnic Affairs Ministry", in *Dateline Irrawaddy*, 12 March 2016 <http://www.irrawaddy.com/factiva/dateline-irrawaddy-desperately-need-ethnic-affairs-ministry.html>.
18. Ibid.
19. See, e.g., Martov (2012), and Karen Human Rights Group, "With only our voices, what can we do? Land confiscation and local response in southeast Myanmar". 2015 <http://khrg.org/2015/06/with-only-our-voices-what-can-we-do-land-confiscation-and-local-response#sthash.DYrrZffz.dpuf>.
20. Taing Day Tha Kyi thot a hote Pyi Nei Asoe Ya Upade, Union Of Myanmar, SPDC, in Burmese.
21. The survey was undertaken on 9 August 2015 during a workshop for NRAMs and administered by the second author. All twelve of NRAMs who attended the workshop participated in focus group discussion, but only eight voluntarily took part in additional survey. All these eight participants in survey — representing Rakhine, Kayin (2), Bamar, Kayan, Shan, Lisu, and Pao minorities — were fully aware of the purpose of the survey.
22. Interview with a Mon regional MP, June 2015. Quite a few people we have talked to offered various explanations for this reduced stipend. Some, such as Naga in Sagaing, said they never received such compensation despite their repeated attempts to meet with regional authorities, while others said the initial budget that was allocated to them was based on the estimated number of teachers, but the amount allotted to individual teachers was reduced because there were more teachers than they previously estimated.
23. First author's conversation with an NRAM in Bago, and with Karen community leaders in Bago, July 2015.

24. The latter view was advocated by a senior official from the Office of the President, as well by as the second author who has worked closely with the ministers.

25. The Union Government has already instructed regional governments to promote the celebration of their respective National Days. However, this does not imply that individual NRAMs have been allocated budgets for this purpose — this remains a decision for the chief minister of the region or state. For example, although Yangon's chief minister has allocated a modest budget for Rakhine Day, he has organized in-kind support from other departments involved.

26. His re-election also reflects the success of ANP which is the only ethnic political party that has successfully merged two rival parties that were vying for the same constituency due mainly to the perceived threat posed by Muslims in the region.

27. There are sub-dialects as well as different types of writing language systems within the subgroups of Kayin. Some Sgaw Kayin Christian for instance use Myanmar scripts invented by missionaries, while others in the border areas have used Roman letters. Pwo Kayin Christian used Myanmar scripts whereas Pwo Kayin Buddhist use Mon scripts for their writing.

28. For instance, Kayan leaders have advocated for the formation of a SAZ for the Kayan minority across Kayah and Shan States (Zaw 2015).

29. These groups and subgroups are: Jing Hpaw (Jing Hpaw, Goree, Khat Khu, Durin); Lao Vao (Ma-u); La Chyik (La Shi); Rawang (Htro, Hta Laung, Rawang); Li Su (Lawrang, Lisu); and Zai Wa (Azi).

References

Andersen, Kirsten Ewers. "Analysis of Customary Communal Tenure of Upland Ethnic Groups, Myanmar". Paper submitted to International Conference on Burma/Myanmar Studies, Chiang Mai, Thailand, 24–26 July 2015.

Barten, Ulrike. "The EU's Lack of Commitment to Minority Protection". *Journal on Ethnopolitics and Minority Issues in Europe* 15, no. 2 (2016): 104–23.

Bertrand, Jacques. *Nationalism and Ethnic Conflicts in Indonesia*. Cambridge: Cambridge University Press, 2009.

Kymlicka, W. *Multicultural Citizenship: A Liberal Theory of Minority Rights*. Oxford: Clarendon Press, 1995.

———. "Multiculturalism and Minority Rights: West and East". *Journal on Ethnopolitics and Minority Issues in Europe* 14, no. 4 (2015): 4–25.

Lee Hock Guan. "Affirmative action in Malaysia". In *Southeast Asian Affairs 2005*, edited by Chin Kin Wah and Daljit Singh, pp. 211–28. Singapore: Institute of Southeast Asian Studies, 2005.

Martov, Seamus. "World's Largest Tiger Reserve 'Bereft of Cats'". *The Irrawaddy*, 16 November 2012 <http://www.irrawaddy.org/z_environment/worlds-largest-tiger-reserve-bereft-of-cats.html> (accessed 25 May 2016).

McCargo, Duncan. *Tearing Apart the Land*. Ithaca: Cornell University Press, 2008.

Robinson, Gwen. "Myanmar parliament moves against judges". *Financial Times*, 6 September 2012.

Silverstein, Josef. *Burmese Politics: The Dilemma of National Unity*. New Brunswick and New Jersey: Rutgers University Press, 1980.

South, Ashley and Marie Lall. *Schooling and Conflict: Ethnic Education and Mother Tongue-based Teaching in Myanmar*. USAID/Asian Foundation, 2016 <http://asiafoundation.org/resources/pdfs/SchoolingConflictENG.pdf> (accessed 25 May 2016).

Taylor, Charles. "The Politics of Recognition". In *Multiculturalism: Examining the Politics of Recognition*, edited by A. Gutmann. Princeton, NJ: Princeton University Press, 1992.

Thawnghmung, Ardeth. *The Other Karen. Ethnic Minorities and the Struggle without Arms*. Lanham: Lexington Books, 2012.

Torbisco-Casals, Neus. "Multiculturalism, Identity Claims, and Human Rights: From Politics to Courts". *Law & Ethics of Human Rights* 10, no. 2 (2016): 367–404.

Transnational Institute. "Ethnicity without Meaning, Data without Context". *Burma Policy Briefing* 13. Washington, D.C.: Transnational Institute, 2014.

———. "The 2015 General Election in Myanmar: What Now for Ethnic Politics". *Myanmar Policy Briefing* 17. Washington, D.C.: Transnational Institute, 2015.

Trudeau, P.E. "The Values of a Just Society". In *Towards a Just Society*, edited by Thomas Axworthy and Pierre Elliot Trudeau. Toronto: Viking Press, 1992.

———. "Me, myself and them". *The Economist*, 12 May 2011.

Yegar, Moshe. *Between Integration and Secession: The Muslim Communities of the Southern Philippines, Southern Thailand and Western Burma/Myanmar*. Lanham: Lexington Books, 2002.

Young, Iris Marion. *Justice and the Politics of Difference*. Princeton, NJ: Princeton University Press, 1990.

Zaw, Maung. "Kayan Leaders Push for Autonomy". *Myanmar Times*, 22 April 2015 <http://www.mmtimes.com/index.php/national-news/14054-kayan-leaders-push-for-autonomy.html> (accessed 25 May 2016).

KARENNI PEOPLE AT A GLANCE

Khu Oo Reh
Vice-Chairman, Karenni National Progressive Party

National identity can be complex in Myanmar due in part to the large number of ethnic groups in the country. Estimates vary, although official sources at various times have listed over 100 diverse groups having distinctive beliefs, customs and language. Members of ethnic groups generally have a strong affiliation to their group, especially so given the history of conflict between a number of major ethnic groups and the central government in modern Myanmar. As the restoration of democracy and the resolution of conflicts proceeds, Myanmar "citizenship" may best be viewed as a layered personal experience, involving both an ethnic and national identity. Some of the larger groups to that are well known are the Chin, Kachin, Shan, Mon, Karen — and the one of concern here, the Karenni.

ORIGINS OF THE KARENNI PEOPLE AND STATE

The Karenni people (also known at times as "Red Karen") are believed to have descended from the Mongolian plateau at a time of food scarcity in the Gobi Desert, and as a result of oppression from other ethnic groups living in Mongolia. The Karenni gradually moved downward along the Yellow River and briefly settled in what today is the Chinese state of Yunnan. They continued moving down along Salween River and finally settled in Dee Maw Soe in 739 BCE (although some historians claim it was not until the early

800s CE). Where the Karenni live today is known as Kayah — formerly called Red Karen or Karenni.

Not long after having established their own Karenni nation, Yeun troops from the north attacked a number of times, finally overcoming them and establishing control of the area for almost a hundred years. During this time of being ruled by the Yeun king, Karenni people were treated as slaves, forced to work their own paddy fields for the benefit of the Yeun king, and taxed unfairly.

Finally, the Karenni people could no longer tolerate the Yeun king's oppression and taxation, and revolted. They collected all available arms, and began a war to expel the Yeun troops. One story from this time concerns the importance of "sticky rice". The Karenni females who were left behind cooked and packed rice with leaves to be sent to the frontline as the main ration for troops in the battlefield. But the packed-rice did not last long in the hot climate, often rotting in one day, which slowed attempts to advance. So they developed an alternative. They cooked the sticky rice and packed it with broom tree leaves, putting three or four pieces together for each fighter. Some were cooked and dried in the sun then flattened to be used as a dry ration. This sticky rice ration lasted much longer, so Karenni fighters were able to advance in their drive to expel Yeun troops.

Finally, the Karenni people drove the Yeun troops from Karenni nation, and were governed by their own chieftains for several centuries. The Karenni subsequently maintained their independence, even during the British colonial era. In fact, the British government's representative and the Burmese king's representative signed an agreement on 21 June 1875 in recognition of Karenni independence during the time of British rule in Burma. It was not until after independence in 1948 that Karenni was taken over by the Burmese government.

THE ORIGIN AND MEANING OF THE DEEKU (STICKY RICE) FESTIVAL OF KARENNI PEOPLES

Following from their victory over the Yeun, Karenni people were grateful for the part that sticky rice had not only in victory over the Yeun, but in unifying the Karenni. From that time on until today, Karenni people celebrate the Deeku (sticky rice) festival once a year, in August or September. They invite all their brothers and sisters near and far to come together to show their unity as a people. The Deeku festival also has another meaning for Karenni people, being a time to pray for to good weather and fruitful crops in the coming year. There is another ancient festival that Karenni people celebrate in March or April each year — the Pole (*Kay Htoe Boe*) Festival. In this festival, the Karenni people erect a pole around which they dance and sing in order to protect their health.

An interesting fact of Karenni culture concerns how the dates for these festivals are chosen, as there is no specific date for either the Pole and Deeku festivals. According to tradition, a rooster's inner leg bone is read to choose the best date — this leg bone sometimes can also reveal whether the year will bring good or bad luck. Reading the rooster's bone can be done only by honest and knowledgeable people who have had considerable practice in this art.

MODERN ERA KARENNI STATE

Modern Karenni State is bordered by Shan State in the north, Karen State in the south and Thailand to the east, with a total area of 4,582 square miles. This is much smaller than the original boundaries before the British demarcation process took place in the days of British colonization. Loikaw, or Thiridaw as it is known by locals, is the capital city located in the northern part of State. It is divided into seven townships: Loikaw, Shadaw, Deemawsoe, Prusoe, Bawlake, Pasaung, and Mae Se. The inhabitants of Karenni are the Kayah, Kayan, Kayaw, Paku Karen, Yintale, Yinbaw, Manu Manaw, Geko, Geba (the original ethnic subgroups), as well as people from neighbouring ethnic groups (such as Shan, Pa-O, Mon and Intha) who have gradually migrated into and settled in Karenni.

THE HISTORY AND ROLE OF THE
KARENNI NATIONAL PROGRESSIVE PARTY

A unit of the first newly formed Burmese government's Union Military Police (UMP) under Prime Minister U Nu, with the help of local men, sneaked into Karenni and attacked the United Karenni State Independent Council (UKSIC) headquarters office in Mya Leh early in the morning of 9 August 1948. Gobi Turee, who was chairman of the council, narrowly escaped the attack with a few bodyguards and took refuge in Pruso, under the care of Sawphya Saw Swe, the last chief of Kyehbogyi sub-state, in the evening of that day.

As a result of that day, thousands of young men across the Karenni State gathered and formed the United Karenni State Independence Army (UKSIA) on 17th of the same month. From then, Karenni people engaged in war with the Burmese governments' troops (*Tatmadaw*) to regain independence. As it became apparent that the struggle was likely to continue for some years, Karenni leaders realized that there was a need for political as well as military leadership. So a congress was convened on 2 May 1957 which led to the formation of the Karenni National Progressive Party (KNPP) as the foremost political party in Karenni. This party developed political goals, objectives and policies as part of the struggle to regain independence. The KNPP engaged in ceasefire talks with former Burmese military regimes, for the first time in 1963 and then in 1995 with military coups' leaders. Both attempts at a ceasefire failed.

The KNPP has been a member of several ethnic armed alliances from the beginning of its armed struggle, including the National Democratic Front (NDF). Now the KNPP is a member of the United Nationalities Federal Council (UNFC), working together with both ethnic armed groups and democratic alliances in order to build a genuine federal union in Burma. Based on the changing political dynamic, in early 2000 the KNPP's leadership changed their political position from regaining independence to forming a federal system together with all other ethnic groups in the hope of a better future for Burma. Following talks with the government of U Thein Sein, the KNPP signed an initial ceasefire agreement at the state level on 7 March 2012 and then again in June at the union level with the aim to engage in a political dialogue together with other ethnic armed organizations to build up a federal union based on democracy, equality and internal self-determination.

THE NEED FOR ETHNIC PEOPLE TO BUILD TRUST, MUTUAL UNDERSTANDING AND UNITY AMONG THEMSELVES UNDER A FEDERAL UNION

The different ethnic groups residing in Burma emigrated from various locations and settled in what is now known as Burma long before the creation of the country itself. Historical records show that most of the non-Burman groups were some of the earliest settlers. The Mon, Arakanese, Chin, Karen, Karenni, Kachin and Shan settled in this land with their own kingdoms and governments independently before the arrival of the Burman ethnic group.

These groups had varying experiences during the British colonial era, with some subject to British rule while others maintained independence within their own territories. Following the dismantling of the British empire following World War II, visionary leaders from the Chin, Kachin, and Shan worked together towards independence and the establishment of a federal union of Burma by signing the Panglong Agreement.

Burma finally gained its independence on 4 January 1948 as a result of the collective efforts of many. Therefore, Burma belongs not only to the Burman ethnic group, but equally and collectively to all the various ethnic groups. Simply because the Burman happen to be the largest ethnic group does not mean they are the owners of the country, despite successive governments since independence that were dominated by the Burman depicting Burma as if it belongs exclusively to the Burman people. This is the type of thinking that led the country to a civil war immediately after independence.

In light of this troublesome history, as we try to end armed conflicts and make peace for an equal and just society, the newly elected government led by the National League for Democracy (NLD) must create opportunity and venues (such as Ethnic Forums or Public Forums or People's Forums) where all ethnic groups — including the Burmans — can come together and exchange experiences, perspectives, and historical knowledge. If we can build an open society through such forums, we will be able to garner mutual understanding, trust, and forgiveness. Consequently, our hope is that in a few years the current peace process will lead to a peaceful federal union, and set our country on the path to full development.

5

MYANMAR'S YOUTH AND THE QUESTION OF CITIZENSHIP

Marie Lall

At its most basic the definition of citizenship is the rights and responsibilities that people have within a nation state. "Citizenship establishes the boundaries of the political community. It establishes that which is public and that which is private. It also tells us who is in and who is outside of the political community." (Kivisto and Faist 2007, p. 13). Citizenship therefore denotes the membership to a polity — in this case a particular state and the membership involves a reciprocal set of rights and duties, sometimes described as a social contract. Generally politically motivated classes or elites decide who can access these rights, working in tandem with the state that has the monopoly on dictating who is in and out. As the introduction and other chapters discuss, there are other elements that are part of citizenship as well — they include identity, participation (see chapter by Walton in this volume) and an element of "moral citizenship" that includes working for the good of society that is expanded upon by McCarthy in Chapter 6. This chapter however focuses much on rights and responsibilities and how these relate to issues of belonging and identity.

Legal citizenship in Myanmar under military rule, as described in the Introduction, has always been defined from above. The 1982 Citizenship Act set out who was a Myanmar national, even if before the 2008 Constitution other rights and responsibilities were rather elusive. How the changes of citizenship were viewed by young people in light of political participation in the 2010 elections has been discussed elsewhere (Lall and Win 2013) This chapter seeks to elucidate views from below — specifically how young people across Myanmar define citizenship in light of the reforms and changes between 2011 and 2015. While few of the conclusions drawn from the survey would provide any great surprises, the aim of the chapter is to allow the voices of the young people who are experiencing the transition to express how they defined their relationship with the state and what underpinned their feelings of belonging in their own words. Beyond being legal citizens of the Myanmar state, how did they define their rights and responsibilities, how did this relate to their identity and what did they feel was important when defining citizenship as their country transitions from a military dictatorship to a more participatory system. In quite a number of cases the themes and issues raised in the quotes reflect and give further credence to what is discussed across this volume.

The research was conducted between 2012 and 2013 using a mixed methods questionnaire that was administered to respondents in seven states (Mon, Karen, Kayah, Shan, Kachin, Chin and Rakhine States) and four regions (Yangon, Bago, Mandalay, Sagain Region) in urban, rural and semi-urban settings.[1] In order to access a significant number of people from across the country, a survey approach was chosen. The survey not only ensured broader participation, but also allowed for greater anonymity. Of the 2007 surveys that were returned (out of 2,050) 47 per cent of the respondents were women and 53 per cent were men. Over 40 per cent were between 18 and 25 and another 22 per cent were under 35. Given that Myanmar is a young nation[2] it is important to prioritize the views of those under 25, as they will be taking the country forward. 60 per cent of the respondents self-identified as Buddhist and 25 per cent as Christian.[3] The occupational breakdown shows that a majority of respondents would be categorized as middle class or lower middle class. Many had their own business or were employed. The third largest category was students. The ethnic breakdown of the sample deliberately included a majority of ethnic groups.[4] The sample was not chosen so as to be representative of the majority Bamar population, but included substantial numbers of all the major ethnic groups so as to be able to have reasonable numbers of each group and be able to represent their views. 24 per cent self-identified as Bamar, 17 per cent as Shan, 12 per cent as Karen, 11 per cent as Chin, 9 per cent as Rakhine, 4 per cent as Mon and Kachin, and 1 per cent as Kayah. 8 per cent self-identified as Mixed and 10 per cent as "Other". The overall research results elucidated views on a large number of issues pertaining to citizenship. However, this chapter explores in more detail the issues pertaining to equality between ethnic groups, nationalism and the role of religion that seems to have become a major issue since 2011, framing this through the lens of Myanmar's education system. The chapter ends with a discussion on the challenges that emerge from this for the government led by the National League for Democracy (NLD) that was elected after the survey was conducted.

CITIZENSHIP IN MYANMAR: RIGHTS, RESPONSIBILITIES AND POLITICAL PARTICIPATION

In Myanmar, citizenship as "status" (Joppke 2007; Kivisto and Faist 2007) existed throughout the time of military rule, as people carried ID cards and could apply for passports. They were, in effect, recognized as citizens by the state. Myanmar nationals resident abroad could secure continued recognition by the state by paying a certain percentage of tax on their foreign income. However, rights — including political participation and access to a "political life" were largely non-existent for most of the years since Ne Win's coup in 1962. The "social contract" was not part and parcel of Myanmar's citizenship at least until 2011 and arguably even beyond.

There has been so much active avoidance of politics over decades that today, even after the 2015 elections, political literacy remains very low.[5] Even though people were very aware of politics, they saw it as dangerous (Kyaw 2007). The crushing of the 1988 uprising created a state of fear, which meant that ordinary citizens preferred to avoid political processes. Consequently there has been little experience with harnessing a multi-party political system for the citizens' advantage and no tradition of holding the government to account. Parts of Myanmar society — such as the Sangha (monkhood) and other religious leaders have been constitutionally excluded from political participation as they are not allowed to vote or stand for elections.[6] Given that most "non-formal" education is provided in monastic schools and that religious leaders of all faiths are seen as pillars of society, it further distances society from political processes.

Traditionally most civil society organizations (CSOs) and non-governmental organizationa (NGOs) have been involved primarily in development work, staying well clear of politics. However prior to the 2010 elections a small number of CSOs started to become actively involved in advocacy and political awareness building as well as basic citizens education.

These CSOs based in the urban centres started to offer courses in voter education, on the content of the Constitution and other election and political related fields so as to try and prepare the wider population for some form of political participation. These were the first steps towards making parts of the (mainly urban and adult) population more conscious of rights, responsibilities and political processes. Individuals were to be empowered to use the limited system which they were being offered and a limited first step towards some form of political literacy that most citizens had not been able to develop. This process has continued to develop. The desire of participation in the political dialogue by CSOs (see chapter by Walton in this volume), as well as increasing "moral citizenship" by young people (as discussed by McCarthy in this volume), complement the contemporary picture of Myanmar citizenship. However it is important to remember that the survey was conducted only 15 months after the 2010 elections, and therefore reflects the views held at that time.

After the 2010 elections the ethnic political parties became the first legitimate opposition in the Union Solidarity and Development Party (USDP) dominated parliaments. Between 2011 and 2015 their role and significance changed as their work in the regional parliaments started to influence policy-making with regard to education and ethnic language use, as well as triggering debates on resource sharing. The concept of the "opposition" was widened as the NLD rejoined the political fold after the 2012 by-elections. Since then membership of a political party is no longer seen as dangerous. Parliamentary debates have been dealing with issues pertaining to rights such as land grabbing, the right for peaceful demonstrations, the right to free speech and press freedom, etc., as well as citizens' responsibilities. The 2015 elections, where over ninety parties contested, brought the first civilian NLD-dominated government to power and with it, the first civilian president, and Daw Aung San Suu Kyi as State Counsellor, the *de facto* head of state. However despite this rapid development towards a more participatory system, political literacy remains low, and therefore people's participation in elections alone do not guarantee the development of a social contract nor an understanding of the concept of citizenship.

Crick develops the concept of political literacy that is imparted through education but is "more than a school educational subject" (Crick 2000, p. 110). He describes political literacy as a combination of knowledge, skills and attitudes, developing alongside each other, each one enforcing the other two. Davies (2008) also believes there are reasons why political literacy should be promoted: "Politics has to connect with young people: it must be taught and learned in ways that are congruent with the essential nature of political education…" (Davies 2008, p. 381). Both agree that society cannot develop a concept of citizenship and a social contract unless this is formally taught. But in Myanmar to date, formal state education has not imparted much with regard to the elements of citizenship, focusing rather on duties and nationalism to support a militarized state (Lall and Win 2013).

THE ROLE OF EDUCATION

In that sense Myanmar is not an unusual case. Education is often used as a tool by the state to inculcate the "state's ideology" in the masses. This is particularly the case with the construction of national identity (Lall and Vickers 2009). However beyond this, education in general and the school curriculum in particular also play a vital role in shaping the concept of citizenship and the role of the state in the minds of people. Kaltsounis and Osborne are of the view that social studies education underpins the understanding of citizenship (Kaltsounis 1994; Osborne 1997). The skills acquired through a curriculum are necessary for "informed participation in a democracy" (Dean 2007). The concepts which Dean refers to include the notions of rights, responsibilities, and political participation, which go beyond the construction of national identity and refer to a "social contract" with corresponding institutional structures that are recognized by society and whose functions are understood. Democracy demands active political participation from citizens and as Crick (2000) explained, political literacy has to be learnt.

In light of the fact that the 2015 elections were the first truly free elections with the NLD participating, it is pertinent to ask what sources of political knowledge were available to voters and what has been the role of the education system in fostering knowledge of political concepts such as citizenship. People living in urban and border areas have been exposed to, and influenced by the globalization process. They have relatively easy access to global news through media and the Internet. However, two-thirds of the Myanmar population live in rural areas where there is limited or no access to those sources. Therefore, the only common source of political knowledge for both the urban and rural population has been through formal basic education provided by the government. Whilst the government between 2011 and 2015 engendered a review and reform process in education, the curriculum itself was not changed before the 2015 elections (Lall 2016).

Given Myanmar's history of military dictatorship, and despite the 2008 Constitution and the 2010 elections, the textbooks do not have notions of rights or of political participation. Salem-Gervais and Metro (2012) have documented how Myanmar's military regime used history textbooks to underpin a Bamar version of state ideology. Current school textbooks reflect and describe the political situation of the last decades. Only the history textbook used for the most senior high school levels include an update of the Myanmar political situation up to the State Peace and Development Council (SPDC) era. Most textbooks were written during the period of the socialist government, with nominal updates. They were purposely created for the working class and promoted social, cultural and national integration and unity. There is little if anything on ethnic diversity as this was considered divisive. The concept of citizenship they present is, therefore one of loyalty to the state and for citizens to be trained to contribute to "nation building" (Aye and Kyi 1998).

Myanmar's literature textbooks throughout all grades are a good guide of the way citizens' thinking is framed because this is a common subject that teaches culture, history and art, which is studied by all students.[7] Instead of citizenship volunteerism is promoted and the books emphasize the importance of socially and morally responsible citizens who are active in community participation. For example, the grade 11 Myanmar literature textbook, describes a strong civil society led by youths promoting the welfare of Burma in the East Asia Youth League (EAYL) led by President U Ba Gyan, who later became Cabinet Minister in 1948. Youth leadership in community service activities is also described as a part of the social activities of the People's Volunteer Organization and EAYL.

Patriotism is another big theme throughout the curriculum. The "Our Blood" poem is taught at grade 7 and aims to condition students to love the country and to be ready to fight against any intruders. The poem goes, "run away evils, don't dare to test our blood, we will defeat any rebels." This is supported by essays and poems written in the colonial period (among them Maung Hmaing aka Thakhin Ko Taw Hmaing's essays and poems and U Ba Gyan's cartoons[8]) that address the poverty issues of those in rural areas and how they are due to exploitation of the colonial government.

The textbooks also advocate militarism by glorifying the times of the Burmese kingdoms across the curriculum. For example, in the grade 11 textbook, the importance of the military is underlined with a quote by a Prince of the Kong Baung dynasty saying, "a country without military is like a person with no legs, it cannot protect itself nor fight back if others invade or insult." Texts promote the idea of joining the military as devotion to the country; and getting prepared to defend the country is a way of showing love for the country. In grade 5 a poem titled "Bamar's son" depicts a mother bragging about her son who is playing with a sword in his young age. She believes he is brave and will one day become a good solider to protect the country.

Given this approach in school, it came as little surprise that when the respondents were asked to describe their country, one of the most prominent cross-cutting themes expressed by the young people across the survey was that of patriotism, nationalism, often linked to culture, religion and sometimes to language. The issue of braveness, strength, protecting culture and/or traditions, came up throughout answers as can be seen below:

> "Myanmar is Buddhist and patriotic." (Bamar, Buddhist, Yangon region)
> "The generation who are quick, brave and strong." (Bamar, Buddhist, Yangon region)
> "All of the Myanmar citizens need to be patriotic spirit. Myanmar citizens must love our culture, country, nation." (Bamar, Buddhist, Mon State)
> "Myanmar means a person who is strong in patriotism and loves his own tradition." (Kayin, Christian, Bago region)
> "Myan means 'easy to be successful in difficult situations'. Mar means 'to get patriotism from everything'. Myanmar people are patriotic and polite with courage and patriotic, brave, honest, empathy, innocent and patriotic." (PaO, Buddhist, Shan State)

The quotes above represent more than simply love for the country and seem to reflect almost a martial tradition, a pride of history, and it was not surprising to find the names of ancient kings mentioned almost as role-models, as reflected in the history lessons:

> "Myanmar country means King Anawyahtar, Kyansisthar, Bayinnoung, Alawngpayar, Banduula have managed our kingdom. We try to keep our traditions and culture all over the world...." (Chin, Christian, Shan State)

In some cases some anti-foreign views were also expressed:

> "Some foreigners moved and resided in some regions of Myanmar. Then, they condensed their population and tried to hold national registration card. If that matter disturb the food, clothing and shelter of our citizens, we must take action against them." (Bamar, Buddhist, Karen State)

These were rare in the this part of the questionnaire, but there were more angry quotes reflecting views on Muslims and the issues in Rakhine State in other parts of the survey as shall be seen later in this chapter.

As well as glowing national pride, politeness was also often emphasized:

> "Polite and smart." (Kachin, Buddhist, Yangon region)
> "Myanmar people are patriotic and polite with courage and patriotism, brave, honest, empathy, innocence and patriotic. All of the Myanmar people follow Buddha's role and are doing well ..." (Rakhine, Buddhist, Rakhine State)

The interesting thing was that these answers emphasizing honour, patriotism and braveness were not limited to Bamar respondents, but also had a number of ethnic representatives who were Buddhist. These kind of statements were remarkably absent from the Kayah, Chin and Kachin samples.

In part, what is taught reflects the traditional cultural and Buddhist trait that being obedient to elders is being polite and that individual opinions need to be demoted in light of what elders or leaders believe.[9] The social hierarchy has to date been reflected in the political and religious culture of the country (also discussed in the chapter by McCarthy in this volume).

When asked about citizenship the role of Buddhism was another prominent theme across the answers given by the young people.[10] The questionnaires had deliberately not asked about religion, so as not to prompt respondents. In one of his speeches, President Thein Sein had mentioned that four major religions including Islam were protected in the Constitution and discrimination against religion and ethnicity would not be accepted in Myanmar.[11] However a very large number of respondents within the Buddhist ethnic groups, i.e., not only Bamar respondents, equated citizenship with religion, or seemed to think that in order to be Myanmar one has to also be Buddhist:[12]

> "Myanmar are Buddhist and have unity." (Bamar, Buddhist, Yangon region)
> "I think Myanmar is better than every countries because there is Buddhism and peace." (Bamar, religion not given, Yangon region)
> "Believing in Buddhist religion, take care of nationality, helping other and having good will." (Bamar, Buddhist, Mon State)
> "Myanmar — believing in Buddhist religion and devout in religion." (Mixed, Muslim, Mon State)
> "I am Buddhist, so I am Myanmar." (Bamar, Buddhist, Mon State)
> "Myanmar is living with Buddha's philosophy." (race missing, religion not given, Sagain region)
> (Myanmar is) "The person who is Buddhist." (Rohingya, Muslim, Rakhine State)

Below was one of the very few quotes that spoke about other religions still being able to be a part of national unity. The freedom of religion mentioned in the president's speech quoted earlier, does not seem to be part of the national consciousness of these respondents:

> "Almost all of Myanmar people's religious are Buddhist and must believe in Buddha's dharma. Myanmar people are polite, kind and hospitable with courage and patriotism, honest, empathic, innocent. Different religions amongst many of the nation races compound as a oneness between each other." (Chin, Buddhist, Chin State)

The responses in Rakhine State were generally even fiercer than those from other Buddhist communities, reflecting the recent riots and communal tensions between Muslims and Buddhists. These quotes reflect the discussions in the three chapters on Rakhine State in this volume by Leider, Tonkin and Nurul Islam:

> "Myanmar and Rakhine are not same. Rakhine always keep their promise but Myanmar are not faithful. Some Myanmar married Muslims but Rakhine don't." (Rakhine, Buddhist, Rakhine State)
> "Rakhine people who is Buddhist are Myanmar." (Rakhine, Buddhist, Rakhine State)
> "The people who is Buddhist, having own culture, not killing another one and polite, are Myanmar." (Rakhine, Buddhist, Rakhine State)

The quotes about patriotism and the ones on the role of Buddhism point to the fact that there is a rise of religious nationalism that could find its way into politics through the debates about citizenship and stand in sharp contrast to Myanmar's multi-ethnic heritage.[13] However the various ethnic identities were never given any prominence across the education system. Many essays, stories and poems across the textbooks endorse the "Unity is Strength" idea that counter internal differences and do not allow separate ethnic identities to emerge. In the grade 10 textbook an essay entitled "Union and Myanmar" explains how the Myanmar nation has been united since the Bagan dynasty and that loyalty requires all ethnic groups to remain united. The same idea is reflected in an essay that explains that a piece of firewood can be broken easily but that a bundle of firewood cannot be broken. It is understood that when all ethnic groups are united, no one can invade the country. The idea of unity across all ethnic groups is underpinned by little information on the culture of other ethnic groups, making this a very Bamar-dominated curriculum.[14]

The focus on unity and the fear of others possibly "invading" the country explains a third set of quotes in the survey that emphasizes the right to reside in the country. Given that Myanmar citizens had few rights in the Western sense of the word, these quotes show particularly interesting positions. Whilst this issue may be more prominent now due to the issues surrounding the Rohingya (see chapters by Tonkin, Leider and Nurul Islam in this volume) demands to be given this right, it clearly predates the riots and has been reflected not only in the citizenship legislation but also in the anti-Indian and anti-Chinese movements (1967) in the past. Colonial history with the British allowing immigration from India is partly to blame, but today there is a consciousness across the country that Myanmar is sandwiched between

very overpopulated neighbours — India, Bangladesh and China. So, linked
to patriotism, religion and pride of the country, the youth quotes now add
ethnic descent or bloodlines to the debates on citizenship:

> "A man resides in Myanmar but we can't say that man is a Myanmar."
> (Rakhine, Buddhist, Rakhine State)

This issue was mentioned across different questions, yet came up mostly
when asked what the respondents understood about citizens' rights and
responsibilities. It is an issue that transcended ethnicity and was represented
across all groups and in all states:

> "The right to belong to my country and the duty is to have patriotism
> and responsible for the duty given by the country." (Bamar, Buddhist,
> Yangon region)
> "Right: want to live peacefully and freedom to reside. Duty: must attack
> aggressors." (Mon Buddhist, Mon State)
> "Citizens have the right to go and reside in Myanmar freely." (Bamar,
> Buddhist, Mon State)
> "A citizen has the right to reside in Myanmar and to do own job. A citizen
> must obey the law of Myanmar." (Karen, Buddhist, Karen State)
> "Right: we have the right to go and reside in any place in Myanmar. Duty: we
> must obey the order of the government." (Rakhine, Buddhist, Rakhine State)

Few responses reflected the position that different ethnic groups or religious
groups cannot live together. However there were still a few, mainly in Rakhine
State.

> "Right: I don't live with Muslims. I cannot receive Muslims in this country."
> (Rakhine, Buddhist, Rakhine State)
> "It is impossible to coexist Rakhine and Rohingya, so must have specific laws.
> Otherwise the problem will go on. Union must give security for people of
> Maungtaw because they feel anxious. And support education, with enough
> teachers for schools. ... I want to live separately with Kalar. I don't want
> chance to live together. All things, we do are only because of their actions.
> I cannot murder like them." (Rakhine, Buddhist, Rakhine State)
> "The right of the race, should not have Rohinga and Muslim." (Rakhine,
> Hindu, Rakhine State)

It is interesting to note that even a few Hindus based in Rakhine State identified
with the anti-Muslim stand and defined their right to live in Myanmar, but
would not concede the same right to Muslims.

CITIZENSHIP IN MYANMAR: ETHNICITY AND IDENTITY

Beyond religion, Myanmar's multi-cultural and multi-ethnic society means that the concept of citizenship differs between ethnic groups. There is a lot of work pertaining to ethnic and religious identities, in particular with regard to the ethnic minorities. (See, for example, Smith 1999; South 2003, 2008; and Thawnghmung 2012.) A great many Myanmar nationals of ethnic minority extraction have come to view their ethnicity as their identity and in many cases see it as more important than their Myanmar citizenship (Tun Aung Chain 2000; South 2008). In contrast, the ethnic Bamar do not see a difference between the word "Myanmar" and the word "Bamar" (or "Burmese"). This chapter does not look in detail at the varying perceptions of ethnic identities across the ethnic groups. However, in light of the quotes above it is pertinent to review how the respondents viewed the issue of equality between the different races.

Equal rights for all was a theme that transcended all questionnaires. However the majority of Bamar and the ethnic communities saw equality quite differently. In demanding equal rights, ethnic minority respondents wanted the same rights as Bamar and self-determination.[15] However there are Bamar respondents who felt that ethnic minorities received more rights than them, especially with regard to business. Some Bamar also mentioned that there are too many Chinese and Indian (Kalar) influences as there are many mosques and both Chinese and Indians are very prominently represented in the business world.

Most ethnic minority respondent wanted resource-sharing, preservation of their cultural heritage including teaching their ethnic literature and language, religious freedom, equal chances, business opportunities, transportation, human and citizens' right, not to be discriminated against, and the right to become public servants. People from some Rakhine areas, especially in the northern, Muslim-dominated areas want freedom of religion, getting an identity card and freedom to travel:

> "All ethnic want equal rights. But everybody knows Bamar get more chances. We lost health, education, development rights." (Rakhine, Buddhist, Rakhine State)
>
> "To get the equality of right, to enact ethnic's literature, custom as a curriculum, to get the equality of right Christian and Buddhist." (Chin, Christian, Chin State)
>
> "(1) Religious freedom. (2) Freedom of learning of language and religious literature. (3) Peacefully living. (4) Freedom of health, economics, social and politics." (Kayin, Christian, Mandalay region)

"According to the constitution, to get equal rights, don't discriminate with regard to religion, culture, gender, living standard, state help and protect Christian, Islam, Hindu, Buddhist and other religions. A citizen can live everywhere in the country. Right to access public servants. Right to do media, to have equal chances, freedom of religious, freedom of marriage and getting baby, education, right to get protection of law." (Mon, Muslim, Yangon region).

The quotes above show that ensuring equality between Myanmar's ethnic groups is complex and linked in with the grievance histories of the different groups. The issue is even more complex when it comes to those who fled their homes because of the ethnic conflict. The peace process and ensuing Nationwide Ceasefire Agreement (see chapter by Kyed and Gravers in this volume) has allowed for a renewed discussion on the citizenship status of internally displace persons (IDPs) and the ethnic people who have lived abroad for many years, many in refugee camps. In some cases, the Ministry of Immigration and Population has agreed to issue citizenship cards for those who want to resettle back in the country. For example, in Kayin, Kayah and Mon States, there has been Myoe Pwin, a government project that served as a "one stop service for issuing citizenship" and is facilitated by Norwegian Refugee Council, and in some places the United Nations High Commissioner for Refugees (UNHCR). That project facilitated the negotiation process and is due to help those who want to get their paperwork done without having to go to the offices in Yangon. In some ways this is a first step in reinstalling "equality" at least with regard to the status of citizenship.

CONCLUSION

The youth voices above have painted an interesting picture of views on citizenship across Myanmar. The quotes show that the issues of rights and responsibilities are closely linked to religious identity. Despite years of military rule inspired education, papering over ethnic differences and ignoring religious issues between communities, these problems are embedded in society. Whilst those of ethnic nationality might feel that there is a need for more equality between ethnic groups, they are considered equal and part of the nation. However many of the discourses around rights and responsibilities clearly exclude non-Buddhist, and especially Muslim communities.

The issues raised also reflect a number of challenges the new government is facing that are discussed below.

The first challenge is to redefine the role of the military in what is a more participatory system. The constitution guarantees the army's place in parliament and control over key ministries. They remain significant stakeholders in the political system. However education must be reformed in a way so that the militarized view of society can be attenuated and that a true definition of citizenship and a social contract can take hold for future generations to be able to imagine their country and politics differently.

No less complicated is to make all citizens feel equal in a united country. Myanmar's ethnic and religious diversity will not make this an easy task. An ultra nationalist Buddhist movement — called Ma Ba Tha (Society for the Protection of Race and Religion) led by monks has gained traction in the last three years and has been fuelling anti-Muslim feelings across the country. Ma Ba Tha's influence did not only result in the four race and religion protection laws being passed in 2015 — which clearly discriminate against Muslims — it has also resulted in Muslim electoral candidates not being able to contest their seats. Not one of the 1,051 NLD candidates was a Muslim. Despite a reasonably large Muslim population, Myanmar's parliament does not have a single Muslim MP. During the electoral campaign the NLD did not speak up for the disenfranchised Rohingya either, in fear of being branded foreigner-friendly. Now in power, the situation in Rakhine State seems to be worsening rather than improving. The country is clearly divided on religious lines and community cohesion is going to be a difficult goal to achieve. The quotes above show that religion is a significant marker for many when it comes to citizenship, and this could result in further religious discrimination, unless the NLD is willing and able to develop an inclusive counter narrative.

The third challenge includes the representation of ethnic people and a discussion around multiple identities that do not threaten the unity of the country. Around 38 per cent of Myanmar's population are ethnic minorities and there are a large number of ethnic parties. Despite local ethnic leaders' misgivings, the NLD fielded candidates in all ethnic majority areas displacing the ethnic parties in their own states. Whilst the NLD has now created an ethnic affairs ministry and ensured that the first vice-president is also of ethnic origin, there is a threat that ethnic issues are subsumed into NLD politics. The issues of equal rights for all, regardless of ethnic group is one that needs to be addressed head on.

However the most important challenge will be the reframing of the debate around who is a citizen of Myanmar through a reformed education system — a challenge that has to listen to many voices from across society if it is to be successful.

Notes

1. Data was collected across the whole country between February 2012 and June 2013. The research was conducted by the Myanmar Egress Research Institute and directed by Marie Lall as a part of a larger EU-funded project. It built on a micro project on the concept of citizenship conducted by Lall and Win in 2010 and 2011 before and after the elections (Lall and Win 2013). The detailed report based on the full dataset was published in Lall et al. (2014). The survey was offered in Burmese. Where there were literacy difficulties the surveyors helped fill out the form. In most cases the respondents filled it out themselves. In the case of language difficulties, especially in Kayah, Kachin and Rakhine States the facilitators arranged for translations and helped fill out the forms in Burmese.

2. According to the CIA Factbook <https://www.cia.gov/library/publications/the-world-factbook/geos/bm.html> 0–14 years: 26.7 per cent (male 7,514,233/female 7,227,893), 15–24 years: 18.6 per cent (male 5,183,653/female 5,060,385), 25–54 years: 42.8 per cent (male 11,724,297/female 11,879,420), 55–64 years: 6.7 per cent (male 1,754,397/female 1,963,051), 65 years and over: 5.2 per cent (male 1,244,758/female 1,615,243) (2013 est.) The median age is total: 27.6 years; male: 27 years; female: 28.2 years (2013 est.)

3. Given that all the regions and a number of the states where research was conducted have a majority Buddhist population, this is not a surprising outcome. However care was taken to increase the Muslim sample after the Rakhine troubles so as to hear the views of the Muslim population, not only in Rakhine State but across the country on issues pertaining to citizenship.

4. But did not include recent conflict-affected areas.

5. This is less the case today in urban centres among the middle classes.

6. This has been the case since the first constitution.

7. Thanks to Hla Hla Win who helped put together this summary during the earlier citizenship project.

8. Both of them were known as "citizen warriors" with a pen who fought against the British government through their nationalist writing.

9. This was also a finding in the ABS survey conducted in 2015. See B. Welsh and Huang Kai-Ping, "Myanmar's Political Aspirations and Perceptions", 2015 Asian Barometer Survey Report, Centre for East Asia Democratic Studies, National Taiwan University, 2016.

10. Again, this finding is reflected in the ABS survey conducted in 2015. See Welsh and Huang (2016). However in their survey Welsh and Huang asked specifically about religion and this survey did not.

11. Mon Tehh Nay, vol. 1, no. 35, 25 August 2013, p. 3.

12. See p. 49 of Welsh and Huang (2016).

13. Dr Matthew Walton whose work also features in this volume has recently (2016) received an ESRC grant to study Buddhist nationalism and the results of this study will greatly elucidate the data gathered as apart of this project.

14. Just one sample page of ethnic riddles, culture or poems that were inserted in some textbooks (such as the Ethnic People's proverb in grade 7).
15. Again, this finding is reflected in the ABS survey conducted in 2015. See Welsh and Huang (2016).

References

Aye, M. and Kyi, T. *National aspects of curriculum decision-making*. UNESCO Press, 1998.

Crick, B. *Essays in Citizenship*. London: Continuum, 2000.

Davies, I. "Political literacy". In *The Sage Handbook of Education for Citizenship and Democracy*, edited by J. Arthur, I. Davies and C. Hahn, pp. 377–87. London: Sage, 2008.

Dean, B.L. *The State of Civic Education in Pakistan*, Research Report. IED, Karachi: Aga Khan University, 2007.

Joppke, C. "Transformation of Citizenship: Status Rights, Identity". *Citizenship Studies* 11, no. 1 (2007).

Kaltsounis, T. "Democracy's Challenge as the Foundation for Social Studies". *Theory and Research in Social Education* 22, no. 2 (1994): 176–93.

Kivisto, P. and T. Faist. *Citizenship: Discourse, Theory and Transnational Prospects*. Oxford: Blackwell Publishing, 2007.

Kyaw Yin Hlaing. *The Politics of State-Society Relations in Myanmar*. South East Asia Research. London: IP Publishing, 2007.

Lall, M. *Understanding Reform in Myanmar, People and Society in the Wake of Military Rule*. London: Hurst, 2016.

——— and E. Vickers, eds. *Education as a Political Tool in Asia*. London: Routledge, 2009.

——— and Hla Hla Win. "Perceptions of the State and Citizenship in Light of the 2010 of the 2010 Myanmar Elections". In *Myanmar's Transition: Openings, Obstacles,* Myanmar Elections." In *Myanmar's Transition: Openings, Obstacles, and Opportunities*, edited by Nick Cheesman, Monique Skidmore and Trevor Wilson. Singapore: Institute of Southeast Asian Studies, 2012.

——— and Hla Hla Win. "Myanmar, the 2010 elections and political participation". *Journal of Burma Studies* 17, no. 1 (2013): 181–220.

Osborne, K. "Citizenship Education and Social Studies". In *Trends and Issue in Canadian Social Studies*, edited by I. Wright and A. Sears. Vancouver: Pacific Education Press, 1997.

Salem-Gervais, Nicolas and Rosalie Metro. "A Textbook Case of Nation-Building: The Evolution of History Curricula in Myanmar". *Journal of Burma Studies* 16, no. 1 (2012): 27–78.

Smith, Martin. *Burma: Insurgency and the politics of ethnicity*. New York: Zed Books, 1999.

South, Ashley. *Mon Nationalism and Civil War in Burma: The Golden Sheldrake*. London: Routledge, 2003.

————. *Ethnic Politics in Burma: States of Conflict*. Oxon: Routledge, 2008.

Tun Aung Chain. "Historians and the Search for Myanmar Nationhood". Paper presented at the 16th Conference of the International Association of Historians of Asia, Kota Kinabalu, International Association of Historians of Asia in Cooperation with Universiti Malaysia Sabah, 2000.

I AM A CITIZEN OF MYANMAR

Aung Naing Oo
Political Analyst

In 2004, when I published my second book in the Myanmar language titled *Compromising with the Burmese Generals*, I quoted a paragraph from Allister Sparks' *Beyond the Miracle: Inside New South Africa*:[1]

> I felt myself to be "emotionally stateless": I could not identify with the land of my birth because it stood for things I abhorred; I felt no sense of pride when I heard my national anthem or saw my national flag.

Sparks, a South African who witnessed and wrote about the brutality of the South African apartheid regime as a journalist, was talking about his feelings regarding apartheid. This was exactly how I felt about "Burma" (which was how I named the country as an exile). Calling Myanmar "Burma" was an act of defiance for me, because I was against what "Myanmar" represented under military rule. Myanmar did not represent me; it was to be abhorred.

There were times that when I was "emotionally stateless". I remember watching the football final between Thailand and Myanmar at the Southeast Asian Games in 1994. It was one of the few exciting games I have ever watched Myanmar play against its rival neighbour. But while my colleagues, led by Moe Thee Zun — a military regime hater himself — wildly cheered for the Myanmar team at the house we rented in Bangkok (through a Myanmar friend who was a legal resident in Thailand), I was quiet because I was not sure if I should support the Myanmar national team. The Myanmar team did very well but was unlucky in the end as a header from Thai striker Kiatisuk "Zico" Senamuang (former Thai football coach) decided the tie.

The match was the talk of the town for both Myanmar and Thais and my colleagues continued to discuss it endlessly. But I was quiet. I was not even sure if I would celebrate if the Myanmar team had won. That was my problem — I could not emotionally connect myself to the Myanmar team because I felt the team represented a regime that I was against. I thought the team itself was also corrupt with its tainted and biased selection and the national football officials bowing to the whims of the ruling generals.

If the Myanmar team had won, I believe that the credit would have gone to the regime. Perhaps that was the reason I could not bear to support the Myanmar national team. My dislike of the military regime unwittingly fuelled my alienation from the country of my birth. I knew it was not healthy but I could not help it. Perhaps this was a trauma that other exiles like me experienced once they had to leave their homeland for political reasons.

But at the same time, I knew it was a denial. I dreamt recurring dreams in which I tried to go home or dreamt that I was home. But even in those dreams, the "home" did not welcome me. In the dreams I was always chased away by some unidentified uniformed officials. Almost always, I woke up sweating and was reassured that I was safe in my bed in Thailand or elsewhere.

As a Myanmar native, the connection was clearly there, as evidenced by my dreams. But what I could not resolve was the conflict within me — the tussle between myself as a citizen of Myanmar and an "oppositionist" who could not identify with the land of his birth. As in my dreams, I tried to belong to Myanmar, my homeland. But sometimes I was overcome with doubt — perhaps, I did not belong to my homeland and it did not want me, the exiled student activist. Perhaps this uncertainty was the reason I did not want to belong to Burma emotionally.

It was a difficult struggle. A constant struggle. Everywhere I went I identified myself as a Myanmar citizen. But everywhere I went I had to say bad things about Myanmar — mostly regarding human rights abuses and denial of democracy. Sometimes, I would describe Myanmar as a "god-forsaken land". And during all of those years in exile — twenty-four years in total — I am not sure if I sang the Myanmar national anthem even once. If I did, or had sung it, it would have been on occasions where I absent-mindedly hummed the rhythm because it had stuck somewhere in my head, having sung it at schools and official ceremonies before I left Myanmar in 1988.

By early 2004, it was getting difficult for me to live in Thailand due to my illegal status. So I managed to successfully apply for political asylum in London. However, it was such a negative experience, one I can never forget. I hated it from the beginning to the end. Especially the first day when I went to the U.K. Asylum Centre in Croydon, I felt at the lowest point of my life, undergoing scrutiny from the guards at the door through to the interviewing officials who regarded me with suspicious eyes. I never considered myself a refugee so it was very difficult for me to say that I was a refugee and that I could not go home for political reasons. But I became a refugee in the United Kingdom and remained a Myanmar citizen. It was indeed a situation in which I had to surrender not just my identity, but my pride and dignity.

In my travels overseas during my exile, I encountered many divided Myanmar communities. Those who were close to the official Myanmar embassies stayed away from exiled or political activists. They went to separate monasteries and their paths did not cross. They talked ill of each other behind their backs. But even among the exiles, there were many divisions. Being a citizen of Burma meant being one of a divided people.

By 1999, all my "official" affiliation with the exiled groups ended. Subsequently, I went back to school. I was lucky enough to get into Harvard Kennedy School in the United States. Following my education, I began to write as a political analyst.

By 2002, I had written a book entitled *Dialogue* in Myanmar language because I wanted the exiles and their opponents to understand the need for dialogue in Myanmar. Despite the call for political dialogue I thought there was little understanding in Myanmar regarding the nature of dialogue with a view to resolving conflicts. By 2004, I had written another book, entitled *Compromising with the Burmese Generals*. It was a step forward, calling not just for dialogue, but for compromise in the Myanmar conflict.

The books were the results of my new insights into and reflections on the politics of conflict in Myanmar. I had come to realize that without dialogue and compromise Myanmar would not break free from its entrenched political quagmire. The best way to get out of such a situation, I thought, was to try to understand each other in order to resolve the problems collaboratively through dialogue and compromise. But for most protagonists these were foolish ideas that could never be realized in Myanmar, and my proposals for empathy in negotiations or dialogue was met with suspicion from all sides.

So what was the problem, why were dialogue and compromise so difficult? In brief, it appears that both sides considered each other enemies. They believed they did not belong with each other. For many ethnic groups, their long-standing belief was that they did not belong to the areas in Myanmar where the majority Bamar lived, or beyond the borders of their ethnic groups within Myanmar. Many of them did not consider themselves citizens of Myanmar. This is down to the fact that the armed conflict had been mainly in the ethnic areas.

But I had no such understanding before the 1988 uprising. Growing up under socialism in a small town near Yangon far away from the armed conflict, I did not see any racial problems, inter-ethnic tensions or understand the effects of the armed conflict. I studied under many (ethnic) Karen teachers in high school and had many Karen friends in my hometown.

My first knowledge of ethnic tension occurred in 1987. It was my final undergraduate year. I distinctly remember arguing with a Karen friend during a drinking session in Yangon. The friend came to live in Yangon from conflict-ridden Karen State and explained to me why he could not work on his land back home. He said there was a constant threat of forced porterage for the army who were fighting the Karen rebels. The choice, he said, was to be drafted into porterage and carry supplies for the army, or pay a bribe to be relieved from the service. I naively argued that he should stand up to such lawlessness in Myanmar.

More importantly, this was when I began to examine if I was a pure Burman, or mixed with ethnic blood. I knew my father was born in a Mon village near Bago, about 2 hours from Yangon, so I thought I certainly had Mon blood in me. But later I found out that my father's grandfather was a Rakhine and had worked in colonial Yangon. However, having grown up in a village near Bago, like most people in Myanmar I describe myself as a Bamar, despite mixed lineage and blood.

As a Bamar, I remember sometimes feeling out of place in some ethnic-controlled areas. I felt as if I did not belong there. At times with the kind of nationalistic rhetoric prevalent in ethnic areas I certainly felt uneasy. But over time, I came to understand the fear and aspirations of ethnic groups. I learned to put myself in their shoes.

I asked myself "What it is like to be an ethnic in Burman-dominated Myanmar?". No doubt, they would feel the same in Burman-dominated Myanmar as I did in ethnic areas, perhaps more so than a Burman because they are the minority in Myanmar. I understand such empathetic realization is not apparent in cities where the majority of the Burman live. But if we are to live together in multi-ethnic and multi-cultured Myanmar we have to understand the ethnic minorities. Likewise, ethnic groups will have to start engaging with issues of national concern and not just their own affairs. I remember President Thein Sein telling leaders of a visiting ethnic armed organization (EAO) last year that they belong to the whole nation, including the capital.

In 2010, long-awaited changes came to Myanmar through what was considered by many to be a controversial election. My colleagues and I, at that time based at Chiang Mai University in Northern Thailand, knew that the 2010 election would bring changes to Myanmar. So we supported it and urged all political parties inside Myanmar to contest the election. Just as we had anticipated, the election paved the way for the return of democracy. It did not matter to me if the changes were labelled as half-baked or a "semi-democracy". All Myanmar needed was an opening for change, and the 2010 election duly provided it.

Importantly, the subsequent reforms from this election paved the way for a return to our homeland for many political exiles, and my colleagues and I returned to Myanmar in February 2012. Then, because of my experience with the ethnic armed groups and my studies overseas on disarmament and other conflict-related issues, I was given the opportunity of a lifetime by the new government — to get involved in the peace process.

Strangely enough by this time all my troubling dreams about going home had disappeared. Indeed, I was home now and there was no need for traumatic nightmares. Within a few months of my return, I got my national ID back and returned the British refugee travel document I had been using to the British embassy in Yangon. Subsequently, I applied for a Myanmar passport. But despite the official acceptance and recognition, I was still not entirely at home. The transition after twenty-four years in exile was not easy. Challenges ranged from adjustment in lifestyle to calling Burma by its official name "Myanmar" for the first time. There were awkward moments when I was introduced to some well-known ministers or generals from the Tatmadaw whose policies I had opposed for many years. I did not get used to these changes immediately, but slowly adjusted to the rhythm of life back in Myanmar.

I slowly began to realize that Myanmar had accepted me back, and that I was embracing Myanmar as my own. Before long, I was cheering for Myanmar national teams — I rejoiced with them when we won and I joined in the collective disappointment shared by my fellow countrymen when we lost. Without doubt, Myanmar's journey towards freedom and democracy is still at the beginning, but even in this beginning I have become one with Myanmar. There are still many things that I do not like about Myanmar, but we are steadily making progress. The military regime I was against no longer exists, and I am now working together with Generals from the Tatmadaw in the peace process. Alongside this, ethnic groups have become part of the efforts at nation-building. Together we will end the armed conflict. Reconciliation is taking place.

Now Myanmar is where I belong. I am no longer stateless. I now have an identity, and a restored emotional attachment to my native country. At long last I feel proud when I see the national flag or sing the national anthem. Indeed, I am a now citizen of Myanmar.

Note

1. Allister Sparks, *Beyond the Miracle: Inside New South Africa* (London: Profile Books, 2003).

6

"THE VALUE OF LIFE"
Citizenship, Entitlement and Moral Legibility in Provincial Myanmar[1]

Gerard McCarthy

After decades of authoritarian rule aimed at ring-fencing everyday people from contentious politics, Myanmar's November 2015 elections saw widespread popular re-engagement with party politics. With the shift from the spectacle of boisterous election campaigning to elite-level negotiation of national political transformation, expectations of what an incoming government can and will deliver for citizens — as well as the ethnic, religious and moral parameters of "the nation" — for many remain deeply rooted in notions of virtuous or moral citizenship popularized through the work of welfare groups and civil society permitted to develop during the dark days of military rule. In this chapter I explore the key social, political and moral ideas that animate people who offer their time, money and resources for these allegedly "apolitical" welfare groups that play an essential role in care for the needy throughout contemporary Myanmar.

Drawing on participant observation and interview research in central Myanmar conducted throughout 2015 with largely Buddhist welfare groups, their beneficiaries and their larger networks of donors, I challenge the fiction that these groups eschew "politics" or operate only in the allegedly "personal" domain of "religion".[2] Building on Andrea Muehlebach's (2012) exploration of citizenship and morality amongst volunteer welfare organizations in austerity Italy, I conceive of these notions, institutions and practices of non-state welfare provision in Myanmar as forms of "moral citizenship". I argue that the exercise of this spiritually imbued citizenship is helping to generate political identities and frames of reference not just about entitlement to social assistance from the state but also about the need to assert and protect Buddhism at a time of rapid social and political transition in Myanmar. These ideas about compassionate citizenship become the basis for excluding minorities from foundational notions of "national values", with virtuousness of their social work compared online and offline with the extremist violence committed by groups such as Islamic State in the Middle East and suggestively tied to Myanmar's own Muslim communities.

The chapter opens with a vignette of blood donations in central Myanmar, before then exploring how the scope of social action for others (*parahita*) in the Buddhist moral universe expanded significantly during the 1990s through the proliferation of Buddhist welfare groups. The notions of moral obligation and entitlement deployed by volunteers, beneficiaries and their extensive networks in contemporary Myanmar is then examined through ethnographic work with these welfare groups and their interaction with the state. The chapter concludes with discussion of how the deployment of these moral frameworks of compassion and good intentions (*cedana*) serve to render Muslims morally illegible to many Buddhists and thereby excise them from the national moral imaginary of Myanmar.

"SOCIAL CONSCIOUSNESS" IN ACTION

Across Myanmar, millions of people offer their money, time and labour on a regular basis for welfare groups. These teams, often linked to religious institutions and spiritualties, play an essential role in providing for some of the neediest people in Southeast Asia's poorest nation. What animates these people, and what do their labours suggest about ideas of citizenship, entitlement and political community after more than five decades of authoritarian rule?

Welfare groups, and the suites of social services which they provide, offer a vivid insight into the notions of merit, virtue and nation that underpin morally imbued welfare in provincial Myanmar. To gain an insight into dynamics of non-state welfare provision and moral ideas animating it outside of Myanmar's big cities, throughout 2015 and 2016 I followed welfare groups and the networks of beneficiaries and patronage linked to them in a mid-sized Bamar Buddhist majority town in central-east Myanmar, Taungoo.

A visit to a local blood bank in Taungoo in mid-2015 provides a prism into these dynamics.

Two students from a newly formed Taungoo University welfare group lay on wooden beds in the donation room. They squirmed a little when looking at the needles stuck into the crest of their arms. The nurse tried to settle them, explaining that it's natural to feel a little dizzy when giving blood.

Accompanying the students was a volunteer from Byama-So, one of a number of local welfare associations that coordinate blood donors and offer a range of other social services including cost-price funerals and free ambulance transportation. Throughout the 45 minutes or so of the students' donation, this volunteer — a trader who took the morning off work to meet the students and provide encouragement — played an essential role in helping to support, and also to frame, their experiences of blood giving.

"What does it feel like to give blood?" I asked one of the students. The volunteer quickly interjected: "It feels fantastic! It is essential that they give blood … People need blood to continue their lives. By giving blood, your happiness is limitless because you save lives!"

The students donating nodded weakly, watching 450 millilitres of their rare AB blood slowly trickle into bags propped up on wooden blocks on the floor. Similar encouragement came from another student who donated the week prior and sat beaming at the end of his friends' bed, loading photos of the students to their group's newly established Facebook page.

The volunteer from Byama-So quietly explained the importance of his role. "If they come alone", he told me, "they get a bit scared and decide not to donate". He then returned to enthusiastically encouraging them, stressing the contribution they are making not just to patients in need of their blood, but also to spreading what is referred to in Burmese as *"parahita seit"* — "a mind for the welfare of others" or more figuratively "social consciousness".

This scene occurs more than ten times a day at Taungoo General Hospital's blood bank. Its protagonists are motivated by a deeply Buddhist conceptualization of obligations to the polity, one which plays an essential role in systems of health, education and subsistence in a country where even despite significant budget growth in recent years less than 3 per cent of GDP was spent on health, education and welfare in 2014–15 (see UNICEF/ MDRI 2014, p. 24). Discursively, this scene also highlights a number of the recurring themes of discussion between beneficiaries, volunteers, committee members and senior monks who frequently serve as the patrons of these groups: that providing assistance to those in need or who are suffering (*doka*) is a fundamental Buddhist virtue, and that this spiritually imbued "value of life" has weakened as a shared national virtue in recent decades. Engaging in meritorious charitable activities is thus seen to strengthen the "affairs of the nation"[3] at a time of dramatic social and political transformation in Myanmar.

NOTIONS OF BUDDHIST MORAL DECLINE AND REJUVENATION

Anxiety about the need to revive popular practice of Buddhist virtues during periods of social turmoil is not a recent phenomenon in Myanmar. Indeed, it has been a recurring feature of Buddhist social action since the late nineteenth century. As Alicia Turner's exploration of the Burmese Buddhist anti-colonial movement highlights, there was widespread moral panic focusing on the "youth" and the reproduction of Buddha's social virtues in the independence movement. This focused particularly on the rejuvenation and state support of monastic schools as well as the cultivation of moral discipline through meditation (Turner 2009; 2011; 2014).

Contemporary expressions and discourses of moral regeneration echo these earlier anxieties. Youth are seen as having little understanding and appreciation for Buddhist virtues — and their exercise as fundamental practices of citizenship — because of what is seen as the deliberate ritualization of Buddhism since the military coup of 1962. "All the children know how to do now is pray", a number of senior monks and Dhamma schoolteachers have explained. "They don't know anything about the Buddha's life and what he taught." Dhamma schools are a major plank of this strategy of reviving knowledge and engagement with Buddhism.[4] In Taungoo, there are now more than ten weekly Dhamma schools across the town, all but one established since 2012. Most schools teach using the textbook provided by the national Dhamma School Foundation, which as of late 2015 only had materials for classes three to six — catering for children aged 5 or 6 through 10 or 11.[5] Every Sunday afternoon, close to 2,000 children from around Taungoo, a mid-sized provincial town of around 160,000 people, flock to monasteries for two hours, including a sermon from a monk, lessons and songs about the life of the Buddha and the virtues he preached, as well as an occasional meal provided by a local donor. Meanwhile, these schools act as a central node of social action, with dozens of lay adults offering their time in various capacity for schools — including (mostly female) teachers as well as committee members, fund-raising teams and weekly donors of snacks and drinks.

The objective of moral rejuvenation is evident in the content of these classes, in particular the focus on the life of the Buddha and his sermons on impermanence and selflessness. Yet there are also newer, more clearly social foci that diverges somewhat from the emphasis on propagation of Buddhist community through study and debate as was envisaged in the independence movement (see Turner 2009; Walton 2012, p. 179). This is clear in the dual emphasis placed in Dhamma school classes of the need for self-less volunteering (*parahita*) and for the protection of "national belief and religion'"(*amyo batha thathana*).[6] Volunteer teachers, senior monks and organizing committee members all focus explicitly upon these three intentions — education about the Buddha; development of a social consciousness (*parahita seit*); protection of "national religion" — when discussing the recent growth of Dhamma schools and their own personal intentions in involvement. These objectives, made evident in the focus given in classes to Buddhist moral virtues of giving with loving kindness, are also found in the booklets provided to every child who attends classes and in promotional materials targeted at parents: "1. To improve knowledge of the life of the Buddha; 2. To instil discipline and virtues of giving (*dana*); 3. To propagate "religious nationalism".[7]

Engaging in social action that preserves life, and to a less overt extent to support or propagate the nationally important character of Buddhism, is also the stated objective of many of Taungoo's biggest welfare groups. All see themselves as possessing, cultivating and putting into practice *parahita seit* or "social consciousness". This draws on the discourse of moral decline and protection of the Buddhist community that dominated concerns of Buddhist civil society during the independence period (Turner 2009; Walton 2012, pp. 179–80). However, it is also deeply imbued with a social-welfare ethic predicated on practices of religious giving (*dana*) in the form of charitable giving and volunteering contributing to national development that has only come to prominence after the protests of 1988 and a subsequent shift in government policy towards civil society in the mid-1990s. A noticeable shift has thus occurred in the scope of moral social action during this period, with substantial implications for contemporary social protection dynamics as well as conceptions of entitlement and the drawing of boundaries of political community to the exclusion of Muslims.

SOCIAL ACTION IN THE BUDDHIST "MORAL UNIVERSE"

Political scientist and scholar of Burmese political thought, Matthew Walton, conceptualizes a Buddhist "moral universe" "that delineates the boundaries of the political as well as what constitutes political subjects and legitimate forms of political authority and participation" (Walton 2012, pp. 3–4). He conceives this Buddhist universe as comprising "a particular conception of human nature, an understanding of the universe as governed by a law of cause and effect that works according to moral principles, a conception of human existence as fundamentally dissatisfactory, and the acceptance of a range of methods to overcome and escape its dissatisfactory character" (Walton 2012, p. 4). Whilst the parameters of this moral universe remain "relatively consistent over time" (Walton 2012, p. 4), specific notions within it are subject to what Peter Jackson terms "interpretative plasticity" or evolution (Jackson 2002, p. 157 in Walton 2012, p. 4).

Drawing on the notion of interpretative plasticity, I focus on a specific component of this moral universe — the logic and scope of moral social action — and its reformulation as a result of the mode of 1990s governance which permitted "apolitical" civil society and offloaded care responsibilities to entrepreneurs. Previously the notion of "work for others" or *parahita* had been enlisted to encourage lay involvement in the propagation of religion in the late colonial period after the British usurping of the monarch. As Turner notes, *parahita* was largely associated with propagation of religion through activities such as teaching the precepts of the Buddha to children (Turner 2009, 2012). Whilst U Nu's Socialist-imbued "Buddhist Revival" sought to consciously cultivate a linkage between social service and good merit (see Walton 2012, p. 180), for much of the period after the coup of 1962 and the subsequent shift to rule by the Burma Socialist Programme Party (BSPP) (1974–88), non-state civil society was largely censored and suppressed. The BSPP regime assumed a significant role in disbursing quotas for basic household goods and foodstuffs. Outside of a handful of allowable class and mass organizations (Taylor 2009, p. 373), all other community or civil society groups not linked to a narrowly defined "religious sphere" were to be suppressed or co-opted by local military commanders and representatives of the BSPP — a directive which led David Steinberg to comment in 1999 that "civil society died under the BSPP; in reality, it was murdered" (Steinberg 1999).[8] This policy endured until the economic crisis of 1988, which sparked mass uprisings across the country, the transition to a highly mediated form of capitalism and a coup from within.

CIVIL SOCIETY AND *PARAHITA SEIT* AFTER 1988

The opposition National League for Democracy's (NLD) victory in the 1990 elections — and particularly in ethnic minority areas — provoked an existential crisis for the new military regime. It embarked on a dual-process of state- and nation-building throughout both the centre and periphery of the territory newly named "Myanmar". Yet the post-socialist focus on forcing insurgencies to ceasefires and building hard, national infrastructure left major gaps in health, social services and local public goods provision (Steinberg 2006, p. 103). Faced with conflicting demands to construct infrastructure whilst managing local affairs, regional military commanders began to permit a liberalization of welfare groups and "traditional" civil society throughout the 1990s (Callahan 2001, p. 41).

Religious and religiously imbued organizations expanded their roles in care in both Bamar majority and ethnic minority areas of Myanmar (Smith 2002, p. 26). Whilst overtly "political" organizations continued to be harassed and surveilled by military authorities, a 2006 study found an estimated 214,000 community-based organizations (CBOs) operating in every corner of the country (Heidel 2006).[9] These groups, given the politically progressive label "civil society" by some Western observers, were largely forced to accept political domination throughout the 1990s and 2000s in exchange for pursuing quotidian coping agendas focused on filling the social welfare gap left by the absence of the state and stagnant economy throughout much of the country.[10]

The proliferation of these mechanisms of informal social protection from the early 1990s resulted in a gradual redefinition of the scope of "work for others" (*parahita*) and giving (*dana*) within the Buddhist moral universe. Key figures in the coalescence of this moral discourse of "socially engaged Buddhism" in Myanmar were two abbots — Sagaing-based Sittagu Sayadaw and Hpaan-based Thamanya Sayadaw. Both encouraged lay charitable action to respond to the welfare crises of the 1990s and 2000s as means of reducing suffering of others in this world whilst simultaneously accruing merit for the next life. Both Sayadaws created significant complexes built off donations of the entrepreneurial class which emerged in the 1990s. Sittagu Sayadaw gained particular renown after establishing a series of free hospitals and clinics in Sagaing in Upper Myanmar in the 1990s where sick patients were treated and lay people from around the country came to offer money and time. After the devastating 2008 Cyclone Nargis, these networks were deployed for disaster relief. Through these projects, a philosophy of "work for others" or *parahita* was modelled whilst the possibilities of engaging in such social work within the context of indirect military rule was demonstrated (Walton 2012, pp. 181–82).

Prominent lay leaders also embraced this expansive moral logic of social action and began to popularize it. For example Aung San Suu Kyi strongly endorsed social work as a means of alleviating suffering and achieving social outcomes, a commitment prominently demonstrated a few weeks after the November 2015 elections when Daw Suu personally picked up trash from a park in Yangon.[11] Meanwhile, famed Myanmar actor and director Kyaw

Thu established a free funeral service in Yangon and drove funeral hearses and ambulances for sick patients.[12]

By the mid to late 1990s, the moral logic and scope of social action had shifted in the mind of many everyday people to seeing individual charitable work as a viable means of achieving social outcomes and simultaneously accruing good merit. For many who supported the long-suppressed National League for Democracy (NLD), demonstrating personal moral fibre through social work also highlighted by comparison the alleged "immorality" of the military junta. As the scope of *parahita* within the Buddhist moral universe broadened, it provided fertile ideational and spiritual grounding for the emergence what Khin Zaw Win (2006), Lorch (2006*a* and 2006*b*) and South (2008) describe as politically bounded though active forms of citizenship.

The association of mechanisms of self-reliance and reciprocity with larger translocal and societal impacts was solidified further after the devastation wrought by Cyclone Nargis in 2008. Welfare groups, often with the support of local entrepreneurs and coordinated by nationally prominent monks such as Sittagu Sayadaw, provided immediate and long-term humanitarian assistance to those worst effected when it was clear that state assistance was woefully insufficient (see Jaquet and Walton 2013; Centre for Peace and Conflict Studies 2009; Human Rights Watch 2010). The spheres of social action offered by both local and trans-local welfare groups combined with the symbolic politics of social work as a mechanism of highlighting the illegitimacy of the regime served to fuse popular associations between religious morality, compassion and active citizenship for many everyday people. Contemporary ethnographic fieldwork highlights that national-level social and political reforms since 2010 have reinforced rather than undermined these mechanisms and logics of citizen moral obligation in ways likely to impact the trajectory of democratic development in Myanmar.

FUSING OF RELIGION, CARE AND CITIZENSHIP IN MYANMAR

Throughout my research in Bamar, Buddhist majority Taungoo in northern Bago Region in 2015 and 2016, I listened to the notions of moral social action, obligation and entitlement that various welfare groups evoked in conducting their work. Previous literature on community-based organizations in Myanmar frame them as "non-contentious" and thus "largely apolitical" (Steinberg 2006, pp. 103–105), noting their tendency to avoid the domain of "big-P" politics and instead emphasize their "purely social content" (Prasse-Freeman 2015, p. 98). I argue that "social" obligation to co-produce welfare and local public goods should be viewed as fundamentally political as it is often seen — especially by democracy activists — as not just a practical necessity but also essential to enacting a deeply moral, compassionate (B: *cedana*) vision of democracy. This social imaginary reinforces an inherently authoritarian conceptualization of rights as "gifts" from the sovereign rather than entitlement, and at least in the conception of the role of the state in welfare is a significant normative shift from the ideology of state-led distributive justice which was hegemonic (though functionally inoperable) during the socialist period until 1988.

One example of this blending of morality, charity and entitlement is the local role of Byama-so, formed in Taungoo in the late 1990s in response to perceived local profiteering in funeral services. The group grew throughout the 2000s, and by 2015 the organization was providing over 1,000 discounted funerals annually, along with a suite of social services including a free ambulance and management of a 4,000 donor blood bank registry used regularly by patients at Taungoo General Hospital. Throughout my fieldwork I observed the expansive logic of social action evoked by those offering their time with both Byama-so as well as other groups more closely aligned with the NLD.

Despite the differing partisan leanings of these local welfare groups, the moral logics underpinning them reflects a configuration of entitlement in which citizens and community-based groups are seen as the locus of care provision. "Everything we do is to try and save lives", a volunteer with NLD-aligned 24 Hours and a prominent member of Buddhist nationalist group Ma Ba Tha explains over tea after supervising a blood donation. "If Myanmar is to become a true democracy (B: *tageh demokrasi*) we need more people to have goodwill/good intentions (B: *cedana*) and be willing to give even their blood for others to reduce suffering (B: *doka*) amongst our family/kin". These types of affective appeals to fictive kinship and "relational empathy" (Bornstein 2012) recurred throughout my fieldwork, especially during the 2015 floods, reframing strangers both near and far as part of a familial community of suffering and compassion which compels individuals to contribute.

Subsequently, the primary focus of these groups is inputs of assistance than outputs or outcomes of aid. For instance, there is no attempt by any of these organizations to measure how many patients' lives are saved by the free pharmacy service, or the number of blood recipients who recover after a transfusion. Rather, emphasis is placed on the transaction of virtuous social action which has larger social ramifications, as seen in the framing role played by the entrepreneurs in the blood bank vignette at the beginning of this chapter.

The imperative to have relational connection — fictive and otherwise — between donor and beneficiary carries with it a scepticism of intermediaries, especially of the state as a mechanism of redistribution. Indeed, throughout my fieldwork "state authorities" (*asohya*) were often cast as incapable or unwilling to effectively deliver necessary help, or were labelled as immoral on the basis of suppressed or disrupted "work for others" in the past. A university student group I followed during Myanmar's 2015 floods framed much of their fund-raising around the metaphor that "brothers and sisters" and family/kin (*amyo/mithazu*) in the Delta were suffering and that the government was not responding. One speech given repeatedly in markets and urban streets around Taungoo rallied: "We are like fatherless children, because our government doesn't give us help. Like orphans we need to support each other to survive."

Beneath this veneer of contention with the state, however, is the notion that good moral conduct compels everyday people and wealthy members of the community to be engaged in social work. This logic of social action does not just see obligations when the state is absent or nefarious. Rather, the vision of political reform propagated by Myanmar's democratic forces sees the co-production of welfare and local public goods as a moral ideal. This was a theme repeated at numerous NLD campaign events in 2015 and shared not just by the grassroots rank-and-file but also current NLD parliamentarians in Myanmar's parliament. As one stated at a rural campaign event:

> After the election you will be able to ask for your rights and try to develop your village …. We can cooperate and work together. The NLD needs to know the needs of the village. But the village also needs to discuss and cooperate with us to lead improvements here" (Author fieldnotes, 20 September 2015, in Burmese).

The notion that state provision of "rights" and "development" requires communities to co-contribute to local social initiatives is not just embraced by NLD members but was also born out in a household survey conducted in two townships of central-east Myanmar in early 2016 (McCarthy 2016*b*). When asked directly whether it was normatively better to receive assistance from government, neighbours/family, or both, almost half (49 per cent) said that both were equally important. Less than 10 per cent of respondents said that it was better for the government to give assistance alone — demonstrating how past experience of co-produced care and public goods shapes the normative preference for such collaboration.[13]

CONTINGENCY OF RIGHTS AND ENTITLEMENT

The specific form of social and economic administration which functioned in provincial Myanmar during the 1990s has thus resulted in a decidedly neoliberal and authoritarian configuration of citizen "entitlement" and "rights". Decades of religious welfare actors and entrepreneurs being tacitly and often explicitly encouraged by military commanders to provide social welfare and public goods as a moral obligation has helped to generate a hegemonic imaginary in which "social outcomes" are achievable through the actions of morally upright individuals. This moral order both atomizes and creates a bond of relational solidarity *beyond* the state as individuals are impelled to engage in "work for others" collectively and with the support of "compassionate-minded" (*cedana*) entrepreneurs and bureaucrats in order to attain "development".

Echoing anthropologist Andrea Muehlebach's (2012) work on Italian welfare groups in the context of austerity state retrenchment, entitlement from the state in contemporary Myanmar relies on satisfying a highly contingent and relational "ethical citizenship" which "encloses citizens within the intimate space of the 'welfare community' or 'welfare society'" (Muehlbach 2012, p. 43). As Muehlebach writes: "Rather than feel attached to the state — and make demands on it — citizens are to attach themselves to each other, through spontaneous, sympathetic acts" (Muehlebach 2012, p. 69).

Similarly, the notion of citizenship which emerges from welfare groups and initiatives in contemporary Myanmar is one that emphasizes both the purity of volunteer intentions and the essential role of this moral attribute in collective life. This is not a configuration of citizenship framed around claiming "human rights" from the state, nor of ensuring citizens receive the public goods to which they are "entitled" (see Prasse-Freeman 2015). Rather, the logic of rights, entitlement and moral obligation shown here have clear synergies with the contingent and "delimited" citizenship rights of the socialist and military periods. As scholar of Burmese legal systems and political thought Nick Cheesman notes, "rights" during these periods sprung from the goodwill or *cedana* of the sovereign ruler. Rights were thus "conditional privileges paternalistically bestowed ... [upon] certain people who deserve them because they conform with the sovereign's vision for the community" (2015, p. 109). Given this understanding of state assistance and reciprocal obligations it is unsurprising that the Burmese notion of "rights" (*akwin aye*) is used colloquially to refer to chance or opportunity for support (Prasse-Freeman 2015, p. 98), rather than the notion of "unfettered right[s] of the sort used to describe fundamental rights or human rights" (Cheesman 2015, p. 109).

For populations in government-controlled areas of Myanmar the requirement of demonstrating *cedana* in order to be deemed worth of rights or assistance is being institutionalized as the state expands in developmental action. Even those most critical of the military regime are embracing these moral responsibilities, with some being willingly enlisted into defending the wealth of the military-linked businessmen who patronize them. The pervasive moral imaginary of welfare-related obligation shapes the possibilities of state-led wealth redistribution as it erodes class-based mobilization, especially against the military-linked elite deeply embedded in these circuits of affect and assistance. Equally pernicious, however, is how this moral economy of welfare and citizenship linked to Buddhism establishes moral parameters around abstract collectives such as "the nation", often rendering Muslims as morally illegible as they are popularly framed as stingy and lacking in compassion.

"MUSLIMS DON'T VALUE LIFE": OPPOSITIONAL MORAL DISCOURSES

The language and identity of moral citizenship frequently recurs in discussions about Muslims, serving to generate new parameters of political community and national reciprocity. Schissler, Walton and Phyu Thi (2015) have observed that narratives of Muslim threat are developing as people manage their understanding of present and past experiences as well as their "relationships with people around them" (Schissler, Walton and Phyu Thi 2015, p. 14). For many people in central Myanmar this iterative process occurs in the social spheres surrounding Buddhist revivalist and welfare groups that are at the centre of moral and social life and which provide essential welfare services. Within these networks, claims and judgements occur about what comprises meritorious action and how these "good intentions" helps to strengthen "the nation" in the face of antithetical philosophies of violence allegedly linked to Islam.

The sentiment that "Muslim's don't value life" was encountered repeatedly in discussion with interlocutors and recurred on social media, especially the Facebook pages of local welfare groups, throughout my fieldwork. Articles and images of violence committed by so-called Islamic State (IS), rumours of Al Qaeda cells within Myanmar, or posts detailing allegedly "coerced" conversion of Buddhist women, featured regularly on these Facebook pages throughout my fieldwork. The process of narrative-making framed around these virulent images of global or local violence and coercion regularly involved universal claims about "the Other" being intrinsically violent or morally deviant. Through the comments function followers of Buddhist revivalist or welfare groups would then take the opportunity to construct narratives about the intentions of Muslims, inserting their own pre-existing grievances and rumours about the greed, aggression or sexual deviancy of Muslim men both near and far (see McCarthy and Menager 2015; McCarthy and Menager 2017; Schissler 2015).

Images of Buddhist volunteers engaging in social work and soliciting donations are a key mechanism through which these moral boundaries of national community were drawn. "Look at my Facebook — there are so many images of Buddhists helping each other", a member of the Buddhist nationalist group Ma Ba Tha told me in the weeks following the 2015 flood appeals. "I never see Muslims making donations or volunteering for these kinds of projects", he said. Ironically, the reverse theme recurred in the Facebook feeds of Muslim contacts about Buddhists during this period with a post being shared repeatedly by Muslim contacts which included six images: five depicted alleged assaults and attacks on Muslims in Myanmar including burning mosques; the final image was a photo of Muslim men wearing religious headwear handing sacks of rice to what appeared to be Buddhists affected by the floods. Above the images was the caption: "They do this to us ... And we do this for their benefit."

Facebook photos shared within insular, largely sectarian social networks can thus become a one-sided battleground where strong in-group social cohesion and out-group boundaries are rhetorically and visually generated. At least on the Facebook groups of Buddhist welfare group many users disparagingly compare the "clean and pure" intentions (*cedana*) of Buddhists with the allegedly "stingy" parochialism of Muslims who, it is claimed, offer help "only to their own kind" (see McCarthy forthcoming).

Through these framing processes the moral deviancy and aggression of self-styled Islamic terrorists around the globe are refracted into local life in provincial Myanmar, with supposed moral distinctions about the value of life and compassionate social action helping to construct a fundamental ethical cleavage between Buddhism and Islam within the context of the "Myanmar nation".[14] It is no surprise given the ubiquitous attempts to render Muslims morally illegible to Buddhists that fear and misunderstanding of Islam and those who practise it is prevalent in provincial Myanmar. For many who offer their time and money to the causes and projects of welfare groups, this fear is compounded by widely propagated narratives that depict Buddhism as having been weakened and ritualized during the authoritarian period and that the country is thus losing moral virtue at a pivotal moment of social transformation.

CONCLUSION

In the context of Myanmar's ongoing social and political reforms, non-state welfare groups are playing an essential role in morally framing charitable social action and cultivating a culture of "social consciousness" (*parahita seit*) focused on the preservation of life. Many of the Buddhist welfare groups that espouse this discourse genuinely do assist large number of people to get by amidst the precariousness of life in one of Southeast Asia's poorest corners (see McCarthy 2016*b*). Their role and prominence is unlikely to fade in the coming years, however, as they envisage themselves increasingly cooperating with, and supplementing, state institutions and agencies that share their objectives. As one doctor told a family of donors at a free, non-government clinic: "No matter how much the government does, it will never be enough. Your contribution is vital!". This philosophy of moral obligation which was popularized throughout the 1990s and 2000s forms the ideational core of many welfare groups in Myanmar, and generates minimalist ideas of citizen entitlement from the state. For most everyday Burmese citizens in central Myanmar, very little is expected of the government, and barely anything received from it — especially in rural and semi-rural communities outside of urban areas. Comparative studies of non-state welfare provision find that reliance on these groups for social assistance weakens participation in state institutions and exercise of citizenship more broadly, with negative consequences for democratic consolidation (MacLean 2010, 2011; Cammett and MacLean 2011).

In Myanmar there is the possibility that moral notions of meritorious social action for others could help to provide a spiritual justification for socio-political participation which, as Walton observes in this volume, is seen by many Burmese people as a morally bankrupt or selfish activity (see also Walton 2012, pp. 178–84). However, embedded within these evolving ideas of virtuous or moral citizenship are also moral parameters and boundaries to the political imagination of Myanmar as a community of shared values of compassion and reciprocity. Meritorious social action engaged in by welfare and civil society groups seeking to "preserve" or "respect" life is thus compared with the atrocities committed by Muslims internationally. Domestic crises such as the 2012 communal violence in Rakhine State as well as local events are repeatedly cited when linking this meta-frame of the differential "value of life" as a national value to Myanmar Muslims, a process aided by culturally embedded practices of narrative-making both offline and online.

This sociology of a highly delimited and contingent welfare state presents Myanmar's Muslim communities with a tremendous challenge: proving they are peaceful and value the preservation of life and engage in compassionate social action to a similar extent and in a cultural vernacular that is morally legible to Myanmar's majority Buddhists. The moral and discursive specificities of Buddhist social work and the distinct rituals of Islamic funerals and religious celebrations at least partially prompt establishment of separate Muslim welfare groups.[15] Segregation of this kind significantly limits the forums or experiences of everyday collaboration through which "the Other" could be humanized and trust built between communities.[16] The need for a genuine religious education both in schools and for adults that can help to dispel myths and develop relationships across people of different religions is essential at this time of social transformation in Myanmar. Whilst many in the Buddhist nationalist Ma Ba Tha movement see all Muslims in Myanmar as "guests" who should be treated as such from the perspective of citizenship rights (see Nyi Kyaw 2015, pp. 57–58), mechanisms for fostering inter-religious collaboration in charitable work certainly do exist and should be explored seriously by the popularly-elected NLD government.

Politically, these ethical subjectivities and notions of citizenship — despite successfully defining the parameters of "the political" in new and often problematic ways (see McCarthy 2016a) — did not lead to support for the regime United Solidarity and Development Party (USDP) at the November 2015 elections. This was despite attempts by Ma Ba Tha networks and the USDP to disseminate materials suggesting that the NLD would weaken the Buddhist character of Myanmar (Kyaw Min 2015). Rather, as a result of the frequent suppression of compassionate social action during the authoritarian period, even those who offer their time for Ma Ba Tha-aligned religious projects and Buddhist welfare groups saw Aung San Suu Kyi as someone who has "endured suffering" at the hands of the regime and has the "needs of the people" in her mind. Meanwhile, major patrons of both the local NLD and the USDP also fund a broad cross-section of Taungoo's Buddhist welfare groups, pointing to a pragmatic political economy of patronage that cuts across opaque partisan lines (see McCarthy 2016a). Perhaps as a consequence of the divergent streams of this complex sociology, many of those who offer their time regularly at Buddhist-imbued welfare groups were unsure for much of 2015 which party they would lend their vote to at the November elections. As the election drew closer and campaigning began, many confidently declared themselves NLD supporters. Others abstained from voting at all, seeing the election simply as a struggle for power between largely immoral, self-interested politicians.

Despite the overwhelming endorsement at the election of the NLDs promise of a more "democratic" Myanmar, it is unlikely that the political culture of non-state welfare from which notions of morally imbued citizenship and the ethnical boundaries of the nation have been popularized will dissipate in the short to medium term. Indeed, as the state expands in welfare and developmental action these patterns of co-production are being reinforced. As such, it may be best to see these groups and the reciprocity and self-reliance practices upon which they are built as "informal institutions" that will form the social basis of important cleavages in Myanmar society and politics during the ongoing democratic transition and must be engaged with as such.[17] These divisions will be of deep pertinence not just to inter-religious relations but also questions of citizenship, entitlement and the boundaries of political community over the coming decades.

Notes

1. Field research was made possible thanks to an Australian Department of Education Endeavour Postgraduate Scholarship. Thanks also to the Department of International Relations at University of Yangon for hosting me as a Visiting Fellow throughout 2015. I am indebted to Justine Chambers, Nicholas Cheesman, Khin Mar Mar Kyi, Benedict Brac de la Perriere, Ashley South, Ardeth Thawnghmung and Matthew Walton for their detailed and insightful comments on earlier versions of this chapter, and to Saw U Ler Moo and Aurnt Bwe Kaung for research and translation assistance.
2. See S. Mahmood on political piety (2005) and secularism in an Islamic context (2015) for exploration of the false distinction between private and public life, especially in debates about the status of religious minorities in supposedly "secular" regimes.
3. The Burmese "*amyotha ye*" was frequently used by my informants to describe one of the key intentions of their work. The term can be translated as "affairs of race" or "affairs of nation" as "*amyo*" is variously used in Burmese to refer to family, type, race or nation depending on context. In the conduct of my fieldwork, "*amyotha ye*" was frequently used by informants to refer to social work strengthening a notion of group membership which transcended ethnicity and religion, for example, in fund-raising for flood and disaster victims at various points in 2015. Thus in the article I render it as "affairs of nation", albeit one very much in generation (see Turner 2016). As will be discussed, these notions of nation often draw explicitly on Buddhist notions of meritorious action that exclude Muslims, complicating the idea that "*amyotha ye*" transcends notion of religious membership and practice. Thanks to Nyi Nyi Kyaw, Elliot Prasse-Freeman and Matthew Walton for their feedback on this interpretation.
4. See Walton (2014) for an overview of the complex relationship between religious education and increasingly ubiquitous narratives of Islamic ascendency in Myanmar.
5. Some, however, teach their own curriculum for students in seventh and eighth class. Two senior monks interviewed in Taungoo mentioned plans for release of a new Dhamma School Foundation curriculum focusing more explicitly on "citizenship" and the role of Buddhism in politics for seventh grade in 2016 and eighth grade in 2017.

6. Following Brac de la Perriere (2015, p. 5), I translate *"amyo batha thathana"* as deployed popularly by Buddhist nationalist group Ma Ba Tha and in the everyday work of Buddhist civil society groups as connecting three forms of belonging: *"amyo"* as nation, *"batha"* as individual belief or faith in religion, and *"thathana"* as institutions of religion.
7. Translation of Burmese leaflet distributed at a prominent Taungoo Dhamma School. Thanks to Saw U Ler Moo for assistance with this translation.
8. This process of institutional domination led Taylor to conclude that at least in central Myanmar, by the time of the 1988 student uprisings, the near bankruptcy of the Burmese State and the consequent military coup, "the state was accepted as inevitable and it dominated other institutions" (Taylor 2009, p. 373).
9. This is a trend also noted by other scholars including James (2005), South (2004), Petrie (2014), and Lorch (2006, 2007, 2008).
10. Navigating the constraints of regime suppression led most organizations to frame their activities and objectives in non-political terms (Heidel 2006, pp. 38–39), a strategy which enabled community groups to both engage and elicit participation from both citizens and state apparatuses. As Elliot Prasse-Freeman observes, their lack of political expression "comprise a spectrum: all the way from being democrats-in-hiding, unwilling to act without the proper conditions; to groups generally indifferent to 'big-P' politics; to groups actively opposed to participating in political processes". Some, such as the Myanmar Maternal and Child Welfare Association, has direct links to the regime but played an important role in delivery of health education and services throughout the country. For a longer discussion of these issues, see Prasse-Freeman (2012).
11. For an account of Aung San Suu Kyi's charitable work and the projects it inspires in provincial areas of Myanmar, see McCarthy (2016*a*).
12. U Kyaw Thu, a prominent Burmese actor, is the founder of the Free Funeral Service that has chapters throughout Myanmar. For more background see Zon Pann Pwint, "Kyat Thu: from actor to funeral director", *Myanmar Times*, 2 December 2013.
13. See McCarthy (2016*b*) for discussion of dynamics of co-production of welfare and public goods as well as explanation of the survey methodology deployed.
14. This is in contrast to the comparatively positive way in which Myanmar Christians are frequently mentioned in these networks. Members of management committees of Buddhist welfare groups and Dhamma Schools in Taungoo interviewed by the author explicitly mentioned Christian welfare groups and especially Sunday Schools as a partial inspiration for their own social and educational work, often invoking the notion that Christians have been successful at maintaining youth involvement in churches whilst youth across Myanmar have been "losing their religion". However, there was also a sentiment amongst Buddhist villagers interviewed that Christians rely too heavily on assistance from foreign religious networks and charities, eroding their ability to organize their community for self-help activities and claim-making from government agencies.

15. Implicit and explicit discrimination and exclusion of Muslims from Buddhist welfare groups is at least partly to blame for this social pillarization, despite the fact that most groups interviews prided themselves on theoretically offering assistance "without regard to age, wealth, ethnicity, or religion".
16. See Varshney's (2002) work on inter-ethnic and inter-religious collaboration in provincial India for a similar argument about the impacts of collaborative work.
17. See Geertz (1959), Auyero (2001), Levitsky (2001, 2003), Helmke and Levitsky (2004), Nishizaki (2004, 2011), MacLean (2010) and Cammett and MacLean (2011) for an overview of the literature on informal institutions, non-state welfare, political process and political culture. See McCarthy (2016*b*) for a longer discussion of prospective mechanisms of engaging with non-state welfare provision to cultivate more functional citizen-state relations in the short to medium term.

References

Auyero, J. *Poor People's Politics: Peronist Survival Networks and The Legacy of Evita.* Durham: Duke University Press, 2001.

Brac de la Perriere, B. "A Generation of Monks in the Democratic Transition". In *Metamorphosis: Studies in Social and Political Change in Myanmar*, edited by Renaud Egreteau and François Robinne. Bangkok: IRASEC Research Institute on Contemporary Southeast Asia, 2015.

Callahan, M. "Cracks in the Edifice? Military-Society Relations in Burma Since 1988". In *Strong Regime, Weak State*, edited by M. Pedersen. Adelaide: Crawford House Publishing, 2001.

Cammett, M. and L.M. MacLean. "Introduction: The Political Consequences of Non-State Social Welfare in the Global South". *Studies in Comparative International Development* 46 (2011): 1–21.

Center for Peace and Conflict Studies. "Listening to the Voices from inside: Myanmar civil society's response to Cyclone Nargis". Siem Reap: Center for Peace and Conflict Studies 2009 <http://www.centrepeaceconflictstudies.org/wp-content/uploads/Listening-to-Voices-from-Inside-Myanmar-Civil-Society.pdf> (accessed 1 June 2016).

Cheesman, N. *Opposing the Rule of Law: How Myanmar's Court Make Law and Order.* Cambridge: Cambridge University Press, 2015.

Geertz, C. "The Javanese village". In *Local, ethnic and national loyalties in village Indonesia: A symposium*, edited by G.W. Skinner. New Haven, Conn: Yale University Cultural Report Series, 1959.

Heidel, B. *The Growth of Civil Society in Myanmar.* Bangalore: Books for Change, 2006.

Helmke, G. and S. Levitsky. "Informal Institutions and Comparative Politics: A Research Agenda". *Perspectives on Politics* 2, no. 4 (2004): 725–40.

Human Rights Watch. *Burma: After Cyclone, Repression Impedes Civil Society and Aid.* Bangkok: Human Rights Watch, 2010.

James, H. *Governance and Civil Society in Myanmar: Education, Health and Environment*. London: Routledge Curzon, 2005.

Jaquet, C. and M. Walton. "Buddhism and Relief in Myanmar: Reflections on Relief as a Practice of Dāna". In *Buddhism, International Relief Work, and Civil Society*, edited by Hiroko Kawanami and Geoffrey Samuel. Basingstoke, UK: Palgrave Macmillan, 2013.

Jesses, K. *Developing relations: Political parties and civil society in Myanmar*. Norwegian Peacebuilding Resource Centre, 2014 <http://www.peacebuilding.no/var/ezflow_site/storage/original/application/1dca6db8cbb10f8810a5146b96715142.pdf> (accessed 1 June 2016).

Khin Zaw Min. "Transition in a Time of Siege: The Pluralism of Societal and Political Practices at Ward/Village Level in Myanmar/Burma". In *Active Citizens Under Political Wraps: Experiences from Myanmar/Burma and Vietnam*, edited by Heinrich Boll Foundation. Chiang Mai: Heinrich Boll Foundation, 2006.

Kyaw Min, A. "Religion looms large over poll as NLD, Ma Ba Tha trade words". *Myanmar Times*, 31 July 2015.

Levitsky, S. "An 'Organised Disorganisation': Informal Organisation and the Persistence of Local Party Structures in Argentine Peronism". *Journal of Latin American Studies* 33 (2001): 29–65.

———. *Transforming Labor-Based Parties in Latin America*. Cambridge: Cambridge University Press, 2003.

Lewis, D. "Civil Society and the Authoritarian State: Cooperation, Contestation and Discourse". *Journal of Civil Society* 9, no. 3 (2013): 325–40.

Lorch, J. "Civil Society under Authoritarian Rule: The Case of Myanmar". *Südostasien aktuell* 2 (2006*a*): 3–37.

———. "Do Civil Society Actors Have Any Room for Maneuver in Myanmar/Burma? Locating Gaps in the Authoritarian System". In *Active Citizens Under Political Wraps: Experiences from Myanmar/Burma and Vietnam*, edited by Heinrich Boll Foundation. Chiang Mai: Heinrich Boll Foundation, 2006*b*.

———. "Myanmar's Civil Society — a Patch for the National Education System? The Emergence of Civil Society in Areas of State Weakness". *Südostasien aktuell* 3 (2007): 54–88.

———. "The (re)-emergence of civil society in areas of state weakness: The case of education in Burma/Myanmar". In *Dictatorship, disorder and decline in Myanmar*, edited by M. Skidmore and T. Wilson. Canberra: ANU E Press, 2008.

MacLean, L. *Informal Institutions and Citizenship in Rural Africa: Risk and Reciprocity in Ghana and Cote D'Ivoire*. Cambridge: Cambridge University Press, 2010.

———. "State Retrenchment and the Exercise of Citizenship in Africa". *Comparative Political Studies* 44 (2011): 1238–66.

Mahmood, S. *Politics of Piety: The Islamic Revival and the Feminist Subject*. Princeton: Princeton University Press, 2005.

———. *Religious Difference in a Secular Age: A Minority Report*. Princeton: Princeton University Press, 2015.

McCarthy, G. "Buddhist welfare and the limits of big 'P' politics in provincial Myanmar". In *Conflict in Myanmar: War, Politics, Religion*, edited by Nick Cheesman and Nicholas Farrelly. Singapore: ISEAS – Yusof Ishak Institute, 2016*a*.

———. "*Building on what's there: Insights on social protection and public goods provision from central-east Myanmar*". Report for International Growth Centre Myanmar, 2016*b*.

———. "Cyberspaces". In *Handbook of Contemporary Myanmar*, edited by A. Simpson, N. Farrelly and I. Holliday. London: Routledge, forthcoming.

——— and J. Menager. "Viral rumours and the quotidian cultivation of political identity in Myanmar's transition." In *Communal Violence in Myanmar*, edited by Nick Cheesman. Yangon: Myanmar Knowledge Society, 2015.

——— and J. Menager. "Gendered Rumours and the Muslim Scapegoat in Myanmar's Transition". *Journal of Contemporary Asia* 47, no. 3 (2017): 396–412.

Muehlebach, A. *The Moral Neoliberal: Welfare and Citizenship in Italy*. Chicago: University of Chicago, 2012.

Nishizaki, Y. "The Weapon of the Strong: Identity, Community and Domination in Provincial Thailand". PhD dissertation, University of Washington, 2004.

———. *Political Authority and Provincial Identity in Thailand: The Making of Banharn-buri*. Ithaca, NY: Cornell Southeast Asia Program, 2011.

Nyi Nyi Kyaw. "Alienation, Discrimination, and Securitization: Legal Personhood and Cultural Personhood of Muslims in Myanmar". *Review of Faith & International Affairs* 13, no. 4 (2015): 50–59.

Petrie, C. and A. South. "Development of civil society in Myanmar". In *Burma/Myanmar: Where Now?*, edited by Mikael Gravers and Flemming Ytzen. Copenhagen: Nordic Institute of Asian Studies Press, 2014.

Prasse-Freeman, E. "Power, Civil Society, and an Inchoate Politics of the Daily in Burma/Myanmar". *Journal of Asian Studies* 71, no. 2 (2012): 371–97.

———. "Grassroots Protest Movements and Mutating Conceptions of 'the Political' in an Evolving Burma". In *Metamorphosis: Studies in Social and Political Change in Myanmar*, edited by Renaud Egreteau and Francois Robinne. Singapore: National University of Singapore Press, 2015.

Schissler, M. "New Technologies, Established Practices: Developing Narratives of Muslim Threat in Myanmar". In *Islam and the State in Myanmar: Muslim-Buddhist Relations and the Politics of Belonging*, edited by Melissa Crouch. Oxford: Oxford University Press, 2015.

———, M.J. Walton and P.P. Thi. *Threat and virtuous defence: Listening to narratives of religious conflict in six Myanmar cities*. Report by Myanmar Media and Society Project, University of Oxford, 2015 <https://www.sant.ox.ac.uk/sites/default/files/m.mas_working_paper_1.1_-_threat_and_virtuous_defence_-_july_2015.pdf> (accessed 28 May 2016).

Smith, M. *Burma (Myanmar): The Time for Change*. Minority Rights Group International, 2002 <http://minorityrights.org/wp-content/uploads/old-site-

downloads/download-133-BurmaMyanmar-Time-for-Change.pdf> (accessed 28 May 2016).

South, A. "Political Transition in Myanmar: A New Model for Democratisation". *Contemporary Southeast Asia: A Journal of International and Strategic Affairs* 26, no. 2 (2004): 233–55.

———. *Civil Society in Burma: The Development of Democracy Amidst Conflict.* Washington, D.C., East-West Center, 2008.

Steinberg, D.I. "A Void in Myanmar: Civil Society in Burma". In *Strengthening Civil Society in Burma: Possibilities and Dilemmas for International NGOs*, edited by T. Kramer and P. Vervest. Chiangmai: Silkworm Books, 1999.

———. *Turmoil in Burma: Contested Legitimacies in Myanmar.* Norwalk, CT: East Bridge. (2006).

Taylor, R. *The State in Myanmar.* London: Hurst Publishing, 2009.

Turner, A. "Buddhism, Colonialism and the Boundaries of Religion: Theravada Buddhism in Burma, 1885–1920". PhD dissertation, University of Chicago, 2009.

———. "Religion Making and Its Failures: Turning Monasteries into Schools and Buddhism into a Religion in Colonial Burma". In *Secularism and Religion Making*, edited by Markus Dressler and Arvind Mandair. New York: Oxford University Press, 2011.

———. "Saving Buddhism: Moral Community and the Impermanence of Colonial Religion". *Southeast Asia: Politics, Meaning and Memory Series.* Honolulu: University of Hawaii Press, 2014.

———. "Myanmar: Contesting Conceptual Landscapes in the Politics of Buddhism". *Kyoto Review of Southeast Asia* 19. Kyoto: Centre for South East Asian Studies, Kyoto University, 2016.

Varshney, A. *Ethnic Conflict and Civic Life: Hindus and Muslims in India.* New Haven: Yale University Press, 2002.

UNICEF/MDRI. *Making Public Finance Work for Children in Myanmar.* Yangon: United Nations Children's Fund and Myanmar Development Resource Institute, 2014.

Walton, M. "Politics in the Moral Universe: Burmese Buddhist political thought". PhD dissertation, University of Washington, 2012.

———. "What are Myanmar's Buddhist Sunday schools teaching?". *East Asia Forum* 16 December 2014 <http://www.eastasiaforum.org/2014/12/16/what-are-myanmars-buddhist-sunday-schools-teaching/> (accessed 29 May 2016).

HOW I BECAME SHAN

Sai Kheunsai
Founder and Editor, Shan Herald Agency for News

Yes, I know. These days it is hard to believe I used to be one of the noted Burmese song writers. That I used to speak Burmese more fluently than Shan. That I used to love wearing Burmese *longyis* than pants.

When I got back to Taunggyi last April to attend a reunion of my extended family, my cousins, nephews and nieces were not only surprised, but also dismayed to find out that I couldn't even remember my own songs. "I remember every song you wrote", said a cousin, who in fact sang for me when I was asked to sing a song.

It wasn't like that when I moved from Lower Burma back to Shan State in 1954. My father who had participated in demonstrations against feudalist Saofas (Sawbwas) had fled to join the First Shan Rifles, formed after Independence under the leadership of Gen Tin Tut, who had worked with Aung San when he came to Panglong in 1947 to participate in the conference that culminated in the signing of the historic treaty.

I was six years old and spoke Shan only with my grandfather and neighbours. Among us brothers and sisters (actually cousins, as all our parents had left us in the care of our widowed grandfather), who had all been brought up in Burma Proper, the lingua franca among us was Burmese. We all read Burmese novels, sang Burmese songs and dressed like Burmese do.

In 1962, following the coup, we moved to Taunggyi where I was reunited with my parents. My father had left the Burma Army, after he, along with his company, was removed from the Shan Rifles to another unit, and spent years being transferred from one place to another. I was 14 that year and, what's more, I was in love — or thought I was, after reading so many romances written by Burmese authors like Tetkatho Phone Naing, who later became the head of the Taunggyi College, where I attended it in 1966. And like every teenager in love, I was desperately in need of an outlet for my pent-up emotions. And I started to write songs in Burmese. (Took me four years to produce the first song)

All in all, I was on my way to becoming a Burman. Without shame. Or without regret.

Then, like most stories in books, disaster struck in the form of a directive from U Tin Ko Ko, said to be a Shan from Pyinmana (Burmese corruption of Piang Mark-na, meaning The Plain of Myrobalan), and appointed by the coup leader Gen Ne Win as a member of the Shan State Executive Council responsible for education. He wanted to continue the Shan language classes, twice a week, and, to my horror, he wanted all male students, both Shans and non-Shans alike, to wear Shan pants to school.

Yes, I remember I didn't like it at all. Why should I learn Shan? Has it become an official language in Shan State? (It hadn't) What good will come out of it by learning it? Such a waste of time.

It was the same sentiments with wearing pants. I thought *longyis* were more convenient for us males on any occasion. What's more, it's cheaper. On the contrary, the baggy Shan pants were really annoying, especially when you have to go to toilet, to relieve yourself, unlike the *longyi*, which all you have to do is to lift the part of it that you need to.

My disgust of the Shan pants reached its zenith the morning when I was cycling to school and came across the girl I had taken a shine on. I thought about chatting with her and if she's interested, which I was sure she was, would ask to sit on my bicycle's backseat to school.

I softly called her name and when she turned her head to look at me, I stopped the bike and lowered my left feet to the ground. Unfortunately, my foot never reached it. My pants were caught in the pedal, and I went crashing down to the ground, with the bicycle on top.

Students then rushed to help me. Someone lifted the bicycle off my back. Another picked up my glasses and handed them back. And everyone was laughing. I was hurt. Moreover my youthful pride was hurt. And I vowed to myself aloud, "I'm not going to be a Shan, ever!".

The vow, like New Year's resolutions, did not last long.

Halfway through the next academic year, the report came that U Tin Ko Ko had been stripped of his positions and detained. Next came the new

Khuensai, 17, in Taunggyi

directive from the education department: From now on, all male students shall no more wear Shan pants to school, but only *longyis*. And, what's more, no more Shan classes.

By all accounts, I should have been happy about the whole affair. Figuratively speaking, hadn't both of my prayers been answered?

But, to my own surprise, I was starting to ask questions:

• Hey, what's wrong with wearing pants? Is it a crime to dress like a Shan coming to school?
• And what about not having to learn Shan? What's wrong with a Shan learning Shan? More than that, if it's all right for non-Burmans to learn Burmese, why shouldn't non-Shans learn Shan, especially when they are in Shan State?

I was young. I was rebellious. Maybe we Shans have some blood akin to the Italians I read in one of *Readers' Digest* funny stories, which goes something like this:

An ocean liner carrying international businessmen holding a business convention is about to sink mid-ocean. The captain calls his chief mate and orders him to inform the passagers that they have to escape by lifeboats now.

After a while, the chief mate returns and informs the captain everyone is refusing to leave. The captain listens and orders him to wait for him at the bridge and goes out. A few minutes later, he is back and tells the mate they are the only people left on the ship and they have to move fast before the ship goes down. The mate asks him how he had pulled it off. And he answers:

It's easy. With the British, I told them it's *sporting* to abandon ship. They went right off. With the French, I said its *chic* and elegant to leave the ship. They happily went away. With Germans, I told them it's an *order*. They obeyed.

With Italians, I said they were *not allowed* to leave the ship, so they went.
Mate: What about the Americans? What did you tell them?
Captain: Simple. I informed them they were *insured*.

Anyway, from then on, I started to learn Shan outside school hours and started wearing Shan pants, at every opportunity offered. To spite the rulers, if not for anything else.

Which started me on the road to politics and in due course rebellion.

In 1983, when I was appointed as a representative to visit the Karen National Union (KNU), my Burmese had become so rusty that I had to ask for an officer who was more at home with the language to prompt me whenever I found myself at a loss for words.

It took me another fifteen years to find out what went wrong.

In 1998, I was at a seminar in Chiangmai, where representatives from different branches of Tai, which includes Shan, Thai, Laotians, Ahom, Leu (Lu), Yon (Muang), and Kheun (Khun), among others, met.

During the break, I had a chance to talk to the Leu representative from Sipsawngpanna (Xixuangbanna, China), whom I told:

"I really envy your situation."
Tai Leu: Why?
I: Because the Chinese government is not only allowing you to learn Tai, but also encouraging and supporting it. The same goes for your efforts to preserve and promote your culture. I wish we in Burma are enjoying the same rights.
Tai Leu: You may be right. But, on the contrary, we too feel envious of your situation."
I: (Surprised) How is that?
Tai Leu: Of course, you know the Tai saying:

The fish lives when the water is hot.
The fish dies when the water is cold.
(Nam Hawn Pa Pen, Nam Yen Pa Tai)

You Shans are living under suppression, like a fish in hot water. You therefore do everything to survive. So your literature and culture live on. However, we Tai Leu, bestowed freedom by the Chinese government to preserve, promote and propagate our literature and culture, face a bigger opponent — our own youth. Given a choice between Tai and Chinese literatures and cultures, they are not interested in their own heritage anymore. To them, the choice is to go the Chinese way. Had our literature and culture been suppressed and strangled like you are, these young people would have been easier to convince.

Since then, I have never stopped wondering: Had successive Burmese governments been as enlightened and magnanimous with the upkeep of Shan literature and culture, like the Chinese government is, would I still choose to be Shan?

7

CONFLICT AND MASS VIOLENCE IN ARAKAN (RAKHINE STATE)
The 1942 Events and Political Identity Formation

Jacques P. Leider

Following the Japanese invasion of Lower Burma in early 1942, the British administration in Arakan[1] collapsed in late March/early April. In a matter of days, communal violence broke out in the rural areas of central and north Arakan (Akyab and Kyaukphyu districts). Muslim villagers from Chittagong who had settled in Arakan since the late nineteenth century were attacked, driven away or killed in Minbya, Myebon, Pauktaw and other townships of central Arakan. A few weeks later, Arakanese Buddhist villagers living in the predominantly Muslim townships of Maungdaw and Buthidaung were taken on by Chittagonian Muslims, their villages destroyed and people killed in great numbers. Muslims fled to the north while Buddhists fled to the south and from 1942 to 1945, the Arakanese countryside was ethnically divided between a Muslim north and a Buddhist south. Several thousand Buddhists and Muslims were relocated by the British to camps in Bengal. The unspeakable outburst of violence has been described with various expressions, such as "massacre", "bitter battle" or "communal riot" reflecting different interpretations of what had happened. In the twenty-first century, the description "ethnic cleansing" would likely be considered as a legally appropriate term. Buddhists and Muslims alike see the 1942 violence as a key moment of their ongoing ethno-religious and political divide.

The waves of communal clashes of 1942 have been poorly documented, sparsely investigated and rarely studied.[2] They are not recorded in standard textbooks on Burma/Myanmar and, surprisingly, they were even absent from contemporary reports and articles that described Burma's situation during and after World War II. From a historiographic point of view, the 1942 atrocities in Arakan may be considered as an example of the academic marginalization of the borderlands of Bengal/East Pakistan/Bangladesh and Arakan/Rakhine State in modern times. In 1952, B.R. Pearn, a professor of history from Rangoon University, wrote a confidential report for the Foreign Office on the Mujahid revolt that consumed North Arakan since 1948. The report contained a historical background that included the 1942 violence. However eight years earlier, Pearn himself had read a paper at the Royal Society of Arts in London ("Burma since the invasion", 14 December 1944) that did not even hint at the forced displacement and the killings that had taken place two years before in Arakan (Pearn 1945; see also Bowerman 1946).

Nonetheless, more recently, following the waves of intercommunal violence in June and October 2012, the events of 1942 have been reinterpreted in the context of background descriptions of the Rakhine State crisis and the plight of the Rohingyas. The prevailing interpretation embeds the violent incidents of 1942 in a record of anti-Muslim persecution, implicitly or explicitly suggesting that Muslims had been victims of discrimination long before the Nagaraja campaign of the Burmese army in 1978 that pushed a quarter million of Muslims over the border into Bangladesh. Such a reading misses relevant facts and important nuances. The terrible confrontation of 1942 had in fact tragic consequences for both communities. The inglorious events have never been a source of contentment or pride for any of the two parties. Actors on both sides of the social and religious divide have to share the responsibility for criminal behaviour. Still, there is regrettably little reliable or detailed information at hand on what triggered the violence in Minbya or Myebon, what happened hereafter and in which exact circumstances a wave of revenge killings occurred. Yet, importantly, what happened during the war had an immediate impact on the political consciousness of the people and the strategy of their leaders.

The present article is an attempt to compile available information on the 1942 violence, the geographical and historical context and the estimations of the number of victims and displaced. It is attentive to the remembrance of the events, their retelling and their impact on the relations and the political ideas of the two groups. Generally speaking, the mutual acts of aggression that led to killings and massive forced displacement increased inter-ethnic hostility. Nonetheless, the article aims primarily at an assessment of the 1942 violence with regard to political identity and supports the argument that the 1942 violence was historically relevant because it determined the civic awareness and the political orientations of Buddhists and Muslims during the early post-war period. In that regard, it provides an input of critical historical awareness that may contribute to a better understanding of the Rakhine conundrum after World War II (see Derek Tonkin's subsequent chapter on citizenship and other Rakhine-related work in the volume).

Over a million Indian migrants had been recorded in the 1931 Burma census. Tensions with the native population were rife in the 1930s. In Burma proper, the anti-Indian riots of 1938 led the government to commission a report on Indian immigration (Baxter Report 1940), but the Japanese invasion cut short the implementation of measures that the report suggested. In Burma, the number of Indians had been steeply growing after World War I and many of them lived and worked in cities, notably in Rangoon. Arakan's situation was different. Seasonal labour was typical for the local rice-growing economy, but Chittagonian agriculturists had settled in growing numbers in North Arakan since the opening of the Suez Canal that had favoured the production and the export of rice. In 1931, three-quarters of the resident Muslim population of Arakan (a quarter million) was born in the country. This number included a small, but much older precolonial community of Arakanese Muslims who were socially well integrated and spread throughout the province.

Muslims in Arakan had not been politically active before the war as the colonial order was a sufficient shield of protection for their economic and political interests. However in 1942, the breakdown of the British rule and a mixed context of physical threats and political opportunities transformed the elite of Muslim land-owners in North Arakan into a politically active group. These men were bound by the same cultural and geographical origins and, pushed by the circumstances, took the conservation of public order into their own hands. They also imagined the project of an exclusive Muslim territory ruled by themselves, a venture that inspired Muslim identity formation throughout the 1940s and 1950s and fired the early Rohingya movement. In the minds of the Buddhist Rakhine, on the other hand, the 1942 expulsion from the north fostered the adamant belief that the Chittagonian settlers, under the guise of labour migration, were bent on pushing the Buddhists out of their homeland.

No enquiry commission ever established a record of the events and the injustice committed. Buddhists and Muslims in Arakan may even have felt that there was no need for any investigation after the war or a preservation of evidence as the bare facts were still at hand for anyone to see and remember. In sum, the lessons were there to be learned by those who had participated or suffered. The ethnic cleansing of 1942 and the three years of ethnic and political division of Arakan certainly conditioned the political beliefs of the local actors and transformed the ethnic and religious differences into a rift that was henceforth perceived as unbridgeable. Therefore, the selective communalist interpretations of the events gained more importance than the need for any elucidation of what had really happened and why. Partisan views were lastly commodified into historical truths.

There is, as we have noted, very little noteworthy writing on the 1942 events.[3] Sources to explore the ethnic cleansing of 1942 are a motley collection of partial Buddhist and Muslim accounts mainly focusing on the losses of their own communities and a few succinct British war memories. Much of the material used for writing this paper is freely available in print or appears on Rakhine or Rohingya websites. Most descriptions of the 1942 events have been written many years after the events took place. They may contain witness accounts, but there is very little verifiable evidence. As a result, the descriptions of what happened, as much as the beliefs of Buddhists and Muslims about the events, seem largely based on extrapolations and interpretations of a mix of facts, guesses, hearsay and prejudice.

VIOLENCE AND ETHNIC CLEANSING IN 1942

Moshe Yegar's description of the 1942 massacres in his work on *The Muslims of Burma* is probably one of the best-known general depictions. However the presentation is very general, it contains no chronology and does not provide a specific context for the actors.

> Gangs of Arakanese Buddhists in southern Arakan, where the Buddhists are in the majority, attacked Muslim villages and massacred their inhabitants. Whole villages were sacked and their inhabitants murdered. Some Arakanese notables attempted to prevent the wholesale massacres, but without success. Muslim refugees streamed to northern Arakan.... The refugees reaching Maungdaw incensed the local Muslim majority with their stories, and the latter began to mete out similar punishment upon the Buddhist minority in their midst. These acts of mutual murder soon caused the Buddhist population in northern Arakan to flee, even as the Muslims had fled from the south.

It was in this manner that Arakan became divided into two separate areas, one Buddhist and the other Muslim (Yegar 1972, p. 95).

In Pearn's (1952) report on the Mujahid Revolt mentioned above, the 1942 massacres are linked to the mounting communal tensions of the 1930s. Strikingly, ten years after the events, Pearn found it easier to *explain* the violence than retrace what had actually happened. Recalling that the townships of Maungdaw and Buthidaung "came to be inhabited more by Muslims whose origins and to a great extent sympathies lay across the frontier", he concluded that "it is not surprising that the Arakanese should feel that they were being driven out of their homeland" and

> communal tension was unavoidable, and was intensified when the development of self-government in Burma from 1923 onwards, with its accompaniment of communal representation in the legislature, tended to emphasise the dissimilarities between communities. The tension found its expression in 1938, when Maungdaw and Buthidaung were involved in the anti-Muslim rioting which spread over Burma in that year.

Construing the events as an argument of historical inevitability, Pearn avoided the issue of political responsibility and agency.

> The collapse of authority in 1942 at the time of the Japanese invasion gave an opportunity for this friction to express itself once more, and in April 1942 Akyab district was the scene of civil war, in which unknown number were slaughtered and many perished of starvation and exposure in attempting to find refuge elsewhere. The devastation caused by the military operations of the next three years caused a continued flight of population: where possible, Arakanese from the north fled southwards, and Muslims fled to Chittagong where refugee camps had to be provided for their accommodation.

Muslim sources, like the ones used by Yegar, agree that violence started with organized Arakanese/Rakhine attacks against Muslims in the rural area of Central Arakan. It broke out allegedly on the 28 March 1942 in either Minbya or Myebon township. Thereafter the aggressions spread over several neighboring townships.

According to A.F.K. Jilani, a veteran Rohingya militant, armed Arakanese attacked their Muslim neighbours in a village of Minbya township, Chanbili. During the next two days, the attacks, including looting and killing, spread to other villages in Minbya ("Lombaissor", "Taungyi Nyo", "Apawka pass") and then to Myebon ("Raichaung", "Pankha"). During the month of April

1942, massacres took place successively in Pauktaw, Mrohaung [Mrauk U], Kyauktaw and Rathedaung. Muslims who fled, joined other communities in Akyab where they acquired arms and defended themselves. Arakanese also led attacks against Muslim villages in Buthidaung township reaching as far north as Taung Bazar (Jilani 2006).

Aye Chan, a Rakhine historian, counters Muslim allegations with a local source stating that the anti-Muslim violence was initially triggered by the killing of the Buddhist village headman of Rak Chaung village (Myebon township) together with his two brothers. This act apparently provoked organized Buddhist attacks on Muslim villages where people were killed (Aye Chan 2005, p. 405).

According to a contemporary Arakanese witness, local Buddhist leaders started by launching attacks against Muslims first in Letma as they suspected them to plan evil (Khaing Myo Saung 2012, p. 105 quoting Maung Kan Htu's notes). Sultan Mahmud, a North Arakan Muslim member of parliament since 1951 and Minister for Health under Prime Minister U Nu in 1956, similarly stated that the violence started in Letma, a village in Myebon township. From there, he said, it spread to six townships including Minbya, Pauktaw, Ponnagyun, Kyauktaw and Rathedaung that were "depleted" of Muslims by "murder and massacre" (Mahmud 1950; Khaing Myo Saung 2012, p. 105).

Muslim sources seem to agree that the violence was prompted by the Thakin leaders in Arakan. The Thakins were a nationalist, anti-colonial organization that had emerged in the 1930s. A small group of them, the Thirty Comrades, received Japanese military training in 1940 and joined the Japanese invasion. They were credited with the creation of the Burma Independence Army (BIA) that grew into a troop of 8,000 in 1942 and supported the advance of the Japanese. Pearn explained that the BIA troops

> fought, bravely enough, alongside the Japanese, and … also took over the administration of the districts which successively fell into enemy hands. Thus, for some months in 1942, an increasing part of Burma was administered by the Burma Independence Army (Pearn 1945, p. 156).

However, according to him, the Thakins also included criminals and the results of their administration "were so disastrous that the Japanese themselves had to intervene. Oppression and corruption reached such an extent that the Japanese suppressed the Burma Independence Army." (ibid.)

Pearn's description thus gives support to the idea that BIA members initiated the anti-Muslim violence. BIA forces coming from the Irrawaddy Valley entered Arakan by the Am road and reached Minbya township after passing the Arakan Yoma ridge and crossing the Lemro River (Bonpauk

Tha Kyaw 1973, pp. 80–82). Yet the BIA had to face first of all retreating British Indian troops, and the sudden prominence of the BIA in the short period between the collapse of the British rule in March and the occupation of Akyab by the Japanese in May 1942 does not answer the question of the underlying causes of the communal violence in the context of central Arakan. Moreover, the fact that in the north and possibly elsewhere the local Muslim communities enjoyed support from British Rajput troops,[4] and were not in favour of the "liberators of Burma" may have had an immediately negative impact on communal relations. Bonpauk Tha Kyaw, who followed Thakin Bo Ran Aung to Arakan, describes a series of encounters with Rakhine local leaders such as Thein Kyaw Aung and Maung Kyaw Ya and men who boasted with their killings of Muslims (Bonpauk 1973, p. 76). Yet while he was discredited in Muslim eyes for cooperating with such people, Tha Kyaw seems to have interpreted the events as entirely detrimental to the cause of the liberation of Burma from the British imperialists (Abu Aneen 2007; Bonpauk 1973, p. 77). His witness account does not suggest that reasonable voices were very successful trying to dissuade the rioteers.

It is reported that a great number of Muslims were killed while a greater number were able to flee to the predominantly Muslim areas in Buthidaung and Maungdaw, and further on to Chittagong. Yegar speaks about 22,000 refugees who fled to India (Yegar 1972, p. 95). Abu Aneen summarizes Muslim views that there were about 100,000 who fled and were relocated to Rangpur in Bengal (Abu Aneen 2007).[5]

Sultan Mahmud goes on to describe what happened thereafter: "These refugees in Maungdaw who had lost their dearest one and all their property now turned against the Rakhine and fell upon them in retaliation" (Mahmud 1950). Ba Tha further explains:

> In turn, the Rohingyas who survived and took shelter in Maungdaw-Buthidaung area wanted to create trouble there. The Maughs [=Arakanese] timely ran away from this area to Kyauktaw and Myohaung [Mrauk U] townships ... (Ba Tha 1960).

Indeed, the next chapter of events took place in the countryside around the town of Maungdaw where the Buddhists formed a small minority among a majority of Muslim villages. Armed Bengali Muslims attacked those villages and thousands of Buddhists took refuge in the town of Maungdaw. An anonymous eyewitness source describes the town under siege:

> The armed Bengalis [Chittagonian Muslims] set up roadblocks, destroyed the bridges, and encircled the Rakhine villages. By then more than 20,000 armed Bengalis had surrounded the Maungdaw town. All the entry and exit

points had been completely blocked and the horrifying news of surrounding Buddhist villages being burnt to the ground and their people slaughtered reached the town constantly. The town was already sheltering hundreds and hundreds of Rakhine refugees from the nearby Buddhist villages. Many were injured or wounded ... But now they were trapped in Maungdaw together with the Rakhine-Buddhists of the town (Anonymous 2012).

Thanks to the intervention of a local magistrate, a detachment of Gurkha troops prevented a massacre and ferried several thousand Arakanese refugees from Maungdaw to Bengal where they were relocated to a camp in Dinajpur (Khaing Myo Saung 2012, pp. 119–26). The eyewitness source concludes:

All the Rakhine villages, there were hundreds of them ... on the extremely fertile strip south of Maungdaw Town between the Naff River and Mayu Ranges, were completely wiped out by the rioting Bengali Muslims within few days. While the Rakhine villagers from the foreshore villages like Nga-khu-ya, Chan-byin, Ywat-hnyo-taung, and Tha-yet-oat villages were able to manage to escape by their sampans across the Naff River, the villages far from the river were burnt down and the whole village slaughtered by the rioting Bengali-Muslims (Anonymous 2012).

The British Commissioner of Arakan had left Akyab in late March 1942, so had the Royal Air Force and the Indian Navy while many soldiers of the Akyab garrison deserted. The Deputy Commissioner, the Arakanese U Kyaw Khine, moved the headquarters to Buthidaung.

The dramatic developments that took place in North Arakan are reported in a few British descriptions mostly written many years after the events. Peter Murray, a British officer who was based in Maungdaw in 1943, took a particular interest in the organization of local Muslim self-government between March and October 1942. According to Murray's sources, Kyaw Khine, the Deputy Commissioner "did what he could to keep the peace and maintain the administration, but everywhere law and order was dissolving into bitter and bloody fighting between CF[6] and Magh" (Murray 1980, p. 3).[7] A contemporary Arakanese/Rakhine source confirms that U Kyaw Khine "tried really hard together with the Muslim leaders Yasein and Sultan Mahmud to prevent the slaughter" (Hla Oo 2012). The Deputy Commissioner was killed when he tried to investigate a looming Muslim attack on Buthidaung. Soon after his murder, Muslim forces assaulted Buthidaung and all the Arakanese were either killed or had to flee.

Murray's summary of the events is based on a collection of contemporary sources, including eyewitness accounts. He explains that the fighting had been "provoked by long-standing racial religious and discords and fuelled by simple greed for loot".

> In the areas nearest the Indian border, the Maungdaw Township down to near Foul Point and the Buthidaung township to about 20 m[iles] south of Buthidaung, the Maghs were killed or driven out (except for small groups in Maungdaw and Buthidaung towns, which had always been predominantly Magh); all Buddhist buildings, pagodas and monasteries, were razed or burnt, and all Magh villages burnt and all Magh property (mainly cattle) seized. Similarly further south, all or nearly all CFs were killed or driven out, mosques destroyed and CF cattle seized (Murray 1980, p. 8).

Murray also mentions the evacuation of 9,000 Arakanese from Maungdaw to Dinajpur thanks to U Kyaw Min, a senior Arakanese Indian Civil Service officer.

Once they controlled the predominantly Muslim areas along the border with the district of Chittagong, the Muslim leaders created a political order of their own though they remained loyal to the British in their opposition to the Japanese. They created the so-called "peace committees" and divided the rule within Maungdaw district among themselves. When BIA emissaries from Akyab approached them in May 1942 to gain the Muslim community over to the Japanese side, the BIA delegation was supposedly massacred after a dinner served in Maungdaw (Murray 1980, p. 7).

Murray lists the Majlis-i-shura of E.D.S. Maracan, a wealthy Indian businessman established south of Maungdaw town, the Maungdaw Central Peace Committee under Omra Meah, a schoolmaster, the Bawli Bazaar Committee under Faruq Ahmed, the Peace Committee ("Anjuman Tahufazzal Islam") of Shabe Bazaar on the Pruma River under Mohamed Luqman that merged subsequently with the Faquira Bazaar Committee. In Buthidaung township there were the Panzai Bazaar Committee on the Kalapanzin Valley under Abdul Salaam, the Taung Bazaar Committee under the schoolmaster Abdul Bari, a committee at Bogrichaung under the reputed landowner Abdul Bari Chowdhury, and an unspecified town peace committee in Buthidaung.[8] Further south towards Rathedaung, there was a robber, Faruq, who ruled the area with his gang.[9] Trade relations with the Chittagong markets took the place of Maungdaw's former connections with Akyab. While the peace committees served the need to establish "law and order and inter-village relations", the various leaders were rivalling and quarrelling with each other. However, their "first and foremost" problem, says Murray, was to get rid of the "hereditary enemies, the Arakanese, a problem which they tackled with vigour and courage and had disposed of by the end of May" (Murray 1980,

p. 5). Murray's understated formulation of the ethnic cleansing suggests that it
was likely perceived by contemporary observers as collateral damage. Anthony
Irwin, the author of a book on the military events in Arakan, sums up the
1942 violence in another minimalist formulation: "Whilst it lasted, it was a
pretty bloody affair" (Irwin 1946). At the time, the British were faced with
the immense challenge to gain ground in the war against the Japanese and
one device was the recruitment of local Muslims to gain intelligence from
behind the Japanese lines. As Pearn explains, the pool of recruits for the
formation of "V Force" were the "local bodies of armed Muslims" that had
been organized under the authority of the peace committees (Pearn 1952).

> In the autumn of 1942, members of these bodies were organised as part of
> a para-military formation known as "V Force", and were trained, clothed,
> armed and paid by the British. The Muslim V Force was active for the
> remainder of the war in Arakan, and became a large and powerful — though
> ill-disciplined — intelligence and intruder agency, which, incidentally, used
> its intelligence duties as a means of smuggling textiles into Japanese-occupied
> territory, much to its own profit (Pearn 1952).

However, before autumn 1942, the same men had been, as Pearn writes,
"engaged in civil war with the Arakanese Buddhists". Pearn, like Murray, thus
suggests that these men had previously been involved in ethnic cleansing and
the forced displacement of Maungdaw and Buthidaung Buddhists. During the
following years of war against the Japanese, the Muslim hostility towards the
Arakanese further increased as the Muslims perceived the Arakanese Buddhists
as traitors while they saw themselves as loyalists.[10] V Force gained fame as an
indispensable support for the British war effort in Arakan between late 1942
and 1945. Its action has been described in glowing terms in Anthony Irwin's
Burmese Outpost and C.E. Lucas Philipps' *The Raiders of Arakan* (Irwin 1946;
Philipps 1971). After the war, their sacrifices for the British served as one
of the main arguments to call for the creation of an autonomous Muslim
zone in North Arakan. The call made by the Jamiat ul-Ulama (Association
of Religious Teachers), the main political body of the Muslim leadership in
North Arakan, was not heeded by the British authorities, though it was not
inconsistent with the British self-perception of Britain's role as the protector
of ethnic minorities in Burma. Informal suggestions and opinions to grant the
Muslims such an autonomous territory had circulated among British military
ranks during the war as they highly valued the contribution of V Force to
the war effort (Mole 2001, p. 193). However, promises were never officially
acknowledged or couched in writing. Claims to designate North Arakan as a
frontier zone, as made by the Jamiat ul-Ulama in the aftermath of the second

Panglong Conference (February 1947), failed as well. They were immediately rejected by the British authorities stating the historical unity of Arakan and the fact that it had never been a "frontier" in the sense of the Shan, Kachin or Chin territories.

POLITICAL COMING OF AGE OF THE MUSLIMS

The political and military developments in 1942 and afterwards had an impact on the political mobilization of the Muslim elite of North Arakan. The war and the collapse of the British rule created an environment where ambitious local leaders could explore the exercise of power in small areas that they ruled by their own means. Murray notes that the Chittagonian migrants under British rule had been "minimal, even-handed and rather dull for 116 years and had on the whole prospered mainly as rice farmers" (Murray 1980, p. 10). The *de facto* autonomy of the Muslim "peace committees" during the critical months of 1942 gave the Muslims a strong awareness of their political interests and potential leverage. Murray makes clear this point when he writes that in his view they "had quite lost their pre-war meekness and were quite prepared to protect themselves". The change of conditions thus produced a novel situation that opened up new political space for a whole generation of North Arakan Muslims. A bird's eye view the organizational mobilization of North Arakan Muslims from the 1930s down to the 1960s reveals the link between the Jamiat ul-Ulama founded in the late 1930s, its political role after the war, the project of a separate Muslim territory that emerged after 1942 and became a central concern of the Mujahid rebels and, lastly, the diffusion of the idea that North Arakan Muslims formed a historical community of mixed ethnicity. The choice of a unifying name to designate this community was critical. Its spelling (Rwangya, Roewhengya, Ruhangya, or Rohingya) was debated among like-minded local leaders and Rangoon University Muslim students from Arakan during the late 1950s and early 1960s. It was an educated elite that formed, in its early stages, the political and ideological "cloud" that one can refer to collectively as the Rohingya movement (Leider 2013*b*).

An embryonic political consciousness of the North Arakan Muslim elite may well have existed since 1937 when Burma was separated from India and the Naf River became the border between two distinct political entities. However, it was the post-1941 experience of several years of a relative autonomy that propelled the political coming of age of the geographically concentrated, but regionally isolated group. Between 1942 and 1945, Muslim landlords and strongmen could effectively exercise administrative control over an area emptied of its Buddhist population, acting on their own or within the context of British military administration. Bursting with self-confidence about the role that they had played either in V Force or in the local administration, at the end of the war, these leaders faced the risk to be politically ignored. So they wanted to strike the iron while it was still hot: preserving the conditions of Muslim political autonomy and staying apart from the Buddhist population. In their letter to A.G. Bottomley, HM's Under-Secretary for Dominions, presented in February 1947, the Jamiat ul-Ulama wrote:

> when the Government protection was withdrawn from this area, we functioned successfully in the interim period as a sovereign State forming a Peace Committee, the Administrative Body, in North Arakan. This conclusively proved our ability to manage our own affairs.... when the Burma campaign was launched in the North Arakan Front, and the advancing Allied forces entered this area, this Peace Committee, the Administrative Body, gained recognition from the military Administrator, North Arakan. And this Administrative Body, was given many pledges towards self determination, on the model of autonomous Muslim State in New Burma (*Representation...* 1947).

Interestingly, the letter refers two times to the "carnage" and the "communal riots" of 1942, but both expressions remain unspecific as to whom was to blame for the violence.

A year later, the Jamiat ul-Ulama pleaded its project of political autonomy with the U Nu government. To no avail. The Anti-Fascist People's Freedom League (AFPFL) leaders and those Burmese politicians who held power throughout the 1950s were strongly attached to the idea of a unitary state where despite the diversity of identities and interests, each ethnic group would freely submit to the consensus of a united nation. When the revolt of the Mujahids spread out in the first half of 1948, the government seems to have taken the sweeping view that North Arakan Muslim leaders were either self-proclaimed or disguised separatists. Under such conditions, the Jamiat ul-Ulama was not in a position to use the damage and the distress of 1942 in its own favor. Nor could it play up the communal aspect of the violence as the Arakanese/Rakhine viewpoints gained a stronger stand after 1948.

Upon Prime Minister U Nu's visit to Maungdaw on 25 October 1948, the Jamiat ul-Ulama changed its approach, pleaded for an "amicable settlement" with the Arakanese and blamed the 1942 violence on the "divide and rule" policy of the British.

> The divide and rule policy of an Alien Govt. had created in the past a large measure of misunderstanding and distrust between our people and

our Arakanese brethrens. This policy culminated in the massacre of 1942 of our people residing in various parts of Akyab District. This unhappy episode brought in, in its tail, communal feuds throughout the whole of Akyab District. We are at pains to rub this unhappy happenings from the minds of us all and come to an amicable settlement between our people and our Arakanese brethren ("Address presented by Jamiat ul-Ulama..." 1948).

Certainly none of the two communities forgot the terrible experience of unbound violence, destruction of the livelihood of thousands of people, slaughters and displacement. Nonetheless, as this extract shows, the Muslim leadership seriously downplayed the 1942 events to safeguard its fragile political interests. Peace-minded Muslim leaders and Mujahidin rebels alike shared the same endeavour for autonomy which they promoted throughout the 1950s while rejecting at the same time the creation of an Arakan State ruled by the Buddhists.

The political situation of Arakanese nationalists, on the other hand, mirrored the one of the divided Muslims of North Arakan. Some argued the case of the creation of an autonomous Arakan State in parliament (like U Kyaw Min) while others fought for an illusory independence by waging a guerrilla war against the government troops (like the monk U Seinda). Both Muslims and Buddhists were keen to reach out for the support of the government. There is no doubt that the ethnic cleansing had, to a certain extent, played in each other's hands, strengthening local ethno-religious domination. However, neither the Buddhists nor the Muslims could hope for any political return playing up the events of 1942. There was nothing to be won by fighting each other. It rather looks as if a veil was silently drawn over the 1942 violence.

In the early 1960s, the winners of the political tug-of-war for a special status were the Muslims, and not the Buddhists, because the Muslims could interpret the formation of the Mayu Frontier Administration (MFA) as a political triumph of the Rohingyas and their core demand for an autonomous zone, free from the potential interference of Buddhist Arakanese/Rakhine (Tha Htu 1962; Leider 2013*b*). The MFA (1961–64) included the townships in the North of Arakan where the Muslims formed an absolute majority. The creation of the MFA marked the golden years of the associative life of the Rohingya movement. However, the Rohingyas indulged in the mistaken belief that following the surrender of the Mujahidin rebellion, the government had officially recognized the Rohingyas as an ethnic group of the Union. This was a delusion. At hindsight, the suppression of the MFA in 1964 marked the premature end of the Rohingya movement in Burma as an officially tolerated tool of Muslim ethnic self-affirmation.[11]

Post-independence government policies towards the Muslim minority in Arakan can at best be called erratic. During the parliamentary period (1948–58; 1960–62), the government and its immigration authorities failed to deal efficiently with the issue of hundreds of thousands of Muslims (often referred to as Pakistanis in the 1950s) as well as Chinese by clarifying their rights and their legal status. Many may have had a demonstrable right to claim citizenship, but it was neither ascertained nor made effective. At the same time, no consistent efforts were made to confront the issue of illegal immigration, a problem that further poisoned inter-communal relations in Arakan and led to the violence and the exactions that accompanied the Nagaraja campaign in 1978, officially started as an immigration control backed by the army.

The increasingly nationalistic Ne Win regime (1962–88) pushed the politically active Rohingyas beyond the borders into East Pakistan and Bangladesh where an important Rohingya community built up during the 1970s. Born as a form of regional Muslim nationalism in Arakan, the Rohingya self-perception of a historical Arakanese Muslim identity survived as an ethno-religious ideology in exile and expanded with Rohingya migrants and refugees to Pakistan and the Middle East. Throughout the 1970s and 1980s, its militants were limited in their action, organizing poorly equipped guerrilla troops in the borderlands. Muslims in Arakan kept on identifying primarily as Muslims.

The claim of Rohingya ideologues that the majority of the Muslims in Arakan had always been "Rohingyas" is an article of faith based on historical and cultural claims. It warrants further critical examination against the background of post-1942 developments (Leider 2013*a*, 2013*b*, 2014). Still, there is little doubt that the Muslim masses in North Arakan underwent a process of ethno-religious identification after 1948 that has remained in motion until the most recent years. The process that led to a sense of shared destiny as victims of state harassment was certainly hastened by the disenfranchisement of Muslims after 1982, the mounting discrimination by the security forces, the exodus of 1978 and 1991–92 and the state's unrelenting oppressive regime, especially since the 1990s. Following its global recognition after 2012, the Rohingya label finally paired a condition of statelessness with an international recognition of refugee status. This was a reversal of the fortune of what it had earlier meant to be a Rohingya. The early Rohingyas pinned their political aims to arguments of historical legitimacy that spoke mainly to an elite. For a long time, these arguments escaped any critical discussion (with the exception of Arakanese/Rakhine writers who contested them, see Phaw Zan 1951) and were increasingly superseded by legal approaches preferred by the international community. After 2012, the prioritization of the human rights perspective enabled powerful dynamics of international support and advocacy for the Rohingyas, but it decontextualized the history of the becoming of the Rohingyas. One example is precisely the thematic marginalization of the 1942 events as a tragic episode of ethnic cleansing where members of the two communities had both been offenders and victims.

The authoritarian state mistrusted the Arakanese nationalists no less than the Muslims. Still, the ethnic identity of the Arakanese/Rakhine was firmly anchored in the 1947 and 1974 constitutions and their dissent with the central state did not raise an issue of political and ethnic legitimacy. Nonetheless, the Arakanese were granted an ethnically labelled state only in 1974, a change that was politically risk-free, as the new constitution that formalized its creation, also entrenched a one-party regime.

The interest of the authoritarian state in Arakan was not the creation of prosperity and welfare, but the maintenance of security and public order along the border. For the rival populations, the administrators and the security organs did not act as arbitrators, but as unpredictable distributors of favours. The state neither intervened to mediate the looming dissent between Buddhists and Muslims nor did it ever appropriate (or say: interpret in its favour or interest) any narrative of the 1942 injustice. Rather it was in the interest of the state to suppress such a narrative as it could upset the public order. Each community, the Arakanese/Rakhine and the self-proclaimed Muslim Rohingyas, recreated their own narrative about what had happened, feeding their mutual disregard, ignoring the victimhood of the rival community and limiting its attention to its own sufferings (Leider 2015*b*).

Before we turn to the later interpretations of "1942", two other subjects need to be briefly presented. The first one is contextual and should not be overlooked. It concerns the painful journey of tens of thousands of Indians, many of whom, in 1942, crossed Arakan to reach their motherland. The second one presents and tries to disentangle some of the figures that have been quoted with regard to the victims of 1942.

JAPANESE INVASION, BRITISH RETREAT AND INDIAN DEPARTURES

Moshe Yegar writes that the Japanese stopped Burmese violence against Indians and tried to win over the Indian minorities in the Southeast Asian states they had invaded (Yegar 1972, p. 68). Still, many Indians in Burma tried to flee the Japanese advance. Arakan was different again as it became a *de facto* lawless zone between the moment the British administration collapsed and the Japanese rule was firmly established. Then it found itself divided into a pro-British Muslim zone in the north and a Japanese-controlled area covering the centre and the south of Arakan. At the same time, Arakan became the theatre of a massive outflow of Indians from Rangoon and Lower Burma. Hundreds of thousands fled the advancing Japanese and tried to reach India either by crossing Arakan or arriving in Manipur passing through the Chindwin valley. According to the British historian Hugh Tinker who studied the "long march" of the Indians, there were between 400,000 and 450,000 refugees who undertook the trek (Tinker 1975, p. 2).[12] The Indians who chose the Arakan road, crossed the Taunggup pass and were taken by boats up to Chittagong. The maritime part of the journey could take between 36 hours and 9 days according to the type of coastal craft. The number of the people who were recorded in Chittagong reached 200,000 in mid-May 1942, as reported by a source of the Indian Overseas Department. Another source estimated the total number of Indians passing through Arakan as between 100,000 and 200,000, noting that casualties on the Arakan road were "infinitely greater" than on other roads (Tinker 1975, p. 6). Yet, though it directly touched Arakan, the Indian exodus was an event that appears as surprisingly unrelated to the violence that took place at approximately the same time further north between Chittagonian Muslim settlers and Buddhist villagers.

FIGURING THE NUMBERS OF THE VICTIMS

The massacres and the ethnic cleansing took place as the British rule collapsed and before the Japanese had established their control over the part of Arakan they conquered successfully. The months from April to June 1942 were a period of chaos and anarchy in Arakan's countryside. Therefore, it is not surprising that the number of people killed or hurt, families dispersed, internally displaced or forced to flee abroad, as well as houses burnt and destroyed, remain unknown, as they were not recorded at the time that the violence took place.

A preceding paragraph has already alluded to the problem of giving an estimation of the number of victims in the two focal areas where ethnic cleansing took place. While the later British reports allow us to imagine the context and the events in the Maungdaw and Buthidaung townships, they do not help us to make conjectures about the number of refugees and people killed. It is very difficult to measure the effect of the violence on the composition of the population in the townships in central Arakan (Minbya, Pauktaw, Myohaung [Mrauk U], Kyauktaw and Myebon) because the record about the first wave of attacks is opaque. Pearn noted that "unknown numbers had been slaughtered and many perished of starvation and exposure in attempting to find refuge elsewhere" (Pearn 1952), a formulation that paraphrases a statement found in an earlier British Foreign Office report of 1949. In his personal record about the last years of British rule, Robert Mole states that "as a result of the communal disturbances which occurred in 1942 after the British evacuation from Arakan … the entire population of this area was now Muslim" (Mole 2001, p. 191). Shortly after the war, North Arakan Muslims indicated the figure of 40,000 people who were allegedly killed (*Representation* 1947). This number was understood as an estimation of Muslim victims who had formerly lived in the centre of the country. It did not include Buddhist victims in the northern border zone. Following Sultan Mahmud's testimonial, Yegar (1972, p. 98) stated that 22,000 Chittagonian refugees fled to Bengal and were relocated in camps in Rangpur. It seems that only the former Muslim residents of Buthidaung could return in a short while to their villages. These approximate figures do not appear as unreasonable when we bear in mind that the population of the townships in the centre must have counted more than 300,000 people. For a deeper analysis of the estimates that have been circulated, one would need to consult the statistics of the number of Muslims and Buddhists at the township level. Unfortunately these data are not extant. Much of what can be said at present remains stuck with the very basic level of understanding of the numerical impact of the violence. The violence had visibly long-lasting material consequences. Buddhist villagers who returned to their properties in Maungdaw and Buthidaung were driven away at their return in 1945, or they left in resignation when the Mujahid revolt, which began in early 1948, shattered the government's control in the area.

In the late 1970s, following the dramatic flight of nearly 200,000 North Arakan Muslims over the border into Bangladesh, Rohingya militants inflated the number of 1942 victims in their propaganda. Figures such as 80,000, 100,000 and even 150,000 were quoted for the number of people killed. None of these figures have been widely reported. The lower number of 80,000 was picked up by authors outside of the community, such as for example Mujtaba Razvi in his report on the problem of Burmese Muslims (Razvi 1978, p. 82). In his article on the 1942 massacre, A.F.K. Jilani, a senior Rohingya militant, provides some detailed figures on allegedly tens of thousands of Muslims killed in certain areas of Central and North Arakan concluding that "more than 100,000 Muslims were massacred and 80,000 fled to Chittagong and Rangpur refugee camps" (Jilani 2006; also *History of Arakan* 1978, p. 36).

Local sources have often referred to impressive arrays of villages that were hit by the violence. Sultan Mahmud listed a total of 294 Muslim villages in the districts of Kyaukphyu (Myebon township) and Akyab (Minbya, Ponnagyun,

Myohaung, Rathedaung, Kyauktaw, Buthidaung and Pauktaw townships) that were "totally destroyed" with Buthidaung, Myohaung and Kyauktaw townships ranking highest with 55, 58 and 78 villages respectively (Mahmud 1950). Ba Tha, another Muslim author, quoted a similar list adding up a total of 307 villages that included villages in Rathedaung and Maungdaw township as well (Ba Tha 1960). Maung Tha Hla, a Rakhine writer, gives the number of 195 villages where the Buddhists were "wiped out" in Maungdaw township (Maung Tha Hla 2004, p. 69). Aye Chan, a Rakhine historian, stated that after the war Arakanese/Rakhine Buddhists could only return to 60 of the 200 Buddhist villages that had existed in Buthidaung and Maungdaw before the Japanese invasion (Aye Chan 2005, p. 410). Another Arakanese source reports a slightly higher number of villages, 213, of which it lists 99 with the number of their households (except 2), totalling 4,081 households, and a second set of 114 villages with an unknown number of households (Hla Oo 2012). Considering an average number of 41 households per village (as derived from the first set) combined with the average number of people per Rakhine household (4 or 5), one could speculate about a total number of between 35,000 and 43,000 people concerned by the violence. The source mentions only Maungdaw, not Buthidaung and the range as indicated here is purely hypothetical. So it would have to be tested against the number of Arakanese who lived in Maungdaw and Buthidaung around 1942. The source states that these villages were burnt down and it names places where "the whole village [was] slaughtered" (Hla Oo 2012). Nonetheless, one may eventually contrast this speculative figure with the number of 20,000 Buddhists allegedly killed in the north that Kyaw Zan Tha suggested in his *Background of Rohingya Problem* (Kyaw Zan Tha 2008).

In sum, none of the figures that have been quoted can be independently confirmed, compared or referred to as fully reliable. More educated guesses would only be possible if the number of Muslims and Buddhists in the respective townships was known in detail.

CONNECTING THE PAST TO THE PRESENT

The violence in 1942 occasioned a shift in the territorial distribution of Muslims and Buddhists in Arakan that lasted throughout the war and deepened the existing ethno-cultural gap. It also left scars on the social memory of the people of Arakan. The territorial redistribution was not revised during the chaotic years of the post-war period when the government and the army struggled to enforce their rule and establish a semblance of political stability. A feeling of injustice lingered on and confirmed the mistrust of the Buddhists towards the Muslim settlers from Chittagong whose itinerant inflows they had viewed with suspicion since the pre-war period. The absence of a factual master narrative, which both Buddhists and Muslims could have agreed upon, barred the emergence of consensual interpretations of the events. Where a neutral observer invariably perceives a causal chain of acute tensions and detrimental actions primarily precipitated by a breakdown of the established political order, each community has singularly re-imagined the record of its own sufferings so that there are only fractional accounts that remain at hand seventy years later. Muslim narratives have very little to say on the massacre and the displacement of the Buddhists, while Buddhist narratives glance over the initial explosion of violence and the persecution of the Muslims. While in Rakhine accounts, the riots appear related to the excesses of certain individuals and the failure of leaders to restrain them, for the Muslim side, as Abu Aneen has put it, it was "not an accidental event", but an "organized campaign" (Abu Aneen 2007).

In the late 1970s, when a quarter million of North Arakan Muslims took refuge in Bangladesh following the harassment and the wanton violence of security personnel that accompanied the authorities' immigration checks, the Rohingya militants that lay in hiding along the border with Bangladesh created a narrative of Muslim persecution in Arakan that linked the displacement of Muslims in 1942 to the flight of 1978. The following quote is from a pamphlet of the Rohingya Patriotic Front (RPF).

> As long as a single Rohingya Muslim lives on earth, the world can never forget that in 1941, when the British government evacuated from Burma and the Japanese did not occupy yet, the Mugh Buddhists equipped with firearms obtained from the British, plundered the Muslim villages and massacred nearly 100,000 Muslims in Arakan. Thousands of men, women and children were burnt alive by locking them up in bamboo houses, and depopulated more than 500,000 Muslims from hundreds of villages. This was the beginning of the present day on-going genocide against the Muslims in Arakan. (Rohingya Patriotic Front 1978)

An undated, but probably more recent Muslim sketch is found in the following extract from another Rohingya tract:

> [they] were brutally killed in the horrific massacre of 1942, that was perpetrated against Rohingya Muslims. More than 20 thousand Muslim scholars and eminent people were killed among one hundred thousand people who met this ruthless fate. The callous killing of Moulana Abdul Jabbar (1868–1942) by Buddhists on 1st April 1942. Their killing was irreparable loss to Jamiatul Ulama. More over, half a million Rohingya

Muslims ... were driven out of their homes .... Fifty thousand of them were in Rangpur refugee camps. (Manifesto n.d.)

Maung Tha Hla's description of the tragic events offers a recent depiction from a Buddhist perspective. For him, "the 1942 ethnic cleansing of Buddhist Rakhaings perpetrated by the Muslims was the most horrible barbarity recorded in contemporary Rakhaing history" (Maung Tha Hla 2009, p. 47). He writes:

> The heavily outnumbered Rakhaings were ruthlessly and wholesomely butchered in the most barbarous manner at their homes, in the ancestral lands as they fled, and in the woods where they sought refuge from the vicious Muslim marauders. They vandalized, raped, and slew. They burned the Rakhaing houses and the Buddhist monasteries... Many thousands, regardless of gender or age, perished in the massacre. The hardest hit being the rural agrarian communities who lived in the outlying villages.... Armies of vultures hovered above the mutilated rotten bodies; the air was heavy with toxic fume; black smoke billowed from places far and wide. (Maung Tha Hla 2004, p. 70)

The present narratives connect the past to the present in ways that serve the validation of opposing identities. They also signal an absence of discursive communication that strikingly mirrors the competing historiographies of Buddhists and Muslims, which have for long divided the communities in their reading of the kingdom's old and early history (Leider 2015*a*).

Nonetheless, one has to bear in mind that the remembrance and the interpretations of "1942" have *not* been a permanent narrative element in the political and historical writing of either Buddhists or Muslims. The events remained an altogether obscure chapter of history, because, as this author would like to repeat, a straightforward and authorized record was never produced after the war. However, as the above citations show, references to 1942 were made during political crises, notably again after the violence in June and October 2012.

A look at recent articles written by Nurul Islam, a prominent Rohingya militant of the old generation and the present leader of the Arakan Rohingya National Organization (since 1998), may illustrate this point. In "Rebuttal to U Khin Maung Saw's misinformation on Rohingya", Nurul Islam stated that "the 1942 massacre of Rohingyas was genocide" (Islam 2012). In an interview given in 2013, he underscored the link between 1942 and 2012: "During a period of 70 years from 1942 to 2012, they carried out countless operations against us, drove us out to other countries or to the sea, made massive Rohingya exodus two times and subsequently made them refugees" (Islam 2013). However, in previous articles "Facts about the Rohingya Muslims of

Arakan" (Islam 2006) and "To bring harmony in Arakan, xenophobic works of the Rakhines must stop" (Islam 2009), he did not even mention the 1942 violence. Pointing out this difference is not an *ad hominem* criticism of Nurul Islam's use of history, but simply one among other examples of the newly re-emerging post-2012 reinterpretation of the aggressions of March–April 1942 as a genocidal crime.

Importantly, recent writers did not simply mention "1942" as a dot on a time-line of communal violence in Rakhine State, but generated interpretations in tune with global discourses on human rights and persistent rumours on real or imagined threats. These post-2012 interpretations allow us to identify contrasting patterns: on the one hand, the Buddhist interpretation of Muslim agency in the form of a pervasive Muslim demographic and political threat; on the other hand, an analytical grid that interprets alleged racism, state discrimination and civic exclusion as a hidden scheme to progressively exterminate the Muslims. "1942" caught the collective power of the Buddhist and Muslim imagination, because its fearful details have fed analyses that exploit both global narratives of Muslim hegemonies and the semantic expansion of the powerful genocide terminology. "1942" has been interpreted as a forerunner of anti-Rohingya violence though there were no self-declared Rohingyas at the time of the events. Still, such an interpretation exemplifies the narrative of the victimization of Muslims worldwide that has been moving public opinion in Muslim-majority countries for decades. True or false reports on the persecution of Muslims worldwide have also been driving Muslim extremism in many countries of the Muslim and Western world.

For the Buddhists, the memory of 1942 matches a Buddhist counter-narrative that associates the demographic strength of the Rohingyas in North Rakhine State and in southeast Bangladesh with the risk of an unchecked transnational Muslim expansion along the border with Bangladesh (and before 1971, East Pakistan). Post-2012 Rakhine nationalist interpretations of "1942" have also interpreted the killings of Maungdaw and Buthidaung Buddhists in 1942 as a genocide against their own community. Once again, this interpretation does not make the events of 1942 any more transparent, but it reflects the current Arakanese fears of a Muslim "invasion" from Bangladesh branding Muslims collectively as Bengalis. It likely serves the dreadful xenophobic propaganda more than the representation of core Rakhine political interests.

> But now these illegal Bengali Muslims, the descendants of those Muslim killers of 1942, are reinventing themselves as so-called ethnic Rohingyas and trying to gain our citizenship so that they and their brothers millions of

Bengali-Muslims from Bangladesh can eventually seep into the proper Burma and swallow us Burmese Buddhists whole to the extinction (Hla Oo 2012).

After 2012, the charge of a state-sponsored genocide against the Rohingyas has become the monopoly of a new group of pro-Rohingya activists who produced international campaigns between 2013 and 2016.[13] It was also strongly echoed by Rohingya activists. Still, such descriptions and allegations were rarely made or emphasized in human rights reports that raised international awareness on the plight of the Rohingyas between 1995 and 2011.[14] Earlier on, the term "genocide" had only been occasionally part of the political vocabulary within the North Arakan Muslim and Rohingya ecosphere. Yet, it did not bear the ideological and legal ballast of the post-2012 interpretation of state–Rohingya relations as the history of a "slow" genocide. "Genocide" in Muslim parlance was first used in a kind of wake-up call on the title page of the Alethangyaw Constitution of Arakani Muslims in 1951, a catalogue of North Arakan Muslim political demands. At the time, it referred to the conditions of civil war created by the multiple rebellions throughout Arakan in 1949 and 1950. It did *not* allude to any anterior events. In the citation from the letter of the Jamiat ul-Ulama to Prime Minister U Nu of 1948 quoted above, the 1942 massacres were merely referred to as an "unhappy episode", not as a genocide. As we have noted, it looks as if, at that time, political actors who had likely been involved in the ethnic cleansing themselves, were keen to understate or pass over the terrible events. No party could claim innocence. Nonetheless, Sultan Mahmud, U Nu's health minister, whose description of the events we have also quoted above, concluded that 1942 had not been a communal riot, but a "pre-planned cold-blooded massacre" (Mahmud 1950). This is probably the strongest expression one could come across in the 1950s. Comparable observations on a tendency to glance over the events could be made on the side of Buddhist writers. Khin Gyi Phyaw's paper on the Mujahidin only mentions the expulsion of Buddhists and Hindus in 1942 (Khin Gyi Phyaw 1959, p. 23) and Pho Kan Kaung elaborating on the danger of Rohingyas for political stability, says simply that Rakhine and Muslims fought each other (Pho Kan Kaung 1992, p. 88). Later on, Arakanese/Rakhine academics such as Aye Chan or Aye Kyaw who have been known for their strong criticism of Rohingya identity claims in the late twentieth and early twenty-first century, barely mentioned the 1942 violence in their writings. The atrocities and the injustice, while never forgotten, rested mostly within each community's partial memory. But as the post-2012 developments show, this memory was mainly susceptible to be revived with reference to newer events and discursive contexts.

THE 1942 EVENTS AND POLITICAL IDENTITY

The present exploration of the 1942 violence and its impact on civic identity is a preliminary investigation hampered by the lack of accessible primary sources and the absence of previous scholarly interest. Nonetheless, it may suggest pathways for further reflection and critical examination. Two analytical frames have to be distinguished to take into account, on the one hand, the 1942 events and their social and political impact, and on the other hand, the construction of commemorative narratives.

The sources that have been quoted illustrate the partial collective memories and the imparted sense of a collective victimhood. The argument proposed in the introduction, namely the link between the events of 1942 and the process of political identity formation cannot be extracted from the testimony of historical memories. It can only be explained with regard to the political behaviour of the leading actors. Nonetheless, while the analytical differentiation provides historical clarity at hindsight, it does not necessarily reflect the self-perception of the actors or the groups of people concerned. The Rohingya leaders have never argued that the political dynamics of their call for territorial autonomy were ignited by the experience of 1942 or that the process of their communal identity was propelled by the concentration and the political isolation of their community increased by what happened between 1942 and 1946. Nor did Arakanese/Rakhine nationalists point to the 1942 events to underscore and possibly rationalize their projection of North Arakan Muslims as people to be excluded and with acclaimed identities that set them outside of the national community.

The links established in this article between the 1942 events and the political behaviour and identities in the post-war period are an attempt of the historian to connect the shock, the ruptures, the displacements and the three years of enforced division with the singular splitting up of the native Buddhist Arakanese/Rakhine community and Arakan's complex Muslim community as evidenced in the sporadic inter-communal violence and the ideological dissent from the late 1970s until 2012. To make this point, one should not look at the ethnic cleansing from March to June 1942 in isolation. The months of anarchy and violence and the ensuing years of ethnic and political division until 1945 should be seen and interpreted as a single complex fact.

The immediate impact of the experience of persecution and the 1942 territorial break-up was the entrenched and durable political division of the Buddhist and Muslim communities and their leaders. There is no hint that the leaders of the two communities ever wanted to work together politically or had a perception of a shared interest in pursuing their goals. This divisiveness certainly had its roots in the late colonial period, but the 1942 events confirmed the communal bitterness.

The present enquiry also makes clear that, besides reinforcing the mutual hostility, the experience of violence and partition did not impact the political ideas of the two communities in the same way. The strongest impact of the 1942–45 experience was what we have called the political coming of age of the Muslims. The upturn of the political conditions (British disaster after the Japanese invasion, anarchy, the British need for local auxiliaries to fight the Japanese) generated the political awakening of the Muslim community's local leaders. The Muslim leadership built on their control of resources and stocks of arms at the end of the war and internally formed a strong, though erroneous sense of the available political space when they stepped forward to claim an independent or autonomous region for the Muslims. The idea that the Muslims could win a separate territory in a short while by clever political manoeuvring was a political delusion. The slightly later production of a specific Rohingya identity (built on the old Muslim presence in the region) was another important element of the political awakening. Though it was slow to take off and to spread, seen at hindsight it has been a more durable outcome of the tidal moment of 1942.

The violence of 1942 had also an impact on the formation of the political ideas and collective identity of the Arakanese/Rakhine. This is not the anti-Rohingya drive that has been a mark of Arakanese/Rakhine nationalism since the 1970s and much more so since the 1990s. To say so would be an anachronism. To state brusquely that the 1942 events made the Arakanese/Rakhine anti-Muslim or more anti-Muslim would misjudge the complex socio-political context that underpinned the migrations during the colonial times. Arakanese nationalism was first of all thriving on an anti-Burmese stance. After independence, the Arakanese nationalist elite fought for a constitutional recognition of a specific Arakanese/Rakhine identity. This was not unlike the Muslim elite who, after 1948, strategically faced the Burmese State (not its Arakanese neighbours) fighting for its political goals. Early on, in the 1950s, the Arakanese nationalists saw the strong Muslim minority with its newly politicized leadership in North Arakan mainly as an annoyance. The 1942 impact lay elsewhere. In the collective psyche of the Arakanese/Rakhine, the experience of 1942 toughened the perception of a demographic threat. Therefore the ethnic cleansing of 1942 smoothly blended into the narrative on illegal immigration and unchecked borders that was and has remained the key political worry for the Arakanese/Rakhine. Rakhine nationalists have often presented the Chittagonian migration as the story of "guests" who betrayed the trust of their hosts as they took the land where they prospered as their own. After the war, Muslim settlers, despite the fact that many may already have been born in Arakan, were still seen as intruders who were not ready to integrate the majority society and failed to adopt local cultural habits unlike earlier generations of Muslims. With our present knowledge, it would thus be difficult to single out the 1942 events as a moment that triggered a certain political turn of the Arakanese/Rakhine identity formation during the post-war period. The interpretation that links the self-perception of the Arakanese/Rakhine as victims of both Burmese oppression and Muslim immigration — a kind of grand historical narrative from 1785 down to the present — rather calls for a deeper investigation of social conditions and inter-ethnic relations in Arakan during the 1920s and 1930s.

Notes

1. Officially named Rakhine State after 1989. Arakan can be used both as a geographical and historical term in contexts where the territory referred to is larger than the modern Rakhine State. Therefore its use should not be entirely discouraged. The terms "Arakanese" and "Rakhine" are used synonymously in this article. An alternate spelling is Rakhaing. An English pronunciation of the term "Rakhine" is closer to the actual ethnonym of the Buddhist majority population than the term "Arakanese". Many Buddhist Rakhine and Muslim Rohingyas writing in English still have a clear preference for "Arakan", while they are strictly divided on the use of respective ethnonyms. Identities and ethnonyms are historically conditioned, but the available space would not allow for a review of a the heated debate that emerged after 2012 about the use of the names "Rohingya" and "Bengali" (see Leider 2013*b*). Nor does the article include a detailed examination of the use of terms such as "Kala" used by Buddhists to designate the Muslims or "Mugh/Magh" used by Muslims to name the Rakhine/Arakanese. Both terms can be used pejoratively.

2. Saya Khaing Myo Saung's Chapters 5–9 in *The bad colonial heritage of Arakan and the expansion of the Bengali Muslims of Chittagong* (Khaing Myo Saung 2012, pp. 94–140) deal with the events to some extent. Abu Aneen's chapter on the 1942 violence (Abu Aneen 2007 [2002]) is an attempt to balance the various accounts and includes instances where efforts were made from leaders of both communities to contain the riots. Both authors draw heavily on Bonpauk Tha Kyaw's war memories (Bonpauk 1973) and other Rakhine authors such as Thein Pe Myint. Abu Aneen's use of diverging Muslim accounts and his comments point to the complexity of competing memories. He also mentions sources in Urdu that he could not access. Khaing Myo Saung and Abu Aneen are pseudonyms, one being a highly regarded Rakhine teacher and the other a respected Rohingya party leader. Defert (2007, p. 130) mentions the request made by a Rohingya to an NGO in Thailand in 2006 for the funding of a historical research project on the massacre of 100,000 Muslims by Buddhists in 1942.

3. A rare exception is the brief mention of "the ethnic cleansing in British-controlled

areas particularly around the town of Maungdaw" by Clive J. Christie in his *Modern History of Southeast Asia* quoted in Aye Chan (2005, p. 408).

4. Thein Pe Myint, as quoted by Abu Aneen, stated that Muslims got support from Indian troops during the riots (Abu Aneen 2007).

5. Conversely this high figure would explain that upon their return from India after the war, the refugees contributed to steep increase of the population in a short while. Abu Aneen argues that the total Muslim population uprooted due to the riots was 200,000, mostly resettling in North Arakan.

6. According to Derek Tonkin, a former British Ambassador, "the designations 'CF' and 'CK' were briefly popularized by the British military administration in Northern Arakan during the Second World War. The probability is that the 'F' and the 'K' reflected the need by the British Army to distinguish Chittagonians", as a British source has put it, "between effers for men and something else for women, but in as genial a way as only the Army would know how". (Email communication with the author 4 February 2016).

7. Khaing Myo Saung (Khaing Myo Saung 2012, pp. 105–107) deals in greater detail with efforts of Arakanese leaders to re-establish public order.

8. According to Abu Aneen, the name of the leader of the Buthidaung peace committee was Zahiruddin (Abu Aneen 2007 [2002]).

9. A detailed list of members of the Maungdaw peace committee is also presented by Khaing Myo Saung (Khaing Myo Saung 2012, p. 113).

10. Abu Aneen makes an effort to counter-balance the impression of exclusive British loyalism by stating that "there [were] Muslims, especially educated ones, who at the first hand help the Japanese and got capital punishment at the hand of British, e.g. Mr. Kala Meah of Kwindaing Village, Buthidaung" (Abu Aneen 2007 [2002]).

11. A slightly more realistic interpretation would be that the MFA was formed after the introduction, in 1960, of a special military administration called "frontier administration" whose primary aim was not the welfare and the political endeavours of the Muslim community, but a stronger control of the border area by the army. It was suppressed in 1964, two years after Ne Win took power, re-igniting in a short lapse of time the Muslim rebellion against the central state. Buthidaung and Maungdaw became, once again, part of Akyab (later Sittway) district.

12. There were a bit over a million Indians in Burma according to the census of 1931. Various authors cite higher numbers for those who fled after the Japanese invasion, but fail to base their guesses on sources. Chakravarti (1971, p. 170) quoted by Aye Chan (2005, pp. 405–406) indicates 900,000 "who attempted to walk over to India". Tinker's paper discusses competing figures, includes his personal testimonial and offers the most detailed and reliable analysis.

13. The most prominent of these activists have been Matthew Smith, the director of Fortify Rights, an NGO, Maung Zarni, a Burmese activist, and Penny Green, a law professor and director of the International State Crime Initiative at Queen Mary University in London. Noted publications of the genocide school are

Cowley and Zarni (2014), Fortify Rights 2014, Fortify Rights 2015 and Green, MacManus and de la Cour Venning (2015).
14. The most prominent international human rights activist doing advocacy for the Rohingya refugees is Chris Lewa, founder and coordinator of the Arakan Project (2005).

References

Abu Aneen. "Towards Understanding Arakan History: A Study on the Issue of Ethnicity in Arakan". 2007 [2002] <http://www.kaladanpress.org/index.php/scholar-column-mainmenu-36/arakan/866-towards-understanding-arakan-history-part-ii.html> (accessed 26 February 2017).

"Address Presented by Jamiat Ul Ulema North Arakan on Behalf of the People of North Arakan to the Hon'ble Prime Minister of the Union of Burma on the Occasion of His Visit to Maugndaw on the 25th October 1948". 1948. Government of the Union of Burma. Foreign Office <http://www.networkmyanmar.org/images/stories/PDF19/J-U-25-October-1948.pdf> (accessed 23 January 2016).

Ahmed, Sultan. "Memorandum to the Government of the Union of Burma 18 June 1948". Quoted in "Rohingya belong to Burma", *Arakan Monthly News and Analysis of the Arakan Rohingya National Organisation, Arakan (Burma)* 6, no. 1 (1948): 10–12.

Arakan, Rohingya and Rakhine. Compiled by Noor Kamal, General Secretary, Arakan Historical Society, Chittagong. N.d. <https://www.scribd.com/fullscreen/49416983?access_key=key-26z11ijlefado2h1sxdw> (accessed 23 January 2016).

Aye Chan. "The Development of a Muslim Enclave in Arakan (Rakhine) State of Burma (Myanmar)". *SOAS Bulletin of Burma Research* 3, no. 2 (2005).

Ba Tha. "Massacre of 1942". 1960 <http://www.arakanbumiputra.com/2013/04/massacre-of-1942-by-ba-tha-buthidaung.html> (accessed 1 October 2015).

Bonpauk Tha Kyaw. *Taw hlan ye khayi way (On the Road of Revolution).* (In Burmese). Yangon: Thatin Journal, 1973.

Bowerman, J.F. "The Frontier Areas of Burma". *Journal of the Royal Society of Arts* 95, no. 4732 (1946): 44–55.

Cowley, Alice and Maung Zarni. "The Slow-Burning Genocide Of Myanmar's Rohingya". *Pacific Rim Law & Policy Journal* 23, no. 3 (2014): 681–752.

Defert, Gabriel. *Les Rohingya de Birmanie. Arakanais, musulmans et apatrides.* Paris: Aux lieux d'être, 2007.

Fortify Rights. "Policies of Persecution Ending Abusive State Policies Against Rohingya Muslims in Myanmar". 2014 <http://www.fortifyrights.org/downloads/Policies_of_Persecution_Feb_25_Fortify_Rights.pdf>.

———. "Persecution of the Rohingya Muslims: Is Genocide Occurring in Myanmar's Rakhine State? A Legal Analysis", by Allard K. Lowenstein International Rights

Clinic, Yale Law School. 2015 <http://www.fortifyrights.org/downloads/Yale_Persecution_of_the_Rohingya_October_2015.pdf>.

Green, Penny, Thomas MacManus and Alice de la Cour Venning. *Countdown to Annihilation: Genocide in Myanmar*. London: Queen Mary University of London/International State Crime Initiative, 2015 <http://statecrime.org/data/2015/10/ISCI-Rohingya-Report-PUBLISHED-VERSION.pdf> (accessed 15 March 2016).

History of Arakan (Burma). Karachi: World Muslim Congress, 1978 <https://www.scribd.com/fullscreen/50268790?access_key=key-2l3yiajlq21nliopdbyw> (accessed 23 January 2016).

Hla Oo. "1942 Genocide of Buddhists in Maungdaw District" (Translation of an eyewitness account of the 1942 Bengali Riots). 8 August 2012 <http://hlaoo1980.blogspot.lu/2012/08/1942-genocide-of-buddhists-in-maungdaw.html> (accessed 26 January 2015).

Irwin, Anthony. *Burmese Outpost*. London: Collins, 1946.

Islam, Islam. "Facts about the Rohingya Muslims of Arakan". 2006 <http://www.rohingya.org/portal/index.php/learn-about-rohingya.html> (accessed 2 March 2016).

———. "To bring harmony in Arakan, Xenophobic works of the Rakhines must stop". 2009 <http://www.bangladesh-web.com/view.php?hidRecord=285470> (accessed 2 March 2016).

———. "Rebuttal to U Khin Maung Saw's misinformation on Rohingya". 2012 <http://www.rohingya.org/portal/index.php/scholars/65-nurul-islam-uk/292-rebuttal-to-u-khin-maung-saws-misinformation-on-rohingya.html> (accessed 2 March 2016).

———. "Interview with Mohammad Noor". 24 May 2013 <http://www.rvisiontv.com/nurul-islam-president-of-arno-with-md-noor-rohingya-roshan-ep-4/> (accessed 9 April 2015).

Khaing Myo Saung, Saya. *The bad colonial heritage of Arakan and the expansion of the Bengali Muslims of Chittagong*. (In Burmese). Tokyo: Arakan Rakkhita Group, 2012.

Khin Gyi Phyaw. "Mugyahein from Rakhine". *Rakhine Tazaung Annual Magazine* 23, no. 4 (in Burmese) (1959–60): 99–100.

Kyaw Zan Tha. "Background of Rohingya Problem". 2008 <https://sites.google.com/site/kogyikyawarakan/arakan-information/Articles-main-page/backgroundofrohingyaproblem> (accessed 2 March 2016).

Leider, Jacques P. "Des musulmans d'Arakan aux Rohingyas de Birmanie: origines historiques et mouvement politique". *Diplomatie Affaires stratégiques et relations internationales,* pp. 70–71. Janvier-Février: 2013*a*.

———. "Rohingya: The Name, the Movement, the Quest for Identity". In *Nation Building in Myanma*, pp. 204–55. Yangon: Myanmar EGRESS/Myanmar Peace Center, 2013*b*.

———. "Identität und historisches Bewusstsein – Muslime in Arakan und die Entstehung der Rohingya". In *Myanmar Von Pagoden, Longyis und Nat-geistern,* edited by Dorothee Schäfer, Wolfgang Stein and Uta Weigelt, pp. 66–73. München: Deutscher Kunstverlag/Museum Fünf Kontinente, 2014.

―――. "Competing Identities and the Hybridized History of the Rohingyas". In *Metamorphosis: Studies in Social and Political Change in Myanmar*, edited by Renaud Egreteau and Francois Robinne, pp. 151–78. Singapore: NUS Press, 2015*a*.

―――. "Background and Prospects in the Buddhist-Muslim Dissensions in Rakhine State of Myanmar". In *Ethnic Conflict in Buddhist Societies in South and Southeast Asia: The Politics Behind Religious Rivalries*, edited by K.M. de Silva, pp. 25–55. Kandy: International Centre for Ethnic Studies, 2015*b*.

Lucas Philipps, C.E. *The Raiders of Arakan*. London: Heinemann, 1971.

Mahmud, Sultan. "The Muslim massacre of 1942". 1950 <http://thevoiceofrohingya. blogspot.lu/2012/07/burma-planned-religious-and-racial.html> (accessed 19 January 2016).

"Manifesto of Rohangya Jamiatul Ulama, Arkan". Rohangya Jamiatul Ulama Arkan. n.d. [A historical record of the Jamiat Ul Ulama from the 1930s until the 1970s] (PDF file searchable on Google in 2014, but not accessible anymore in 2016.)

Maung Tha Hla. *The Rakhaing*. New York: Buddhist Rakhaing Cultural Association, 2004.

―――. *Rohingya Hoax*. New York: Buddhist Rakhaing Cultural Association, 2009.

Mole, Robert. *The Temple Bells Are Calling: A Personal Record of the Last Years of British Rule in Burma*. Bishop, Auckland: Pentland Books, 2001.

Murray, Peter. "North Arakan 1942, detailing the collapse of British Administration in the area, with a brief historical introduction and a short account of subsequent events". British Library. IOC, Mss Eur E 390 (1980).

Pearn, Bertie Reginald. "Burma Since the Invasion". *Journal of the Royal Society of Arts* 93, no. 4686 (1945): 155–64.

―――. "The Mujahid Revolt in Arakan. 31 December 1952". National Archives. British Foreign Office. FO 371/101002 – FB 1015/63 (1952).

Phaw Zan. "Sudeten Muslims". *The Guardian [?]*. (Typewritten text in the hands of the author. 1951[?]).

Pho Kan Kaung. "The Danger of Rohingya". *Myet Khin Thit Magazine* 25 (in Burmese) (May 1992): 87–103.

"Representation by the Muslims of North Arakan Claiming for an Autonomous State in the Buthidaung and Maungdaw Areas". Home Department, Government of Burma, 24 February 1947 <http://www.networkmyanmar.org/images/stories/PDF18/Representations-1947-rev.pdf> (accessed 12 January 2016).

Rohingya Patriotic Front. "Genocide in Burma against the Muslims of Arakan". Pamphlet, 12 April 1978.

Tha Htu. "The Mayu Frontier Administrative Area". *The Guardian Monthly*, February 1962, pp. 29–30.

Tinker, Hugh. "A Forgotten Long March: The Indian Exodus from Burma, 1942". *Journal of Southeast Asia Studies* 6, no. 1 (1975): 1–15.

Yegar, Moshe. *The Muslims in Burma*. Wiesbaden: Harassowitz, 1972.

8

EXPLORING THE ISSUE OF CITIZENSHIP IN RAKHINE STATE

Derek Tonkin

There are over 1 million Muslims in Rakhine State whose legal status is obscure. They are generally referred to as "Rohingya", an ethnic designation unknown to the former British administration. Though the Rohingya are primarily located in the northern part of the state, there are many thousands, if not tens of thousands, of Muslims of Chittagonian origin living elsewhere in Myanmar who are likely to be inhibited from claiming openly to be Rohingya. There are in addition another million or more Rohingya said to be living overseas, as refugees in Bangladesh and elsewhere, or as workers in Saudi Arabia and other Gulf States.

For some time the international community has been urging the Myanmar Government to grant full citizenship rights to the Rohingya, and to review the controversial 1982 Citizenship Law in this context. But this is easier said than done as the extent of illegal immigration from Bangladesh into Rakhine State since independence in 1948 is difficult if not impossible to assess. I also argue that it is not so much the Law itself which is at fault as the failure to implement the Law in Rakhine State in a timely and responsible manner. The longer the government delays action to resolve the impasse, the more entrenched and potentially explosive the situation is likely to become.

* * *

Controversy surrounds the designation of some 1 million or more people of Islamic faith who live in Rakhine State in Myanmar. For some, this controversy is as unwelcome as it is unnecessary, since the issue at stake is the human rights, and especially the citizenship status of the people concerned. For others, the designation of the community as "Rohingya" is vital to their very survival and is not to be dismissed as a distraction.

The designation "Rohingya" is used, particularly by support organizations overseas, to refer to some reported 3 million or more Muslim residents and former residents of Rakhine State in Myanmar.[1] These numbers should however be treated with caution. Tens of thousands of former residents of Arakan are said to have sought sanctuary overseas from the early 1940s onwards, not only in what is today Bangladesh but as far afield as Saudi Arabia and the Gulf states. In Saudi Arabia alone there are reported to be some 300,000 or more "Rohingya"[2] longer term residents, though the Saudi authorities do not use this designation to describe them, and another 50,000 in the United Arab Emirates.[3] The precise origins of many of these people must however be suspect as some are known to have travelled on restricted Bangladeshi and Pakistani passports.[4]

In recent years the flow of refugees out of Rakhine State has continued. The United Nations High Commissioner for Refugees (UNHCR) has reported[5] that:

> Bangladesh has experienced two influxes of refugees from Myanmar, the first in 1978 and the second in 1991–92. Around 250,000 people were involved both times. Both influxes were followed by large-scale repatriation exercises whose voluntariness was seriously questioned. Some of those who were repatriated subsequently fled again to Bangladesh, but many were unable to recover their former and government-acknowledged refugee status.

There are currently thought to be some 200,000 undocumented cases of Rohingya refugees in Bangladesh, as well as some 32,975 documented cases (2015 count) from the 1991–92 exodus in two UNHCR assisted government camps and another exodus of several thousands in the wake of insurgent attacks in October 2016. Others have sought sanctuary in Malaysia, Thailand, Indonesia, Pakistan and India. Since the communal violence of July 2012, some 120,000 are estimated to have fled by boat to Malaysia and Indonesia.

Inside Myanmar, some 1.1 million persons in Rakhine State were omitted from the 2014 Census because they declined to be enumerated other than as "Rohingya". But elsewhere in Myanmar there are thought to be many thousands, if not tens of thousands of residents of nineteenth and twentieth century Chittagonian (Bengali) origin — stevedores, riverboat crew, construction workers, small traders and artisans rather than farm workers — who might claim to be Rohingya, but understandably did not seek to be so enumerated at the 2014 Census. In 1960 speakers at a meeting of "Ruhangya" (sic) organizations in Rangoon claimed that there were some 700,000 "Ruhangya" in Burma, of whom 300,000 lived outside Arakan.[6] The majority of Muslims[7] who live outside Rakhine State seem lukewarm towards Rohingya aspirations, apart from a dedicated core in Yangon who may aspire to the political leadership of the community in Rakhine State.

In this article, I consider primarily the position of those claiming to be Rohingya who live either in Rakhine State or who have a valid case to seek repatriation from elsewhere in Southeast Asia where they have sought refuge in recent years. Those who have been overseas for thirty years or more can have little prospect of ever returning to Myanmar. So the total number under consideration might be as high as 1.5 million, but at least one-third of this number could be illegal immigrants into Arakan from East Pakistan/Bangladesh since 1948 and by now impossible to identify as such as they would have long ago destroyed any Bengali documentation about their origins, and are by now indistinguishable from longer term residents.

THE ROHINGYA DESIGNATION

I have found not a single reference to the term "Rohingya" in any shape or form in any documents or correspondence, official or private, recording the 124 years of British rule in Arakan from 1824 to 1948. Those who support the Rohingya narrative of a specific ethnicity going back many centuries invariably do so on the basis of a very few unconnected historical events, like Dr Francis Buchanan's fortuitous meeting in 1795 in the Burman capital of Amarapura with a group of deported Muslims who "call themselves *Rooinga* or natives of *Arakan*" (Buchanan 1799). But Buchanan never made use again of this designation, though he wrote prolific accounts until his death in 1829 about his travels along the Bengal-Arakan frontier where he met many Muslim refugees from Arakan.[8] Nor was the designation used by any of his contemporaries. Nor did the British encounter any "Rooinga" when they arrived in Arakan in 1824.[9]

The reason for this must surely be that the word means no more than "Arakaner" and is derived from the Bengali word for Arakan which is "Rohang" with a family taxonomic suffix — "gya". All the group wanted to tell Buchanan was that they came from Arakan, and not from Bengal. For that reason, the British never heard the word inside Arakan, because it was obvious that the Muslims living in Arakan were Arakaners. Buchanan was also told that the "real natives" of Arakan, the Buddhists, called both Muslims and Hindus "Kulaw Yakain" or stranger *Arakan*, that is, they were regarded as settlers.

The British initially designated the Muslims simply as "Mohamedans", but by the 1921 Census had decided on the name "Arakan-Mohamedans" as a race category; this became "Arakan-Muslim" in the 1931 Census. The 1921 Census had this to say about the Arakan-Mohamedans:

> The Arakan-Mahomedans are practically confined to Akyab district and are properly the descendants of Arakanese women who have married Chittagonian Mahomedans. It is said that the descendants of a Chittagonian who has permanently settled in Akyab district always refuse to be called Chittagonian and desire to be called Arakan-Mahomedans; but as permanent settlement seems to imply marriage to an Arakanese woman this is quite in accordance with the description given. Although so closely connected with Chittagonians racially, the Arakan-Mahomedans do not associate with them at all; they consequently marry almost solely among themselves and have become recognised locally as a distinct race. The Arakanese Buddhists asked the Deputy Commissioner there not to let the Arakan-Mahomedans be included under *Arakanese* in the census. The instruction issued to enumerators with reference to Arakan-Mahomedans was that this race-name (in Burmese *Yakaing-kala*) should be recorded for those Mahomedans who were domiciled in Burma and had adopted a certain mode of dress which is neither Arakanese nor Indian and who call themselves and are generally called by others *Yakaing-kala*.

It will be clear that the term "Kulaw Yakain" which Buchanan had heard in 1795 is the "Yakaing-kala" of the 1921 Census. The Rooinga met by Buchanan at Amarapura outside Arakan are indeed the Arakan-Muslims of the era of British rule. They are differentiated from the Chittagonian and other Bengali migrants of the nineteenth and twentieth centuries.

Financial Secretary James Baxter noted in his 1941 Report on Indian Immigration that in Akyab District (present-day Sittwe and Maungdaw districts combined) no less than "79 per cent of the Indian population was born in Burma, evidence of the presence of a large and established Chittagonian agricultural community". Tables in his report show that as many as 82.43 per cent of all 186,327 Chittagonians and 15,586 Bengalis recorded in the 1931 Census as living in Akyab District (present-day Sittwe and Maungdaw districts combined) gave Burma as their place of birth. In the 1931 Census Chittagonian migrants from Bengal ("Indians") outnumbered indigenous Muslims in Arakan ("Indo-Burmans") by at least four to one.[10]

Charney (1999, p. 264) in his seminal 1999 dissertation,[11] noted "the surprisingly low percentage of Muslims (20 per cent) in the Arakan Littoral found by the British at the close of Burman rule".[12] The first properly conducted peace-time census for the capitation tax in 1829 assessed the population of Arakan at 121,288 by which time many of those, both Muslims and Buddhists, who had sought refuge in Bengal during Burman rule, had returned home. By 1832 the population had risen to 195,107 and by 1842 to 246,766. The Rev GS Comstock (1847) recorded that the 1842 Annual Census estimated the population at the time at some 257,000. "Of these about 167,000 were Mugs [Rakhine], 40,000 are Burmese, 20,000 are Mussulmans, 5,000 are Bengalese, 3,000 are Toungmroos, 2,000 are Kemees, 1,250 are Karens and the remainder are of various races, in smaller numbers and sundry other ethnic groups." This would indicate an 8 to 1 ratio of Buddhists (Rakhine and Burmese) to Muslims in Arakan as a whole.[13]

The population of Arakan trebled during the first twenty-five years of British rule from 100,000 or so to more than 350,000 (352,348 recorded in the 1852 Annual Census). This was, as former Chief Commissioner of Burma Lt. Gen Albert Fytche put it,[14] "due to immigration from provinces under Burmese government, and notably from Pegu". This meant "the desertion of their own sovereign and country by these masses, and their voluntarily placing themselves under an alien rule, coupled with the vast increase of prosperity in every shape of the portion of Burma which has become British". These migrants were overwhelmingly Buddhist, not Muslim.

This process however was later reversed in Akyab district (that is, Northern Arakan) when the migration of Muslims from Bengal started in earnest after 1870. By the time of the first full census of 1872, the population of Arakan as a whole had reached 484,673. Buddhists (364,023) still exceeded Muslims (64,313) by a ratio of nearly 6 to 1. However, in Akyab district 185,266 Buddhists were counted against 58,203 Muslims, a ratio of nearly 3 to 1. From then on, the ratio of Buddhists to Muslims in Akyab District showed a steady decline as migration from Bengal into the district gradually increased. By the time of the 1931 Census there were still more Buddhists (448,288) in Akyab District than Muslims (244,398).[15] But the ratio had fallen to less than 2 to 1.

1948: THE START OF THE CITIZENSHIP DILEMMA

The Japanese invasion of Burma brought massive inter-communal violence which saw the flight in 1942 of most Muslims in southern Arakan to the north, or into Bengal itself, and of most Buddhists to the south (see, for example, Leider in this volume). By the time of independence in 1948, Arakan was in a state of ferment. There was however no doubt about the

Burmese citizenship of Muslims in Arakan after independence. They qualified provided they belonged to an indigenous group like the Yakaing-kala (in English "Arakan-Muslim"), Myedu, Kaman and Zerbadi (from 1941 renamed "Burmese Muslim"), tracing roots back before the British invasion in 1823; or provided they could trace family history back at least three generations even if they arrived in Arakan after 1823;[16] or provided their application for naturalization, based on a minimum five years' residence, was approved; or finally provided that they had been resident, like some later Chittagonian immigrants, for eight years out of ten prior to 1 January 1942 (the time of the Japanese invasion) or 4 January 1948 (Independence Day). The relevant texts are the 1947 Constitution, the 1948 Union Citizenship Act (for "indigenous" and third generation residents as well as applicants for naturalization) and the 1948 Union Citizenship (Election) Act (for those eligible to elect for citizenship by 30 April 1950 by reason of eight out of ten years' residence).

Only indigenous residents were automatically citizens. All others had to make application. That indigenous ("pre-1823") groups included the Muslim groups mentioned above is confirmed in the list of 144 ethnicities approved for the 1973 Census[17] which classified them as Rakhine-Chittagong, Rakhine Kaman, Burmese Muslim, Other Burmese Indian, Burmese Chinese and Myedu.

On independence in 1948, the Muslim communities of Arakan understandably felt that they needed to redefine their ethnicity, not least in order to demonstrate their loyalty to the newly independent Burma. The designations which the British had used to describe Muslims in Arakan were felt to be out of date and out of place. This was an issue, indeed a dilemma for many Indians — Hindu, Sikh and Muslim — who had crossed the Bay of Bengal in the nineteenth and twentieth centuries in search of a better life. Should they return to an India which some had never seen and which was reluctant to accept their return, or should they declare their loyalty to the newly independent states of Ceylon, Malaya, Singapore and Burma (see, e.g., Amrith 2013)?

An approach in early 1947 by the quasi-political Muslim Council (Jamiatul Ulama or "Council of Religious Leaders") of North Arakan to the Parliamentary Under-Secretary of State Arthur Bottomley seeking an autonomous Muslim district for North Arakan and the same status accorded under the Panglong Agreement to certain other frontier areas fell on deaf ears.[18] More pointedly, on 18 June 1948 the President of the Council, Sultan Ahmed, in a Memorandum to the Burmese Government[19] recorded the objections which had been made to the use of the designation "Chittagonians" to describe the Northern Arakan Muslim community. He reminded the government that Prime Minister U Nu had apologized and had directed that the correct designation should be either "Arakanese Muslims" or "Burmese Muslims". It should be noted however that he did not ask that the community should be designated "Rohingya" as the term was not at that time in use or even known.[20]

"Burmese Muslims" was, Sultan Ahmed recalled, a term which the former British administration had approved in 1941 at the request of community representatives of those who had previously been designated "Zerbadis", a designation applied mostly to Muslims of mixed race or parentage, though other explanations exist.[21] Sultan Ahmed also recalled in his Memorandum[22] that:

> When Section 11 of the Constitution of the Union of Burma was being framed, a doubt as to whether the Muslims of North Arakan fell under the section sub-clauses (i) (ii) and (iii), arose and in effect an objection was put in to have the doubt cleared in respect of the term "indigenous" as used in the constitution, but it was withdrawn on the understanding and assurance of the President of the Constituent Assembly, at present His Excellency the President of the Union of Burma (Sao Shwe Thaik), who when approached for clarification with this question, said, "Muslims of Arakan certainly belong to one of the indigenous races of Burma which you represent. In fact there is no pure indigenous race in Burma, and that if you do not belong to indigenous races of Burma, we also cannot be taken an indigenous races of Burma". Being satisfied with his kind explanation, the objection put in was withdrawn.

Four months later, in an address to visiting Prime Minister U Nu on 25 October 1948, the Council laid the blame on the British for the rise of inter-communal tensions over the years, citing as the improbable cause their alleged "divide and rule" policy which supposedly "culminated in the massacre of 1942" of Muslims in the central and southern regions of Arakan. In this address the Council again sought an autonomous Muslim district. They also recorded, though without providing any sources, that the descendants of early Muslim settlers were known as "Ruhangyas" or "Rushangyas". The Council however denied, to the astonishment of the Government and everyone else, that there had ever been any substantive immigration from the Chittagong region into Arakan at any time:[23]

> We are dejected to mention that in this country we have been wrongly taken as part of the race generally known as Chittagonians and as foreigners. We humbly submit that we are not. We have a history of our own distinct from that of Chittagonians. We have a culture of our own. Historically we are a race by ourselves.... Our spoken language is an admixture of Arabic, Persian, Urdu, Arakanese and Bengali.

In a despatch dated 22 December 1949 to the Foreign Secretary, Ernest Bevin, on the Muslim insurrection, British Ambassador James Bowker reported that: [24]

> publicity has been given to protestations of loyalty to the Union Government made to U Aung Zan Wai[25] on his visit in October by the "Rwangya" Community (Arakanese as opposed to Chittagonian Muslims); it is doubtful whether these represent the true feelings of more than a small fraction of the North Arakan Muslims.

Soon after, the settled "Chittagonians" also felt that they no longer wished to be designated by the name used in British censuses and cloaked themselves in the "Rwangya" mantle as well.[26] Thompson and Adloff (1955) wrote:

> The postwar illegal immigration of Chittagonians into that area (Arakan) was on a vast scale, and in the Maungdaw and Buthidaung areas they replaced the Arakanese.... The newcomers were called Mujahids (crusaders), in contrast to the Rwangya or settled Chittagonian population, and though they were economic differences between them, both groups were Muslims and together came to outnumber the Arakanese Buddhists.

In Bengal, a number of "Rwangya" (aka "Rawangya") support groups had indeed emerged, and the cross-border origins of and support given to the Mujahid rebellion were no secret. Van Schendel (2001) referred to the "All-Burma Rwangya Refugee Organisation (East Pakistan)" at the border settlement of Nhila which had in 1951 sought the support of the Burmese Consul to introduce a "permit system to facilitate their going to Burma for earning their bread".

THE SEARCH FOR A BETTER DESIGNATION

In the 1950s other possible designations in addition to "Rwangya" emerged, and we can find in Burmese periodicals a number of articles by the Muslim scholarly and political elite putting forward various designations with differing etymologies, all based on words beginning with "R". Apart from Rwangya and its variant Rawangya, we find Roewenhnya, Roewengya and Rushangya, as well as Rohingya and its variants Rohinja, Ruhangya and Rohangya.[27] The Rakhine scholar Khin Maung Saw has also drawn attention to other variants including Rwahaung Ga Kyar ("Tiger from Old Village"), Rahingya/Rahinja (descendants of Prince Rahin, a Mogul Emperor), Roan Ane Gya (from a Sultanate "Roang" said to be feudatory to Arakan), Rowunhnyar (from the Rakhine words Ro Wan Hnyar meaning "honest and brave people"), and Ronjan/Rohan (a plea for mercy from Arab seafarers wrecked in the eighth century on Ramree Island).[28] The above list of Muslim and Rakhine references, though, is by no means exhaustive. Controversy exists about when the first reference to "Rohingya" was made. This is most recently attributed to Abdul Gaffar, Member of Parliament for Buthidaung, in a letter dated 20 November 1948[29] to the Minister for Home Affairs, but I have seen no original text and doubt that "Rohingya" was the word actually used, more probably "Rwangya" which was then current, though both words could be etymologically related.

Rohingya is today still more of a political label seeking to associate a number of Muslim communities rather than an established ethnic designation. Its political purpose was to seek acceptance of the designation as a "national race" and thus as an indigenous ethnicity. Rohingya might however also be seen to reflect an emerging, coalescing ethnic process among persons of Bengali racial origin designed as much as anything for self-protection in an increasingly hostile environment. But in the process, the former quasi-indigenous Muslim communities — the Arakan-Muslims (aka Yakaing-kala), the Myedus, the former Zerbadis now designated "Burmese Muslims" — have faded as the non-indigenous Chittagonians moved to centre stage. Only the Kaman have remained distinct. The Myedus have already been subsumed.

Calls for unity among the Muslim population of Arakan were a particular theme in the 1960s. Writing in the *Guardian* magazine of August 1960 on the need for understanding in Arakan between Buddhists and Muslims, Mohammed Akram Ali was moved to say:

> I feel very sorry to mention that there is also a lack of unity among the Arakanese Muslims themselves. The main causes of the disruption of unity among them are racial and sectional prejudices. Some of them style themselves as Rowengyas while others call themselves Kamans and yet others Chittagonian descendants etc.... Some of them have a deep-seated sense of localism and therefore take pride in their birth places, such as Maungdaw, Buthidaung, Akyab, Mrohaung, Kyaukpyu, Sandoway. If we go on in this way, I can say with certainty that we will not be able to achieve any good work, nor will we be able to get unity among ourselves. I should therefore like to request my people that they should forget the past and make their future bright by sinking their racial differences.

The writer however makes no mention of "Rohingya". That designation had scarcely come on to the radar screen. It was to make its most important appearance the following year. The (Rangoon) *Guardian* recorded the surrender of Mujahid insurgents at formal ceremonies at Maungdaw, Mayu frontier district, Rakhine State, on 4 July and 15 November 1961. The ceremonies were presided over by the Vice-Chief of the General Staff, Brigadier (later

Brigadier General) Aung Gyi. At the ceremony on 4 July 1961, the *Guardian* reported under the headline "Rohinja (sic) is one of the minorities of the Union and Rohinjas must be loyal":

> The VCGS (Brigadier Aung Gyi) pointed out that like all other minorities such as Nagas, Shans, Yingphaws, Lisus, people of Chinese origin in Kokang and others who live on both sides of the 2,000 mile long frontier, there are people of Chittagonian origin living on both sides of the border. As Lisus on the Burmese side of the frontier is taken as Burmese citizens, similar status applies to the Rohinjas who have been residing on Burmese side of the border for generations. But those minorities must be loyal to the Union, Brigadier Aung Gyi emphasized…

I should add that I am intrigued by the arguments of one "Abu Anin" (the pseudonym, I understand, of a Rohingya politician) who in 2009 wrote that:

> Here as people of Chittagong are called Chatghannya, so do people of Rohang are called Rohangya. It is very comprehensive from linguistic point of view of Bengali language….
>
> Rohingya classified the Rakhine as Rohingya Magh and Anaukiya Magh, which means Rakhine from Arakan and Rakhine from Anouk Pyi (Bengal). So here Rohingya means settlers of Rohang alias Arakan. Thus Rohingya is synonymous to Arakanese.[30]

According to this interpretation, Rohingya/Rwangya means, as I have already concluded above, no more than "Arakaner" in Bengali-related languages and applies to all permanent residents of Arakan, whatever their race or ethnicity.

Despite the debate among the scholarly and political Muslim elite about the future designation of Muslims in Arakan, their status as citizens of Burma was accepted internationally and was not challenged at home. In a despatch to the Foreign Office in January 1965[31] reporting on the visit to Burma of the ill-fated Pakistani Foreign Minister Zulfiqar Ali Bhutto, British Ambassador Gordon Whitteridge referred to the "extremely oppressive measures" which the local Burmese authorities had been using to root out illegal immigrants from what was then still East Pakistan. Mr Bhutto had promised General Ne Win Pakistan's maximum cooperation in dealing with any "genuine illegal immigrants". The Ambassador recorded in his despatch:

> The Moslems in that portion of Arakan which adjoins the border with East Pakistan number about 400,000 and have lived there for generations and have acquired Burmese nationality. But they are patently of Pakistani origin and occasionally some Pakistanis cross into Arakan illegally and mingle with the local population.

The extent of this illegal migration was noted in the same year by the West German Ambassador to Pakistan. In his report on General Ne Win's return visit to Pakistan a few weeks later, Günther Scholl told the Auswärtiges Amt in Bonn:[32]

> Also discussed was the problem of the roughly 250,000 Moslems resident in the Province of Arakan whose nationality is unclarified because the Burmese regime regards them as illegal immigrants from East Pakistan. A majority of these Pakistani immigrants who are unable to prove that they have been resident in Burma for at least three generations are being and will be deported by the Burmese authorities to East Pakistan.

The extent of illegal immigration had become very apparent to the diplomatic communities in both Burma and Pakistan. This flow of migrants did not unfortunately abate, and at the time of the creation of Bangladesh in 1971 the problem was exacerbated. By December 1975 the British Ambassador had recorded a conversation with his Bangladeshi colleague in which this matter had come up:[33]

> He (Mr Kaiser) admitted that there were upward of 1/2 million Bangalee trespassers in Arakan whom the Burmese had some right to eject. He had implored the Burmese authorities not to press this issue during Bangladesh's present troubles[34] and had been pleased that the Burmese had not taken advantage of his country's misfortunes in this respect. He denied that there had been any fresh exodus into Burma.

Not surprisingly the Burmese government decided to carry out a process of citizenship verification in the border regions. Operation Naga Min ("Dragon King") was accordingly launched in late 1977. This passed off without trouble in the Karen, Mon, Shan and Kachin States, but in Arakan the campaign initiated in Sittwe in early 1978 led to the early deportation of over 1,250 illegal migrants. The heavy-handed action of local police and officials caused consternation among the local Muslim population further north, and within a matter of days the headlong flight began into Bangladesh of the mostly rural populations from Maungdaw and Buthidaung townships.

There is no reliable evidence however that this flight was deliberately instigated by the Burmese authorities. The view among UN and diplomatic observers at the time was that there may even have been a measure of Muslim instigation for political reasons. Whatever the case, whole villages decamped in a display of what UN Development Programme Director for Bangladesh Zagorin described in May 1978 as "mass hysteria",[35] inspired perhaps by memories of the communal savagery of 1942. The U.S. Embassy in Rangoon typically[36] reported on 14 June 1978:[37]

At dinner on June 13, the Ambassador discussed Burmese-Bangladeshi issues with the British, Australian, West German and Malaysian Ambassadors. To a man the other diplomats agreed that on the basis of their information the Bangladesh charges (of deliberate expulsion) appeared to be considerably exaggerated and inconsistent. They also noted that journalists ... saw normally functioning Muslim villages in the Arakan which were not being harassed by GUB (Government of Burma) authorities.... We remain sceptical that the GUB has embarked on a systematic campaign to drive Muslims of Chittagonian ancestry from the Arakan or that the refugee-alleged atrocities have occurred.

Some 170,000 out of an estimated 200,000 refugees who had fled to Bangladesh were eventually repatriated under Agreements concluded in Dacca on 10 July 1978[38] and Maungdaw on 10 October 1978.[39] British Ambassador Charles Booth reported the history and outcome of these events in a despatch to London dated 3 July 1979.[40] The Ambassador noted in his despatch that some 65 per cent of all returnees held National Registration Cards (NRCs) issued under the authority of the 1948 Citizenship Acts or Foreign Registration Cards. It was however widely suspected that some NRCs had been improperly obtained and that others may well have been forgeries.[41] The Ambassador's Bangladeshi colleague Zaniruddin had already confirmed in February 1979[42] that NRC holders amounted to 105–110,000 and FRC holders to "some 3,000 at the most".

THE 1982 CITIZENSHIP LAW

Indeed, two years before Operation Naga Min was launched, the Government had begun consideration of a revised citizenship law. As early as October 1976 the National Assembly was informed that a draft law was already under preparation. However, progress was slow. By May 1979 a Law Commission had been established under Dr Maung Maung, the principal drafter of the 1974 Constitution. The Commission sought the views of local and regional authorities. In July 1980 a process of public consultation began which lasted six months.[43] A draft of the proposed legislation was finally published on 21 April 1982.[44] In a report to the Foreign and Commonwealth Office in May 1982,[45] British Ambassador Charles Booth noted that the proposed bill "is far more restrictive than existing legislation". He enclosed a highly critical opinion from his Indian colleague who "took an apocalyptic view of this legislation". Asked however whether he would be protesting about the discriminatory provisions of the bill, Indian Ambassador Swell replied in the negative: this was a strictly internal affair, from which Ambassador Booth concluded that "the Indians are not at present at any rate considering the possibility that the legislation may be in breach of international human rights declarations and that Burma may be vulnerable to criticism in human rights fora".

In his covering letter to London, however, Ambassador Booth concluded that:

> The new bill reflects little credit on the legislators and ultimately on the regime as a whole, and I see it as another move in Burma's policy of keeping itself 'pure' of foreign involvement. Its immediate concern, I assume, is with illegal Bengali immigration into Arakan.

When the bill was finally enacted on 15 October 1982,[46] Acting Head of Mission Roger Leeland reported to London on 25 November 1982 that:

> The new Law is blatantly discriminatory on racial grounds. If the new procedures that are being prepared turn out to be as rigorous as we suspect they will be, then the Law may in practice be even more discriminatory than its text pretends.

> On the other hand it would be possible to argue that the new Law is a generous and far-sighted instrument to resolve over a period of time an awkward legacy of the colonial era.

These views were generally reflected in a detailed analysis enclosed with Leeland's letter to London and prepared by the Australian Embassy in Rangoon. Political Officer Roland Rich noted that a lengthy speech by General Ne Win on 8 October 1982[47] shed considerable light on the intentions of the legislators. I would in particular quote one passage from General Ne Win's address:[48]

> We are, in reality, not in a position to drive away all those people who had come at different times for different reasons from different lands. We must have sympathy on those who had been here for such a long time and give them peace of mind. We have therefore designated them *eh-naingngan-tha* (associate citizens) in this law. Why have we given them this name? Because, we were all citizens in the beginning; then these people came as guests and eventually could not go back and have decided to go on living here for the rest of their lives. Such being their predicament, we accept them as citizens. We can leniently give them the right to live in this country and to carry on a livelihood in the legitimate way. But we will have to leave them out in matters involving the affairs of the country and the destiny of the State.

Rich pointed out that the concept of "associate citizens" was a late addition to the law and had not been included in the draft released in April 1982.

He wrote:

> It deals with a limited category of persons who applied for citizenship
> under the 1948 Union Citizenship Act but, presumably, have not yet
> been granted it. We have been told that there are 80,000 to 90,000 such
> applicants who, for one reason or another, have not had their application
> processed. It is likely that bureaucratic inertia is a major contributing factor
> in this state of affairs.

This "bureaucratic inertia" however spread beyond unprocessed claims under
the Union Citizenship Act 1948. Many who applied to register as Foreign
Nationals in order to obtain Foreign Registration Certificates were never called
for interview. Others who qualified for citizenship as indigenous Muslim
citizens and were not required to submit an application (Myedu, Kaman,
Arakan Muslim, Other Indian Muslim, Burmese Muslim and Chinese Muslim
recognized as categories even as late as the 1973 Census)[49] never received
their ID documentation on various excuses, such as that they were not at
home when the registrar called at their village, or that there were details or
discrepancies which needed to be checked. Some, not many, might unwisely
not have regarded the acquisition of an ID under the 1948 Act as a priority,
but as persons resident in a border region most would have understood
instinctively the importance of certification.

There is another aspect of the 1982 Law (whose provisions are well
summarized in Nurul Islam's contribution to this volume and are accordingly
not repeated here) which merits attention. Article 6 of the Law reads that:
"A person who is already a citizen on the date this Law comes into force is a
citizen." The explanation of this provision given in the April 1982 draft is that:
"Under Article 145(b) of the (1974) Constitution, persons who are already
citizens according to law on 3rd January 1974, the day the Constitution came
into force, are citizens." However because of the prevalence of forged IDs,
it seems that the decision was taken that, exceptionally in Arakan, no new
IDs would be issued to Muslims at all until their documentation had been
checked, even in cases where valid IDs issued under either of the 1948 Acts
were legitimately held. Elsewhere in Myanmar it would seem that the many
thousands of "Chittagonians" who might claim to be Rohingya had little
or no difficulty in exchange their old IDs for new IDs and thus continuing
their full citizenship, including voting rights and access to state welfare
and educational facilities. Although in 1960 some 300,000 out of 700,000
Ruhangyas/Rohingyas in Burma were said to live outside Arakan (see note 6),
it is noteworthy that neither the 1982 Citizenship Law nor the 2014 Census
would appear to have affected them and their descendants detrimentally.

There is yet another issue which may not be widely understood. Although much attention has been paid to the provision in Article 3 of the 1982 Law (paralleling a similar article in the 1948 Act) that: "Nationals such as the Kachin, Kayah, Karen, Chin, Burman, Mon, Rakhine or Shan and ethnic groups as have settled in any of the territories included within the State as their permanent home from a period anterior to 1185 B.E., 1823 A.D. are Burma citizens", this does not mean that membership of one of these races — an illustrative and not a definitive list — is essential for eventual full citizenship. The Law makes clear in Article 7, and General Ne Win confirmed this in his 8 October 1982 speech, that the third generation (the first generation only resident, the next two actually born in Burma) of descendants of both associate and naturalized citizens would indeed become full citizens, regardless of their race or ethnicity.[50] In other words, any problems affecting the granting of less than full citizenship through "associate" and "naturalized" status would largely disappear with the arrival of the third generation who would be full citizens.[51]

It is not true to say, as is frequently alleged, that Arakan Muslims have been deliberately excluded by the 1982 Law from citizenship. At the time this law came into force, the most recent list of officially recognized ethnicities was not the present list of 135 ethnicities which was first published only in 1990[52] but the list used for the 1973 Census which included several indigenous, even non-indigenous Muslim ethnicities, though not "Rohingya". A critical test is surely whether "Rohingya" has ever been formally recorded as an ethnicity by the Myanmar authorities and as an option for use during any census held since independence in 1948. The answer is that this has never been the case, even though the term may on infrequent occasions have been used by persons in authority or even noted on isolated ID cards.[53]

It does not appear that the 1973 list was used for the 1983 Census, but what list if any was used is not apparent from the census returns in English which listed only the main ethnic groups, with indigenous Muslim communities seemingly recorded as "Indian" and non-indigenous as "Bangladeshi".[54] Muslims in Arakan apparently agreed to be enumerated as "Bengalis" which was after all for most their heritage and racial ancestry. They would however have been most unhappy if they discovered that in the English-language census report their ethnicity had been classified as "Bangladeshi", which is not an ethnicity but a nationality which they neither claimed nor wanted. (As Robert Taylor has also pointed out[55] "the confusion over ethnicity and race in Myanmar is compounded by the fact that one word, 'lumyo', is normally used to express both concepts"). Finally, there is the provision in Article 8(a) of the 1982 Law that: "The Council of State may, in the interest of the State, confer on any person citizenship, or associate citizenship or naturalised citizenship." This gives the Executive today the right to grant citizenship to anyone it chooses, whatever their race or ethnicity.

As both I and Nick Cheesman have shown,[56] whereas under the 1948 Act belonging to a "national race" was the least complicated path to citizenship, there were other channels. The 1982 Law however, as Cheesman writes, made "ethnic identity, which is to say, membership in a 'national race' category, the primary basis for citizenship". Belonging to a "national race" became "the gold standard for membership in the political community 'Myanmar' and also a guarantee of membership." Rohingya claims to membership however were rejected; the Rohingya ethnicity was not formally accepted in law as a pre-1823 indigenous identity. The political objective of achieving this had thus failed totally, despite broad uncritical acceptance of the designation internationally.

As "the law of each State primarily determines who are its nationals",[57] and as a reasonable interpretation of the provisions of the 1982 Law discussed above gives the State the right to grant citizenship to all those Muslims in Rakhine State who meet certain basic criteria, and even to those who do not, frequent calls from the international community for "reviewing the 1982 Citizenship Law"[58] and related regulations[59] are in my view not altogether justified because they reveal an ignorance of the provisions of the Law itself.[60]

It is not so much the law itself which is at fault as the failure to implement the law in Rakhine State in a timely and responsible manner. This is indeed the primary cause of current tensions.[61]

REPERCUSSIONS OF GOVERNMENT INACTION ON CITIZENSHIP APPLICATIONS

What had been lacking from 1948 to 1982 was the political will to tackle the problem of some 2 million residents[62] with foreign ancestry. Since 1982 the authorities have likewise shown no urgency or even serious interest in taking those measures needed to grant citizenship to Muslims in Rakhine State on the basis of the 1982 Law, to dispense with the impossibly strict level of documentary evidence currently demanded, and to cease the chicanery and obstructionism to which Muslims both as candidates and voters in the recent elections have been subject.

Insistence on use of the term "Rohingya" by their international backers has however made it difficult for the authorities to apply the Citizenship Law in a liberal and constructive manner, even if they had the political will to do so. Myanmar is a party to neither of the UN Conventions on Statelessness,[63] neither the 1954 Convention to which 83 countries have so far acceded, nor the 1961 Convention which has so far attracted 61 signatories from among the UN's 193 members. Nor has it yet acceded to the International Convention on Civil and Political Rights. Article 15 of the Universal Declaration of Human Rights adopted by the UN General Assembly in December 1948 however provides that: "Everyone has the right to a nationality" and that: "No one shall be arbitrarily deprived of his nationality nor denied the right to change his nationality", while Article 7 of the 1989 Convention of the Rights of the Child provides that: "The child shall be registered immediately after birth and shall have the right from birth to a name, the right to acquire a nationality and, as far as possible, right to know and be cared for by his or her parents." Myanmar may well be in breach of their Article 15 (1948) obligation through their prolonged delay in issuing new IDs under the 1982 Law and possibly also in breach of their Article 7 (1989) obligation through the alleged unwillingness of local authorities on occasions to register new Rohingya births, especially of the third or subsequent child in a family, though Myanmar has denied this allegation.[64]

Minister for Immigration and Population Khin Yi, when asked about the problem of "White Card" (temporary registration card) holders, told the *Irrawaddy* in February 2015: "This has not happened during our term. It was in 1990 when their NRCs were seized, as there were reports of people obtaining fake cards. We have now allowed them to reapply for citizenship. When they apply, we issue them the appropriate documents...." The strong suggestion in the Minister's remarks is that what happened from 1988 to 2011 when the country was under military rule is not the responsibility of subsequent administrations. This is not a satisfactory answer. Most "White Card" holders have waited over twenty-five years for their applications for new IDs to be considered. Some 800,000 cards were issued, mostly to Arakan Muslims, and a pilot citizenship verification process was for a time suspended.[65] As a result, many Rohingya have existed for far too long in a stateless limbo. "White Cards" have in any case been invalidated and those who have handed them in have received green-turquoise coloured receipts valid for only two years.[66] This happened in the context of the disenfranchisement of "White Card" holders prior to the elections held on 8 November 2015, which was for many Rohingya the last straw.[67]

The Myanmar authorities have viewed with some concern the transformation and coalescence of a rich historical kaleidoscope of Muslim communities in Arakan, encouraged by a vociferous and well-coordinated international lobby[68] and enhanced by substantial illegal emigration from Bengal, into a monolithic political community. The Rohingya narrative, which denies any significant immigration from Bengal, implies an astonishing, almost 100-fold natural increase in the Rohingya population in Arakan as a whole since the Rev. Comstock's recording of some 20,000 "Mussulmans" of 1842, and an increase since the end of the Second World War in Sittwe and Maungdaw Districts (former Akyab District) twice the rate of neighbouring East Pakistan/Bangladesh where the rate of natural increase is now declining. This is not credible unless the large-scale migration from Bengal into Arakan since 1948 is recognized.

INTERNATIONAL IMPLICATIONS

The United Nations and Western governments are under pressure to accept the Rohingya identity. That is a political decision which only they can take. It is important though that their unqualified recognition of the Rohingya identity in Myanmar and overseas should not provide moral and political support to a highly questionable and pretentious narrative. Such an uncritical acceptance damages the prospects for reconciliation by further polarizing the Buddhist and Muslim communities.

British Ambassador Andrew Patrick in Myanmar made his own position clear when he said in an interview with *Mizzima Business Weekly* on 8 May 2014:

> Generally in the UK, and in Europe, ethnic groups are allowed to call themselves by the name they want to use, whether or not that name has any historic validity. Of course when we use it, that's not to say we're expecting some sort of special status or a recognition of the Rohingya as an ethnic group. That is for the Burmese parliament to decide.[69] What I would say, is that it's obviously very important for that community to have the rights they are entitled to. And the Government has made a commitment to ensure that everyone who is entitled to citizenship under the 1982 law gets that.

The British Government itself, however, has been reluctant to provide such a nuanced clarification. The Ambassador would only state what he knows or believes to be the position of his government. In this context, Western governments surely have a responsibility to ensure that, if they use the designation "Rohingya" in their statements, they should also make it clear that this does not imply any recognition of the Rohingya as an ethnic group, nor any view about precisely who they are and where they might be living in Myanmar.

As Robert Taylor has also noted,[70] the Rohingya issue is not simply a Myanmar responsibility. There is an international dimension to the problem, and especially a Bangladeshi one. It is impossible to say just how many

Bangladeshis have migrated illegally into Myanmar since 1948, but the number may run into tens if not hundreds of thousands. Yet in most cases even these illegal migrants have now been in Myanmar for thirty years or more, and so it is difficult to see, on a purely practical basis, how they could now be forcibly removed to Bangladesh, especially as up to 200,000 Rohingya refugees currently in Bangladesh might reasonably claim repatriation to Myanmar.

The International Crisis Group (ICG) in "Myanmar: The Politics of Rakhine State" (2014) highlighted the dilemmas facing all parties, and the anxieties of both Buddhist Rakhine and Muslim Rohingya. ICG quote a Rohingya elder as saying: "The violence in 2012 changed the situation. Before the violence our Rohingya name was not something we thought about every day. Since the violence, everything has been stolen from us — now all we have left is our Rohingya identity. All of us are united on this." The ICG commented: "Rohingya leaders see defending their political identity as vital to gain Myanmar citizenship and ease discrimination and denial of rights. They see international use of the term as an important source of legitimacy and support for their rights."

It would make it much easier for the international community to promote this usage if the Rohingya lobby could at least try to explain, if indeed they know, how the designation emerged in the late 1950s, rather than proclaiming a dogmatic historical narrative which is scarcely credible and is based on an almost if not total absence of documentary sources.[71] Emerging ethnicities cannot reasonably be backdated many hundreds of years in support of a political agenda.

Many ordinary Rohingya people are fearful, impoverished, poorly educated and in many cases now unable to earn their traditional living as farmers and fishermen. But as the ICG report of last October noted: "Camp leaders have considerable coercive powers, and there is widespread fear, limiting the possibility for individuals to break with the political orthodoxy." Furthermore, as Crouch (2014) reported in *New Mandala* of 4 November 2014:

> Some religious leaders from the Indian Muslim community issued a *fatwa* (Islamic legal opinion) to their community members to instruct them on how to list their identity in the census. They emphasized that Muslims should not be afraid to list their religious identity on the census. Some Indian Muslim leaders even argued that it was *haram* (forbidden) for a Muslim to fail to list their religion on the census.

Western governments tend to lament that this problem over the designation "Rohingya" is a distraction. In August 2015 it was reported that U.S. Secretary of State John Kerry had told Myanmar's leaders that the name issue should be set aside and that to force any community to accept a name they consider to be offensive is to invite conflict. Yet the matter of designation is of the very essence of the dispute and should not in my view be swept under the carpet. While Rohingya may well say they find it offensive to be called "Bengalis", Rakhine Buddhists find it equally offensive that Rakhine Muslims should call themselves "Rohingya".[72]

THE SIGNIFICANCE OF THE 2012 STATEMENT BY PRESIDENT THEIN SEIN TO THE UNHCR

On 11 July 2012 President Thein Sein met the then UN High Commissioner for Refugees António Guterres (now UN Secretary-General) and in a statement issued through the Presidential Office the following day, in the Burmese language only, we read: [73]

> The President said that Bengalis came to Myanmar because the British colonialists invited them in prior to 1948, when Myanmar gained independence from Britain, to work in the agricultural sector. Some Bengalis settled here because it was convenient for them to do so, and according to Myanmar law, the third generation of those who arrived before 1948 can be granted Myanmar citizenship. He added that, if we look at the situation in Rakhine State, some people are the younger generation of Bengalis who arrived before 1948, but some are illegal immigrants claiming to be Rohingyas and this threatens the stability of the state. The Government has been looking seriously for a solution to this problem. The country will take responsibility for its native people, but it cannot accept illegal immigrant Rohingya in any way. So in the end the solution to the problem is to set up refugee camps for them so that UNHCR can look after them. If a third country accepts them, we will send them there.

No official English version of this statement has appeared, and it was almost universally reported, inaccurately, that the President was telling the UN High Commissioner that all those who claimed to be Rohingya were illegal Bengali immigrants. The President was rather seeking to make the point that in his view the "Rohingya" designation had cross-border origins and that those claiming to be "Rohingya" could not claim to be pre-1948 legal migrants. The President also made it clear that Bengalis who had settled in Burma under British rule were legal migrants and that their descendants at the third generation could apply for citizenship.[74] It seems possible, even likely, that pressure among Muslims in Arakan to use the designation "Rohingya" in preference to several other "R" words mooted at the time indeed came from Mujahid rebel sources.[75]

People of Islamic faith have indeed been in Arakan for a very long time. Even so, over 90 per cent of the Muslim population of Arakan, whenever and however they arrived, are likely to have Bengali ancestry. Myanmar's borders extend to over 6,150 kilometres. There are Malay, Karen, Mon, Shan, Kachin, Jingpaw, Yao, Naga and many other historical ethnic communities on both sides of Myanmar's borders with Malaysia, Thailand, Laos, China, India and Bangladesh. The Bangladeshi position is that, despite the cultural, linguistic, ethnic and family ties between Bengal and Arakan, there are no, and never have been any historical, indigenous "Rohingya" communities on their side of the 270-kilometre border with Myanmar, although other minor ethnic groups are to be found on both sides of the same border in the Chittagong and Arakan Hill Tracts, such as the Daignet, Maramagyi, Mro, Chakma and Mrama.

I have no reason to question the Bangladeshi position. But the only possible explanation I can offer for this quite remarkable state of affairs affecting what was for centuries one of the most porous borders in the region is that just as there are no historical ethnic "Rohingya" communities in Bangladesh, so there are no historical ethnic "Rohingya" communities on the Myanmar side of the border either. The Rohingya in Myanmar may well exist today, but they are not an indigenous community, otherwise they would be found in Bangladesh as well. In the words of Brigadier Aung Gyi in 1961, however, there are Chittagonians on both sides of the border, and Bangladesh would at least agree that there are Chittagonians on their side.

Western governments are hoping that the new National League for Democracy (NLD) administration in Myanmar which took over at the end of March 2016 in the wake of the 8 November 2015 elections will seek to resolve the Rohingya citizenship issue as a matter of urgency.[76] It is fortunate that on 26 January 2016 the Joint Bill Committee of the Union Parliament voted by a narrow margin against the merger of the Ministry of Immigration and Population with the Ministry of Home Affairs. The Ministry of Home Affairs is a military sinecure, as are defence and border affairs. All three departments have been active historically in Rakhine State and are very influential there. The merger of Immigration and Population with Home Affairs would have removed citizenship matters from the NLD's orbit of responsibilities and created a serious problem.

The resolution of these complex issues will test the powers of negotiation and compromise of the civilian and military branches of the administration to the utmost. Recently the authorities resumed a citizenship verification project suspended before the elections. Although the NLD said soon after the elections that they did not see the Rakhine issue as a priority,[77] the new administration announced on 31 May 2016 a comprehensive initiative at the highest level: a "Central Committee" of twenty Cabinet Ministers chaired by State Counsellor Daw Aung San Suu Kyi, with four working groups on security and stability, immigration and citizenship, resettlement and socio-economic development, and cooperation with UN and international agencies. Since then the administration has agreed to the establishment of an Advisory Commission under the chairmanship of former UN Secretary-General Kofi Annan, but its international membership has aroused controversy. The insurgent attacks which began on 9 October 2016 are also under scrutiny by a government-appointed Investigation Commission.

It is not the objective of this chapter to suggest what needs to be done. But it is appropriate to draw attention to matters which are at the heart of the current repression and discrimination against the Rohingya community. These include in particular three issues, which are in the nature of broken promises, are all directly related to citizenship and affect a substantial majority of all those claiming to be Rohingya in Rakhine State:

- the guarantee in Article 6 of the 1982 Citizenship Law that no one would lose their citizenship already held prior to the enactment of the Law;
- the assurance given by President Thein Sein on 11 July 2012 to then United Nations High Commissioner for Refugee, and now UN Secretary-General, António Guterres, that Myanmar accepts as Burmese citizens descendants of Bengali (Chittagonian) immigrants under British rule.
- the restoration of voting rights to all those Muslims in Arakan who were entitled to them from 1948 to 2015 when they were summarily disenfranchised.

The public recognition of these legal entitlements and the restoration of what are basic political and human rights are long overdue, especially when it is apparent that Muslims of the same heritage living elsewhere in Myanmar have lost none of these entitlements as a result of the 1982 Citizenship Law.

APPENDIX

BURMA CITIZENSHIP LAW PROMULGATED ON 15 OCTOBER 1982[78]

Chapter I — Title and Definition

1. This Law shall be called the Burma Citizenship Law.
2. The expressions contained in this Law shall have the following meanings:
   (a) "State" means the Socialist Republic of the Union of Burma;
   (b) "Citizen" means a Burma citizen;
   (c) "Associate Citizen" means an associate citizen prescribed by this Law;
   (d) "Naturalized Citizen" means a prescribed by this Law;
   (e) "Foreigner" means a person who is not a citizen or an associate citizen or a naturalized citizen;
   (f) "Certificate of citizenship" means a certificate of citizenship granted under the Union Citizenship (Election) Act, 1948 or the Union Citizenship Act, 1948 or this Law;
   (g) "Certificate of Associate Citizenship" means a certificate of associate citizenship granted under this Law;
   (h) "Certificate of Naturalized Citizenship" means a certificate of naturalized citizenship granted under this Law;
   (i) "Central Body established under this Law.

Chapter II — Citizenship

3. Nationals such as the Kachin, Kayah, Karen, Chin, Burman, Mon, Rakhine or Shan and ethnic groups as have settled in any of the territories included within the State as their permanent home from a period anterior to 1185 B.E., 1823 A.D. are Burma citizens.
4. The Council of State may decide whether any ethnic group is national or not.
5. Every national and every person born of parents, both of whom are nationals are citizens by birth.
6. A person who is already a citizen on the date this Law cones into force is a citizen. Action, however shall be taken under section 18 for infringement of the provision of that section.
7. The following persons born in or outside the State are also citizens:
   (a) persons born of parents, both of whom are citizens;
   (b) persons born of parents, one of whom is a citizen and the other an associate citizen;

    (c) persons born of parents, one of whom and the other a naturalized citizen;

    (d) persons born of parents one of whom is

        (i) a citizen; or

        (ii) an associate citizen; or

        (iii) a naturalized citizen;

        and the other is born of parents, both of whom are associate citizens;

    (e) persons born of parents, one of whom is

        (i) a citizen; or

        (ii) an associate citizen; or

        (iii) a naturalized citizen;

        and the other is born of parents, both of whom are naturalized citizens;

    (f) persons born of parents one of whom is

        (i) a citizen; or

        (ii) an associate citizen; or

        (iii) a naturalized citizen;

        and the other is born of parents, one of whom is an associate citizen and the other a naturalized citizen.

8. (a) The Council of State may, in the interest of the State confer on any person citizenship or associate citizenship or naturalized citizenship.

    (b) The Council of State may, in the interest of the State revoke the citizenship or associate citizenship or naturalized citizenship of any person except a citizen by birth.

9. A person born in the State shall have his birth registered either by the parent or guardian in the prescribed manner, within year from the date he completes the age of ten years, at the organizations prescribed by the Ministry of Home Affairs.

Proviso. If registration is not possible within one year from the date he completes the age of ten years, application may be made by the parent or guardian, furnishing sufficient reasons to the organizations prescribed by the Ministry of Home Affairs.

10. A person born outside the State shall have his birth registered either by the parent or guardian in the proscribed manner within one year from the date of birth at the Burmese Embassy or Consulate or organizations prescribed by the Ministry of Home Affairs.

Proviso. If registration is not possible within one year from the date of birth, application may be made by the parent or guardian, furnishing sufficient reasons to the Central Body through the Burmese Embassy or Consulate or organizations prescribed by the Ministry of Home Affairs.

11. (a) A parent or guardian who fails to comply with section 9 or section 10 shall be liable to pay a penalty of kyats fifty per year to the Burmese Embassy or Consulate or an organization prescribed by the Ministry of Home Affairs.

    (b) A parent or guardian who fails for five years in succession to comply with section 9 or section 10 shall be liable to a penalty of kyats one thousand.

12. A citizen shall
    (a) respect and abide by the laws of the State;
    (b) discharge the duties prescribed by the laws of the State
    (c) be entitled to enjoy the rights prescribed by the laws of the State.

13. A citizen shall not as well acquire the citizenship of another country.

14. A citizen shall have no right to divest himself of his citizenship during any war in which the State is engaged.

15. (a) A citizen shall not automatically lose his citizenship merely by marriage to a foreigner.
    (b) A foreigner shall not automatically acquire citizenship merely by marriage to a citizen.

16. A citizen who leaves the State permanently, or who acquires the citizenship of or registers himself as a citizen of another country, or who takes out a passport or a similar certificate of another country ceases to be a citizen.

17. The citizenship of a citizen by birth shall in no case be revoked except in the case of cessation of citizenship due to infringement of the provision of section 16.

18. A citizen who has acquired citizenship by making a false representation or by concealment shall have his citizenship revoked, and shall also be liable to imprisonment for a term of ton years and to a fine of kyats fifty thousand.

19. A citizen who has committed abetment of obtaining, in a fraudulent manner, a certificate of citizenship or a certificate of associate citizenship or a certificate of naturalized citizenship for another person shall be liable to imprisonment for a term of seven years and to a fine of kyats ten thousand.

20. (a) The certificate of citizenship of a person whose citizenship has ceased or has been revoked shall be cancelled. A person holding such a cancelled certificate shall surrender it in the manner prescribed by the Ministry of Home Affairs.

(b) Failure to surrender a cancelled certificate of citizenship or continued use of it or transfer of it in a fraudulent manner to another person shall entail imprisonment for a term of ten years and a fine of kyats twenty thousand.

(c) Whoever holds and uses a cancelled certificate of citizenship or the certificate of a deceased citizen shall be liable to imprisonment for a term of ten years and to a fine of kyats twenty thousand.

21. Whoever forges a certificate of citizenship or abets such act shall be liable to imprisonment for a term of fifteen years to a fine of kyats fifty thousand.

22. A person whose citizenship has ceased or has been revoked shall have no right to apply again for citizenship or associate citizenship or naturalized citizenship.

Chapter III — Associate Citizenship

23. Applicants for citizenship under the Union Citizenship Act, 1948, conforming to the stipulations and qualifications may be determined as associate citizens by the Central Body.

24. A person who has been determined is an associate citizen by the Central Body shall appear in person before an organization prescribed by the Ministry of Home Affairs, and shall make an affirmation in writing that he owes allegiance to the State, that, he will respect and abide by the laws of the State and that he is aware of the prescribed duties and rights.

25. The Central Body may include in the certificate of associate citizenship the names of children mentioned in the application. The child whose name is so included is an associate citizen.

26. The child whose name is included under section 25, and who has completed the age of eighteen years shall make an affirmation in accordance with section 24, along with the parents.

27. (a) The child whose name is included under section 25 and who has not completed the age of eighteen years shall, within one year from the date he completes the age of eighteen years appear in person before an organization prescribed by the Ministry of Home Affairs and make an affirmation in accordance with section 24.

(b) A person who fails to comply with sub-section (a) shall be liable to pay a penalty of kyats fifty per year to an organization prescribed by the Ministry of Home Affairs.

28. If affirmation is not possible within one year, application may be made, furnishing sufficient reasons to the Central Body, through the

organizations prescribed by the Ministry of Home Affairs. If there are no sufficient reasons after the date on which he completes the age of twenty-two years, he shall lose his associate citizenship.

29. (a) When both the parents, of the children included in their certificate of associate of associate citizenship, lose their associate citizenship, the child who has not completed the age of eighteen years, and the child who has completed the age of eighteen years, but has not made an affirmation cease to be associate citizens.

   (b) Where one of the parents, of the children included in the certificate hold by her or him, is an associate citizen and the other a foreigner, and if the mother or father who is an associate citizen loses her or his associate citizenship the child who has not completed the age of eighteen years, and the child who has completed the age of eighteen years, but has not made an affirmation cease to be associate citizens.

30. An associate citizen shall
   (a) respect and abide by the laws of the State;
   (b) discharge the duties prescribed by the laws of the State;
   (c) be entitled to enjoy the rights of a citizen under the laws of the State, with the exception of the rights stipulated from time to time by, the Council of State.

31. An associate citizen shall not as well acquire the citizenship of another country.

32. An associate citizen shall have no right to divest himself of his associate citizenship during any war in which the State is engaged.

33. An associate citizen shall not automatically acquire citizenship merely by marriage to a citizen.

34. An associate citizen who leaves the State permanently or, who acquires the citizenship of or registers himself as a citizen of another country, or who takes out a passport or a similar certificate of another country ceases to be an associate citizen.

35. The Central Body may revoke the associate citizenship of a person if he infringes any of the following provisions:
   (a) trading or communicating with enemy countries or with countries assisting the enemy country, or with citizens or organizations of such countries during a war in which the State is engaged or abetting such an act;
   (b) trading or communicating with an organization or with a member of such organization which is hostile to the State, or abetting such an act;

(c) committing an act likely to endanger the sovereignty and security of the State or public peace and tranquillity or giving rise to the reasonable belief that he is about to commit such an act;

(d) showing disaffection or disloyalty to the State by any act or speech or otherwise;

(e) giving information relating to a state secret to any person, or to any organization, or to any other country or countries,, or abetting such an act;

(f) committing an offence involving moral turpitude for which he has been sentenced to imprisonment for a minimum term of one year or to a minimum fine of kyats one thousand.

36. An associate citizen who has acquired such citizenship by making a false representation or by concealment shall have his associate citizenship revoked, and shall also be liable to imprisonment for a term of ten years and to a fine of kyats fifty thousand.

37. An associate citizen who has committed abetment of obtaining in a fraudulent manners a certificate of citizenship or a certificate of associate citizenship or a certificate of naturalized citizenship for another person shall have his associate citizenship revoked; and shall also be liable to imprisonment for a term of seven years and to a fine of kyats ton thousand.

38. An associate citizen who has personal knowledge of an offence committed by any person under section 36 or section 37, or as an accomplice who has committed such an act, discloses or admits the offence before organizations prescribed by the Ministry of Home Affairs within one year from the date this Law comes into force, or within one year from the date of commission of the offence shall be exempted from the penal provisions relating to such offence.

39. (a) The certificate of associate citizenship of a person whose associate citizenship has ceased or has been revoked shall be cancelled. A person holding such a cancelled certificate shall surrender it in the manner prescribed by the Ministry of Home Affairs.

(b) Failure to surrender a cancelled certificate of associate citizenship or continued use of it or transfer of it in a fraudulent manner to another person shall entail imprisonment for a term of ten years and a fine of kyats twenty thousand.

(c) Whoever holds and uses a cancelled certificate of associate citizenship or the certificate of a deceased associate citizen shall be liable to imprisonment for a term of ten years and to a fine of kyats twenty thousand.

40. Whoever forges a certificate of associate citizenship or abets such act shall be liable to imprisonment for a term of fifteen years and to a fine of kyats fifty thousand.

41. A person whose associate citizenship has ceased or has been revoked shall have no right to apply again for associate citizenship or naturalized citizenship.

Chapter IV — Naturalized Citizenship

42. Persons who have entered and resided in the State anterior to 4th January, 1948, and their offsprings born Within the State may, if they have not yet applied under the union Citizenship Act, 1948, apply for naturalized citizenship to the Central Body, furnishing conclusive evidence.

43. The following persons born in or outside the State from the date this Law comes into force may also apply for naturalized citizenship:
    (a) persons born of Parents one of whom is a citizen and the other a foreigner;
    (b) persons born of parents, one of whom is an associate citizen and the other a naturalized citizen;
    (c) persons born of parents one of whom is an associate citizen and the other a foreigner;
    (d) persons born of parents, both of whom are naturalized citizens;
    (e) persons born of parents, one of whom is a naturalized citizen and the other a foreigner.

44. An applicant for naturalized citizenship shall have the following qualifications:
    (a) be a person who conforms to the provisions of section 42 or section 43;
    (b) have completed the age of eighteen years;
    (c) be able to speak well one of the national languages;
    (d) be of good character;
    (e) be of sound mind.

45. A person married to a citizen or to an associate citizen or to a naturalized citizen, who is holding a Foreigner's Registration Certificate anterior to the date this Law comes into force shall have the following qualifications to apply for naturalized citizenship:
    (a) have completed the age of eighteen years;
    (b) be of good character;
    (c) be of sound mind;
    (d) be the only husband or wife;

(e) have resided continuously in the State for at least three years is the lawful wife or husband.

46. (a) A person who has been determined as a naturalized citizen by the Central Body shall appear in person before an organization prescribed by the Ministry of Home Affairs, and shall make an affirmation in writing that he owes allegiance to the State, that he will respect and abide by the laws of the State and that he is aware of the prescribed duties and rights.

(b) A person who has been determined as a naturalized citizen by the Central Body and holding a Foreigner's Registration Certificate shall appear in person before an organization prescribed by the Ministry of Home Affairs, and shall make an affirmation in writing that he renounces his foreign citizenship, that he owes allegiance to the State, that he will respect and abide by the laws of the State and that he is aware of the prescribed duties and rights.

47. The Central Body may include in the certificate of naturalized citizenship the name of a child mentioned in the application. The child whose name is so included is a naturalized citizen.

48. The child whose name is included under section 47, and who has completed the age of eighteen years shall make an affirmation in accordance with sub-section (a) of section 46, along with the parents.

49. (a) The child whose name is included under section 47, and who has not completed the age of eighteen years shall, with in one year from the date on which he completes the age of eighteen years appear in person before an organization prescribed by the Ministry of Home Affairs and make an affirmation in accordance with sub-section (a) of section 46.

(b) A person who fails to comply with sub-section (a) shall be liable to pay a penalty of kyats fifty per year to an organization prescribed by the Ministry of Home Affairs.

50. If affirmation is not possible within one year, application may be made, furnishing sufficient reasons to the Central Body, through the organizations prescribed by the Ministry of Home Affairs. If there are no sufficient reasons after the date on which he completes the age of twenty-two years, he shall lose his naturalized citizenship.

51. (a) When both the parents, of the children included in their certificate of naturalized citizenship, lose their naturalized citizenship the child who has not completed the age of eighteen years, and the child

who has completed the age of eighteen years, but has not made an affirmation cease to be naturalized citizens.

(b) Where one of the parents of the children included in the certificate held by her or him, is a citizen and the other a foreigner, and if the mother or father who is a citizen loses her or his citizenship, the child who has not completed the age of eighteen years and the child who has completed the age of eighteen years, but has not made an affirmation cease to be naturalized citizen.

(c) Where one of the parents, of the children included in the certificate hold by her or him, is an associate citizen and the other a foreigner, and if the mother or father who is associate citizen loses her or his associate citizenship, the child who has not completed the age of eighteen years, and the child who has completed the age of eighteen years, but has not made in affirmation cease to be naturalized citizens.

(d) Where one of the parents, of the children included in the certificate held by her or him, is a naturalized citizen and the other a foreigner, and if the mother or father who is a naturalized citizen loses her or his naturalized citizenship, the child who has not completed the age of eighteen years, and the child who has completed the age of eighteen years, but has not made an affirmation cease to be naturalized citizens.

52. If a person married to a citizen or to an associate citizen or to a naturalized citizen, who is holding a Foreigner's Registration Certificate anterior to the date this Law comes into force applies for naturalized citizenship and the husband or wife of such a person dies or is divorced from such a person before acquiring naturalized citizenship, the application for naturalized citizenship of such a person shall lapse.

53. A naturalized citizen shall
(a) respect and abide by the laws of the State;
(b) discharge the duties prescribed by the laws of the State;
(c) be entitled to enjoy the rights of a citizen under the laws of the State with the exception of the rights stipulated from time to time by the Council of State.

54. A naturalized citizen shall not as well acquire the citizenship of another country.

55. A naturalized citizen shall have no right to divest himself of his naturalized citizenship during any war in which the State is engaged.

56. A naturalized citizen shall not Automatically acquire citizenship or

associate citizenship merely by marriage to a citizen or to an associate citizen.

57. A naturalized citizen who leaves the State permanently, or who acquires the citizenship of or registers himself as a citizen of another country, or who takes out a passport or a similar certificate of another country ceases to be a naturalized citizen.

58. The Central Body may revoke the naturalized citizenship of a person if he infringes any of the following provisions:

    (a) trading or communicating with enemy countries Or with countries assisting the enemy country, or with citizens or organizations of such countries during a war in which the State is engaged, or abetting such an act;

    (b) trading or communicating with an organization or with a member of such organization which is hostile to the State, or abetting such an act;

    (c) committing an act likely to endanger the sovereignty and security of the State or Public peace and tranquillity or giving rise to the reasonable belief that he is about to commit such an act;

    (d) showing disaffection or disloyalty to the State by any act or speech or otherwise;

    (e) giving information relating to a State secret to any person, or to any organization, or to any other country or countries, or abetting such an act;

    (f) committing an offence involving moral turpitude for which he has been sentenced to imprisonment for a minimum term of one year or to a minimum fine of kyats one thousand.

59. A naturalized citizen who has acquired such citizenship by making a false representation or by concealment shall have his naturalized citizenship revoked, and shall also be liable to imprisonment for a term of ten years and to a fine of kyats fifty thousand.

60. A naturalized citizen who has committed abetment of obtaining in a fraudulent manner, a certificate of citizenship or a certificate of associate citizenship or a certificate of naturalized citizenship for another person shall have his naturalized citizenship revoked, and shall also be liable to imprisonment for a term of seven years and to a fine of kyats ten thousand.

61. A naturalized citizen who has personal knowledge of an offence committed by any person under section 59 or section 60, or as an accomplice who has committed such an act, discloses or admits the offence before

organizations prescribed by the Ministry of Home Affairs within one year from the date this Law comes into force, or within one year from the date of commission of the offence shall be exempted from the penal provisions relating to such offence.

62. (a) The certificate of naturalized citizenship of a person, whose naturalized citizenship has ceased or has been revoked, shall be cancelled. A person holding such a cancelled certificate shall surrender it in the manner prescribed by the Ministry of Home Affairs.

   (b) Failure to surrender a cancelled certificate of naturalized citizenship or continued use of it or transfer of it, in a fraudulent manner, to another person shall entail imprisonment for a term of ten years and a fine of kyats twenty thousand.

   (c) Whoever holds and uses a cancelled certificate of naturalized citizenship or the certificate of a deceased naturalized citizen shall be liable to imprisonment for a term of ten years and to a fine of kyats twenty thousand.

63. Whoever forges a certificate of naturalized citizenship or abets such act shall be liable to imprisonment for a term of fifteen years and to a fine of kyats fifty thousand.

64. A person whose naturalized citizenship has ceased or has been revoked shall have no right to apply again for naturalized citizenship.

Chapter V — Decision as to Citizenship, Associate Citizenship or Naturalized Citizenship

65. Any person may apply to the Central Body when it is necessary for a decision as to his citizenship, associate citizenship or naturalized citizenship.

66. The Central Body shall
   (a) permit the applicant the submission of application with supporting evidence;
   (b) decide in accordance with law;
   (c) inform its decision to the applicant.

Chapter VI — Central Body

67. The Council of Ministers shall form the Central Body as follows:
   (a) Minister Chairman Ministry of Home Affairs
   (b) Minister Member Ministry of Defence
   (c) Minister Member Ministry of Foreign Affairs

68. The Central Body has the authority:
    (a) to decide if a person is a citizen, or an associate citizen or a naturalized citizen;
    (b) to decide upon an application for associate citizenship or naturalized citizenship;
    (c) to terminate citizenship or associate citizenship or naturalized citizenship;
    (d) to revoke citizenship or associate citizenship or naturalized citizenship;
    (e) to decide upon an application regarding failure as to registration or affirmation.
69. The Central Body shall give the right of defence to a person against whom action is taken

Chapter VII — Appeals

70. (a) A person dissatisfied with the decision of the Central Body may appeal to the Council of Ministers in accordance with the procedure laid down.
    (b) The decision of the Council of Ministers is final.
71. Organizations conferred with authority under this Law shall give no reasons in matters carried out under this Law.

Chapter VIII — Miscellaneous

72. Except under any of the provisions of this Law, no foreigner shall have the right to apply for naturalized citizenship from the date this Law comes into force.
73. A foreigner who is adopted by a citizen or by an associate citizen or by a naturalized citizen shall not acquire citizenship or associate citizenship or naturalized citizenship.
74. Except on penal matters, all matters relating to this Law shall be decided by the only organizations which are conferred with authority to do so.
75. The Council of Ministers, shall, for the purpose of carrying out the provisions of this Law, lay down necessary procedures with the approval of the Council of State.
76. The following Acts are repealed by this Law:
    (a) The Union Citizenship (Election) Act, 1948;
    (b) The Union Citizenship Act, 1948.

Notes

1. It is often not clear whether communities accept the designation Rohingya by which they are described, nor whether self-identification as Rohingya is as voluntary as it might appear.
2. See photographic essay at <https://www.flickr.com/photos/nayeem_kalam/sets/72157625071796986/>.
3. <http://www.kaladanpress.org/index.php/seminar-and-event-mainmenu-38/61-the-first-rohingya-consultation-in-bangkok-2006/752-the-situation-of-rohingya-in-uae.html>.
4. A letter ref. 020/16/49 of 28 February 1949 from the British Embassy in Rangoon to the British High Commission in Karachi reported that "from information available it seems likely that the number of Muslims in the whole of Akyab District [present-day Sittwe and Maungdaw Districts combined] may be something like 200–250,000" and that a UK Foreign Office estimate for the number of Muslims in the Maungdaw-Buthidaung area alone was about 100–120,000. The Scotsman special correspondent Michael Davidson in a despatch from Akyab (Sittwe) published on 18 May 1949 noted that: "The great majority of Arakan Muslims are said to be Pakistanis from Chittagong, even if they have settled here for a generation. Of the 130,000 Muslims here, 80,000 are still Pakistani citizens." The 1931 census estimate of 250,000 Muslims in Arakan under British rule was generally accepted by the Muslim Council of North Arakan in an Address on 25 October 1948 to Prime Minister U Nu — see later.
5. <http://www.unhcr.org/cgi-bin/texis/vtx/home/opendocPDFViewer.html?docid=4ee754c19&query=rohingya>.
6. "Ruhangyas against Statehood", *The Guardian*, 3 August 1960.
7. The 2014 Census Volume 2-C released in July 2016 lists the total enumerated population at 50,279,900 of whom 1,147,495 were Muslim, or 2.28 per cent of this total. This included Kaman and other Muslim persons in Rakhine State. An estimated 1,090,000 Muslims in Rakhine State who wished to be enumerated as "Rohingya" were not allowed to do so. The Census estimated the total population, numerated and not enumerated, at 51,485,253, of whom 2,237,495 or 4.34 per cent were Muslims.
8. Records I investigated included British census reports between 1826 and 1948. I have not yet been able so far to track down the original annual "capitation-tax" censuses which were carried out jointly by revenue officers and local officials, in the case of Arakan from 1829 onwards. However extracts from these annual records are available in other documents. I have been impressed by the detail, clarity and intellectual integrity of the full censuses held in 1872, 1881, 1891, 1901, 1911, 1921 and 1931. I also found other reports from the British era of invaluable assistance, including local and national gazetteers and official as well as private papers and correspondence and personal reminiscences.

9. There are isolated references in encyclopaedias and other reference works published during the ninetheenth century to Buchanan's account, but none of these references is a new or independent source.

10. This ratio is disputed by some who argue that the British could not distinguish between the descendants of indigenous and immigrant families. However, as Moshe Yegar observes in a footnote on p. 91 of his highly respected 1972 publication *The Muslims of Burma*: "According to the 1931 census, there were 130,524 Muslims in the regions of Maungdaw and Buthidaung. A significant section of these were not Arakanese Muslims, called Rohingya (see above page 25) — but Chittagongs who came from Bengal with the annual stream of immigrating cheap labour brought by landowners and merchants. Many of them remained and settled in Arakan." In the 1921 and 1931 Censuses, the indigenous Muslim groups in Arakan were classified by the British as "Indo-Burman" which thereby recognized both their Indian and Burmese heritage, while the nineteenth and twentieth century migrants from Bengal were classified as "Indian".

11. <http://www.scribd.com/doc/97188422/Where-Jambudipa-and-Islamdom-Converged-Religious-Change-and-the-Emergence-of-Buddhist-Communalism-in-Early-Modern-Arakan-15th-19th-Centuries-by-Mic>.

12. In volume XVI of *Asiatic Researches* of 1828, Charles Paton, Sub-Commissioner in Aracan, recorded on p. 372 that: "The population of *Aracan* and its dependencies (sic), *Ramree*, *Cheduba* and *Sandoway*, does not, at present, exceed a hundred thousand souls, and may be classed as follows: Mugs [Rakhine], six-tenths, Musselmans, three-tenths, Burmese, one-tenth : Total 100,000 souls."

13. Lt. Phayre estimated "the present *Kola* (foreign) population ... [at] about 15% of the whole population" of Arakan — "Account of Arakan", *Journal of the Asiatic Society*, p. 681, no. 117 of 1841. *Kola/Kala* includes both Muslim and Hindus.

14. <https://archive.org/details/burmapastandpre02fytcgoog>.

15. 1931 Census — Provincial Table II, p. 274.

16. Section 4(2) of the 1948 Citizenship Act: Citizens include: "Any person descended from ancestors who for two generations at least have all made any of the territories included within the Union their permanent home and whose parents and himself were born in any of such territories shall be deemed to be a citizen of the Union."

17. Instruction Book "How to fill up the Census Form" issued by the Immigration and Manpower Department on 9 December 1972 for the 1973 Census.

18. Letter dated 24 February 1947 signed by all members of the Jamiatul-ulama North Arakan to the Hon. A.G. Bottomley.

19. Text in vol. 1, Issue no. 6 of "Arakan" — News and Analysis of the Arakan Rohingya National Organisation, June 2009.

20. When the designation "Rohingya" eventually came into use, according to Brig Gen Aung Gyi writing in 1992: "Specifically, the Rohingya leaders asked us not to call the Rohingya (pejorative terms such as) 'Khaw Taw', nor 'Bengali',

nor 'Chittagonian Kalar' nor 'Arakan Muslims'." <http://www.dvb.no/analysis/suu-kyi-govt-must-not-continue-state-persecution-of-rohingya/60196>.

21. See, for example, the explanation of "Zairbaidis" on p. 111 of the 1901 Census Report.

22. This report is probably apocryphal, in the sense that it has not been formally recorded in any parliamentary assembly or committee proceedings, though the content is credible. Sao Shwe Thaik, a Shan Sawbwa, would not however have wished to include later settlers from Chittagong who were not third-generation residents, though such persons were entitled, if eligible, to elect for citizenship or to apply for naturalisation.

23. This archaic dialect was indeed spoken by those enumerated as "Arakan-Muslims" or "Yakaing-kala" by the British and was recorded by Francis Buchanan in 1795. But it is not the dialect of most Muslims in Rakhine State today which is close to the Chittagonian dialect. In claiming that this was the lingua franca of the Muslim population generally, the Council could already have taken a conscious decision to deny the Indian roots of the population and to cloak everyone protectively in an indigenous minority Muslim culture. In his Memorandum "The Mujahid Revolt in Arakan" of 31 December 1952, Foreign Office historian Professor Bertie R. Pearn wrote that the Council was "largely composed of *Rwangyas*", including the Members of Parliament for Maungdaw and Buthidaung — Council Members Sultan Ahmed and Abdul Gaffar were at the time Members of Parliament for Maungdaw (North) and Buthidaung (North), respectively.

24. "Rwangya" is a word whose etymology was at one time thought to be related to the words "rwam and kya", meaning "in-between", according to Foreign Office historical advisor Professor Bertie Pearn in an internal Foreign Office memorandum "The Mujahid Revolt in Arakan" Bur/24/52, dated 31 December 1952. A less complicated explanation is that "Rwangya" is but another version of "Rooinga", used by the same community of indigenous Arakan Muslims whom Francis Buchanan met in 1795. In the 1931 Census, some 51,612 Arakan-Muslims aka Yakaing-kala aka (later) Rwangya were recorded as living in Akyab District compared with 186,327 Chittagonians and 15,586 Bengalis. Buchanan noted that both *Rooinga* and the *Hindus* of Arakan, "by the real natives of *Arakan, are called Kulaw Yakain* or stranger *Arakan*". That is, they were regarded by Rakhine Buddhists as settlers from India, not indigenous.

25. Minority Affairs Minister, himself a Rakhine Buddhist.

26. In June 1978 the U.S. Embassy in Rangoon still classified Rakhine refugees in Bangladesh as "Chittagonian" <https://search.wikileaks.org/plusd/cables/1978RANGOO02140_d.html>.

27. The Bengali word for Arakan is "Rohang" with variants noted by Francis Buchanan in his 1798 account of his journey in Southeast Bengal such as: "Rossawn, Rohhawn, Roang, Reng or Rung for by all these names is Arakan called by the Bengalese" (van Schendel 1992).

28. See, for example, Khin Maung Saw, *Arakan a Neglected Land and her Voiceless*

People and *Behind the Mask — The Truth behind the Name "Rohingya"*: both books published in Yangon in 2016.

29. Posting on the Facebook of the Ministry of Religious Affairs and Culture on 12 December 1948.

30. A study on the issue of ethnicity in Arakan: Abu Anin — 2009 <https://merhrom. wordpress.com/2009/03/04/towards-understanding-arakan-history-part-i/>.

31. I was Burma Desk Officer in the Foreign Office at the time and processed the despatch on receipt in London.

32. Federal German Ambassador to Pakistan Günther Scholl reporting from Karachi in his letter (German original) dated 22 February 1965 to the Auswärtiges Amt on the visit to Pakistan by General Ne Win, Chairman of the Revolutionary Council: 12–19 February 1965. German original at <http://www.networkmyanmar.org/ images/stories/PDF20/Karachi-Scholl-1965.pdf>.

33. National Archives: Folio 35 on File FCO 15/2041. Extract from record by U.K. Ambassador Terence J. O'Brien of his call in Rangoon on the Bangladesh Ambassador to Burma Khwaja Mohammed Kaiser on 23 December 1975.

34. The military coups of August and November 1975.

35. U.S. Embassy Dacca <https://search.wikileaks.org/plusd/cables/1978 DACCA02901_d.html>.

36. For a comprehensive account of these events, see Fleischmann (1981), "Vorgeschichte und Folgen des Flüchtlingstroms von 1978", Hamburg, 1981. Fleischmann himself concluded (translated from the German original) that: "From everything that we know about this operation, there is nothing to suggest that an expulsion of all Muslims from Arakan was planned."

37. U.S. Embassy Rangoon <https://search.wikileaks.org/plusd/cables/ 1978RANGOO02140_d.html> — "Chittagonian Refugees from Arakan State", U.S., British, Australian and UN reports at the time contain no references to "Rohingya".

38. Transcript at <http://dataspace.princeton.edu/jspui/handle/88435/dsp01 th83kz538>.

39. Main provisions reported in *The Guardian* (Rangoon) of 11 October 1978.

40. Despatch dated 3 July 1979 from British Ambassador Charles Booth reference 020/1 on FCO 15/2468.

41. The Final Report of the Inquiry Commission on Sectarian Violence in Rakhine State issued on 8 July 2013 put the number of returnees at 31,505 families comprising 186,968 persons, though according to the Inquiry Commission's figures only 25,905 families comprising 156,630 persons had actually left Arakan in the first place.

42. Letter of 6 February 1979 Charles Booth to South-East Asian Department reference 020/1 on FCO 15/2468.

43. See Fleischmann (1981), pp. 194–96 for further details of the process of public and parliamentary consultation 1976–81.

44. Supplement to *The Guardian* of 21 April 1982.

45. Letter of 12 May 1982 to Robert Flower, South East Asia Department on File FCO 15/3177, 1982.
46. Text at <http://www.ibiblio.org/obl/docs/Citizenship%20Law.htm> and in Appendix.
47. Text at <http://www.burmalibrary.org/docs6/Ne_Win's_speech_Oct-1982-Citizenship_Law.pdf>.
48. To my knowledge, the only associate citizenships awarded to date are those few hundred granted in the Myebon pilot scheme launched in June 2014.
49. See note 15.
50. The principle of "third generation" eligibility is to be found not only in the 1948 Act and 1982 Law, but also in pronouncements made by senior ministers from time to time.
51. Under the 1948 Citizenship Acts, citizens enjoyed exactly the same rights, whether citizenship was acquired through birth, ancestry, election or naturalization. Under the 1982 Law, associate and naturalized citizens enjoy full citizen rights except as later stipulated by the Council of State. To date, I am not aware of any such stipulation. According to General Ne Win in his speech of 8 October 1982, "we will have to leave them out in matters involving the affairs of the country and the destiny of the State".
52. *Loktha Pyithu Neizin* (*Working People's Daily*, in Burmese) of 26 September 1990.
53. See <http://www.rohingyablogger.com/2013/05/the-official-evidence-of-rohingya.html> by Maung Zarni.
54. In his informative presentation: "A genealogy of *taingyintha*, Myanmar's national races" at the Australian National University on 27 October 2015, Nick Cheesman noted that the Loktha Pyithu Neizin of 26 September 1990 stated that the 1983 Census used the list of the 135 national races then published for the first time. I cannot myself confirm that the 1983 Census in fact did so.
55. "The Politics of Ethnicity in Myanmar Today", *ISEAS Perspective* 12/2015, footnote 1.
56. "Problems with Facts about Rohingya Statelessness" <http://www.e-ir.info/2015/12/08/problems-with-facts-about-rohingya-statelessness/>, 8 December 2015.
57. Anthony Aust, *Handbook of International Law* (Cambridge University Press, 2005), p. 179. It is generally agreed that by international custom each sovereign state has the right to determine who it will recognize as its nationals and citizens.
58. Resolution of the Human Rights Council A/HRC/Res/29/21 of 22 July 2015.
59. There are references to published "Procedures" introduced in 1983, but no text has yet been found.
60. Surprisingly, on 20 January 2014, Baroness Warsi, the Senior Minister of State in the Foreign and Commonwealth Office told the House of Lords in response to a Question that: "The Burmese government view is that over 90% of the Rohingya will be eligible for citizenship under the existing 1982 law". Hansard House of Lords, 20 January 2014.

61. In her report A/HRC/31/71 of 8 March 2016 to the Human Rights Council, Special Rapporteur Yanghee Lee nonetheless called in para. 82(c) for a review and the amendment of the 1982 Law "to bring it into line with international standards. In particular, remove any provisions that provide for the granting of citizenship on the basis of ethnicity or race." This is a counsel of perfection, in that other nationality laws have similar provisions. China, for example, provides in para. 2 of its 1980 Nationality Law that: "Persons belonging to any of the nationalities in China shall have Chinese nationality." Indeed, I doubt that there are any international standards in this context.

62. Estimate by British Embassy in Rangoon. Letter from Chancery to the Foreign Office dated 21 January 1958 reference DB1821/1.

63. <http://www.unhcr.org/pages/4a2535c3d.html>.

64. On 14 March 2016 the Myanmar delegate to the interactive dialogue on Myanmar at the Human Rights Council described as "false information" reports by the UN Special Rapporteur Yanghee Lee "that couples in northern Rakhine State needed permission to marry and were limited to two children".

65. At a refugee camp in Myebon in Sittwe District, out of 1,280 applications only some 97 persons have reportedly received full citizenship (presumably as Kamans) and another 360 naturalization as citizens.

66. These receipts appear to have been followed by the issuing of what was described by the Presidential Office on 27 December 2016 as an "Identity Card for National Verification". However, by 23 December 2016 only 6,077 such IDs had been issued out of 397,497 "White Cards" surrendered in Rakhine State, or about 60 per cent only of the total issued in Rakhine State judged against 469,183 surrendered out of 759,672 issued throughout the country. Otherwise known as National Verification Cards (NVDs), they represent only the next stage in the process of citizenship recognition.

67. Noted particularly by the International Crisis Group in their report of 15 December 2016, "Myanmar: A new Muslim insurgency in Rakhine State": "Disenfranchisement prior to the 2015 elections severed the last link with politics and means of influence."

68. <http://www.bt.com.bn/2011/06/10/arakan-rohingya-union-aru-formed>.

69. The new NLD administration has already stated that they do not accept the "Rohingya" designation — <http://www.the-american-interest.com/2016/05/06/suu-kyi-kicks-the-rohingya/>.

70. <http://www.iseas.edu.sg/documents/publication/iseas_perspective_2015_12.pdf>.

71. It may also depend on whether you interpret Francis Buchanan's "Rooinga" as a geographic locator, as I do, or as an ethnicity.

72. At a press conference with U.S. Secretary of State John Kerry on 22 May 2016, Daw Aung San Suu Kyi made the same point: "There are two terms which are emotive, and we've got to face them fairly and squarely. The Rakhine Buddhists object to the term 'Rohingya', just as much as the Muslims object to the term

Bengali, because these have all kinds of political and emotional implications which are unacceptable to the opposing parties."

73. Unofficial independent translation made at my request by news media in Yangon.

74. As indeed provided for in Article 4(2) of the 1948 Citizenship Act and Articles 23 and 42 of the 1982 Citizenship Law (for associate and naturalized citizenship respectively). The *Myanmar Times* report of UNHCR's press conference in Yangon on 12 July 2012 at <http://www.mmtimes.com/index.php/national-news/yangon/395-unhcr-seeks-true-community-reconciliation-in-rakhine-state.html> quotes Mr Guterres as observing that "it is important to say that it [Rohingya] is not the designation that the government of Myanmar uses for the population".

75. Radio Free Asia, <http://www.rfa.org/english/news/rohingya-07122012185242.html>, was one of the very few media reports to highlight the distinction between Bengalis who arrived legally before independence and those who arrived illegally after independence.

76. In their report at <http://theconversation.com/myanmars-new-leaders-could-end-rohingya-conflict-by-tapping-into-reserves-of-goodwill-51465>, dated 6 December 2015, Anthony Ware and Ronan Lee of Deakin University have shown that the desire exists among both Muslim and Rakhine communities in Rakhine State to resolve the predicament of the "Rohingya" community, provided only that the political will also exists to seek a solution. VOA quoting Rohan Lee on 28 December 2016: "What's actually going on is that there is a difference of opinion as to which group of people should be allowed to use the name 'Rohingya'. But then when you ask the Muslims how much do you believe that the name Rohingya is really, really important to your identity, their attitude was very much: 'Look, we just want our rights and our citizenship — we want to be part of Myanmar — we have lived here for generations, we have a heritage here that goes back hundreds of years'."

77. NLD Spokesman U Win Htein said the Rohingya' Muslims' plight was not top of the agenda for his party. "We have other priorities. Peace, the peaceful transition of power, economic development and constitutional reform.", *The Telegraph*, 19 November 2015.

78. Text taken from <http://www.ibiblio.org/obl/docs/Citizenship%20Law.htm>.

References

(To be read in conjunction with the Bibliography to Chapter 7.)
Amrith, Sunil. *Crossing the Bay of Bengal*. Harvard: Harvard University Press, 2013.
Ba Tha. "Shah Shujah in Arakan". *The Guardian* magazine (Rangoon), September 1959, pp. 26–28.
———. "Roewengyas in Arakan". *The Guardian* magazine (Rangoon), May 1960, pp. 33–36.

————. "Rowengya Fine Arts". *The Guardian* magazine (Rangoon), October 1960, pp. 20–22.

————. "Slave Raids in Bengal or Heins in Arakan". *The Guardian* magazine (Rangoon), October 1960, pp. 25–27.

————. "The Coming of Islam to Arakan". *The Guardian* magazine (Rangoon), March 1963, pp. 9–13.

Buchanan, Francis. 1799. "A comparative vocabulary of some of the languages spoken in the Burmese Empire". *Asiatick Researches*, Volume V (Calcutta edition 1799; London edition 1801), pp. 219–41.

Charney, Michael W. "Where Jambudipa and Islamdom Converged: Religious Change and the Emergence of Buddhist Communalism in Early Modern Arakan". PhD dissertation, University of Michigan, 1999.

Cheesman, Nick. "Problems with Facts about Rohingya Statelessness". *E-International Relations*, 8 December 2015.

————. "How in Myanmar 'national races' came to surpass citizenship and exclude Rohingya". *Journal of Contemporary Asia* (forthcoming).

———— and Nicholas Farrelly, eds. *Conflict in Myanmar: War, Politics Religion*. Singapore: ISEAS – Yusof Ishak Institute, 2016.

Comstock, G.S. "Notes on Arakan: By the Late Rev. G.S. Comstock, American Baptist Missionary in That Country from 1834 to 1844". *Journal of the American Oriental Society* 1, no. 3 (1847): 219 and 221–58.

Crouch, Melissa. "Myanmar's Muslim mosaic and the politics of belonging". *New Mandala*, 4 November 2014.

Fleischmann, Klaus. *Arakan: Konfliktregion zwischen Birma und Bangladesh*. Hamburg: Institut für Asienkunde, 1981.

International Crisis Group (ICG). "Myanmar: The Politics of Rakhine State". *Asia Report* No. 261, October 2014.

———— "Myanmar: A New Muslim Insurgency in Rakhine State". Asia Report No. 283, December 2016.

Leider, Jacques. "Competing Identities and the Hybridized History of the Rohingyas". In *Metamorphosis: Studies in Social and Political Change in Myanmar*, Ch. 6. Singapore: NUS Press, 2015.

————. "Rohingya: The Name. The Movement. The Quest for Identity". In *Nation Building in Myanmar*. Myanmar Egress and Myanmar Peace Centre, January 2014, pp. 204–55.

Thompson, Virginia and Richard Adloff. *Minority Problems in Southeast Asia*. Stanford: Stanford University Press, 1955.

van Schendel, Willem. *"Making a living in the Bengal Borderlands"*. International Review of Social History 46 (2001): 393–421.

van Schendel, Willem, ed. *Francis Buchanan in Southeast Bengal (1798): His Journey to Chittagong, the Chittagong Hill tracts, Noakhali and Comilla*. Dhaka: The University Press, 1992.

Zarni, Maung and Alice Cowley. "The Slow-burning Genocide of Myanmar's Rohingya". *Pacific Rim Law and Policy Journal* 23 (2014): 683–754.

ROHINGYA AND NATIONALITY STATUS IN MYANMAR

Nurul Islam
Chairman of the Arakan Rohingya National Organization

EMERGENCE OF THE UNION OF BURMA/MYANMAR

Myanmar, also called Burma, is a multi-cultural and multi-lingual country. "In fact, much of Myanmar and all its borderland regions are multi-ethnic, and they have historically remained in a state of social and political flux" (Smith 1995). Based on the precept of ethnic togetherness, the independence hero the late General Aung San articulated the agreed upon union principle or policy of "unity in diversity" as the foundation of which the "Union of Burma" came into existence on 4 January 1948.

WHO ARE ROHINGYA?

Rohingya, a predominantly Muslim community, are a borderland people with a long history of living in Arakan (Rakhine) State of Myanmar. They are a people developed from diverse stocks of people over many centuries. The Rohingya have historical connections to the high cultures of Bengal, Persia and Arabia. Due to their origin and culture, as well as their present geographical location, there is no doubt that, historically, they have mixed more with Indian people than with the Burmese. The Chandra dynasty was an ancient Bengali kingdom of Arakan. Thus, Maurice Collis, who worked and lived in Burma from 1912 to 1934, writes: "Arakan was then an Indian land, its inhabitants being Indians similar to those resident in Bengal" (Collis 1985,

p. 135). The group identity of the Rohingya is marked by a shared religion, geography, language and culture. They believe they are culturally distinctive and different to outsiders. They are distinguishable from the surrounding communities. However, Rakhine chauvinists and other extremists in Burma do not necessarily agree with these views: like the former military regime, most of them reject Rohingyas' right to exist in Myanmar.

ARAKAN IN HISTORICAL PERSPECTIVE

The historical situation of Arakan in terms of the growth of its Muslim population cannot be looked at in isolation, but should be considered in the regional context. Situated in the tri-border region between modern-day Burma, India and Bangladesh, Arakan is on the frontline between the Islamic and Buddhist worlds of Asia, and amidst the Indo-Aryan and Mongoloid races.

Throughout history Arakan maintained very close ties with Muslim Bengal, which had always helped and stood by the people of Arakan in the event of any natural disaster or external aggression. Particularly, the relation between Arakan and Chittagong is influenced by geographical, ethnological, cultural and historical considerations. There are plausible historical references that hint that Arakan was Greater Chittagong and Chittagong was Greater Arakan. "Because of the political, cultural and commercial links between those two territories, Arakan used to be called 'extended Chittagong'." (Bangladesh Institute of Law and International Affairs).

History testifies that the heyday of Arakan began with the development of Muslim civilization, which reached its zenith during the most successful period of the Mrauk-U dynasty:

> It was a new golden age for this country — a period of power and prosperity — and creation of a remarkably hybrid Buddhist-Islamic court, fusing tradition from Persia and India as well as Buddhist worlds to the east.... Several of the kings took Islamic as well as Pali titles, patronizing Buddhist monasteries and erecting Buddhist pagodas while also appearing in Persian-inspired dress and the conical heads of Isfahan and Mughal Delhi, and minting coins with the *kalima*, Islamic declaration of faith (Myint-U 2006, pp. 72–73).

The then Chairman of the Burma Historical Commission, Col. (Rtd) Bashin writes: "Arakan was virtually ruled by Muslims from 1430 to 1531" (Ba Shin 1961, p. 4). Many thronged to Mrauk-U city — Muslim ministers, administrators, statesmen, artists, men of literature, court poets, civil and military personnel, who all contributed to the kingdom. Muslim influence and rule in Arakan lasted for more than 350 years until the kingdom was invaded and occupied by Burmese king Bodawphaya in 1784 A.D.

Martin Smith (1995) writes:

> What, however, cannot be disputed is that, for the last thousand years or so, Muslims and Buddhists have historically lived on both sides of the Naf River which marks the modern border with Bangladesh. As a result, the present cultural and ethnic distinctions — between Buddhists and Muslims or Rakhine and Rohingyas — were not always so clear. As recently as 1955, for example, in his classic history of South-East Asia, D.G.E. Hall described the Arakanese of today as basically Burmese with an unmistakable Indian admixture.

Harvey (1929, p. 90) writes: "Doubtless it is Muhammadan influence which led to the women being more secluded in Arakan than in Burma." Aung San Suu Kyi (2010, p. 64) writes: "There is, however, one Arakanese custom which is very alien to the Burmese. The Arakanese favour marriage between cross cousins. (Children of one's mother's brothers or of one's father's sisters are known as cross-cousins.) This is a reflection of Islamic influence."

INSTITUTIONALIZED PERSECUTION AND EXTERMINATION OF ROHINGYA

In post-independence period the successive Burmese administrations actively practised policies of exclusion and persecution against the country's Muslims. Particularly the Muslim Rohingya have been subjected to institutionalized persecution, ethnic-cleansing, ethnocide, and slow genocide. They have been rendered stateless by the oppressive Burma Citizenship Law of 1982, enacted by late dictator General Ne Win.

Unfortunately, the policies and actions of the military encouraged hostile Rakhines into giving support to the military-backed regime so as to expel all Muslims from Arakan and thereby to achieve the cherished goal of "Arakan for the Rakhine only". In this hostile environment, Rohingya culture and language were not accommodated, but considered as practising a foreign way of life that had no origin in Myanmar. Instead, a percept has been promoted that "to be a Burmese is to be a Buddhist" and "Arakan, Rakhine and Buddhism are synonymous".

ROHINGYAS' HELPLESSNESS IN MYANMAR'S DEMOCRATIC TRANSITION

It is regrettable that Rohingya are not benefiting from Myanmar's democratic transition. In 1990, Rohingya were permitted to form political parties and vote in multi-party elections. They had participated in all elections held in Burma/Myanmar from 1936 to the 2010 military-held elections, and voted their representatives to the parliaments and state assemblies, including the 2008 referendum for the adoption of the constitution of the state. In spite of that they were effectively disenfranchised for the first time in Myanmar when were stripped of their right to vote and to stand for office in the general elections of November 2015, and were also excluded from the recent national census and continue to be denied their legal right to citizenship.

Daw Aung San Suu Kyi has in the past pledged to prioritize national reconciliation and protection of human rights for all. But days after her party clinched victory in the country's historic elections, U Win Htein, a spokesman and leading figure in her National League for Democracy (NLD) said that helping the persecuted Rohingya minority is not a priority. Their plight was not on the agenda for his party, echoing the previous military-backed Thein Sein government's rhetoric about the Rohingya that suggests they are illegal immigrants from Bangladesh. Sadly, the continued persecution of these defenceless people has not prompted Daw Aung San Suu Kyi to break her long silence on this issue. This has been disappointing for Rohingya people, as apparently they can expect little from the NLD government in the immediate future. Nonetheless, the Rohingya continue to believe that something can be expected under her leadership.

NATIONALITY

Citizenship is the social and legal link between individuals and their democratic political community (Patrick 1999). Citizenship is arguably the same as nationality but Burmese law uses the expression of citizenship and not nationality (Verma 1961). Nationality is often described as the connecting link between the individual and international law (see, e.g., Evans and Newnham 1998, p. 349). Nationality indicates the status of belonging to a particular state. By virtue of this, an individual may be entitled to certain benefits and obligations under municipal and international law. There is no accepted definition of nationality. As a general rule each state is free to define who its nationals are, although this description can be circumscribed by specific Treaties, such as those concerning the elimination of statelessness. Thus Article 1 of the 1930 Hague Convention on the Conflict of Nationality Laws stated that: "it is for each state to determine under its own law who are the nationals. This law shall be recognized by other states in so far as it is consistent with international conventions, international custom and principles of law generally recognized with regard to nationality." Thus a state's nationality laws are required to conform to international law, international human rights law, international conventions, customs and practices. The most important of these principles concerning acquisition of nationality are first, descent from parents who are nationals (*jus sanguinis*) and secondly, the territorial location of birth (*jus soli*). Nationality may also be acquired by marriage, adoption, legalization, naturalization (the proceeding whereby a foreigner is granted citizenship) or as a result of transfer of territory from one state to another. It should be noted that since international law recognizes the primacy of the state in this regard, the practice of acquiring nationality varies considerably.

THE BURMA CITIZENSHIP LAW OF 1982 IS AN OPPRESSIVE LEGAL WEAPON AGAINST ROHINGYA

From the time of independence in 1948, the Rohingya were treated as the same as other people in Burma/Myanmar. There was one form of citizenship, and citizens were issued cards called National Registration Cards (NRCs). They were issued to the Rohingya from 1955 onwards. But their citizenship became questionable with the promulgation of the "Burma Citizenship Law" on the 15 October 1982 by the former dictator General Ne Win. This can be seen as being one of the most restrictive citizenship laws in the world. Unlike the 1948 Citizenship Act, the 1982 law is essentially based on the principle of *jus sanguinis* and has repealed the Union Citizenship (Election) Act of 1948 and the Union Citizenship Act of 1948. Based on how one's forebears obtained citizenship, since 1982 Ne Win's law has stratified citizenship into three status groups: full, associate and naturalized.

Full citizenship is restricted to nationals of 135 named ethnic groups deemed to have settled in Myanmar prior to 1823, the start of British colonization of Arakan, or who were born to parents who were citizens of Burma at the time of birth. According to Ne Win (1982), "racially, only pure-blooded nationals will be called citizens". Burma does not consider the Rohingya to be a national ethnic group. Rohingya are therefore excluded from full citizenship under this provision.

Associate citizenship only applies to individuals who had already applied for citizenship under the Union Citizenship Act 1948 and was pending on the date the 1982 Act came into force. The deadline for applying for associate citizenship passed on 15 October 1982. So far no Rohingya had applied since they believed they were already citizens. Most were unaware of the 1948 Act or of its significance. Now no new application can be made.

Naturalized citizenship may be applied for by individuals (and their offspring born within Myanmar) who can furnish "conclusive evidence" that they entered and resided in Myanmar prior to 4 January 1948, who could speak one of the national languages well. Thus, naturalized citizens refer to persons who lived in Burma before 4 January 1948 and applied for citizenship after 1982. Foreigners cannot become naturalized citizens unless they can prove a close familial connection to the country.

Full citizenship is denied to Rohingya as "Rohingya" was deleted from the list of Burma's national races in 1982. Naturalized citizenship is denied to Rohingya as the Rohingya language does not feature as one of the so-called "national languages". As few Rohingya speak any of those other languages that the government recognized, hardly any Rohingyas could fulfil these requirements. Furthermore, whether one is citizen or not is to be decided by the single authority, the "Council of State", rather than a court. "Moreover, the wide powers assigned to a government-controlled Central Body to decide on matters pertaining to citizenship mean that, in practice, the Rohingyas' entitlement to citizenship will not be recognized" (Lewa 2009).

This oppressive law effectively excludes almost all Rohingya, since they are in practice unable to furnish or fulfil those trammel-net like "conclusive evidence" of requirements. But this law was not fully implemented immediately. It appeared to be gradually introduced and implemented over the following decades. NRCs were still being issued to Rohingya into the mid 1980s.

Colour-coded Citizen Scrutiny Cards

In 1989 the dictatorship began replacing the NRCs with colour-coded Citizens Scrutiny Cards: pink cards for full citizens, blue for associate citizens, and green for naturalized citizens. Rohingya were not issued with any identity cards, which are essential for everyday life and all national activities. It is important for ownership of property, transport, studies, dealing with the law and even staying at home. The withholding of national identification documents since the 1970s has become a mechanism for discrimination and persecution for those of Rohingya ethnicity. "The law continues to create outflows of refugees, which overburden other countries posing threats to peace and tranquillity within the region" (Islam 1999, p. 3).

Temporary Registration Cards (TRCs)

In 1995, Temporary Registration Cards (TRCs) — also known as white cards — were issued to Rohingya by the Burmese government through a programme funded by the United States and initiated by UNHCR pursuant to the 1949 Residents of Burma Registration Act. "The TRC does not mention the bearer's place of birth and cannot be used to claim citizenship.

The family list, which every family residing in Burma possesses, only records family members and their dates of birth. It does not indicate the place of birth and therefore provides no official evidence of birth in Burma — and so perpetuates statelessness" (Lewa 2009). By *jus sanguinis* rule or any accepted concepts of citizenship, the Rohingya should be issued no documents other than full citizenship certificates.

Although "white cards" were irrationally issued in lieu of seized NRCs — as well as given to the younger generation of ethnic Rohingya — in the absence of any other documents these IDs were somewhat helpful, even allowing a right of franchise. But white cards were invalidated on 31 March 2015 depriving the holders of voting rights for the first time in Burma since the voting system introduced during the British colonial period in 1936. It also excluded holders from the recent UN-sponsored national census and continues to be part of the methods for denying a legal right to citizenship.

MILITARY'S MAKING OF ETHNIC RACES IS NOT JUSTIFIED

The military's construction — or recognition — of 135 so-called ethnic groups in Myanmar is whimsical and lacks consistency. In 1960 U Nu's parliamentary government estimated ethnic groups to be about fifty.[1] (Rohingya were one of them as their representatives were invited to Union Day Celebration every year together with all other ethnic nationalities of the country.) But Ne Win's administration "listed 144 ethnic groups in the country".[2] After 1990 the military State Peace and Development Council (SPDC) put only 135 groups or national races on a short list, deleting the three groups of Muslims in Burma: Rohingya (Muslim Arakanese), Panthay (Chinese Muslims), and Bashu (Malay Muslims) as well as six other smaller non-Burman groups.

On 11 March 2016, ten days before U Thein Sein's presidency ended, his military-backed government announced that an ethnic Chinese group with a population of 60,000 residing in northern Shan State were named as the latest addition to Bamar ethnic nationality. They were designated as "Mong Woon Bamar" ethnicity on their ID cards despite their language being Chinese and their culture being Chinese. Nonetheless, with this addition, there are now 136 officially recognized ethnic groups in the country. Earlier in Shan State, on the border of China, Kokang (who are ethnically Han Chinese, speak Mandarin, and who are not unlike the Mong Woon group) were recognized as an ethnic group by the military. As a matter of fact, the birth or recognition, and demise or rejection of an ethnic group is done not on accepted norms but is solely in the hands of a powerful elite in Myanmar.

This capricious creation/abolition of ethnic groups by the military is clearly not justifiable.

THE ROHINGYA CITIZENSHIP QUESTION IS NOT AN ISSUE OF ILLEGAL IMMIGRATION BUT A DENIAL OF EXISTENCE

Rohingya are peace loving and aspire to serve the country as responsible citizens. Yet they are not tolerated in Myanmar because of their ethnicity and religion, and for their South Asian appearance in contrast to Southeast Asian appearance of the dominant Burman group. During the long military rule from 1962, they have been persecuted and rendered stateless within Burma, and have become refugees beyond its borders. The seed of Islamophobia and prejudice towards the Rohingya was systematically orchestrated and institutionalized by the dictator General Ne Win and his military cronies.

Despite being indigenous to Arakan with a long and celebrated history, Burmese government neither recognizes Rohingyas as citizens nor as foreigners, but treat them as non-nationals, describing them as "illegal immigrants from Bangladesh". They are in a situation of permanent limbo. While repatriating Rohingya refugees from Bangladesh the Burmese government had only accepted them as "Burmese residents" which is not a legal status. Thus "the law made the Rohingya ethnic group a stateless one in the country where they have been living for generations" (Razzaq and Hague 1995, p. 53).

In 1998, in a letter to UNHCR, Burma's then Prime Minister General Khin Nyunt wrote: "These people are not originally from Myanmar but have illegally migrated to Myanmar because of population pressures in their own country" (Lewa 2009). In February 1996, UN Special Rapporteur on Burma Professor Yozu Yokota quoted Lt. General Mya Thinn, the then Home Minister of SPDC, as saying:

> (The) Muslim population of Rakhine (Arakan) State was not recognized as citizens of Myanmar under the existing naturalization regulations and they were not even registered as so-called foreign residents ... Their status situation did not permit them to travel in the country ... They are also not allowed to serve in the state positions and are barred from attending higher educational institution (Islam 2012).

The government authorities and xenophobes, including some Rakhine academics, are engaged in systematic vilification against Rohingya. They dishonestly claim that the name "Rohingya" is non-existent, unheard of, a creation of Mujahids (Muslim rebels) and/or Rohingya leaders in 1951.

But historical evidence from the Scottish doctor Francis Buchanan (1799) rebuts this politically motivated claim. He explained "Mohammedans, who have long settled in Arakan, and who called themselves Rooinga, or native of Arakan." Dr Michael Charney states, "it can be asserted, however, that one claim of the Buddhist school in Rakhine historiography, that Rohingya was an invention of the colonial period is contradicted by the evidence" (Charney 2005, p. 132).

ANALYSIS OF THE MYANMAR CITIZENSHIP LAW OF 1982

General Ne Win and senior military officials often expressed extremely negative views toward Rohingyas. Accordingly, the military dictatorship introduced the Citizenship Law of 1982, a three-tier form of citizenship in Myanmar. But "the timing of its promulgation shortly after the refugee repatriation (from Bangladesh) of 1979, strongly suggests that it was specifically designed to exclude the Rohingya" (Lewa 2009) who had previously been recognized as citizens as well as a national race of Burma.

The 1982 Citizenship Law violates several fundamental principles of international customary legal standards, offends the Universal Declaration of Human Rights and leaves Rohingyas lacking legal protection of their rights. The law has perpetuated the Rohingya citizenship crisis making them objects of persecution and of discrimination, and as stateless people in their native country. Such persecution and discrimination constitute a total disregard of the most elementary humanitarian principles and is contrary to the purposes of the United Nations (UN). Myanmar, as a UN member state has an obligation to follow UN resolutions. One such resolution — unanimously adopted at 48th plenary meeting of the General Assembly — reads as follows:

> The General Assembly declares that it is in the higher interests of humanity to put an immediate end to religious and so-called racial persecution and discrimination, and calls on the Governments and responsible authorities to conform both to the letter and spirit of the Charter of the United Nations, and to take the most prompt and energetic steps to that end (United Nations 1946).

There is a wholly arbitrary deprivation of the fundamental rights to citizenship of native Rohingya in Myanmar. Provisions of the 1982 law have excluded most Muslims from their country, including those whose ancestors came to Burma from the sub-continent, and who had been living in Burma for generations and considered themselves patriotic Burmese.

The 1982 Citizenship Law offends, *inter alia*, the following laws of humanity:

1. Article 15 of the Universal Declaration of Human Rights (UDHR) states that "everyone has the right to a nationality" and that "no one shall be arbitrarily deprived of his nationality nor denied the right to change his nationality". But the Rohingyas are declared non-nationals, rendering them stateless in the homeland where they have been living for centuries.

2. This conflicts with the government's obligation to fulfil the rights of the child as stipulated by Article 7(1) of the UN Convention on the Rights of the Child, 1989 which states that the child shall be registered immediately after birth and shall have the right to a name, and to acquire a nationality. The Burmese government ratified this convention in 1991 and is obliged to grant citizenship to Rohingya. Article 24(3) of the UN International Covenant on Civil and Political Rights 1966 also states, "Every child has the right to acquire a nationality". But most Rohingya children were denied registration and hundreds and thousands of Rohingya children have been effectively blacklisted — the reason given being that their parents had not married with official permission.

3. Under Myanmar's 1982 Citizenship Law, Rohingya children — both registered and unregistered — are stateless, and hence face limited access to food and healthcare, leaving them susceptible to preventable diseases and malnutrition. Many are prevented from attending school and used for forced labour, contributing to a Rohingya illiteracy rate of 80 per cent. More than 60 per cent of children aged between five and seventeen have never enrolled in school (The Arakan Project 2011). Article 9 of the UN Convention on the Elimination of All Forms of Discrimination Against Women (CEADAW), 1979 states: "(a) States Parties shall grant women equal rights with men to acquire, change or retain their nationality ... (b) States Parties shall grant women equal rights with men with respect to the nationality of their children." The Burmese government ratified this convention. But Rohingya women and their children have been deprived of their Burmese nationality forcing them to live in segregation and squalid apartheid like semi-concentration camps and ghettos inside Arakan as well as living as refugees or displaced people outside of Myanmar, wandering from place to place with an uncertain future.

4. Article 5(d)(iii) of the UN Convention on the Elimination of All Forms of Racial Discrimination 1965 states that "States Parties undertake to prohibit and to eliminate racial discrimination in all its forms and to guarantee

the right of everyone, without distinction as to race, colour, or national or ethnic origin, to equality before the law...[and to] the enjoyment of ...the right to nationality." But the Rohingyas are discriminated against and excluded from their ancestral homeland on grounds of ethnicity and religion. They have been subjected to "systematic racism".

5. The law promotes discrimination against Rohingya and arbitrary deprivation of their Myanmar citizenship. The deprivation of one's nationality is not only a serious violation of human rights but also an international crime. The law does not oblige the state to protect stateless persons (i.e., victims of a serious human rights violation), thus largely ignoring state's "obligation to respect the right to nationality".

THE LEGAL STATUS OF ROHINGYA IN MYANMAR

During the British colonial period the Rohingya were recognized as an indigenous race of Burma. Paragraph 7 in the Baxter report of 1940 recommended: "The Arakanese Muslim community settled so long in Akyab District had for all intents and purposes to be regarded as an indigenous race". The British Military Command declared the northern part of Arakan as the "Muslim National Area".[3] This area was later created as Special Mayu Frontier District for the development of the Rohingya people by former Parliamentary Government of U Nu.

Under Article 3 of the Nu-Attlee Agreement of 17 October 1947, and under section 11(i) (ii) (iii) of the Constitution of the Union of Burma 1947 — effected 4 January 1948 — the Rohingyas are citizens of Burma. They are a people settled in Arakan as a compact community anterior to 1823 or before British colonization of it and so by definition of the Constitution as well as under all legal standards they are an indigenous ethnic nationality:

> Any person who at the date of the coming into force of the present Treaty is, by virtue of the Constitution of the Union of Burma, a citizen thereof and who is, or by virtue of a subsequent election is deemed to be, also a British subject, may make a declaration of alienage in the manner prescribed by the law of the Union, and thereupon shall cease to be a citizen of the Union (Nu-Attlee Agreement 1947, Article 3).

Let us have a look what the two leaders of the country said. When section II of the Constitution of the Union of Burma was being framed, in regard to the indigenous status of Rohingya, the President of the Constituent Assembly, who became the first President of the Union of Burma, Saw Shwe Theik said (ARNO 2009, p. 10):

> Muslims of Arakan certainly belong to one of the indigenous races of Burma ... In fact there are no pure indigenous races in Burma, if they do not belong to indigenous races of Burma, we also cannot be taken as indigenous races of Burma.

Recognizing the Rohingya as an indigenous ethnic group the former parliamentary government of Prime Minister U Nu officially announced on 25 September 1954 in clear and unambiguous terms: "The people living in northern Arakan are our national brethren. They are called Rohingya. They are on the same par in the status of nationality with Kachin, Kayah, Karen, Mon, Rakhine, Shan. They are one of the ethnic races of Burma." As such, like other ethnic nationalities, Rohingya participated as "state guests" in the Union Day Celebration held in Rangoon on 12 February every year.

By Cabinet decision Rohingya language was relayed thrice a week from the official Burma Broadcasting Service (BBS) Rangoon, in its "Indigenous Race Broadcasting Programme" from 15 May 1961 to 30 October 1965. Such facts were given in p. 71 of the book *30 years of Burma Radio* published by the Ministry of Information and Broadcasting. The Rangoon University Rohingya Students Association was one of the ethnic student associations that functioned from 1959 to 1961 under the registration numbers 113/99 December 1959 and 7/60 September 1960 respectively.

The Burma official encyclopaedia *Myanmar Swezon Kyan* records that in 1964 75 per cent of the population in Mayu Frontier District was Rohingya. Even the current *Text Book of Module No. Geog-1004 Geography of Myanmar*[4] records that Rohinggas (Rohingyas) are one of the minority ethnic groups that had settled in Northern Rakhine State close to the border with Bangladesh from early days.

Who are indigenous races was defined in Article 3(1) of the Burma Citizenship Law 1948, which states:

> For the purposes of section 11 of the Constitution the expression any of the indigenous races of Burma shall mean the Arakanese, Burmese, Chin, Kachin, Karen, Kayah, Mon or Shan race and such racial group as has settled in any of the territories included within the Union as their permanent home from a period anterior to 1823 CE (1185 BE).

However, the 1982 Law altered the word "Arakanese" to "Rakhine", thus effectively excluding the minority Rohingya of Arakan from their previously shared national status. The 1982 Burma Citizenship Law, Article 3, records indigenous ethnic groups (*taing yin thar*) as "Nationals such as the Kachin, Karen, Chin, Burma, Mon, Rakhine or Shan and ethnic groups as have settled in any of the territories included within the States as their permanent home from a period anterior to 1185 BE, 1823 CE". Unlike the 1948 Union Citizenship Act, the word "Rakhine" is unilaterally used for Buddhist Arakanese at the expense of the Muslim Rohingya Arakanese.

Article 44(c) of the 1982 Citizenship Law states an applicant for naturalized citizenship shall have "to be able to speak well one of the national languages". This clause is a tool designed to denationalize marginalized groups like Rohingya, and will generate many internally displaced people (IDPs) and refugees. It should be permanently deleted so as to acknowledge the reality of Myanmar as an ethnically diverse country. In the case of Hasan Ali vs. Union of Burma, Supreme Court Criminal Miscellaneous cases No. 155 and 156 of 1959, their Lordships of the Supreme Court remarked (Verma 1961, pp. 121–22):

> Today in various parts of Burma there are people who, because of their origin and isolated way of life, are totally unlike the Burmese in appearance or speak of events which had occurred outside of the limit of their habitation. They are nevertheless statutory citizens under the Union Citizenship Act ... Thus mere race or appearance of a person or whether he has a knowledge of any language of the Union is not the test as to whether he is a citizen of the Union.

Article 71 of the 1982 law states "Organisations conferred with authority under this law shall give no reasons in matters carried out under this law." This clause is not at all compatible with democracy and human rights — everything should be answerable to law and constitution.

Unlike the 1947 Constitution and 1948 Citizenship Law, the 1982 Citizenship Law, which established a three-tiered system of citizenship — full, associate and naturalized — is an instrument of discrimination and oppression against so-called non-indigenous racial groups, and the Rohingya. There should be only one kind of citizenship that is, citizenship of the Union of Myanmar, in conformity with generally accepted citizenship practices and provisions of international law. Associate citizenship should be abolished. All citizens whether natural citizens or naturalized citizens should be constitutionally treated as equal in dignity, rights and privileges. No special privileges should be accorded to any individuals or groups on grounds of ethnicity and religion etc. or in the name of indigenous ethnic nationalities.

With respect to its inherent nature, the Rohingya are natural citizens of Myanmar. Their forefathers were once a welcome elite in the kingdom of Arakan, but now they have become unwanted aliens and have been reduced to serfdom. Being natives by virtue of originating naturally in Arakan, by all legal standards, their citizenship rights cannot morally or in accord with accepted legal principles be revoked. The oppressive, discriminatory — and internationally condemned — Citizenship Law of 1982 is not compatible with a democratic Myanmar. It must be scrapped or amended to conform to international human rights law and citizenship standards.

Last but not least, if the 1982 Citizenship Law is applied to Rohingya without discriminatory or prejudicial attitudes, the Rohingya are automatic citizens of Myanmar, as Article 6 of the Law which reads: "A person who is already a citizen on the date of this Law comes into force is a citizen." Had not Arakan been under Burmese occupation the question of Rohingya citizenship and their indigenous status would never arise in Arakan. Thus, Rohingya merit indigenous status with indigenous citizenship rather than citizenship by naturalization.

Notes

1. A 1960 publication of the Ministry of Culture.
2. *Botataung Daily* (Burmese newspaper), Rangoon, 23 February 1973.
3. Order No. 11-OA-CC/42 (31 December 1942), of the Office of the Military Administration, North Arakan.
4. Textbook prepared for First Year Arts students specializing in History and Myanmar Studies, published in 2008 by the Department of Geography, Yangon University Distance Education, under the Ministry of Education, p. 61.

References

Arakan Project, The. *Submission to the Committee on the Rights of the Child: Issues to be Raised Concerning the Situation of Stateless Rohingya Children in Myanmar (Burma)*. Bangkok: The Arakan Project, January 2012 <http://www.burmalibrary. org/docs12/AP-CRCMyanmar-12-01.pdf> (accessed 28 May 2016).

Arakan Rohingya National Organisation (ARNO). "Rohingya Belong to Burma". *Arakan Monthly* 1, no. 6 (2009): 10–12 <http://www.burmalibrary.org/docs08/ mag_arakan01-06.pdf> (accessed 1 June 2016).

Atlee, C.R. and Thakin NU. *The Nu-Atlee Burma Independence Agreement*. London, 1947 <https://burmastar1010.files.wordpress.com/2011/06/nu-atlee-agreement. pdf> (accessed 2 June 2016).

Aung San Suu Kyi. *Freedom from Fear*. London: Penguin Publication, 2010.

Ba Shin. "Coming of Islam to Burma 1700 A.D.". Paper presented at Azad Bhavan, New Delhi, 1961.

Bangladesh Institute of Law and International Affairs. "Arakan in Historical Perspective". *Monthly Bulletin of the Bangladesh Institute of Law and International Affairs* 1, no. 4 (1978).

Buchanan, Francis. "Francis Buchanan in Southeast Bengal (1798): His Journey to

Chittagong, the Chittagong Hill tracts, Noakhali and Comilla". In *A comparative vocabulary of some of the languages spoken in the Burmese Empire. Asiatick Researches* V. Calcutta edition 1799, London edition 1801.

Charney, Michael. W. "Buddhism in Arakan: Theory and Historiography of Religious Basis of the Ethnonym". Paper submitted to the Forgotten Kingdom of Arakan Workshop, Bangkok, 23–24 November 2005.

Collis, Maurice. *The Land of Great Image*. Reissued with additional illustrations. New York: New Directions, 1985.

Evans, Graham and Jeffrey Newnham. *The Penguin Dictionary of International Relations*. London: Penguin Books, 1998.

Harvey, G.E. *Outline of Burmese History*. London, New York & Bombay: Longmans, Green & Co., 1947.

Islam, Nurul. *The Rohingya Problem*. Arakan: Arakan Rohingya National Organisation. 1999.

———. "Rohingya tangled in Burma citizenship politics". Kaladanpress Network, 2012 <http://www.kaladanpress.org/feature-mainmenu-28/45-kaladan-news/3669-rohingya-tangled-in-burma-citizenship-politics> (accessed 2 June 2016).

Lewa, Chris. "North Arakan: An open prison for the Rohingya in Burma". *Forced Migration* 32, 2009 <http://www.fmreview.org/sites/fmr/files/FMRdownloads/en/FMRpdfs/FMR32/FMR32.pdf> (accessed 2 June 2016).

Myanmar Swezon Kyan (Burmese Official Encyclopedia) 1964. *Myanmar Swezon Kyan* 9, Rangoon: Sabeybikman Publication, 1964.

Myint-U, Thant. *The River of Lost Footsteps: Histories of Burma*. New York: Farrar, Straus and Giroux, 2006.

Patrick, John J. "The Concept of Citizenship in Education for Democracy". ERIC Digest, August 1999 <http://www.ericdigests.org/2000-1/democracy.html> (accessed 30 May 2016).

Razzaq, Abdur and Mahfuzul Haque. *A Tale of Refugees: Rohingyas in Bangladesh*. Dhaka: Centre for Human Rights, 1995.

Smith, Martin. "The Muslim Rohingya of Burma". Paper delivered at Conference of Burma Centrum, Nederland, 11 December 1995.

United Nations. General Assembly Resolution 103(1). 19 November 1946 <http://www.worldlii.org/int/other/UNGA/1946/41.pdf>) (accessed 27 May 2016).

Verma, S.L. *The Law Relating to Foreigners and Citizenship in Burma*. Mandalay: The George Printing Works, 1961.

Working Peoples' Daily (Rangoon). "Speech by General Ne Win". 9 October 1982.

9

MYANMAR'S OTHER MUSLIMS[1]
The Case of the Kaman

Nyi Nyi Kyaw

INTRODUCTION

The story of rather chronic discrimination and persecution by successive governments of Myanmar meted out against Muslims — especially the world-famous statelessness of the Rohingya — before and after transition started in 2010 is taken for granted. Questions relating to eligibility, recognition, and protection of Muslims' citizenship have therefore been raised. Largely informed by a meta-narrative of the plight of the Myanmar Muslim minority, those questions have been answered by making generalizing arguments that governments and Buddhists in Myanmar discriminate against and/or persecute a Muslim *minority*. This tendency has unfortunately led to lack of sophistication and nuance in making academic and/or journalistic arguments about Myanmar's Muslims.

By conducting a case study of the Kaman that is now the only government-recognized Muslim ethnic group in Buddhist Myanmar, this article suggests that there are two or more Muslim minorities with different relationships with the state and society in Myanmar that have significant impact on their identity and citizenship in Myanmar. Attention to those intra-communal differences even within the so-called Muslim minority of Myanmar is expected to contribute not only to research on Muslims in the country but also to policy advice for betterment of diverse minority groups that constitute Myanmar's Muslims.

ANTI-MUSLIM VIOLENCE AS CHALLENGE OF TRANSITION

Myanmar's political and social liberalization post-2011 could be traced back to the sham general elections in November 2010[2] held by the previous military regime (State Law and Order Restoration Council/State Peace and Development Council [SLORC/SPDC]). The quasi-civilian government headed by President U Thein Sein, ex-general and ex-prime minister during the previous military rule, came to power in late March 2011. After the election the government initiated a series of political reforms, including the release of Nobel Laureate Daw Aung San Suu Kyi from house arrest on 13 November (six days after the election, following a period of detention of fifteen years from 1989).

Besides her release, other significant political and social reforms included but were not limited to: release from prison of many other prominent political dissidents, such as Min Ko Naing; removal of the clause in the Political Parties Registration Law which banned ex-prisoners from joining political parties, paving the way for National League for Democracy (NLD) to re-enter the electoral scene, compete (and eventually win in a landslide in the by-elections of April 2012); elimination of the notorious draconian press censorship and emergence of a largely free private press; holding of ceasefire and peace negotiation talks with ethnic armed organizations (EAOs); and allowing ordinary people to enjoy political and civil rights to a significant extent, especially in the areas of expression, association, and assembly.

Due to these significant reforms, the years 2011 and 2012 were an unprecedented time of jubilation for President U Thein Sein and his administration as they garnered praise from various corners of the international community. The mantra of "Burma (or Myanmar) is changing!" was repeatedly chanted in the media and at international policy tables. This political euphoria unfortunately did not last long. Myanmar faced a series of unprecedented events of sectarian violence, and a rise of inter-religious tensions between Rakhine Buddhists and Rohingya/non-Rohingya[3] Muslims in Rakhine State in 2012 and in other places in 2013 and 2014: Meiktila (March 2013); Okkan (April 2013); Lashio (May 2013); Kanbalu (August 2013); and Mandalay (July 2014). This has been called "one of the darkest aspects of Burma's political transition" by Min Zin (2015, p. 375). Depending on the system of quantification adopted, the number of those largely anti-Muslim violent episodes from June 2012 through June 2015 ranges from ten to sixteen (Min Zin 2015). Since Muslims bore the brunt of violence during and after all of these violent episodes, the international community started portraying what happened as "anti-Muslim". Again, even among Muslims, the Rohingya, whose Myanmar citizenship and legal belonging to the country has been questioned and rejected over the last four years, were disproportionately affected.

There are a number of contextual factors which include both causes and causers (following the designation of Huntington 1991), which led to the outbreak of those conflicts. A few organizational and individual authors have pinpointed factors such as the adverse impact of transition (International Crisis Group 2013); direct involvement of the state (Maung Zarni 2013); the authorities' failure to control hate groups and indirect involvement in the groups (Min Zin 2015; Nyi Nyi Kyaw 2016); failure of the state to protect (Human Rights Watch 2012; Physicians for Human Rights 2013); the role of the "hidden hands" (Justice Trust 2015); chauvinist nationalist media (Dolan and Gray 2014); and Islamophobic mobilizations by Buddhist nationalist groups such as 969 and Ma-Ba-Tha (Nyi Nyi Kyaw 2016; Walton and Hayward 2014).

ANTI-MUSLIM HATE CAMPAIGN

Many observers may be of the opinion that violent episodes in Rakhine State and elsewhere in Myanmar only directly affected Muslims in those violence-stricken places alone. For example, the Rakhine violence may be assumed to have not affected Muslims in Yangon. However, it is truer to say that Myanmar Muslims in general were either directly or indirectly affected not only by violence but also by anti-Muslim hate campaigns. Historically speaking, many, if not most, people in Myanmar have harboured anti-Muslim prejudices since the colonial period (Egreteau 2011). Violent anti-Muslim episodes have occurred often in the past, especially in the late 1980s, 1990s and 2000s. However, the nationwide hate campaign targeting Muslims as a community from 2012 to 2015 is unprecedented (Min Zin 2015). The hate campaign, which is believed to have played at least an indirect, if not direct, role in all those above-mentioned anti-Muslim violence, is led by 969 and Ma-Ba-Tha (Organization for Protection of Race, Religion, and Sasana). The former was established on 30 October 2012 by a monks' network based in Mawlamyine a few days after the outbreak of the second round of violence in Rakhine State and the latter on 27 June 2013 by monks and lay Buddhists, both clamouring to defend Buddhism from Islamization. 969 was later subsumed under the umbrella of the larger Ma-Ba-Tha since the leaders of the former all are senior members of the latter. Monastic leadership of Ma-Ba-Tha, supplemented by lay leadership and membership, and their professed social and nationalist nature, have enabled them to evade the restrictions normally imposed by Ma Ha Na (State Sangha Maha Nayaka Committee), the supreme body of Myanmar's Buddhist Sangha, that rules no monks-only religious organizations can be formed apart from the nine sects officially recognized by the state since 1980.

This recent hate campaign propagated a popular conspiracy theory that claimed polygamous and hyper-fertile Muslim men have a mission to Islamize Myanmar by luring Buddhist women into interfaith marriage and converting the latter to Islam. This conspiracy theory claims that the religious and demographic threat of the Muslim plot is financially endowed by the practice of Muslims buying only from shops owned by fellow Muslims. This then creates more Muslim wealth that enables Muslims to lure Buddhist women, especially those of low socio-economic backgrounds, who are forced to convert to Islam through interfaith marriage. The hate campaign claims that it is imperative that the plot be immediately exposed and stopped to protect Buddhist Myanmar from this grand scheme of Islamization. Therefore, 969 and Ma-Ba-Tha campaigners requested ordinary Buddhists to stop dealing with Muslims, to buy from other Buddhists only, and for the government and parliament to legislate for protection of Buddhism against rampant polygamy, forced religious conversion, lax interfaith marriage, and uncontrollable childbirth (Nyi Nyi Kyaw 2016).

The principal strategy of the 969 and Ma-Ba-Tha-led hate campaign has been incessant and militant bombardment of their message through sermons by Buddhist monks and talks by laypeople, together with photo shows, weekly and bi-weekly journals, pamphlets, statements, pictures, songs, conferences, stories, books, movies, and social media (mainly Facebook). Those materials circulating in the streets, on social media and at bookshops and meetings which are extremely inflammatory and may in theory instigate conflicts, have largely created a siege mentality among Muslims across Myanmar. Muslims have been called illegal migrants, dogs, African caps, Jihadists, ungrateful guests, kalas, etc. Ironically, a Muslim siege mentality seems to have emerged and been strongly felt, despite the professed goal of the hate campaign to check the Muslim threat due to a centuries-old Buddhist siege mentality (Kyaw San Wai 2014). Commenting on a recent anti-Muslim incident which occurred in Bago Region on 23 June 2016, Yanghee Lee, the UN Special Rapporteur on the Situation of Human Rights in Myanmar, characterized such instances of anti-Muslim violence as "an attack on the past, present and future of one community" (Lee 2016).

Governmentally speaking, despite repeated promises by President U Thein Sein that he would not allow hate speech, the anti-Muslim campaign remained unchecked and grew exponentially at least until late 2015, when the NLD won in a landslide in the general elections held on 8 November. It was reported that U Thein Sein himself, and his subordinates were in close touch with the leaders of the movement, including Ashin Wirathu, according to reliable sources (Min Zin 2014, 2015). Apparently succumbing to the demand made by Ma-Ba-Tha with the support of 1.3 million signatures of the people, in February 2014 U Thein Sein asked the parliament to draft four race and protection bills — known in Myanmar as "Myo Saung Upade" (Lawi Weng 2014*a*). When the parliament responded that it was the government's responsibility to draft such bills, in March U Thein Sein formed a special commission to draft the bills on religious conversion and population growth control and suggested that the Supreme Court of the Union of Myanmar draft the other two on interfaith marriage and monogamy (Lawi Weng 2014*b*). All four bills became law in 2015. All of these — the anti-Muslim violence, the hate campaigns, and legislative reforms to "protect" Buddhism — strongly support the argument that Muslims in general, regardless of their background, legal citizenship and residence, have been subject to social or communal harassment and securitization due to being seen as a threat to Buddhist Myanmar during the bumpy transition of the past few years.

For this reason, the international community has tended to homogenize Muslims of Myanmar and construct a besieged Muslim minority being terrorized by a Buddhist majority in Myanmar. As noted above, it is largely true that Myanmar's Muslims in general experienced social suffering and an identity crisis as a community. The issue of the Rohingya, who have suffered most, has understandably become the dominant topic in most talks and writings on Myanmar Muslims. However, there are a few other Muslim minorities whose experiences in the transition have been different depending on their identity and dwelling place. This article highlights the experience of the ethnic Kaman who have also been affected by the rise of anti-Muslim sentiments and violent/non-violent conflicts and argue that their suffering differs from the Rohingya's, implying that there are Muslim minorities, not a Muslim minority, in Myanmar. It then discusses how the Kaman identity has been constructed, problematized and reconstructed largely due to the impact of sectarian violent conflicts in Rakhine State in 2012, and analyses how the tiny Kaman community has striven for political and ethnic survival due to their status, sandwiched between Rakhine Buddhists and Rohingya

Muslims. Finally, it analyses citizenship of the Kamans and their negligible representation in formal electoral politics.

KAMAN MUSLIMS DURING AND AFTER SECTARIAN VIOLENCE IN RAKHINE STATE IN 2012

The Kaman is a Muslim ethnic group which is recognized by the Myanmar government as one of 135 groups entitled to full citizenship at birth. Their exact population is not known; it has been estimated as a few tens of thousands or more. Two rounds of unprecedented sectarian violence rocked Rakhine State in June and October 2012.[4] The violence and its aftermath presented itself as an intractable obstacle to Myanmar's further political liberalization because it led to the re-emergence of old issues and the emergence of new ones, all concerning the Muslim question that has proven to be extremely emotive and sensitive for the government and people of Myanmar, especially Rakhines. Let us first see what happened in Rakhine State in 2012 before moving on to discuss the trajectory of Kaman identity.

A number of contextual factors, including both causes and causers, seemed to lie behind the violence in Rakhine State, a detailed discussion of which is beyond this article. However, there is now an almost universal consensus that the first round of violence was provoked by the alleged rape, robbery, and murder of a Rakhine Buddhist woman, by the name of Ma Thida Htwe, by three Muslim men, on 28 May 2012 in Kyauknimaw, in Yanbye township. A hate campaign followed when the news of the crime along with a gruesome picture of the body of Ma Thida Htwe covered in blood circulated on social media. A pamphlet which graphically described the case and demonized Muslims of Rakhine State was reportedly distributed in Taungup, another town in Rakhine State. Tragically, this is believed to have led to the lynching by a Rakhine Buddhist vigilante mob of ten Muslim bus passengers (eight from the middle of Myanmar travelling on a religious itinerary and two from Thandwe) in Taungup on 3 June 2012. Gruesome pictures of the ten Muslims again appeared in social media. On 5 June 2012 three state newspapers[5] reported the killing by referring to "kala", which Muslims find vulgar and derogatory, especially when it is used in public by the state.[6] A group of Muslims protested against the use in front of a central mosque in downtown Yangon on the same day. The newspapers the next day issued a correction and changed "kala" to "Muslims living within Myanmar".

The tensions did not subside, but in fact worsened. A serious riot broke out in Maungdaw, where Rakhine Buddhists constitute a numerical minority, in the afternoon of 8 June 2012, when Muslims burned Rakhine Buddhist-owned houses and properties and killed a number of Rakhine Buddhists. This resulted in revenge by Rakhine Buddhists upon Muslims elsewhere in Rakhine State where the latter are the minority. Eventually, the riotous conflicts turned out to be the most serious sectarian episode in Myanmar's or Rakhine State's history since independence.[7] The first round of violence was seemingly spontaneous although various questions may be asked about the hidden role of the State, which apparently failed to manage its spread across the whole of Rakhine State. It should be noted that, largely, this did not affect the Kaman.

A second round of violence broke out in October in which Muslims were disproportionately affected. This time the Kaman found themselves on the receiving end, a number of them being killed by the police and by Rakhine Buddhists (Human Rights Watch 2013). However, the Final Report of the government-established Inquiry Commission on Sectarian Violence in Rakhine State (2013) does not provide a separate figure of Kaman lives lost and Kaman properties destroyed, although it mentions a Kaman killed in Yanbye in June (p. 11), attacks upon the Kaman in Kyaukphyu in October (p. 24), and the Kaman being encamped as internally displaced peoples (IDPs) despite their government-recognized ethnic identity status (p. 25). In one year after the second round of violence, five Kaman Muslims including a 94-year old woman were killed in Thabyu Chaing in Thandwe District in October 2013, one year after the second round of violence (Fuller 2013). Despite sporadic mention of the Kaman suffering as noted above, the Final Report eventually gives figures of loss of human lives and properties by dividing them into the Rakhine side and the Bengali (the preferred name for all non-Kaman Muslims in Rakhine State used by the government and people of Myanmar) side. It means that the report tries to portray the conflict as an occurrence which only affected Rakhine Buddhists and Bengali Muslims (or Rohingyas). The suffering of the Kaman, who are a recognized minority group, has then been largely lost in all of this Rakhine- and Rohingya-centric reporting.

The Inquiry Commission on Sectarian Violence in Rakhine State (2013, p. 20, Appendix C) reports two separate occasions of violence that resulted in: the loss of lives of 192 people (98 the first time [32 Rakhines and 66 Muslims][8] and 94 the second time [26 Rakhines and 68 Muslims]); injuries to 265 people (123 the first time [51 Rakhines and 72 Muslims] and 142 people the second time [97 Rakhines and 45 Muslims]); destruction of 8,614 houses (5,338 houses the first time [1,150 Rakhine-owned houses and 4,188 Muslim-owned houses] and 3,276 houses the second time [42 Rakhine-owned houses and 3,234 Muslim-owned houses]); destruction of 120 businesses on the two occasions (45 Rakhine-owned businesses and 75 Muslim-owned businesses). The Final Report also reports the loss of lives and properties as claimed by the two sides: 128 dead and 169 injured (Rakhines) and 219 dead and 242 injured (Muslims) (2013, p. 22).

A casual look at these figures provided by the Inquiry Commission may lead one to conclude that the conflict was inter-communal as both sides apparently suffered. However, it is more accurate to say that Muslims, including the Kaman, disproportionately suffered for two main reasons. The National Democratic Party for Development (NPDP), a registered political party mainly composed of Muslims from Rakhine State, claimed that it has a detailed list (name, age, address, and type of weapon used in killing) of about 500 people killed during the two rounds of violence, most of whom were Muslims (Aye Nai 2012). Although the NPDP did not distinguish between Kaman, Rohingya, and other Muslims, at least a small percentage of them most probably would have been Kaman, because the second round of violence occurred in Kaman-populated areas such as Kyaukphyu, Mrauk-U, Myebon and Thandwe. Also, 4,000 displaced Kaman Muslims were still confined to camps as of July 2015 (Yen Snaing 2015), a fact which was neither recognized nor stated in the Inquiry Commission's Final Report, the draft Rakhine State Action Plan[9] nor by the Myanmar government. Despite a few media reports, ethnic Kaman Muslims' suffering has gone largely unnoticed and unrecognized by both the Inquiry Commission and the Myanmar government who apparently tried to "Bengalize" all Muslims in Rakhine State. Those 4,000 Kaman Muslims in camps have also been subject to travel restrictions. Indeed, the travel restrictions that the Kaman Muslims in camps face nowadays are not new; in the 1990s and 2000s the community also met the same fate.

As seen above, the Inquiry Commission provided all of the statistics of casualties, injuries, and displacement in terms of only two categories — Rakhines and Bengalis — a rhetoric also adopted by the Myanmar government. This Bengalization of all Muslims of Rakhine State has effectively helped the government to evade its responsibility to protect the Kaman, which is one of the recognized national groups. This is more obvious when seen in light of the use of taing yin thar (native or indigenous) affixed to Rakhines throughout the Final Report, and in several pronouncements and publications by the government on the conflict. It has effectively meant that Rakhines are indigenous whereas Muslims are not, that the two sides are not equal and that the former must be given priority. For example, in his latest media interview, Maung Maung Ohn, then Chief Minister of Rakhine State, stated: "There are two major ethnic groups in the State of Rakhine, those who have inhabited this land for a very long time and those who migrated from another country, the Bengalis" (Outlook India 2015).

In terms of displacement, about 140,000 Muslims were made homeless or displaced in 2012 either due to loss their homes or due to their inability to return to their original places, even when these remained intact. On the other hand, there were only 3,500 Rakhine IDPs in November 2012 (Inquiry Commission on Sectarian Violence in Rakhine State 2013, p. 28). According to the Rakhine State Action Plan, there were 1,738 Rakhine and 138,724 Muslim IDPs to be resettled as of September 2014 (Rakhine State Action Plan n.d., p. 7), meaning half of the Rakhine IDPs had been resettled. Although there have been offers by the international community to build new houses for Muslim IDPs, the main obstacle was the demand by the Myanmar government and Rakhine Buddhists that all Muslim IDPs undergo a special citizenship check prior to their resettlement. This demand, while appearing reasonable, is actually unacceptable, since almost all of the Rohingya in Myanmar had been deprived of permanent identity documentation, many holding only temporary identity certificates known as "White Cards", all of which expired at the end of March in 2015.

KAMAN IDENTITY AND ETHNO-HISTORY

The Kaman, originally a Persian term meaning "bow and arrow", are different from the Rohingya in terms of possession of an officially recognized identity. Admittedly, the terms "identity" and "ethnic groups" are fluid concepts open to question and controversy, especially in the context of government use and recognition. It is more reasonable to characterize Myanmar's 135 indigenous or national groups (Hla Min 2013, pp. 171–74) as ethnic categories, following the classification of Smith (1999, p. 13) who defines the groups as "populations distinguished by outsiders as possessing the attributes of a common name or emblem, a shared cultural element (usually language or religion), and a link with a particular territory."

Kaman (or Kamein, as it was often spelled) is recognized as one of seven ethnic sub-groups under the umbrella of the Rakhine super-group, the others being Rakhine, Mro, Thet, Khami, Daingnet, and Marmagyi. More importantly, the Kaman are the only Muslim community in Myanmar who is recognized as an ethnic group by the government. One version of the origin of the Kaman is that their history is traceable to the retreat of the Mogul prince Shah Shuja, second son of Emperor Shah Jahan, and his family and soldiers to Arakan in 1660, where they permanently settled (Yegar 1972). However, by drawing upon several Rakhine sources, the now almost definitive history of the Kaman (or accepted as such by the Kaman leaders), was written by a non-Kaman Buddhist writer Maung Sanda (Le Way) (2005). He questions this

above version of Kaman history, and instead traces the Kaman to the times of
the Rakhine kings in the thirteenth century, and claims that the Kaman are
Rakhines who are only different from present-day Rakhine Buddhists in terms
of religious affiliation. This claim is very important because in recent years
a notion of Rakhine supremacy has emerged that asserts that the Rakhines
are the original owners of the land now existing as Rakhine State. Claiming
that the Kaman are Rakhines too will have put the former on a par with the
latter — subject to acceptance by Rakhines.

Despite this lengthy history, Islam and its adherents (Muslims) have
been assumed to be alien to Rakhine State and Myanmar generally. This
homogenization has led to loss of diversity of Myanmar's Muslims. More
importantly, this has also created a notion of Muslims as "guests" with
Buddhists (including Rakhines) as "hosts", regardless of how long Muslims
have resided in Myanmar. As I argue elsewhere, this situates Buddhists and
Muslims of Myanmar "in a relational social milieu in which the former is
the benefactor and the latter the debtor" (Nyi Nyi Kyaw 2015, p. 57). Also,
due to the occurrence of sectarian conflicts in Rakhine State and elsewhere,
Muslims have been largely blamed by Rakhines and other nationalist Buddhist
groups and forces as the primary perpetrator. The Muslim identity is further
problematized by this perspective, since they are "ungrateful guests who try
to bite the hand that feeds them" (Nyi Nyi Kyaw 2015, p. 57). This religious
othering by Rakhines seems to have pushed the Kaman into claiming that
they are racially, ethnically, and culturally Rakhines. Although the Rakhine
origin of the Kaman has not been recognized by Rakhines as yet, the Kaman
identity is one of the 135 government-recognized ethnic groups. This has
been frequently emphasized by the government, politicians and activists from
across Myanmar, who use this fact to argue that what happened in Myanmar
from 2012 through 2014 is not religious persecution per se.

Maung Sanda (Le Way)'s history (2005) portrays the Kaman as a
community who linguistically speak the Rakhine dialect, culturally practise
Rakhine norms and traditions, and politically ally with the Myanmar State and
Rakhines. Kaman leaders I interviewed emphasize that the book was written
in 2005, by which time it was almost impossible to get clearance from the
State Press Censorship Board for publications on ethno-histories, indicating
acceptance by the government of Myanmar of the history of the Kaman as
presented in the book. This official acceptance is highly relevant since the
state has discretionary powers to decide whether an ethnic group is national
or indigenous according to section 4 of the Myanmar Citizenship Law (1982).

Moreover, Maung Sanda (Le Way)'s work consists of very interesting
facts about the Kaman ethno-history which is expected to have significant

demographic implications on the size of the community. By drawing upon Rakhine sources, Maung Sanda (2005, pp. 25–53) states that there existed a sizeable Kaman archer corps serving Rakhine kings as early as the thirteenth century, and that the size of the corps and their families reached 200,000 in the seventeenth century. By writing this Kaman ethno-history, Maung Sanda (Le Way) questions the well-accepted history of the origin of the Kaman from Shah Shuja's followers and soldiers, who were around 300 in number, and claims that it is more sensible to claim that those Mogul soldiers and their families were absorbed into the already existing Kaman community. Besides this trajectory of the Kaman community in Arakan, by drawing upon Burmese historical sources, Maung Sanda (Le Way) (2005, pp. 54–58) provides another interesting fact about the Kaman history by tracing the transfer of a sizeable number of the Kaman from then Arakan to central Myanmar (then under the Bamar kings) from the seventeenth century onwards. Those Kaman, who were mainly professionals, and their families were given lands by the Bamar kings for permanent settlement in places such as Shwe Bo, Taung Ngu, Meiktila, Myedu, and Depayin in middle Myanmar. This segment of the Kaman history is revealing in terms of construction of ethnicity because those Muslims, claimed as Kaman by Maung Sanda (Le Way), later became known and identified by the Bamar kings as "Pathi" (or "Bamar Muslims" from the 1920–30s onwards).[10]

Putting the Kaman in Rakhine State who still identify as Kaman, and those elsewhere who seem to have forgotten their Kaman roots and identify in other ways under the ethnic umbrella of the Kaman, would create a large indigenous Kaman community. This raises many questions for the Rakhines and other Bamar Buddhists who view Muslims as "guests", as will having a sizeable indigenous Muslim community with the special rights that are constitutionally provided for official ethnic minorities (or "national races" as they are called in the Constitution of the Republic of the Union of Myanmar). The demographic implications and debates surrounding the actual size of the Kaman community are discussed in the next section.

SIZE OF THE KAMAN COMMUNITY AND ITS PROBLEMATIC RELATION TO ETHNICITY

The 1931 census recorded 2,686 Kaman in Arakan (Yegar 1972, 1982, 2002). The exact Kaman population nowadays is not known as yet, as up until the end of its rule in early 2016 the U Thein Sein administration had not released statistics on ethnicity and religion from the last census, which was conducted in 2014. The now ruling NLD government has stated that it would release data on religious demography by August 2016 — although data on ethnicity is yet to be finalized in consultation with respective ethnic groups (Ye Mon 2016). However, Kaman leaders estimate the size of their community at around 50,000 or more, although it must be noted that this does not include those Muslims in middle Myanmar who are originally Kaman.

Indeed, the size of the Kaman community in Rakhine State and in Yangon has been a highly politicized issue due to the claims by Rakhines that Bengalis have used the Kaman identity to secure Citizenship Scrutiny Cards (CSCs). This claim is often echoed by Kaman leaders themselves. U Tin Hlaing Win, general secretary of the Kaman National Development Party (KNDP), alleged that Bengalis[11] had penetrated into the Kaman in one of his interviews in November 2013 with Narinjara, a Rakhine news agency — possibly to satisfy and make peace with Rakhines (Narinjara 2013).

The Kaman identity, which was little known beyond Rakhine State until 2012, became a "political" subject for the Kaman themselves, Rakhines, the government, and many other people. In other words, Kaman found themselves being and becoming Kaman[12] in public imagination or knowledge. However, becoming known seems to have had its own drawbacks because the "Kaman" identity and the acceptable number of people associated with it have been increasingly problematized. For example, U Aye Thar Aung, a prominent Rakhine politician appointed as Deputy Speaker of the Upper House by the NLD government, stated in June 2016 that as many as 150,000 Muslims had acquired CSCs although there are only 30,000 Kamans (U Kyaw Zan Tha 2016).[13] Due to their ethnic identity, listed as one of the seven sub-groups under the Rakhine category, and to their religious identity, shared by the Rohingya, the tiny Kaman community saw themselves sandwiched between the two largest ethnic groups living in Rakhine State, i.e., 2-million-strong Rakhines and 1-million-strong Rohingyas (Ministry of Immigration and Population 2015). Kaman leaders I interviewed in Yangon seem to be bitterly aware of their sandwiched status.

Amidst re-emergence, or in other words re-reification, of ethnicity as an important channel for calling upon the government to provide group rights (Taylor 2015), Kamans have also been found to emphasize their indigenous status to secure protection from the government — albeit largely in vain. Despite their ethnic status and Myanmar citizenship, several Kaman people are still confined to IDP camps in Rakhine, although all citizens are entitled to the right to settle and reside anywhere in Myanmar, according to section 355 of the Myanmar Constitution.[14]

Due to their sandwiched status between the two demographic giants and growing politicization of their ethnic identity, the Kaman, especially their leaders, have resorted to employing a number of political strategies for survival. Especially worth noting here are two discursive strategies increasingly used by the Kaman for their political and social survival as a tiny minority in Rakhine State, where Rakhines have come to occupy a role more dominant than ever. They are: a re-emphasis of their indigeneity and loyalty to the Myanmar State, including Rakhine Buddhists; and distancing themselves from their fellow non-Kaman Muslims in Rakhine State. It is notable that all of these emerged in response to increasingly aggressive problematization by Rakhines of the Kaman identity and Rakhines' tendency to homogenize all Muslims in Rakhine State into a single community.

Despite these rhetorical strategies employed by the leaders of the KNDP, the Kaman have fallen victim to "Bengalization" by both the Rakhine leadership and the government. Besides Bengalization, the Kaman as a Muslim community have also found themselves subject to another increasingly popular conceptualization of Muslims as "guests" and of Buddhists as "hosts" (Nyi Nyi Kyaw 2015). This is most probably why Maung Maung Ohn called Kamans "guests" during one of his visits to a Muslim IDP camp in Myebon in May 2014 (Nan Mya Nadi 2014). On another occasion, he also told a meeting held in Sittwe in July 2014 that there are Muslims who have used fake Kaman identity to secure citizenship scrutiny cards or IDs (Maung Kan 2014). Rakhines have been more blunt and aggressive. For example, in the wake of the second round of violence, U Bat Di Ya, a Rakhine Buddhist monk, contended: "Kaman are also Kular (another spelling of kala). They are a kind of Kular race. They are the same blood. When incidents happen they unite with Kular, they don't stay on the Rakhine side" (Schearf 2012). On another occasion, a Rakhine man in his interview with Voice of America (Burmese) contended that Kaman is not a genuine indigenous ethnic group, but a naturalized one, because it was made to be so by the government, implying that Rakhines are the owners of Rakhine State (Voice of America 2012). When the issue of inclusion of "Rohingya" as a right of self-identification became highly volatile amidst Rakhines' protests before the 2014 census was taken, Kamans joined with the other six groups — including Rakhine — and called for non-inclusion of the controversial ethnonym (Radio Free Asia 2014).

Since before 2012, Kaman leaders have adopted these rhetorical strategies, apparently for community survival and self-protection. For example, the late U Shwe Bye, a Kaman ex-school headmaster, in his unpublished manuscript (n.d.) written in the 1990s on the history of his community,[15] emphasizes cultural "Rakhinization" or "Burmanization" and loyalty to the state. Likewise, Maung Sanda (Le Way) (2005, pp. 61–76) portrays the Kaman as a community whose cultural norms and practices are similar to those of the Rakhine. Maung

Sanda (Le Way) (2005, pp. 79–83; 101–34) also provides several biographical sketches and career histories of Kaman individuals who have occupied senior positions in the public sector, to prove that the Kaman has been consistently loyal to the Myanmar State. One of these is U Si Bu, who was appointed as one of the three judges of the Special Crimes Tribunal which adjudicated on the high-profile case of the assassination of Myanmar's national hero Aung San and his cabinet on 19 July 1947. In short, these histories portray the Kaman as a model minority which has culturally adapted to, and politically allied with, the majority.

Although Maung Maung Ohn reportedly promised Kaman leaders that he would arrange rebuilding of houses for 4,000 Kamans, this did not occur. One-third of Kamans still do not possess Citizenship Scrutiny Cards (Su Min Ko 2014). The other two-thirds of the Kaman population who are supposed to have CSCs are being accused of including those with fake identity. Rakhines did not even agree when 209 Muslims from an IDP camp in Myebon were given CSCs following official scrutiny in September 2014 (Aung Ye Maung Maung 2014), let alone 15,000–20,000 Kamans outside the IDP camps that are yet to be documented.

Therefore, the Kaman identity is expected to continue to be a highly charged issue in the politics of Rakhine State. Part of the community is being denigrated as having fake identity, and the Kaman themselves are expected to continue to fall prey to Rakhine nationalism and Rohingya vs. Rakhine competition. Both the Union and Rakhine State governments during the U Thein Sein era neglected the rights and plight of the Kaman, who occupy a special position as a tiny minority sandwiched between the dominant Rakhine community and the beleaguered Rohingya community. If and how the NLD government will guarantee and protect the rights of the Kaman is yet to be seen. The Kaman, especially their leaders, are also expected to continue to strive to make peace with Rakhines by rejecting their fellow Muslims in order to regain their lost rights both as citizens and as a recognized ethnic group. How all of these dynamics will play out in the near to middle future is yet to be seen, and is subject to political, social, cultural, and religious changes both in Rakhine State and elsewhere across the country.

KAMAN IDENTITY, CITIZENSHIP AND POLITICAL PARTICIPATION

So far, we have seen historical construction of Kaman ethnicity and the contested notions of their identity, which have been problematically influenced by demography and religion. Let us now first take a look at their citizenship as legally defined in the 1982 Citizenship Law. Since they are among 135 government recognized ethnic groups, the Kaman possess a type of citizenship superior to that held by all other non-Kaman Muslims in Myanmar. The 1982 Citizenship Law designates members of those ethnic groups or national races as citizens by birth whose citizenship can only be revoked when such citizens permanently leave Myanmar or take up citizenship of another country. In addition, there are Citizens, Associate Citizens, and Naturalized Citizens whose citizenship is revocable by the state. Non-Kaman Muslims in Myanmar nowadays belong to one of these three classes of citizens.[16] In marked contrast to Western ideals of democratic citizenship and legal egalitarianism of all citizens, those 135 national races or *taing yin thars* constitute the state itself, as argued by Nick Cheesman (2017), effectively excluding other non-*taing yin thar* citizens from the body politic. Despite this political superiority of the Kaman in terms of citizenship and their entitlements, as we have seen above, the Kaman have been increasingly subject to several restrictions which are only meant for non-citizens or Rohingya whose citizenship is undecided yet or unrecognized.

Finally, I turn to the issue of political participation of the Kaman, and analyse how this community has been electorally represented, at least since 1990 when three general elections have been held (in 1990, 2010 and 2015). The Kaman have been able to establish political parties and contest all three general elections: three candidates were fielded and one seat won by Kaman National League for Democracy in the 1990 elections; six candidates and no seats won by Kaman National Development Party in the 2010 elections; four candidates fielded and no seats won by Kaman National Development Party; and three independent candidates fielded and no seats won by All Myanmar Kaman National League for Democracy Party whose registration was not approved in the 2015 elections. So, formal political representation has been consistently negligible since 1990.

Due to their tiny size and demographic concentration in Rakhine State, the Kaman are, unlike other Muslims, not known to have joined in large numbers in the nationwide political parties such as NLD and Union Solidarity and Development Party. Despite little prospect of success, the Kaman have persistently established political parties and fielded a few candidates in every general election since 1990. For them, having a political party under the ethnonym of "Kaman" seems to serve as a reminder to the peoples of Myanmar of the former's recognized ethnicity and status. Kaman leaders emphasize that having a Kaman political party has enabled the community to hold political capital — however small that is — and to report their problems to the government and to the press.

Probably due to political insignificance of the Kaman, their ethnicity has often been used by Rakhines and other people of Myanmar in recent years to reject the criticisms made by the international community of their alleged ill-treatment of the Rohingya, and claim that there is a well-accepted Muslim ethnic group in Myanmar. The Kaman seem to be well aware of the growing importance of their ethnic identity. Therefore, the Kaman National Development Party, in the years since the 2012 Rakhine conflict, have used the press to increase public awareness of their ethnic identity, which was almost totally unknown beyond Rakhine State prior to the conflict. However, due to their religious identity commonly shared with other Muslims of Myanmar, the Kaman have been subject to some level of the popular discourses of Muslims as guests or as "kala", according to Kaman leaders.

CONCLUSION

To be Muslim in Myanmar nowadays is, arguably, the most difficult time in Myanmar's history, at least since independence. Never has anti-Muslim violence occurred at such levels. Never have Muslims of Myanmar, Rohingya and non-Rohingya, faced such a time in which their identity is so aggressively and emotionally problematized and alienated. Never have they lived with everyday Islamophobia and hate messages being spread across Myanmar by a nationwide campaign, such as Ma-Ba-Tha and 969. Never have they lived with such uncertainties and concerns about the future.

This chapter has warned that sweeping claims and generalizing arguments miss a very important fact about Muslims of Myanmar: the diversity of this minority community. Due to the discrimination and persecution of the Rohingya since the 1970s, which has increased markedly in recent years, the international media and a few scholarly writings have largely focused on the Rohingya. These narratives effectively overlook the other side of the Myanmar Muslim coin. By highlighting the experience of Kaman Muslims, who have also been torn apart by violent and non-violent sectarian conflicts since 2012, this paper concludes that there is not a Muslim minority, but rather Muslim minorities, in Myanmar. Moreover, by discussing the Kaman, it is also argued that different Muslim groups have had different relational issues and problems with the Buddhist majorities in their respective places, and with the state as well, subject to their constructed identities and space in which they live.

I believe that my argument has two important implications for policy and for further academic research. In terms of policy, any substantive prescriptions or suggestions on how to tackle present and future violent and non-violent conflicts between Buddhists and Muslims should keep in mind that different Muslim groups of Myanmar are embedded in different social and political relations with the state and also with neighbouring Buddhist communities. Academically, the paper suggests that intercommunal tensions should be seen in terms of both state-minority relations and majority-minority relations. Timing and context should be included in studying those dynamic relations. Admittedly, my argument would have been stronger if it could be buttressed by anthropological and sociological field research in Myanmar on how identities are constructed, deconstructed, and reconstructed on one hand, and how identities are shared or confrontationally constructed by different groups in different locales. Therefore, two projects on Muslims of Myanmar in general, and on how Buddhist-Muslim relations have fared over the last five decades, seem to be two most worthwhile efforts for researchers.

Notes

1. The conceptualization of "other Muslims" draws on Ardeth Maung Thawnghmung's *The "Other" Karens in Myanmar* (2012).
2. U.S. President Barack Obama said of the 2010 election in Myanmar: "It is unacceptable to steal an election, as the regime in Burma has done again for all the world to see." (Voice of America 2010).
3. Use of "Rohingya" has over the last four years become one of the most controversial issues to the extent that any meaningful discussion of the decades-long statelessness of the Rohingya will be blocked once one uses the ethnonym. For detailed discussions of the naming issue and citizenship of the Rohingya, see chapters by Leider, Tonkin, and Islam in this volume and Nyi Nyi Kyaw 2017. "Rohingya" is used here simply because it is the better known ethnonym now. Also, the term "non-Rohingya Muslims" is used here to denote other Muslims communities who also live in Rakhine State and include the Kaman. For further discussion of these issues, see the chapters by Tonkin, Leider and Islam.
4. The period between June and October in 2012 also saw small-scale incidents pitting Rakhine Buddhists against Rohingya and non-Rohingya Muslims in August and September (Inquiry Commission on Sectarian Violence in Rakhine State 2013, pp. 12–13).
5. The *Myanma Alinn Daily* (p. 7); *The Mirror* (p. 5) published by the Ministry of Information; and the *Myawady Daily* (p. 9) published by the military.
6. Despite this Muslim perception of the term, whether use of *kala* is totally and consistently derogatory from the viewpoint of non-Muslims is still open to dispute because it is used by different people in different social settings. However, *Muslim kala* was used by those three state newspapers whose religious profiling appears unquestionably derogatory and racist in that context.

7. Serious inter-communal conflict occurred in Rakhine State in 1942. See Leider in this volume for details of that conflict.
8. "Muslim" is used consciously here for two reasons: to dispute Bengalization of all Muslims by the Final Report and to include Rohingya, Kaman, Myedu and other mixed Muslims in Rakhine State.
9. The draft Rakhine State Action Plan was drawn by the Myanmar government in consultation with the international diplomatic and humanitarian assistance organizations. The plan leaked out in late September or early October 2014 but was never finalized due to inclusion of controversial content and practically impossible suggestions.
10. The origin of *Pathi* and *Bamar Muslims* as ethnonyms and construction of ethnic identities under those names is another interesting aspect of Muslim identity in Myanmar, which will not be discussed at length here. It is, however, important to note here that neither name is recognized by the Myanmar government. It means that although there are a large number of people in present-day Myanmar who identify themselves as *Pathi* or *Bamar Muslims*, there are no such ethnic groups officially recognized. It is also important to note that the issue of *Pathi* as an ethnic category emerged mainly among Muslims in middle Myanmar in the months prior to the most recent population census conducted in late March and early April in 2014.
11. Kaman leaders I interviewed also use "Bengali" in colloquial settings to refer to the Rohingya. However, this does not necessarily mean that the Kaman also claim a large percent of the Rohingya are illegal migrants from Bangladesh, as Rakhines and successive Myanmar governments do.
12. This term "being and becoming Kaman" is derived from Mandy Sadan's study of the Kachin ethnicity (2013) titled *Being and Becoming Kachin: Histories beyond the State in the Borderworlds of Burma.*
13. This numerical difference is understandable since most, if not all, of the Rohingya have not been issued CSCs since at least the late 1980s.
14. This right is subject to law according to Section 355 although what is meant by "according to law" has not been sufficiently explained.
15. There are less than a handful of written accounts of the community by the Kaman themselves among which U Shwe Bye's is one. All of them are unpublished manuscripts. However, Maung Sanda (Le Way)'s work draws upon those manuscripts and is said to be a definitive history by the Kaman leaders.
16. For details of legal definitions of different classes of citizens and their entitlements, see Nyi Nyi Kyaw (2015).

References

Ardeth Maung Thawnghmung. *The "Other" Karen in Myanmar: Ethnic Minorities and the Struggle without Arms.* Lanham: Lexington Books, 2012.
Aung Ye Maung Maung. "naing ngan tha pyit kvin pe hmu Myebon hma kan kvet

hmu twe shi (*There are protests against naturalisation in Myebon*)". *Voice of America.* 23 September 2014 <http://burmese.voanews.com/content/rohingya-burma-naturalization/2459369.html> (accessed 24 September 2014).

Aye Nai. "Group Says Death Toll in Arakan Higher than Government Figures". *Democratic Voice of Burma.* 13 November 2012 <http://www.dvb.no/news/group-says-death-toll-in-arakanhigher-than-gov't-figures/24723> (accessed 14 November 2012).

Cheesman, Nick. "How in Myanmar 'National Races' Came to Surpass Citizenship and Exclude Rohingya". *Journal of Contemporary Asia* 47, no. 3 (2017): 461–83.

Dolan, Theo and Stephen Gray. *Media and Conflict in Myanmar: Opportunities for Media to Advance Peace.* Washington, D.C.: United States Institute of Peace, 2014.

Egreteau, Renaud. "Burmese Indians in Contemporary Burma: Heritage, Influence, and Perceptions since 1988". *Asian Ethnicity* 12, no. 1 (2011): 33–54.

Fuller, Thomas. "Elderly Woman's Killing Lays Bare Myanmar's Religious Divisions". *New York Times,* 9 November 2013 <http://www.nytimes.com/2013/11/10/world/asia/elderly-womans-killing-lays-bare-myanmars-religious-divisions.html> (accessed 10 November 2013).

Hla Min. *The Way I See it: Myanmar and Its Evolving Global Role.* Yangon: Myanmar Consolidated Media Co. Ltd., 2013.

Human Rights Watch. *The Government Could Have Stopped This: Sectarian Violence and Ensuing Abuses in Burma's Arakan State.* New York: Human Rights Watch, 2012.

———. *All You Can Do Is Pray: Crimes Against Humanity and Ethnic Cleansing of Rohingya Muslims in Burma's Arakan State.* New York: Human Rights Watch, 2013.

Huntington, Samuel P. *The Third Wave: Democratization in the Late Twentieth Century.* Norman: University of Oklahoma Press, 1991.

Inquiry Commission on Sectarian Violence in Rakhine State. *Final Report of Inquiry Commission on Sectarian Violence in Rakhine State.* Nay Pyi Taw: Inquiry Commission on Sectarian Violence in Rakhine State, 2013.

International Crisis Group. *The Dark Side of Transition: Violence against Muslims in Myanmar.* Brussels: International Crisis Group, 2013.

Justice Trust. *Hidden Hands behind Communal Violence in Myanmar: Case Study of the Mandalay Riots.* New York: Justice Trust, 2015.

Kyaw San Wai. *Myanmar's Religious Violence: A Buddhist "Siege Mentality" at Work.* Singapore: S. Rajaratnam School of International Studies, 2014.

Lawi Weng. "Thein Sein Asks Parliament to Discuss Interfaith Marriage". *Irrawaddy,* 27 February 2014*a* <http://www.irrawaddy.org/burma/thein-sein-asks-parliament-discuss-interfaith-marriage.html> (accessed 1 July 2015).

———. "Thein Sein Orders Commission, Court to Draft 'Protection of Religion' Law". *Irrawaddy,* 7 March 2014*b* <http://www.irrawaddy.org/burma/thein-sein-orders-commission-court-draft-protection-religion-law.html> (accessed 1 July 2015).

Lee, Yanghee. "End of mission statement by the Special Rapporteur on the situation of human rights in Myanmar". *United Nations Information Centre*, 1 July 2016 <http://yangon.sites.unicnetwork.org/> (accessed 3 July 2016).

Maung Kan. "Rakhine pyi-nè-twin Kaman a-tu-mya shi-ne-thi-hu than-tha-ya-shi-kyaung pyi-nè-wan-kyi-kyôk pyaw (State Premier says he suspects that there are fake Kamans in Rakhine State)". *7 Day Daily*, 7 July 2014 <http://www.7daydaily.com/story/15128> (accessed 7 July 2014).

Maung Sanda (Le Way). *Kaman-myo-nwè-su tha-maing (History of the Kaman Ethnic)*. Yangon: U Ohn Maung, 2005.

Maung Zarni. "Religious Violence and the Role of the State in Myanmar". In *Myanmar in Transition: Polity, People, and Processes*, edited by Kerstin Duell. Singapore: Konrad-Adenauer-Stiftung, 2013.

Ministry of Immigration and Population. *The 2014 Myanmar Population and Housing Census: The Union Report: Census Report Volume 2*. Nay Pyi Taw: Department of Population, Ministry of Immigration and Population, 2015.

Min Zin. "Why Burma is Heading Downhill Fast". *Foreign Policy*, 28 March 2014 <http://foreignpolicy.com/2014/03/28/why-burma-is-heading-downhill-fast/> (accessed 6 January 2015).

———. "Anti-Muslim Violence in Burma: Why Now?". *Social Research* 82, no. 2 (2015): 375–97.

Nan Mya Nadi. "Rakhine pyi-nè a-ye-paw paung-sat-hnyi-hnaing-ye sin-ta-a-pwè Myebon dôk-ka-thè sa-kan sit-se (Rakhine State Emergency Coordination Center inspects Myebon IDP camp)". *Democratic Voice of Burma*, 15 May 2014 <http://burmese.dvb.no/archives/56670> (accessed 22 May 2014).

Narinjara. "Kaman lu-myo ma-hôk-bè Kaman taing-yin-tha-kat kaing-pyi hluttaw-tè-yauk-ne" [Those who are not Kaman hold Kaman national IDs and are now in the Hluttaw]. *Narinjara*, 25 November 2013 <http://www.narinjara.com/burmese> (accessed 2 July 2015).

Nyi Nyi Kyaw. "Alienation, Discrimination, and Securitization: Legal Personhood and Cultural Personhood of Muslims in Myanmar". *Review of Faith & International Affairs* 13, no. 4 (2015): 50–59.

———. "Islamophobia in Buddhist Myanmar: The 969 Movement & Anti-Muslim Violence". In *Islam and the State in Myanmar: Muslim-Buddhist Relations and the Politics of Belonging*, edited by Melissa Crouch. New Delhi: Oxford University Press India, 2016.

———. "Unpacking the Presumed Statelessness of Rohingyas". *Journal of Immigrant & Refugee Studies* 15, no. 3 (2017).

Outlook India. "Interview: 'There's No Persecution, Just That Govt Will Not Use Rohingya In Official National Documents'." *Outlook India*, 13 July 2015 <http://www.outlookindia.com/article/theres-no-persecution-just-that-govt-will-not-use-rohingya-in-official-national-documents/294782> (accessed 5 July 2015).

Physicians for Human Rights. *Massacre in Central Burma: Muslim Students Terrorized and Killed in Meiktila.* Cambridge, Massachusetts: Physicians for Human Rights, 2013.

Radio Free Asia. "Rohingya a-mi ma-te-thwin-po myo-nwè-su 7-ku kaung-saung-twe taung-so" [Leaders of seven sub-ethnic groups call for non-inclusion of "Rohingya"]. *Radio Free Asia*, 20 March 2014 <http://www.rfa.org/burmese/news/rakhine-againt-rohingya-name-03202014104524.html> (accessed 22 March 2014).

Sadan, Mandy. *Being and Becoming Kachin: Histories beyond the State in the Borderworlds of Burma.* Oxford: Published for the British Academy by Oxford University Press, 2013.

Schearf, Daniel. "Kaman Muslims Raise Concerns of Wider Conflict". Voice of America, 29 November 2012 <http://www.voanews.com/content/burmas-kaman-muslims-cite-religious-ethnic-conflict-in-rakhine-state/1555524.html> (accessed 4 July 2015).

Smith, Anthony D. *Myths and Memories of the Nation.* Oxford: Oxford University Press, 1999.

Su Min Ko. "Kaman taing-yin-tha-mya-a hmat-pôn-tin tôk-pe-yan la-wa-ka-thui tin-pya-mi" [Matter of issuing national IDs to Kaman ethnics to be submitted to Immigration]. *Messenger Daily*, 13 September 2014, p. 3.

Taylor, Robert H. "Fog of Ethnicity Weighs on Myanmar's Future". *Nikkei Asian Review*, 4 December 2015 <http://asia.nikkei.com/Viewpoints/Viewpoints/Fog-of-ethnicity-weighs-on-Myanmar-s-future> (accessed 5 December 2015).

U Kyaw Zan Tha. "*Rakhine ngyein-chan-pwin-pyp-ye a-la-a-la*" [Prospects of Peace and Development in Rakhine]. *Voice of America,* 8 June 2016 <http://burmese.voanews.com/a/weekly-news-analysis-interview-with-uayetharaung/3367526.html> (accessed 9 June 2016).

U Shwe Bye. *Rakhine Kaman tha maing* [History of the Kaman]. Unpublished manuscript, no date.

Voice of America. "Obama: Burma's Government Steals Election". 7 November 2010 <http://www.voanews.com/content/obama-says-burmese-government-stole-election-106881289/130098.html> (accessed 29 June 2015).

———. "*Rakhine-Kaman a-kyan-pet pa-ti-pa-ka*" [Rakhine-Kaman Violent Conflict]. *Voice of America,* 7 November 2012. <http://burmese.voanews.com/content/news-analysis-kaman-rakhine/1541636.html> accessed 10 November 2012.

Walton, Matthew, J. and Susan Hayward. *Contesting Buddhist Narratives: Democratization, Nationalism, and Communal Violence in Myanmar.* Honolulu: East-West Center, 2014.

Ye Mon. "Controversial Census Data on Religion to be Released within Two Months". *Myanmar Times*, 1 June 2016 <http://www.mmtimes.com/index.php/national-news/yangon/20597-controversial-census-data-on-religion-to-be-released-within-two-months.html> (accessed 1 June 2016).

Yegar, Moshe. *The Muslims of Burma: A Study of a Minority Group*. Wiesbaden: O. Harrassowitz, 1972.

──────. "*The Muslims of Burma*". In *The Crescent in the East: Islam in Asia Major*, edited by Raphael Israeli. London: Curzon Press, 1982.

──────. *Between Integration and Secession: The Muslim Communities of the Southern Philippines, Southern Thailand, and Western Burma/Myanmar*. Lanham: Lexington, 2002.

Yen Snaing. "Kaman IDPs in Arakan State Ask Govt to Rebuild Homes". *Irrawaddy*, 24 April 2015 <http://www.irrawaddy.org/burma/kaman-idps-in-arakan-state-ask-govt-to-rebuildhomes.html> (accessed 25 April 2015).

INTERVIEW WITH P'DOH KWEH HTOO WIN
General Secretary, Karen National Union (KNU)

Interviewed by Ashley South, Chiang Mai, 11 August 2016

1. What does citizenship mean to you?

I was born in Myanmar, and so I am a citizen of Myanmar. Even after I joined the Karen revolution, I still felt that I was a citizen of my country, Burma. After all, I hold a citizen's ID card (Citizenship Scrutiny Card).

Being a citizen is like being a member of the family, and family members don't always get along peacefully! All citizens should have rights, equal with each other. This is particularly important for Karen people, who live spread across the country, and not just in Karen State. It's important that Karen and other ethnic people have rights to self-determination in their own homeland territory and also in other parts of the country.

2. What are the problems Karen people face as citizens of Myanmar/Burma? How have Karen people been treated by the state/government in the past, and present? What are the main challenges?

In the past, during the long years of armed conflict, Karen people faced many difficulties. Issues of citizenship were particularly difficult for people living in areas under the control or influence of the KNU, and other armed groups. They often did not have a chance to receive ID cards, or be recognized as full citizens of Myanmar. The government, and particularly the Myanmar

Army, thought of them as KNU supporters, and often treated very badly. It was difficult for villagers to get even basic services from the government, and they were often abused and marginalized. Even for Karen people living "inside" the country, in areas under government control, it was difficult for them to learn their language, as ethnic languages were not used in government service or in schools. Karen and other ethnic nationality people were often looked down on by members of the majority community, and there was great prejudice and widespread racism. Things have started to improve in the last few years, particularly because of the peace process — but there is still a long way to go. Many people in the government and the military are still suspicious of ethnic minority communities.

3. What is the relationship between Karen people and other citizens of the country?
(Relations with the Bama community:) I come from a Christian family in the Tanintharyi Region. Our community has suffered many long years of oppression. When I was growing up, we experienced prejudice and lack of equality, and racism by members of the Burman community. They did not respect our language, culture or religion. I was taught that Karen people cannot trust the Burmese. However, I have grown to realize that we are all human beings, and essentially the same. How people behave depends so much on their surroundings and circumstances. People from any community can be wonderful human beings, or can behave badly. It doesn't depend on which ethnic group you are, but what type of person you are, and your circumstances.

(Relations with the Mon community:) Historically, the Burman and Mon kings used to oppress the Karen people, who were often pressed into service and abused during their wars. Since the start of a revolution however, Karen and Mon have worked together. Sometimes, we felt that Mon groups were not sincere — and there have been problems on the ground between Karen and Mon communities, for example, with contested claims for ownership of land and natural resources. Generally however, we have been able to work this out, as we are brother ethnic nationalities and work together in a political alliance.

(Relations with the Muslim community:) There is widespread prejudice against Muslims in Myanmar, including among some Karen people. However, this is not such a big issue in Karen State. We need to find ways to live and work together.

4. What are the challenges that need to be addressed so the Karen people can be full citizens of Myanmar?

Karen villagers need proper documentation, particularly those living in remote and conflict affected areas. We also need to have our rights recognized, and to be treated equally with other ethnic communities. For example, the government and military should not discriminate against Karen people, in favour of Bama; they should respect our language and culture, and social and political organizations.

The KNU and other ethnic armed organizations, and ethnic communities across the country, have been struggling for federalism. This is partly about territory, but also ethnic people need rights to study their language and for self-determination, wherever they live in the union. Therefore, federalism should be about territorial autonomy, and also about nationality rights.

Another challenge we face is how to build trust. Sometimes leaders in the peace process have been criticized, as our people ask how we can trust the Burmese leaders after so many years of suffering and violent conflict. However, we realize that if we wait until we trust the other side, there will never be peace. We have to negotiate with them and reach agreements, and then to see whether these are really honoured. That way, we can begin to build mutual trust step-by-step.

INDEX

Note: Page numbers followed by "n" denote endnotes.

www.ingramcontent.com/pod-product-compliance
Lightning Source LLC
Chambersburg PA
CBHW060145280326
41932CB00012B/1635